THE

LIFE OF BISMARCK,

PRIVATE AND POLITICAL.

"Mit Gott für König und Vaterland."

LONDON:
WOODFALL AND KINDER, PRINTERS,
MILFORD LANE, STRAND, W.C.

0

THE

LIFE OF BISMARCK,

PRIVATE AND POLITICAL;

WITH

DESCRIPTIVE NOTICES OF HIS ANCESTRY.

BY

JOHN GEORGE LOUIS HESEKIEL,

AUTHOR OF "FAUST AND DON JUAN," ETC.

TRANSLATED AND EDITED,
WITH AN INTRODUCTION, EXPLANATORY NOTES, AND APPENDICES,

BY

KENNETH R. H. MACKENZIE, F.S.A., F.A.S.L.

With Upwards of One Hundred Illustrations by Diez, Grimm,
Pietsch, and Others.

LONDON:
JAMES HOGG AND SON, YORK STREET, COVENT GARDEN.
MDCCCLXX.

CONTENTS.

𝔅𝔬𝔬𝔨 𝔱𝔥𝔢 𝔉𝔦𝔯𝔰𝔱.

THE BISMARCKS OF OLDEN TIME.

LONDON:

WOODFALL AND KINDER, PRINTERS,

MILFORD LANE, STRAND, W.C.

Book the Third.

LEARNING THE BUSINESS.

Book the Fourth.

ON THE VOYAGE OF LIFE.

Book the Fifth.

MINISTER-PRESIDENT AND COUNT.

LIST OF TONED PAPER ILLUSTRATIONS.

———

EDITOR'S PREFACE

TO THE ENGLISH EDITION.

THE life of Count Bismarck has been so much misinterpreted, by interested and disinterested persons, that it is thought the present publication, which tells "a plain unvarnished tale," will not be unwelcome. In these days of universal criticism, no person is exempt from the carping mood of the envious, or the facile unreasoning of the ready-made theorist. Should we feel disposed to credit vulgar report, noble motives and heroic lives are no longer extant in our present state of society. The eyes of detractors are everywhere curiously—too curiously—fixed upon the deeds of men of mark, and mingled feelings pull down from the pedestal of fame every man who has ascended to the eminence awarded to the patriot and statesman. Truly, such a condition of things bodes no good to the commonweal of society, either in England, Prussia, or in any part of Europe. The present writer can see no utility in this practice of soiling the reputations and actions of men who, by slow degrees, have worked their way into positions of merit and mark.

The evil, however, does not wholly rest with the detractors. An erroneous theory about universal equality gives the spur to this spirit of criticism. A sort of feeling arises in the mind to the effect of, "Had I been in his place, I should have acted otherwise!"—the bystander proverbially seeing more of the game than the players. It is, however, a great matter of doubt whether this is universally true. It might be true, if every circumstance, every motive, every actuation, could be laid bare to positive vision. In the conduct of life, however, this is rarely possible, even in the crudest way; especially is it so in the intricate and tortuous paths of politics. Politicians, we all know, are many; statesmen, unfortunately for the well-being of the world, are few.

Some few years since England lost a statesman named Henry Temple, Viscount Palmerston. He had the rare happiness of being popular during his life, although it is perhaps more certain of him than of any modern statesman, that his inflexibility as to issues was remarkable. Apparently he would bend, but he had, upon fixed principles, determined to rule, and his happy method of conciliation, in which he was clad as in a garment, veiled from the eyes of friend or foe that wonderful spirit of determination permeating all the actions characterizing his political career. And when Palmerston died, a wild wail of sorrow arose from all England, a regret which will never be abated so long as England's history remains intelligible.

Of similar materials to Palmerston, Count Bismarck is composed. Otherwise put together, it is true, in accordance with the genius of the nation amongst which his life-destiny has cast him; but as to the generic likeness there can be little doubt. The policy of Palmerston was "thorough;" so is that of Bismarck. But it is not the "thorough" of a Strafford; it is rather the enlightened "thorough" of a man cast into modern society, and intensely patriotic. Though Bismarck has consistently upheld the prerogatives of his royal master, he has not been neglectful of the interests of the nation of which he is the Minister. A spirit of candour breathes through all his actions, and displays him in the light of an emphatically honest man. Unlike the present remarkable

occupant of the French throne, he is not tided along by
public events; nor, like that potentate, does he extract
fame from an adroit bowing to the exigencies of the hour.
The French sovereign has eliminated a policy, and gained
a kind of respect from others, in consequence of a masterly
manipulation of passing occurrences. The Prussian
Premier, on the other hand, has observed fixed principles.
The latter has his political regrets—he can shed a tear
over the grave of the meanest soldier who died at Sadowa.
The former looks upon human life much as chess-players
look upon pawns—to be ruthlessly sacrificed on occasion,
should it happen that a skilful flank movement may
protect the ultimate design in view. Chess-players, however, know that the pawns constitute the real strength of
the game, and that it would be worse than folly to sacrifice
the humble pieces. Political sagacity is ever displayed in
judicious reserve, and this quality is eminently evinced in
all Bismarck's activity. Perhaps the most singular
triumph of Bismarck's life consists in the neutralization
of Luxemburg—an episode in his career of which he has
greater reason to be proud than of the battle-field of
Sadowa, or the indirect countenance afforded by him to
Italy. It can scarcely be doubted that so peaceful a
victory is a greater merit than the massing together of
thousands of armed men, for trying a right by ordeal of
steel and gunpowder.

Astute as Napoleon may be, Bismarck certainly was
wiser than he. The former has dynastic reasons for maintaining a pre-eminence in the face of Europe; but the
latter, with comparatively inadequate means, had a far
more difficult problem to solve. For Bismarck has a heart
large enough to entertain feelings of kindliness towards
the whole of Germany, as well as towards that section of
it known as Prussia alone. There is a generous aspiration
in him for German nationality, overruling petty animosity
towards his enemies.

In all his contests he has ever been ready to hold out
the hand of reconciliation, although, in no instance, has
he deviated from the strict line of duty pointed out by his
special nationality. Indeed, it was a paramount necessity
to raise Prussia in the scale of nations, ere a German
nationality could emerge into healthy political being.
Prussia's rise, therefore, comprehended within it the
elements of German political existence. Geographically,
the consolidation of a great kingdom in the north was a
necessity; and considering how well and prudently Prussia
sia has used its great position, no one can regret the result
of the events of 1866. Prussia, as a Protestant country,
as a land of education and intellectual refinement, has no
equal on the face of the globe. But that single position
depends on the race-character of the nation evinced in its
utilitarian spirit. Bismarck will perpetuate his policy in
time to come.

"Great acts," says the old dramatist, "thrive when
reason guides the will." This application of reason, so
continuously, consistently, and quietly exercised, pre-
dicates a great national future. That future is bound up
with the fame of this great loyal statesman and dutiful
subject, who has had insight enough to see how far the
prerogative of the crown of Prussia was consistent with the
happiness of its people, foresight enough to rationally
contend for such prerogative, and faithful courage adequate to the fearless execution of a grand design, compre-
hending within itself elements of consolidation and
enduring strength. What Germany owes to Bismarck
can as yet be scarcely calculated, but very few years need
elapse ere the sum will become intelligible.

It is, however, necessary to descend from generalities into
particulars; to discuss, as briefly as may be, some objections
that have been urged, and to expose the fallacy of certain
historical parallels, sought to be drawn in reference to Bismarck's position towards his King and his country.

We have not to contrast Bismarck with any hero or statesman of antiquity. Society, although not human nature, has so changed, that what our modern men do for the common weal, changes with the circumstances and the extension of the circle of population. One man could then address a nation—now the nation must rely upon Camarillas. Democracy, in these days, either vaguely advocates desperate political experiments, or, stung to madness by real or fancied wrongs, determines them—as hot-headed non-thinkers usually determine—by violence.

Our modern Cleons use the press, which, truth to be spoken, is not unwilling to be used; and hence anything not to be twisted before the law courts into libel, represents the license and not the freedom of the press. But the man of antiquity at least had to exercise the courage of meeting his fellow citizens, and thus either swayed them or was lost. Assent or dissent was given by acclamation. Bismarck presents rather a contrast than a likeness to Greek or Roman statesmen—they sought the Agora or the Forum; he has no time for claptrap.

But let us turn to the political doctrine, partly known as that of divine right, for which Bismarck has been thought to fight.

The doctrine of a divine right of possession to the Crown of Prussia is one not readily comprehensible to an English subject, under the circumstances of the modern constitution of the United Kingdom, for the reason that modern society has accustomed itself to look upon the results of the revolutions of 1649 and 1688 as final, and settled by events, and the contract entered into between the parliament, or representative body, on the one hand, and the constitutional sovereign on the other. We may recur to an earlier period, when the Crown was devisable by will in England, or when at least the succession was settled in accordance with the desires of a dying sovereign, for some kind of parallel. Although this absolute right of leaving the

Crown by will has not often been exercised, it has found
its defenders; for instance, in the case of Queen Jane, a
minority held that Edward was justified in devising his
Crown; therefore, while the theory was not actually
substantiated by the right of peaceable possession, it was
not regarded as wholly illusory. If Henry VIII. might,
by his prerogative, bar certain members of his family from
the succession, the Crown advisers of that day must have
been justified in supporting such a prerogative, and could
not have regarded the sovereign as *ultra vires* in the matter
of a transmission of the Crown. It is certainly, from the
logic of facts, an impossibility to effect any such change
in the order of succession now, and in itself would be as
fatal a step as any political theorists could attempt; and
if so fatal in a country where feudalism is a mere historical
eidolon, how far more unwise in a country such as Prussia,
where feudalism has still a practical, though not an avowed,
existence? In the very nature of things, the sovereigns
of Prussia hold their Crown upon a principle of divine
right, as proprietors of the fee-simple of the soil, which
divine right has ever been construed to impose certain
obligations towards their vassals, the holders of the
usufruct, and their subjects, agents, and traders—which
obligations, to their honour be it spoken, the sovereigns of
Prussia have ever attempted to fulfil. This divine right
differs in its nature and mode of action from the mere
arbitrary will of a tyrant. There, as here,—

> " Not Amurath an Amurath succeeds,
> But Harry, Harry."

Their divine right to the soil, which they swear to
defend, and seek to improve, for the benefit of all, differs
essentially from the divine right as understood by a
Charles Stuart. Fiscal arrangements are again of a widely
different character, and a vassal like Bismarck, who main-
tains the prerogative of his sovereign liege, is merely
carrying the legitimate consequences of an enduring and

progressive system, akin to, but not identical with, ancient feudal theories, into action. It is clearly false to seek a parallel in Charles and Strafford; the parallel would be more just if drawn between Henry and Wolsey. But parallels are ever suspicious, as the course of historical sequence is not identical, and presents only delusive points of contact.

Any adequate explanation must be sought in another direction, and that direction is best pointed out by the very essential features of Prussian history itself. From this cause, a prominence, by no means undeserved, has been assigned to the early history of the family whence Bismarck sprang. In the brief sketch given in the first book; it may be plainly seen that impulses of duty guided, and a kind of hierarchy of rank sustained, the active energy in the vassal on behalf of the sovereign, and that in fighting for the supremacy of the Prussian Crown, Bismarck was at the same moment upholding the real solidarity and ultimate rights of the subjects of that Crown. Surely by maintaining the rights of the father against all comers—those rights held by the father in trust—the interests of the children are best consulted.

For there is a mesne power between absolutism and republicanism, tyranny and democracy; this is not constitutionalism. This is Honour, higher than all.

"The divinity that doth hedge a king," from which a true king's impulses flow, must be founded on a higher instinct, and derived from a higher plane. True kingship is very rare, often falls short of its standard in the very best of men—for humanity has always its faults; but rightly guided, it is possible, nay, probable, that the office of kingship may be justly and nobly exercised. A constitutional monarch, although irremovable, save by the process of revolution, can only be governed by the impulses of the man himself, while an absolute sovereign may arrest, correct, and mitigate much that is evil in the State. In civil affairs, we require such an ultimate per-

sonage, one whose honour and self-respect will be a
sufficient safeguard against abuses. Any king not evi-
dencing that honour in his private life as well as public
acts, is liable, and justly so, to deposition; every king who
faithfully performs the difficult and delicate duties of his
position, has a right to expect the true and loving submission of his subjects. The combination of an honest
minister with a noble-minded king, however, is rare. In
Frederick the Second of Prussia, as to some extent in the
first Napoleon, there was a will to be honest; but where
the latter failed in his task, the former prevailed in the
hearts of his people, and the admiration of the world. Have
we not the exquisite book of Mr. Carlyle as evidence of it?
Real statesmen know how infinitely difficult the problem
of administration must be, and hence it is that so many
real wrongs are accidentally committed, when the right is
sought through the agency of unscrupulous ministers.
The axiom that the king can do no wrong, simply means
that if he inadvertently do a wrong, he is bound to repair
it so soon as he is possessedof the truth of the wrong.
On this fact—and no polity is built up with safety without
resting on facts—is based the right of petition, as well in
oriental as in occidental countries. Now, here is the
political lever, nor is the standpoint far off. The King is
bound to do justice, because his position, being founded on
divine right, relies upon divine protection. In any country
where God, under whatever form, is honoured, no king,
conscious of his deep obligations for his position, can
hesitate to throw himself fearlessly into the midst of his
subjects, always regarding such monarch, as is the case in
Prussia, as the steward of the Unseen Governor of all.
Legally and politically, the king represents the ultimate
court of appeal, and honestly fulfilling the duties imposed
upon him, no sovereign need fear, as in Prussia would be
absurd, the hand of the assassin. It is the everlasting
curse entailed upon large States, that for petty motives

there exists an alarming system of bureaucracy, in which the voices of the honest servants are drowned in the din of the general throng for distinction, wealth, ease, and enjoyment. Hence public servants, of whatever degree, fear to speak; hence the public fumes, hence stoppage of trade, discredit by capitalists, ultimate want of employment, lassitude of patriotism, conspiracy, crime—with its load of expense—famine, and the fall of States ensue.

Now, a practical king, conscious of his office, and able-bodied enough to undergo the exertion, can be the greatest of philanthropists, if supported by an honest ministry, fearless enough to repress undue expenditure, either by his sovereign or the lieges. Wary to draw the sword, eager to substitute the ploughshare, should such a monarch be; and such a monarch we find in Prussia, and have found before. Fearless and honourable should be his minister; and such a minister we find, fortunately not without parallels, in Count Bismarck.

Bismarck had not only this abstract duty, as some may like to call it, to perform towards his own Sovereign. There was another duty of no less importance and delicacy to fulfil as a German—as a member of the body corporate of the Teutonic nation. Had Austria continued in its peculiar position of pre-eminence, derived from an association of its rulers with the extinct Holy Roman Empire, the real power of self-government would have passed from the German nations to that mixture of Slavs and Czechs, Huns, Magyars, and Poles, making up so large a proportion of Austrian subjects; and could Prussia, emphatically German in all its regions, have permitted a supremacy so at variance with—I will not say common sense,—but ethnical affinity? Is it not more in conformity with natural sympathy that the German kindred races of the North should be consolidated in a truly German national sense, than remain a loosely-constructed federation of petty princedoms, under the guidance of a Power whose main strength lay in races alien, and even hostile, if we are to trust present events, in their interests, instincts, and sympathies?

There was, of course, underlying all this, the cardinal fact of a difference of religious sympathies. So eminently Roman Catholic, ruling over nations outwardly, and perhaps sincerely, attached to the Papal forms of ecclesiastical government and doctrine, Austria could not hold out a faithful hand of fellowship to Protestant Prussia, with its stern Calvinistic self-assertion: so attached to all that is ancient in reference to birth, family tradition, and historical fame, Austria could not but be jealous of a nation which had robbed it of its warlike glory, and set up a new nobility in opposition to its ancient semi-oriental princely families: so wedded to all that was archaic and statuesque in form and stationary in its character, how was it possible to tolerate a neighbour whose spirit is remarkable for its restless activity and love of innovation; so practical in science and utilitarian in its aims? A contest between two such Powers, and in such a cause, and as a consequence of such various processes of development, was inevitable, while the ultimation of the strife could scarcely be doubtful. The Imperial nation, so proud, profuse, and old-fashioned, must receive a lesson, intended in the utmost spirit of candour, from the patient, practical, and untiring nation of North Germany, who looked upon its Sovereign and institutions with kindly affection, as the outcome of the labours of their immediate fathers, and to the fruits of which those subjects were honestly entitled. Nor, as having resided in both Prussia and Austria, am I disposed to think that Prussian tendencies do not receive hearty approval in the German sections of the Austrian people. Let the events accompanying the siege of Vienna, in 1848, be properly valued, and the fact is patent. The cowardice of Ferdinand is the key to the history of that siege, as well as its justification.

We have not here, however, so much to do with the policy of the Prussian people, and their relations towards Austria, as with a consideration of the effects wrought upon Bismarck's mind by his position, education, personal character, and the events of his era. We here rather want to get an intelligible picture of Bismarck himself—to learn why Bismarck is the actual Bismarck he is, and not another Bismarck, as it were, altogether.

Let us therefore glance at his early life, and see how his strong, daring, and somewhat headlong youth has gradually moulded him into the astute, unbending, and progressive statesman we now see him to be in the latter days of his remarkable life.

The first thing that strikes us must be his opportunities of birth and of lineage. Education, it cannot be doubted, is materially influenced by these two considerations. An indulgent father and an ambitious mother may help a lad along. Next comes the necessary process of estrangement; that emergence into actual life from which so few come forth proudly; and, finally, the attainment of self-consciousness, but without direction and without an aim. This usually results, as with Bismarck, in an appreciable amount of obloquy, from which the strong spirit desires emancipation. In the case now in point, his aspirations of the better sort had the mastery. Application to his distressed fortunes led him to think of others, and while he tested other men he applied the same stern acid to his own soul.

The empty affection of dissolutism assailed him, and he fled from it with the disgust of a noble mind: he longed for a more exquisite grace of beauty and dignity, and attained it. From that time forward he could apply; the serious element in his nature obtained the upper hand, and he perceived that life was not intended as a mere puppet scene. Patriotism, one of the grandest impulses of human nature, led him to a recognition of his duties as a man, and comforted in his domestic relations, he stood for his King. He became the King's man—to that fealty he vowed himself, and that fealty he has nobly accomplished. He saw at once he was the King's man, but policy he had none. Policy, of whatever sort it might prove to be, was yet to come; but the historical guide-line of a relation between the highest post of dignity and his own rank, fashioned it into a policy into which perforce the idea of aristocracy necessarily entered. Had Bismarck not been so vehemently attacked at the onset of his political and representative career, it is very probable that the stout resistance he made would not have proved so strenuous. But the attack was one which roused the dormant elements of his nature. Very proud, like most of the Pomeranian and Brandenburg Junkers, he resolved upon showing that his pride was not false, and was not so greatly leavened with personal ambition as some tauntingly averred. But it must be confessed that there is a vast difference between his early speeches and his later policy—in itself a proof that his career was not that of a political adventurer, resolved for notoriety at any price. The crudeness of his earlier speeches has formed an absolute boon to his opponents, who scarcely anticipated that a man who honestly cared for the point at issue, rather than the airing of a more or less inflated eloquence—seasoned with a philosophy of a very unpractical kind—was about to enter into the political arena. Looking at Bismarck in his earliest stages of development as a statesman, the present writer cannot say there was much beyond a general adhesion to the Prussian traditions to recommend him. It is for this reason that certain documents have been reprinted in the latter pages of this book, not furnished by the German compiler. In these documents, appealing as they do to his family pride as a liegeman, may be found the key of Bismarck's subsequent violent declaration on the side of the monarchy. " That a King should voluntarily propose to set aside what, in my contract, inherent in my birth, with that King, contravenes my family pride, makes me sorry for that King, but vehement against his advisers. But being sorry, I must fight for him, or his successors."

Prussia was, like a nation or two more in Europe, in a "parlous state" in 1848. But these days of March were a natural result of facts pressing on the people : they passed, however. In those events, misunderstood even at the present time—misunderstood as all revolutions must be—Bismarck took no part save that of thinking that a replacement of the army by an ununiformed corps was another insult to Prussia—and her lieges.

His political education had advanced to a point when it would either resolve itself into a total abnegation of political activity, or an aspiration towards some ameliorations of the matter in hand. This signified itself, not by individual actions after a time, but rather by the centralization of a party existing in fortuitous atoms into clubs—adding the printing press as a powerful aid.

Suddenly the Ambassadorial post at Frankfurt was offered him. Light-hearted and willing—to all appearance—he accepted it. The world has yet to be made acquainted with the positive result of this Frankfurt mission. That his instructions were accurate there can be little doubt, and that all his energies were bent upon the humiliation of Austria as the powerful rival of Prussia, is equally true. That his diplomatic facility had at this time acquired any great amount of strength is doubtful. He was an excellent host, and a sincere adviser; but it is due to him rather again to cast away any delusion as to the diplomatic grandeur of his actions—unless, which may be the case, honesty pure and simple is diplomacy.

He therefore remained a good friend, a good host, a kind master, a most loving husband and brother. Perhaps nothing in connection with the man who has been thought so harsh, is so interesting as his care, his love, not only for his own family, but for his humbler dependants. In his correspondence, which really forms the feature of this volume, we find the careful and truthful expression of a mind seeking to set itself right with the world and its duties, and consistently adopting utter straightforwardness as the efficient means to this end. In times of trouble he sympathizes deeply with the bereaved; in seasons when most aspersed he shows a firm reliance on the goodness of his cause, and his innate sense of right; and he ever displays a confidence in the ultimate realization of the object held in view.

The various letters written during seasons of holiday travel display a keen delight in natural objects, and are written with a simple eloquence denoting frankness and candour.

Before closing this Preface, already somewhat lengthy, it is perhaps not out of place to refer to a recent review of the two first German sections of this book, in the October number of the *Edinburgh Review*. The reviewer will perceive that the blemishes to which he alludes have been removed, so far as may be, from the text. Any one, acquainted with German literature, is aware that its genius admits of the expression of many simple *naïvetés*, very far from consonant with the dignity and spirit of the English language. For these reasons a rearrangement and compression of the earlier parts of the book has been effected, and notes have been added of interest to the English reader, whose acquaintance with some of the personages named would necessarily be limited. Nothing, however, tending to illustrate the character and purposes of the chief personage, has been omitted. So far as the materials could serve, a faithful picture of Count Bismarck is here presented, and it is anticipated that the Prussian Premier will be seen to far greater advantage than through the medium of the Edinburgh reviewer.

That gentleman will perhaps forgive the writer for differing from him in his general estimate of Bismarck's character. The estimate taken by the critic is very severe, and scarcely just. It is also so curious that the writer cannot refrain from transcribing it here, that the reader may have both sides of the picture before him.

" To govern," says the critic,* " is, according to his ideas, to command, and parliamentary government is to command with a flourish of speeches and debates, which should always end in a happy subserviency with the ruling Minister. This arbitrary disposition is, of course, strengthened by his success of 1866; but he will be grievously deceived in believing that only stubborn resolution is wanted to triumph again. He is a man of the type of Richelieu and Pombal; but this style of statesmanship is rather out of place in our century, at least for obtaining a lasting success.

" We cannot, therefore, consider him as a really great statesman, though he has certainly gifts of the highest order. He is a first-rate diplomatist and negotiator. No man can captivate more adroitly those he wants to win; nobody knows better to strike at the right moment, or to wait when the tide is running in his favour. His personal courage is great, physically as well as morally; he shrinks from nothing conducive to his end. He is not naturally eloquent; but his speeches are generally impressive, and full of terse argument. He is a capital companion in society—witty, genial, sparkling in his conversation. His private life is pure; nobody has accused him of having used his high position for his pecuniary advantage. It is natural that such qualities, backed by an indomitable will, a strong belief in himself, and an originally robust constitution, should achieve much. But by the side of these virtues the darker shades are not

* *Edinburgh Review*, vol. cxxx., pp. 457, 458.

c

wanting. We will not reproach him with ambition; it is
natural that such a man should be ambitious. But his
ambition goes far to identify the interests of his country
with his own personal power. Everything is personal
with him; *he never forgets a slight, and persecutes people
who have offended him, with the most unworthy malice.* His
strong will degenerates frequently into absurd obstinacy;
he is feared by his subordinates, but we never heard *that
anybody loved him.* Driven into a strait, his courage
becomes the reckless daring of the gambler, who stakes
everything on one card. *He can tell the very reverse
of the truth with an amazing coolness;* still oftener he will
tell the plain truth when he knows that he will not be
believed. He is a great comedian, performing admirably
the part he chooses to play. He knows how to flatter his
interlocutors, by assuming an air of genuine admiration
for their talents; they leave him charmed by his con-
descension, *whilst he laughs at the fools who took his fine
words for solid cash. His contempt of men is profound;* he
dislikes independence, though he probably respects it.
*There is not a single man of character left in the Ministry or
the more important places of the Civil Service* (!). Few
things or persons exist at which he would not venture a
sneer.

"At present he has chosen to retire, for an indefinite
period, from a perplexing situation which he has himself
created. Nobody can tell in what direction he is going
to steer his vessel. He likes to strike the imagination of
the public by sudden resolutions. Nobody can prophecy
what will be the final result of the great political experiment upon which he has entered, for it depends on the
working of so many different factors, that even the boldest
will scarcely venture to calculate the issue."

Those passages italicized above, form a specimen of the
kind of attacks, by no means honourably or reasonably
made, upon Count Bismarck, and it is somewhat lament-

able to read, in the pages of so important a Review, views quite incompatible with truth, and so calculated to sway the minds of many who have little leisure to analyze historical phenomena.

Time has triumphantly cleared up much that seemed vaguely ominous in Bismarck's policy, and the progress of events will doubtless throw clear light on that which still remains dark and unintelligible to those who care little for light.

KENNETH R. H. MACKENZIE.

4, St. Martin's Place, Trafalgar Square,
    6th December, 1869.

Book the First.

—●—

THE BISMARCKS OF OLDEN TIME.

B

CHAPTER I.

NAME AND ORIGIN.

Bismarck on the Biese.—The Bismarck Louse.—Derivation of the Name Bismarck.—Wendic Origin Untenable.—The Bismarcks in Priegnitz and Ruppin.—Riedel's Erroneous Theory.—The Bismarcks of Stendal.—Members of City Guilds.—Claus von Bismarck of Stendal.—Rise of the Family into the Highest Rank in the Fourteenth Century.

 N the Alt Mark, belonging to the circle of Stendal, lies the small town of Bismarck on the Biese. It is an old and famous place, for south of the town stands an ancient tower, known as the Bismarck Louse; tradition states that the tower received its name from a gigantic louse which inhabited it, and that the peasants of the district had every day to provide huge quantities of meat for the monster's food. In this legend we can trace the popular spirit of the sober Alt Mark—it laughs at the pilgrimages which were made in the thirteenth century to Bismarck in honour of a holy cross, said to have fallen from heaven. These pilgrimages, at first greatly encouraged by the lords of the soil, as they found in them a rich source of income, soon came to a sanguinary end, from the severe strife occasioned by these very revenues.

Bismarck does not, as some assert, derive its name from the Biese, because in the year 1203, when it is first mentioned in the records, it is called Biscopesmarck, or Bishopsmark, afterwards corrupted into Bismarck. It belonged to the Bishops of Havelberg, who erected a fort here as a defence of their Mark, on the frontiers of the Sprengels of Halberstadt. From the little town the noble family of Bismarck has its name.

It is a tradition of later times, by no means historically confirmed, that the Bismarcks were a noble family of Bohemia, settled by Charlemagne in the Alt Mark, and the founders of the town of Bismarck, which received its name from them. It is further erroneously asserted, that the Bismarcks, after the decease of the very powerful Count von Osterburg, had shared the county with the family of Alvensleben; and thus the town of Bismarck passed into the possession of the Alvenslebens.* This last is only stated to account for the circumstance of the holding of Bismarck in the fourteenth century as a fief by the Alvenslebens; it being

---

* *Alvensleben.* This family was of noble origin in the Alt Mark, and has been partly elevated to the rank of Count. Its annals extend to 1163. The original seat of the family was Alvensleben on the Bever; the lines consisted of three—red, black, and white. Of these the red line died out in 1534 and 1553, at Erxleben and Kalvörden. The white line, divided into three, through Joachim Valentine, at Isernschnippe, Eirnersleben, and Erxleben—the first expired in 1680, the second in 1734—the third, founded by Gebhard Christoph, still flourishes. The black line was always the most extensive. It divided into two branches, that of Ludolf and that of Joachim. Only a portion of this family exists at the present day. Of the branch of Ludolf, there existed Philip Karl (b. 1745, 16th Dec.), who became a Prussian diplomatist and was a favourite of Friedrich II. and Minister of Foreign Affairs. He died a Count, 21st Oct., 1802, at Berlin, unmarried. Johann Aug. Ernst was born at Erxleben, 6th Aug., 1758; he was Minister for Brandenburg and Privy Councillor of Prussia; died 27th Sept., 1827, a Prussian Count. The black line died out with his son, the Prussian Minister Albrecht v. A. The white, or Gardelegen line, was elevated to the rank of Count in the persons of Fried. Will. Aug. (b. 31st May, 1798; d. 2nd Dec., 1853), and Ferd. Friedr. Ludolf (born 23rd Jan., 1803), at the ascension of Fried. Wilh. IV., 15th Oct., 1840. Albrecht, the representative of the black line, was distinguished for his devotion to his king, much as Bismarck has been. He died 2nd May, 1858; his large property went to his sister and her children.—K. R. H. M.

forgotten that in those days the title went with the office, and that a county could not therefore be in the possession of two families.

As groundless is the tradition of the Wendic descent of the Bismarcks. According to this, the actual name of this noble family should be Bij-smarku, in Wendic, "Beware of the Christ-thorn." Not very happily has the double trefoil in the arms of the Bismarcks been identified with the Christ-thorn — as a proof of their Wendic descent.

The Bismarcks are rather, as are all the families of knightly rank in the Alt Mark, the descendants of German warriors who, under the Guelph, the Ascanian, or other princes, had conquered the Slavic lands on both banks of the Elbe for Christianity and German civilization, and had then settled themselves on those lands as fief-holders. The Bismarcks belonged to the warrior family of Biscopesmarck - Bishopsmark - Bismarck, and when surnames came into use, called themselves after their dwelling-place—von Bismarck. Of course they retained the name after the loss or cession of their original seat.

Like many other knightly families of the Alt Mark, the Bismarcks gradually spread towards the East, conquering greater space for German Christian culture, subduing the Wends or driving them back towards the Oder. Thus the Bismarcks also appear, at the beginning of the fourteenth century, as warrior knights in Priegnitz and the region of Ruppin.

We cannot understand how an historian of such general intelligence as Riedel, can object to this course of development, presenting so many analogies in the series of other races of nobility in the Alt Mark. According to this writer, it appears "credible and plausible" that the chivalric race of Bismarck, found at the beginning of the fourteenth century in the region of Priegnitz and Ruppin, should have descended from the Castellans at

Bismarck, who were provided with some territorial fiefs on the downfall of the episcopal castle. "On the other hand," says Riedel, "those citizen families to be found in the cities of the Mark, and in Stendal, bearing the name of Bismarck, whence that branch arose, the energy of which not only equalized the Von Bismarcks with the highest nobility of the Mark, but has surpassed all of them, by the principles of unprejudiced historical inquiry, are proved to be self-distinguished, and the descendants of plain citizens of the little town Bismarck, which had flourished so well under episcopal protection."

This is, however, an assertion supported by nothing, except, perhaps, by an accidental negative—the circumstance that up to the present time no seal has been found of the undoubtedly chivalric Bismarcks in Priegnitz and Ruppin; for the identity of armorial bearings would necessarily establish the common origin of the knightly Bismarcks, and those of Stendal, beyond all question. But we do not understand Riedel's objection, as he does not deny that the Bismarcks entered the first rank of the aristocracy of the Alt Mark in the same fourteenth century. It would be almost puerile, by means of fantastic explanations respecting the races bearing the name of Bismarck, to deprive the Minister of the rank of Junker,* and thus claim him as a plebeian.

For if the Bismarcks of Stendal appear in the character of citizens since the thirteenth century, it proves nothing as to their chivalric descent, but may almost be used as an argument in favour of it. It is well known and unquestioned that a whole series of knightly families have settled themselves in towns, and taken part in municipal government, in all places at first more or less

---

* This rank in Germany, and especially in North Germany, is held to be noble. We have no corresponding title in English; it is higher than esquire, but not exactly that of a knight or baronet. Perhaps it corresponds to honourable."—K. R. H. M.

patrician in character. Thus it fared with the Bismarcks in Stendal, and not with them only, but with the Schadewachts and other Alt Mark knightly races, members of which took their places in the municipal government of Stendal. The Bismarcks were then attached to the most distinguished, honourable, and influential Guild of Tailors (cloth merchants), because every inhabitant of a town was obliged to belong to some guild. But to infer from this that the Bismarcks were of citizen birth, would be as absurd as to deny the nobility of the Iron Duke, the victor of Waterloo, because the Worshipful Company of Merchant Tailors in London, as recognizing his fame, made him free of their guild. It is in the thirteenth and fourteenth centuries, in fact, and especially in the towns of the Marks, that we find the noblest families—even the Margrave himself—associated with citizen guilds. At the same time it mattered not at all whether such members occupied themselves with the trade ; for we are not, in this place, speaking of position, but descent. And if the practice of handicrafts and commerce were not then, as later, held to be incompatible with noble birth—although, in general, the practice was uncommon —the descendants of noble houses, on leaving the towns, naturally re-entered their own rank of territorial lords.

It is, therefore, explicable that Claus von Bismarck, Freeman of the Guild of Tailors in Stendal, could step from that position into the first rank of the Alt Mark nobility.

Riedel is also the only historian who, in contradiction to earlier and later authorities, asserts the descent of the Bismarcks from a citizen family in Stendal, instead of from the Castellans of the episcopal castle of that name. Even, however, had he been able to determine this beyond a doubt, it would not have proved the plebeian descent of the Minister-President, but only that the nobility of his family reaches no higher than the fourteenth century—in itself a sufficiently long pedigree.

CHAPTER II.

CASTELLANS AT BURGSTALL CASTLE.

1270—1550.

Rulo von Bismarck, 1309–1338.—Excommunicated.—Claus von Bismarck.—His Policy.—Created Castellan of Burgstall, 1345.—Castellans.—Reconciliation with Stendal, 1350.—Councillor to the Margrave, 1353.—Dietrich Kogelwiet, 1361.—His White Hood.—Claus in his Service, while Archbishop of Magdeburg.—The Emperor Charles IV.—The Independence of Brandenburg threatened.—Chamberlain to the Margrave, 1368.—Subjection of the Marks to Bohemia, 1373.—Claus retires into Private Life.—Death about 1377.—Claus II., 1403.—Claus III. and Henning.—Friedrich I. appoints Henning a Judge.—Ludolf.—His Sons.—Pantaleon.—Henning III. *obiit circâ* 1528.—Claus Electoral Ranger, 1512.—Ludolf von Bismarck.—Electoral Sheriff of Boetzow, 1513.—His Descendants.

S the ancestor of the race of Bismarck, we find among the Bismarcks in Stendal, where they had been known since 1270, a certain Rule or Rulo, otherwise Rudolf von Bismarck, whose name appears in the records from 1309 to 1338. This personage was a respected member of the Guild of Tailors, often its guide and master, as also a member of the Town Council of Stendal.

In the sparse notices contained in the records concern-

Die alten Bismarcke.

Heil dem Manne, der die Blicke
Gern zu seinen Ahnen kehrt!
Seiner Väter soll sich freuen,
Wer sich fühlt der Väter werth!

THE BISMARCKS OF OLD.

Book the first.

———◆———

THE BISMARCKS OF OLDEN TIME.

the front of the aristocratic conservative party in Stendal. But in the country he sided more and more with the Margrave, at that time of Bavarian origin, and gradually became one of the leaders of that patriotic Brandenburg association, which sought to reunite the Marks, separated by the death of Waldemar the Great, under one government.

The political activity of Claus von Bismarck in the fourteenth century, offers many points of similarity to that of his descendant Otto von Bismarck in the nineteenth century.

In his contest with the democratic party in Stendal, Claus von Bismarck was not very successful. After a long and obstinate fight, the aristocratic Guild of Tailors was worsted. The members of it, and among them Claus von Bismarck, were driven out and banished. He now returned to the country, where he possessed numerous estates, inherited from his father; but he did not remain quiet. We see him in continued activity on behalf of the Margrave Ludwig, for whom he conducted the most intricate negotiations, and to whom he lent considerable sums of money.

The reward of his political assiduity was proportionate to its importance. On the 15th of June, 1345, the Margrave granted the Castle of Burgstall, one of the strongholds of the country, protecting the southern frontier of the Alt Mark towards Magdeburg, to Claus von Bismarck and his descendants, and their brothers, as a fief. Thus the Bismarcks entered the first rank of the nobility of the Alt Mark, as Castellans.*

These Castellan families in the Alt Mark, although they could not claim any right to a higher rank, formed a privileged class of the chivalric nobility, which maintained itself by the possession of castles—then of great importance for the defence of the country. The Castel-

---

* In the original, *Schlossgessessen*, literally "seized of or seated at a castle." —K. R. H. M.

lans under the Luxemburg dynasty, like the members of the Bohemian nobility, were called *nobiles*, while other classes of the nobility were only denominated "worshipful," or *strenui*. They had ingress and precedence at the Diets before the others, were not summoned to those assemblies by proclamation, but by writ, and were immediately under the jurisdiction of the Land Captain, while ordinary knights were subject to the Courts of Justice of the Province. Although the Castellans maintained a portion of these rights to very recent times, they were never anything more than Alt Mark Junkers, whose families possessed some privileges beyond the rest.

Among the Castellans of the fourteenth century were the Von der Schulenburgs, the Von Alvenslebens, the Von Bartenslebens, the Von Jagows, the Von Knesebecks,* and the Von Bismarcks of Burgstall.

On the outbreak of the terrible storm which accompanied the appearance of the pretender Waldemar —whose claims have, however, not yet been disproved— Claus von Bismarck prudently withdrew himself, and awaited the conclusion of these troubles at the Castle of Burgstall. It was the only thing he could do, for, in the position of circumstances, he could afford no assistance to the Bavarian Margrave, with whom he was intimately connected, and on the general question he could give no decision, as the person of Waldemar the Great had never been known to him.

About this time, 1350, a reconciliation took place

* *Knesebeck.* Of this family one was celebrated as Prussian Field Marshal (b. 5th May, 1768, at Carwe, near New Ruppin, of an ancient Brandenburg family). He fought with distinction in 1792–94, and was placed on the staff by the Duke of Brunswick. He fulfilled a singular diplomatic mission to Petersburg in 1811–12, which had for its real motives an incitement to the Russian emperor to withstand Napoleon to the utmost, and to decoy him into the interior of Russia. The world knows the rest. He was an enthusiast in poetry, as well as war. Many poems of his have been privately printed—the chief of these is one in praise of war (*Lob des Kriegs*). Think of a Tyrtæus in a Prussian general's uniform! He died 12th Jan., 1848. —S. R. H. M.

between the banished aristocratic party and the town of Stendal. Some of the members returned thither, but Claus von Bismarck, as may be supposed, remained at Burgstall; but it would appear that from that time forward he stood on friendly terms with his native city.

In the year 1353, he became still more closely connected with the Margrave, in the capacity of Privy Councillor; and in this post, which carried no emolument with it whatever, he exhibited energy of such a wise character that Bismarck's government, despite of the wretched and sorrowful state of things at the time, bore rich fruits, not only for the Alt Mark, but for miserable Brandenburg in general.

In the year 1361, Claus quitted the service of Brandenburg, for that of the Archbishop of Magdeburg, in consequence of his near relative, Dietrich von Portitz, known as Kagelwiet or Kogelwiet—i.e., White Kogel or hood—having ascended the archiespiscopal throne of St. Moritz.*

Dietrich von Portitz, whose relationship to Claus is unquestionable, but whose precise affinity is not clear, was a native of Stendal. He had embraced the ecclesiastical profession, and had shown such a genius for government, even as a monk at Lehnin, that the Bishop of Brandenburg, Ludwig von Neiendorff, entrusted him with the administration of his diocese, much to his own advantage. The Emperor, Charles IV., early recognized the importance of this man; created him Bishop of Sarepta and Chancellor of Bohemia, subsequently procured him the Bishopric of Minden, and finally the Archbishopric of Magdeburg. The cognomen of Kagelwiet or Kogelwiet this distinguished person received from a castle of this name in Bohemia, but according to some, from the white

* The Archbishopric of Magdeburg took its rise from a Benedictine convent in honour of St. Maurice, founded by Emperor Otto I. in 937; and in 967 it was made an archbishopric, and the primacy of Germany was given by Pope John XIII., with Havelberg, among others, as a dependency.—K. R. H. M.

hood which he had assumed in orders at Lehnin. A tradition asserts that the Bohemian magnates, envious of the eminence of the Chancellor, accused him of fraud, and referred the Emperor to the iron chest which stood in Dietrich's private chamber. When Charles IV. had this chest opened by Dietrich, there was only found within it the monk's frock, the white hood of Brother Dietrich of Lehnin.

As to the relationship between the Archbishop Dietrich Kogelwiet and Claus Bismarck, it must be admitted that it has not been clearly established by the records. But we think we do not err in assuming that Dietrich Kogelwiet was also one of the Bismarcks of Stendal of the same family as Claus von Bismarck. He certainly is called Dietrich von Portitz, but we must not consider this singular in an age when brothers even existed with different surnames; and, on the other hand, an identical name by no means establishes any relationship, or places it beyond doubt.

Common armorial bearings were a much surer index to
family affinity between their wearers than identical names.
We cannot, as before stated, absolutely prove from the
records that the Archbishop Dietrich Kogelwiet was a
Bismarck : it may be decided by later researches, but
there are several reasons for considering this to be the
case.   There was no family of Portitz at Stendal, to claim
the Archbishop as a scion of their house—an important
fact, as the birthplace of Dietrich is ascertained to have
been Stendal.

When Dietrich Kogelwiet entered on the government
of the Archbishopric of Magdeburg, he immediately
summoned his relative, Claus Bismarck, to assist in his
administration.   Such an invitation might have been the
more welcome, in consequence of the hopeless condition
of the Margrave's affairs.   It must not be forgotten
that Claus was not only a vassal to Brandenburg, but to
Magdeburg, and was connected by blood and friendship
with many members of the Cathedral community.

Thus Claus von Bismarck, in conjunction with the
knight Meinecke von Schierstaedt, became General
Commandant of Magdeburg.   The duties were so shared
between them that Von Schierstaedt fulfilled the office of
Minister of War, while Von Bismarck was Minister of the
Interior and of Finance.   Foreign affairs, and especially
those relating to Brandenburg, the Archbishop had reserved for himself—why, we shall presently see..   We
must not, however, regard the various duties in those
days as so clearly defined as in a modern government ;
the distinctions were less obvious, and thus we see
Claus von Bismarck in many a battle - field, fighting
bravely beside Schierstaedt.   Dietrich Kogelwiet and his
two chief servants, in fact, carried on a · really model
government.   In the course of a few years the very
considerable debts of the Archbishopric were liquidated,
estates pawned or wholly alienated were redeemed, and

the security of the subjects of the See fixed in a manner rarely known in Germany at that era. Bismarck's constant care was devoted to the protection of the peasantry against the frequent outbreaks, usually ending in the plunder or destruction of property; for his clear insight had perceived that the safety of the life and property of the subject was bound up with that of the liege lord's income—apparently a secret to most rulers of that time.

Thus this six years' administration of the See by Bismarck became a great blessing to it, and Dietrich Kogelwiet recognized the fact by implicit confidence, although—a very remarkable circumstance, impossible at the present day—he was opposed to Bismarck in his foreign policy.

The politic Emperor Charles IV. had especially seated his Bohemian Chancellor upon the archiepiscopal throne of St. Moritz, with the absolute intention of securing in him an efficient co-operator in his extensive plans. Dietrich Kogelwiet was to aid in the conquest of the Mark of Brandenburg for the great Bohemian empire which Charles IV. sought to erect from Lübeck to the coast of the Adriatic for the house of Lützelburg. Dietrich Kogelwiet had from of old been a chief supporter of these aims, and, as Archbishop of Magdeburg, he succeeded only too well, considering the weakness and poverty of the Bavarian Margrave, in ensnaring him and bringing him into relations which rendered him an unconditional and very abject dependant of the Emperor. At the death of the Archbishop, after a reign of six years, the independence of Brandenburg was lost, and the councillors of the Margrave consisted of imperial servants alien to Brandenburg.

Claus von Bismarck held utterly aloof from this policy of his chief, for his Brandenburg patriotism desired the maintenance of the independence of the Marks. He saw no safety in the division of his native land, and its final subjection to the crown of Bohemia. Despite of these differences, the Archbishop held fast to his " dear uncle "—a designation applied in those days as cousin is now—bequeathed to him the greater part of his wealth, appointed him his executor, and a member of the inter-regnum provided to exist until the enthronement of his successor in the See.

When Bismarck had acquitted himself of his duties towards the Church of Magdeburg, and had overcome the many obstacles towards a settlement of the inheritance of Dietrich Kogelwiet, he did what he had probably long since designed. He returned to the service of the Mar-grave of Brandenburg. This step can only be explained by the high patriotism which actuated this excellent man. For himself he had nothing to gain by such a step, and he must have been aware of the sacrifice he was making, for the affairs of the Margrave at that time were in the utmost confusion, and in a ruinous condition. The national income had long been anticipated, money was rare, and the partially justified concurrent government of the imperial councillors seemed to render it impossible to save the autonomy of Brandenburg.

The Emperor Charles, to whom Bismarck's conduct was sufficiently intelligible, sought with great pains to win him to his party, but in vain. The faithful Alt Mark Junker, in 1368, became administrator of the Margrave's government in the capacity of Chamberlain, and con-ducted his patriotic labour with such energy and wisdom, that by the October of that year the imperial councillors placed about the Margrave were dismissed, and their posts entirely filled by Brandenburgers of Bismarck's party. In this new Council there sat Dietrich von der Schulenburg, Bishop of Brandenburg, the noblest prelate in the land; Count Albert von Lindau, Lord of Ruppin, the chief vassal of the Margrave; Bismarck himself was

Chamberlain for the Alt Mark; Marshal Sir Lippold von Bredow for the Middle Mark; and Justice Otto von Moerner represented the New Mark.

Bismarck and his friends now actively promoted the safety of Brandenburg independence by every means in their power, during a period of five years. Bismarck was the soul of this patriotic struggle against the policy and rapacity of the mighty Emperor. His wisdom and energy were visible in every department of the State; his immense wealth he freely sacrificed in every direction; and the results were so important that they forced the disconcerted Emperor to a measure which even Bismarck had not been able to foresee as a wholly unexpected proceeding

The politic Charles, who had never speculated upon an appeal to arms, and who depended on the cunning, of which he was so great a master, before displayed in his counsels, suddenly seized the sword. He perceived that he was unable to outwit Bismarck, and was compelled to emerge from his lair and break up the independence of Brandenburg by force. Bismarck could not oppose his mighty army, and thus by the treaty of Fürstenwald the independence of Brandenburg was lost, on the 13th of August, 1373; the Marks fell into the hands of Bohemia.

After this destruction of his patriotic plans, Claus von Bismarck retired into private life, most probably to Burgstall; but the proximity of the great Emperor, who held his court at Tangermünde, forced him to retreat from the former place. Neither Claus nor his sons ever served the house of Lützelburg. He then retired to his native city of Stendal, and occupied himself with religious duties and the affairs of the Hospital of St. Gertrude, which he had founded at the Uengling Gate of Stendal in 1370. Probably this foundation again embroiled the aged man with the ecclesiastical authorities during his closing years, and he seems to have died in excommunication, like his

c

The four sons of Ludolf were Günther, Ludolf, George, and Pantaleon. They were ennobled, together with their cousins, in 1499, by the Elector Joachim I., but the two elder brothers soon died without male heirs, and the third brother, George, was childless; it does not appear that he was ever married. Pantaleon alone left a son, Henning III., by his wife Ottilien von Bredow, who died before 1528, leaving four sons behind him—Henry, Levin, Frederick, and Laurence. Levin and Laurence soon disappear from the records, and Henry, married to Ilse from the Kattenwinkel, and Frederick, wedded to Anna von Wenckstern, appear as the representatives of the elder stock of Ludolf. All these Bismarcks lived in peaceful retirement, on the best terms, at Burgstall, with their cousins of the younger Henning-branch of the family.

Henning II. and his wife Sabine von Alvensleben had as sons, Busso, Claus, Dietrich, and Ludolf. Dietrich and Busso dying in early youth, Claus became in 1512 the Electoral Ranger of the great estate of Gardelegen (the forests of Jävenitz and Letzling). The rangers were in those days high officials (chief foresters); the title, however, they did not obtain until the time of King Frederick William I., with considerable privileges. The foresters were then literally called heath-runners (*Haide-laüfer*)—rangers, in fact.

Ludolf von Bismarck in 1513 became Electoral Sheriff of Boetzow, the present Oranienburg. His activity appears to have been applied to the protection of the Electoral game preserves. Ludolf was reckoned one of he best horsemen and warriors of his era, although we do not learn anything respecting his prowess. He seems to have been very active in the establishment of the militia of the Alt Mark, and died in 1534. His wife, Hedwig von Doeberitz, long survived him. In the year 1543, the Elector Joachim owed her a thousand thalers, and she was still alive in 1562. Ludolf's sons were Jobst, Joachim, and George.

Joachim was killed at the siege of Magdeburg, at which he was present with his brothers. Jobst married Emerentia Schenk von Lützendorf. George married Armengard von Alvensleben.

We thus see the castle of Burgstall in the middle of the sixteenth century inhabited by two pairs of brothers, with four households; Henry and Frederick representing the elder or Ludolf branch of the Bismarcks, and Jobst and George the younger one through Henning. Ludolf's widow also resided at Burgstall.

CHAPTER III.

THE PERMUTATION.

1550—1563.

Changes.—The Electoral Prince John George and Burgstall.—Forest-rights.
—The exchange of Burgstall for Crevese.—Schönhausen and Fischbeck.—
The Permutation completed, 1563.

DOOMED to a sorrowful termination was the peaceful life of the family of the Bismarcks at Burgstall. All the Bismarcks were eager sportsmen, and there was no spot in the whole of the Brandenburg country better adapted for sport than their castle, situated in the midst of the great preserve of Gardelegen, the woods of the Tanger, and of the Ohre.

These preserves were not only the most considerable, but also the most well-stocked in the Marks; and although only a small portion belonged to the Bismarcks, they enjoyed forest privileges conjointly with their neighbours to the fullest extent. It was not remarkable, therefore to find the Castellans of Burgstall "mighty hunters;" but a still mightier hunter was destined to overwhelm them, and compel them to give up their privileges in forest and moor.

Every one of the descendants of the great Frankish prince, the Burgrave Frederick von Nürnberg—all the powerful Electors and noble Margraves of Brandenburg—were considerable sportsmen. They had early perceived

that no place was more convenient than Burgstall Castle, when they desired to hunt near the Tanger, through the forest of Gardelegen, the Drömling, and other preserves of the Ohre. They often visited their trusty vassals at Burgstall, and for weeks together were welcome guests of the Bismarcks, whose wealth could well maintain the expensive hospitality of princely guests. The Electors John Cicero and Joachim Nestor were frequently at Burgstall. We know that the Bismarcks were one of the first families of the country, allied to the new Frank rulers; even at a later time the Bismarcks were proud of their loyalty to their liege lords; but the intimate personal relations which the Bismarcks maintained with the Electors John Cicero, Joachim Nestor, Joachim Hector, and the Electoral Prince and Margrave John George, engendered feelings of personal affection and respect, far surpassing the ordinary loyalty of vassals.

This has to be remembered when it is sought to understand the events which took place in 1562 among the Bismarcks in their right light.

When the hunt-loving Electoral Prince, the Margrave John George, became administrator in the year 1553 for his youthful son, the postulated Bishop of the See of Havelberg, he followed the chase more enthusiastically than ever, and founded the hunting-box in Netzlingen, purchased from the Alvenslebens in 1555, known as Letzlingen. In order to establish wider preserves for the new edifice, he everywhere attacked the privileges of the Bismarcks; and his object was to abridge or to abrogate their forest rights in all directions. The Bismarcks, known to us as zealous sportsmen, did not wish to dispose of their forest rights; their position at Burgstall did not admit of pecuniary compensation; but they, nevertheless, from a feeling of respect for the Electoral Prince, consented to a treaty which considerably circumscribed their privileges, much to their disadvantage. This treaty was signed at Zechlin, on the 1st July, 1555, in person, the Prince residing at that place. They asked for no compensation from the Prince, but allowed him to fix it as he pleased, accepting without a murmur a deed acknowledging a debt of three thousand *gulden*, a sum by no means representing the amount of their loss. By this sacrifice they purchased peace, however, for but a very short time; for while the differences continued between the Margrave's huntsmen and those of Bismarck, the Electoral Prince could not but perceive that the Castellanship of Burgstall stuck like a wedge in the centre of his preserves. He desired to have the entire control from Letzlingen, where John George habitually held his court, to the castle of Tangermünde; hence it was necessary to dispossess the Bismarcks of Burgstall.

This honourable and faithful family suffered deeply, when, in the beginning of the year 1562, the Electoral Prince proposed to them to exchange Burgstall for other lands. He first offered them the convent of Arendsee; but the Bismarcks, who could not, at first, contemplate the resignation of their ancient family seat, declined to this procedure. The affair was of such an unusual character that it created the greatest excitement. Even the Chapter at Magdeburg, to whom the Bismarcks were lieges for several possessions at Burgstall, was set in commotion. They dreaded an enlargement of the boundary of Brandenburg, beyond this purchase of Burgstall, to the detriment of the archiepiscopate. The Archbishop of Magdeburg, the Margrave Sigismund, and brother of the Electoral Prince also wrote, apparently at the instance of his Chapter, to him, "that he hoped he would desist from his intention, and leave the Bismarcks in peaceful possession of their lands, and allow other folks to have a hare, a buck, or a stag."

John George, however, was not the man to be so easily dissuaded from his purpose. He continued to ply the Bismarcks with propositions of exchange, which they as

steadily rejected, being unwilling to resign Burgstal.
But their rejection was of no advantage to them, for their
loyal principles were outraged at this difference with their
liege lord ; and, besides, it became very evident to them
that the Electoral Prince had no intention of abandoning
his plans. If the brothers and cousins Von Bismarck
had possessed a spark of speculation, they might, under
the circumstances, have obtained compensation of such
magnitude as to have formed an enormous revenue for
their house ; but such thoughts were remote from these
loyal and simple-minded country Junkers.

The Electoral Prince, who knew his men, employed
measures which he saw must lead to his object without
fail. On the 12th of October, 1562, he wrote, from Letzlingen, a letter in very ungracious terms, in which he
gave up his project of exchange in the greatest anger,
but allowed a whole series of minor difficulties to become
apparent for the future.

The Bismarcks replied in a highly respectful manner,
and reminded the Electoral Prince, in almost touching
accents, " that their ancestors and themselves had for a
long time sate worthily under the Electoral Princes, had
served them with blood and substance willingly, and
testified themselves to be honest, upright, and true subjects, and would willingly have met the estimable Elector
and Prince, the Margrave of Brandenburg, in these very
matters ; although they might be forgiven for hesitating
at an exchange which would transport their ancient race
to other places, and they would prefer to remain in their
ancestral seat, granted them by Almighty God, rather
than idly to depart therefrom."

This letter, however, was the limit of the powers of the
Bismarcks. The Electoral Prince had taken his measures
only too well. There now · ensued very active and
weighty negotiations as to the compensation to be given

for Burgstall. This was not easily to be found, and these negotiations prove, as also their final result, that the Bismarcks agreed to the surrender of Burgstall out of respect to the Prince, and from an apprehension of setting themselves in actual hostility to the authorities as the result of any further refusal.

The representatives of the elder race — Henry and Frederick—first assented, and took for their shares in Burgstall the Abbey of Crevese, a foundation of Benedictine nuns. The income of this property, with all its appurtenances, did not amount by far to those enjoyed by the brothers in Burgstall; but no better estate could be found, and the Prince therefore commanded the payment of considerable sums in satisfaction—not, however, exceeding the moderate amount of two thousand *thalers.*

The ladies of the house of Bismarck seemed even more disconsolate at the loss of Burgstall than the men. To terminate their lamentations, the Prince allowed each of them the sum of one hundred *gulden.*

The representatives of the younger branch—Jobst and George von Bismarck—were still more unfortunate. They hesitated longer than their cousins, not from want of will, but because the proffered compensation was still more incommensurate with what they lost. But at last, moved by the instances and promises of the Prince, they agreed to accept Schönhausen and Fischbeck.

On the 14th December of the year 1562, all the Bismarcks had met together at Letzlingen with the Prince, and the agreements were here executed by which they surrendered Burgstall for Crevese and Schönhausen. The grandchildren of the first Claus von Bismarck might well be sorry at this surrender. The exchange expressly excluded the Hospital of St. Gertrude at Stendal, as well as their possessions at Wolmirstädt, Burg, and other remote places in the Archbishopric of Magdeburg. The Permutation, as it was called, did not alter the vassaldom of the Bismarcks; they continued to be lieges of Magdeburg for the fiefs abandoned with Burgstall, and vassals of Brandenburg, as before, belonging to the Alt Mark nobility in respect of Schönhausen and Fischbeck.

The Bismarcks still remained a very considerable family after the permutation, but their original position was lost by the cession of Burgstall, and their former wealth much decreased. That the permutation also had its effect in manifold way on the character of the family cannot be denied. It was a great sacrifice to bring to the governing house, although the Bismarcks very likely under-estimated the magnitude of this sacrifice.

By the Easter of 1563 the Bismarcks had quitted Burgstall, and taken possession of Crevese. The Electoral Prince had hurried their departure in consequence of the breeding season of the game and the advance of spring. On the third day after Easter he granted them Schönhausen, in the name of his son, the Bishop of Havelberg, having obtained the consent of the Chapter on the previous day.*

* Briest was also included in the permutation.—K. R. H. M.

CHAPTER IV.

THE BISMARCKS OF SCHÖNHAUSEN.

1563—1800.

Further Genealogy of the Bismarcks.—Captain Ludolf von Bismarck.— Ludolf August von Bismarck.—His remarkable Career.—Dies in the Russian Service, 1750.—Frederick William von Bismarck.—Created Count by the King of Würtemberg.—Charles Alexander von Bismarck, 1727.— His Memorial to his Wife.—His Descendants.—Charles William Ferdinand, Father of Count Otto von Bismarck.

 F the four families of the race of Bismarck, who quitted Burgstall at the Easter of 1563, three had perished in the male line in the first generation; the youngest branch had completely died out with Jobst and George; and in the elder, Henry had left behind his only daughter, Anna Ottilie, who married Fritz von der Schulenburg at Uetz. Frederick alone perpetuated the race, and all the property of the elder and younger branches at Crevese and Schönhausen fell to his line. He was known in early days as the Permutator. Perhaps he had represented his family in the negotiations with the Electoral Prince respecting Burgstall; we have seen that the two brothers of the elder

line preceded the younger ones in conceding the property. But the designation is unfitting, as he was rather permutated (bartered) than a permutator.

On his death in 1589, he left behind him, by his marriage with Anna von Wenckstern, three sons and a daughter. The race of the youngest son, Abraham, and of his wife Anna Schenck von Flechtingen, perished in the next generation. The second son, Pantaleon, married to Anna von der Schulenburg, is the ancestor of the flourishing and numerous branches of the Bismarcks of Crevese.

The Schönhausen branch was continued by Frederick's eldest son, the Captain Ludolf von Bismarck. In 1560 he joined in a campaign against the Turks under the command of Wolff Gleissenthaler, who commanded a troop of 1,300 horse in the name of the Elector of Saxony, in the Imperial army. Ludolf married Sophie von Alvensleben in 1579, and died in 1598. He was succeeded in the possession of Schönhausen by his only son Valentine, who married Bertha von der Asseburg * in 1607, and died on the 12th of April, 1620. His second son August von Bismarck succeeded him at Schönhausen. He was born on the 13th of February, 1611, and died the 2nd of February, 1670, a Colonel in the Elector of Brandenburg's army, and Commandant of the fortress of Peitz. Having entered the army in his earliest youth, he took service under the Rhinegrave in 1631. After the battle of Nördlingen, in 1634, he served in the army of Duke Bernhard of Weimar; served also till 1640 in Lothringen, Burgundy, and France, but then passed over into the service of Brandenburg. He was

---

* *Asseburg.* This family is noble and well endowed in Prussia Proper and Anhalt. The name is derived from Asseburg in Brunswick, a noble structure of considerable antiquity. It was finally sacked in 1492, and destroyed altogether in the Brunswick troubles. The present family hold the lesser countyship of Falkenstein in the Mansfeld district and the knight's fee of Eggenstadt.—K. R. H. M.

thrice married, first to Helene Elizabeth von Kottwitz, then to Dorothea Elizabeth von Katte,* and lastly to Frederica Sophia von Möllendorff.†

A young brother of this August was Valentine Busso; born 1622, died 18th of May, 1679; had issue by his wife, a Von Bardeleben,‡ the General Frederick Christopher von Bismarck, who died in command of Küstrin in 1704. The second son of the first marriage of Christopher Frederick with Louise Margarethe von der Asseburg, was Ludolf August, the only adventurous member of the family of the Bismarcks of Schönhausen.

Ludolf August von Bismarck was born on the 21st of March, 1683, entered the army at an early age, and as a valiant soldier, a handsome person, of rare intellect, he made a great figure. Something uneasy and adventurous was early observed in his character. On the 22nd of November, 1704, he married Johanna Margarethe von der Asseburg, who died in 1719, only leaving him a daughter, Albertine Louise, and who married, in 1738 or 1739, a Prussian officer, named Frederick William von der Alben. When a lieutenant-colonel in garrison at Magdeburg, Ludolf August had the misfortune to kill a footman, either in anger or when intoxicated. He concealed the corpse under the bed, and fled. Nevertheless, he obtained a pardon through his great patron

---

* *Katte.* This remarkable family needs scarcely anything at my hands. It is ancient and aristocratic, and has continued to exist despite all kinds of mutations till now. There was in the line of Wust, John Henry von Katte, whose unfortunate son was beheaded for undue zeal towards Frederick the Great: of him some account is presented—the date of his murder being 6th November, 1730. Other members of the family have distinguished themselves to recent days.—K. R. H. M.

† *Möllendorff.* One of the Möllendorffs was a Prussian field-marshal, Richard Joachim Henry von M. (b. 1725; d. 1816). He was with " *der olle Fritz,*" and was even respected by his enemies. Napoleon gave him the Grand Cross of the Legion of Honour.—K. R. H. M.

‡ *Bardeleben.* This family exists in the best condition, and has done good service to the Prussian state. The most distinguished member of this family is Kurt von Bardeleben, jurist and judge at Minden.—K. R. H. M.

General Field-Marshal Gneomar Dubislaw von Natzmer,[*] who possessed great influence with King Frederick William I., and had won great fame in battle against the Swedes, Turks, and French, and was also distinguished for exemplary piety. He was the step-brother of Count Zinzendorf, the founder of the Moravians, through his second wife, born a Von Gersdorf. Bismarck was pardoned for his desertion, and reinstated; but promotion did not ensue. Bismarck was thrice passed over on regimental changes; for the King entertained some anger against him, despite of his experience. Bismarck did not bear this long; he sold his estate of Skatiken in Prussian Lithuania, quitted the army, and entered the Russian service in 1732. In the next year, on the 26th of May, 1733, he married a Mademoiselle Trotte von Treyden, whose sister was the wife of Biron,[†] the favourite of the

[*] Gneomar Dubislaw von Natzmer was a field-marshal in the time of King Frederick William I., and frustrated the flight of the Crown Prince, afterwards Frederick II. Among his proximate descendants, through the mother, was a distinguished Prussian general, Oltwig Ant. Leop. v. Natzmer, born 18th April, 1782, at Villin in Pomerania. He took part in the many illustrious struggles of the growing kingdom of Prussia—was present at the battle of Auerstädt, 1806; taken prisoner at Prenzlau and exchanged in 1807. He received promotion to the staff after the peace of Tilsit, accompanied the King to the conference of princes at Dresden, and was sent on a secret mission to Russia. He was also in action at the battles of Gross-görschen (1813), Hainau (1813), Bautzen, and others down to Leipzig. He was also in the campaign of 1815, in high command. After a life of devotion to his sovereign, he died 1st Nov., 1861. It may be as well to state here that my object in these notes is to show how entirely devoted the military officials of Prussia are to the house of Hohenzollern, and that these side-illustrations throw a light upon the central figure of this book, Count Bismarck himself, and the motives of his steady, although apparently inconsistent, patriotism.— K. R. H. M.

[†] Biron (Ernst Johann von), Duke of Courland, was born in 1687, the son of a landed proprietor named Bühren. He was the favourite of the Duchess of Courland, Anna Iwanowna, niece of Peter the Great, from his elegant manners and attainments. She ascended the Russian throne in 1730, and though it had been expressly stipulated that Biron should not be allowed to come to Russia, he soon made his appearance at the court. Assuming the arms of the French Dukes of Biron, he governed Russia, through Anna. His life was stormy until near its close, when he returned to his Duchy of Courland, which he governed wisely. In 1769 he abdicated in favour of his

D

Empress Anna, and afterwards Duke of Courland. He combined his fortunes with those of that remarkable personage; but shared his disgrace, and was banished to Siberia. But by means of his considerable talents he seemed to have made friends outside of the Biron party, for he was soon recalled, and appointed a General. Bismarck governed several districts with ability, and fulfilled some diplomatic missions, especially at the court of London, to the perfect satisfaction of all, and seems to have conducted himself with peculiar tact, so as to come into collision with no party; and he succeeded in maintaining the position he had earned in the service of the State. He finally became General in the Ukraine, and died in October, 1750, at Pultawa. He left no issue by his second marriage, with the sister of the Duchess Biron of Courland.

A century after Ludolf August, a second Bismarck of Schönhausen visited Russia, under specially honourable circumstances. This was Frederick William von Bismarck, the famous Cavalry General of Würtemberg, also known as an esteemed military author. He was born on the 28th of July, 1783, at Windheim on the Weser, and joined the Brunswick service in 1797. He afterwards served in England, and finally in Würtemberg, where he very greatly distinguished himself, and rose to the rank of General. He was the Würtemberg ambassador to Berlin, Dresden, Hanover, and Carlsruhe. He aided in the reconstruction of the Danish army in 1826, and was

son Peter, and died 28th December, 1772. This son Peter governed till 28th March, 1795, then resigning Courland to the Czarina Catherine, but retaining all his sovereign rights. He then passed his time alternately at Berlin and his estates of Sagan and Nachod, dying 12th Jan., 1800, at Gellenau in Silesia. One of the collateral descendants of Biron, Prince Gustav Calixt von Biron, born 29th Jan., 1780, died in the Prussian service, a Lieut. General and Governor of the fortress of Glatz, 20th June, 1821. He had three sons. The second, Calixt Gustav, born 3rd Jan., 1817, is alive, having married 1845 the Princess Helene Meschtscherskii, by whom he has issue Gustav Peter Jon, born 17 Oct., 1859.—K. R. H. M.

esteemed so high an authority on cavalry matters, that the Emperor Nicholas summoned him, in 1835, to Russia, to inspect his cavalry. In 1818, Bismarck was created a Count, by the King of Würtemberg, which title he transmitted after his marriage with the Princess Augusta Amalia of Nassau-Usingen (born 30th December, 1778; died 16th July, 1846, the last of the line Nassau-Usingen),* on her bringing him no issue, to the descendants of his deceased elder brother, John Henry Ludwig. On the 3rd of April, 1848, he again married Amalia Julie Thibaut, and died on the 18th of June, 1860. His descendants by this marriage, a son and a daughter, form the second lines of the Count Bismarcks of Würtemberg, the other line existing in the family of his deceased brother.

The third Bismarck of Schönhausen, who went to Russia as the representative of His Majesty the King of Prussia, is our Minister-President.

Colonel August von Bismarck was succeeded in Schönhausen by his second son, also named August;—born the 15th of May, 1666; married the 24th of April, 1694, to Dorothea Sophie von Katte; died the 18th of June, 1732. He was Councillor and Land Commissioner to the Elector of Brandenburg, the builder or restorer of the present mansion of Schönhausen. He was succeeded by the eldest of his seven sons, August Frederick—born the 2nd of April, 1695—who met a hero's death as Colonel and Commandant of the regiment of Anspach-Baireuth Dragoons in the year 1742, at the battle of Chotusitz.† It is said that the Minister-President in person is extremely like this

* Nassau-Usingen, Princess Aug. Amalia, was married 2nd Aug., 1804, to Louis William, Landgrave of Hesse-Hombourg (died 19th Jan., 1839); separated 1805. She was the daughter of Duke Frederick Augustus (died 24th March, 1816, the last of his house) and of Louise, born Princess of Waldeck (died 17th Nov., 1816). The Almanach de Gotha does not recognize the subsequent marriage with Count Bismarck.

† The battle of Chotusitz was fought the 17th May, 1742, by Frederick II., when he obtained a victory over the Austrians under Prince Karl of Lorraine.

Bismarck, his great-grandfather, who was an excellent soldier, and high in favour with Frederick the Great. August Frederick was twice married, first to Stephanie von Dewitz, and then to Frederica Charlotte von Tresckow.

The second son of the first marriage of this brave soldier was the intellectual Charles Alexander von Bismarck, born in 1727. He was about to accompany his maternal uncle, one of the Von Dewitz family, to his post, which was that of Prussian Ambassador to Vienna, when

Charles Alexander von Bismarck.

Frederick the Great appointed his future to be otherwise. Charles Alexander entered the Royal chamber an attaché of the embassy, but quitted it as a cavalry officer. He was averse to the military art, and soon obtained his discharge as a Captain. On the 5th of March, 1762, he

The place has some 1,200 inhabitants, and is situated near Czaslau in Bohemia. This decided the cession of almost the whole of Silesia.— K. R. H. M.

married Christine Charlotte Gottliebe von Schönfeld—
born the 25th of December, 1741; deceased on the 22nd
of October, 1772—her mother having been a sister of
his mother, one of the Dewitz family. An elegant
French composition, by Charles Alexander, is preserved;
a spirited and touching memorial of his departed wife,
in the inflated style of those days. The title of this
composition—of greater merit than usually the case

Christine von Bismarck.

with such writings—is as follows: "Eloge ou Monu
ment érigé à la Mémoire de C. C. G. de Bismarck, né
de Schoenfeld, par Charles Alexandre de Bismarck.
Berlin, 1774."

We select a few passages therefrom:—

"My friend lost her mother (Sophie Eleonore von
Dewitz) in her earliest childhood, and her maternal grandmother (Louise Emilie von Dewitz, born a Von Zeethen
of the family of Trebnitz) took her to live with her at

Hoffelde. She was there nurtured in retirement and innocence, and already won my heart by her filial gentleness. There I found her once more, after years of war and life in a distant garrison, in perfect innocence, the charming picture of a blushing rose. O! that ye could return, ye hours of rapture! when the society of this sweet creature, who in her solitude had received nothing from art, but everything from the hand of nature, filled my soul with such celestial joy, that in possessing her I forgot, not alone every evil of life, but even every minor grief! Return at least for an instant to my remembrance, ye sweetest of hours, for alas! the pang of sorrow will needs drive you away too soon! Above all, return, thou memory of yon magnificent spring night, upon which I wandered, between my best beloved and her dear sister, in the outskirts of a majestic and peaceful forest, under the silvery moonlight, while the brooks trilled and the nightingale raised her sorrowing tones. My heart was instinct with love, and attuned to the enchanting prospect. I felt the beauty of the earth, and the still greater loveliness of innocence, indwelling those hearts so full of affection for me! But, no! this reminiscence is now too powerful for my feelings, and my tear-bedewed eye is too weak to bear the dazzling glory of joy! No other evening is destined for me on earth such as that was! She exists no longer who made that evening more charming to me than all the beauties of nature. She has left me for ever! Soon afterwards our society was interrupted, our supposed felicity was bitterly destroyed. Our grandmother, the refuge of her grandchildren, the sustainer of all the poor of her neighbourhood, died. My friend and I were parted, and the sorrow which succeeds all evanescent joy became our portion.

"Still it was not that terrible misery which now oppresses my heart. Well founded hopes comforted and the tenderest affection aided us. My hopes were not in vain. The slight cloud which had veiled the morning sun—which gave me life—passed away, and his ray soon shone forth with accustomed glory. With anxious unrest I yearned to associate myself with my friend to the brink of the grave. Could I but have done so for eternity! Our compact, however, is not yet broken, and will endure as long as my tears can flow, and the soul of my beloved was too beautiful to prevent their flowing for ever. Her excellent father, who might have bestowed her on a better and a richer man, gave her to me because my beloved would not have a better or richer man, nor any man save myself. What words, my father, could express my thanks for this favour, unless they could to some extent mark the value of your daughter, and stand in some relation to my lost happiness and my present grief! The silent tears that overflow my cheeks are more eloquent than words. You cannot see my tears, but perchance God beholds them, and your daughter also. A tear is the only gratitude I can offer. May the conviction cheer you that you could not have given your virtuous daughter to any one who loved her more affectionately, faithfully, and unselfishly than I did!

"You then gave her to me, my father. The 5th of March, 1762, was the happiest day of my life. I still hear the words which my tender bride selected for herself: ' *Intreat me not to leave thee or to return from following after thee, for whither thou goest I will go, and where thou lodgest I will lodge : thy people shall be my people, and thy God my God. Where thou diest will I die, and there will I be buried : the Lord do so to me, and more also, if aught but death part thee and me* ' (Ruth i., 16, 17). I cherish the hope, the only hope now animating me, that even death does not part us.

"With what delight, my friend and my father, did I then receive her from your hand. Alas! that I had left her with thee! I declare with the sincerity of one who is comfortless that I should have done so, had I known that death would so soon have withdrawn her from my arms!

"I should then have lost eleven years of a life such as angels only lead; but I would willingly have sacrificed these happiest years of my earthly life. Then I felt as secure from such thoughts of death as if I were to retain her for ever! but she left thee and her relatives in tears, and her peerless heart impelled her to ask my pardon for these very tears. Of this nature were all her imperfections. What happiness did I not anticipate in the future on the revelation of such tender sentiments; and the realization was still greater than my expectation. Our days passed away in happiness and peace. Could this state of things last for ever? It was heaven upon earth, for me at least; for what can be preferred to this intimate association with a charming, joyous, tender, intelligent, and virtuous woman? Exclusively to love! exclusively to be beloved!

"Nature had endowed my friend with beauties of person and mind, by which she could not fail to please. The first would immediately fascinate the eye, the second preserved that fascination for ever. Perhaps I ought only to dwell upon the last as the fountains of her virtues. But it would be ungrateful to be silent respecting the once visible half of the charming whole, by which alone we learn to know the other invisible portion, causing virtuous thoughts to grow into virtuous deeds, and without which I cannot even realize any picture of my beloved friend. She was of noble form, pleasant and well formed. Her expression was exactly equivalent to its necessary power of pleasing. Her hair of dark yellow tint. Her forehead was prominent, which she herself regretted, but which made her more beautiful in the eyes of others. Her brow never betrayed pride or passion. Her eyes were bluish-grey — their expression was attentive and watchful, but joyous. Her heart was light, mild, and ever open, and ever performed what her eye promised. Her nose was very handsome, somewhat high in the centre, but not to the extent visible in ambitious or passionate women. Her cheeks were breathed upon by the happy bloom of health, and the still more lovely blush of shame readily rose. Her mouth, which never gave an untrue kiss, which never uttered a word of vanity, of slander, or of lust, displayed handsome, well-arranged teeth, and balmy lips. The gentle smile of this mouth, the seat of innocence, how soon, alas! was it to pass away! The outlines of the lower part of the face were soft, the chin well formed. The profile was artistic, and so excellent that a famous Berlin painter desired to sketch it for that alone. Her manners manifested a noble freedom, neatness, and good taste." *

Thus does Bismarck's grandfather depict his wife. There certainly is much of the sentimentality of the times in these characteristic sentences, but there is more —true affection and a cultivated sense. It evinces a well of poesy in the individual, that we grieve to find these thoughts clothed in the choicest French. The poet in him is then first justified when these periods are re-translated into German, for that they were thought in German is not to be doubted.

The four sons of Charles Alexander are:—Ernst Frederick Alexander, born the 14th of February, 1763; died a Colonel and Brigadier in 1813; his eldest son by a marriage with Louise von Miltitz is Theodore Alexander Frederick Philip von Bismarck, created Count Bismarck-Bohlen, the 21st of February, 1818. He is the second Bismarck of Schönhausen who gained the rank of count; for the General Frederick von Bismarck, who obtained a similar dignity in the same year and month (the

* This rhapsody will convey a good idea of what was thought fine writing in those days, but it is fulsome to the last degree.—K. R. H. M.

17th February, 1818), from the King of Würtemberg, was also a Schönhausen. His line still endures in one son, while the title was also ceded to the descendants of his elder brother, the present Count von Bismarck-Schierstein.

The second son of Charles Alexander was Frederick Adolf Ludwig, born the 1st of August, 1766; he died in 1831, a retired Lieut.-General. In 1813 he was Commandant of Leipzig, in 1814 of Stettin, and owned the knight's fee and estate of Templin, near Potsdam.

The third was Philip Ludwig Leopold Frederick, born the 21st February, 1770, a Major in the Mecklenburg Hussar Regiment; he died on the 25th October, 1813, at Halle on the Saale, of his wounds received at the battle of Möckern.

The fourth and last, Charles William Ferdinand, was the father of the present Minister-President.

CHAPTER V.

ARMORIAL BEARINGS.

Up with the banner in the morning air!
Raise high the ancestral shield up there!
For these loved symbols bid us know
That joyfully we van-ward go!

THE shield of the Bismarcks exhibits a device, which, although it has not materially changed in the course of centuries, has at different times been variously blazoned. It displays a double trefoil, or, more exactly speaking, a round-leafed trefoil, flanked in its corners by three long leaves. The centre device has altered in the seals of various times, sometimes resembling a rose leaf, sometimes a clover leaf; finally it has remained a clover leaf. The other trefoil has been treated in the same way, the leaf being sharply serrated and shorter, or sometimes longer and but slightly serrated, finally becoming an oak leaf. The colours have also only been decided in later years. The shield is thus described :—

" In a field azure a golden clover leaf supported in the three angles by three silver oak leaves." As to the crest, the arms of Ludolf von Bismarck exhibit two stags' antlers on the helmet, evidently alluding to his official position as Ranger to the Margrave, for the buffalo horns now in use also often appear at a very early period. The present emblazoning of the crest is thus given :—" On a coroneted helmet displayed two buffalo horns proper in azure and argent crosswise—the helmet is azure and argent."

The small gold coronet, which, contrary to every rule of good heraldry, is represented hovering between the horns, is a more recent addition. We are unable to decide when and how this coronet became part of the crest. Brüggemann, in his description of Pomerania, describes it as a Count's coronet—for what reason we do not perceive.

On inspection of the earliest seals it is evident that the round trefoil was unquestionably the peculiar and original device, the elongated leaves having been subsequently added, disputing precedence with the clover leaf. Thus it is that afterwards we find the oak leaves small and the centre trefoil large—and contrariwise. If the clover be regarded as the principal device, it would be more heraldically true, as it is always emblazoned in gold, to blazon the horns in azure and or. Indeed, the heraldic ensigns of the Prussian Monarchy (Vol. I. p. 19.) give the correct crest of the Bismarcks in the Armorial Bearings of the Counts of Bismarck-Bohlen.

The seal of the first Nicholas von Bismarck (1365) displays the device in a neat border, with a string of pearls within the inscription. This inscription, no longer very legible, is *S. (Sigillum) Nicolay de Bismark*. This border disappears on the seals of his three sons : the shield lies within a string of pearls on a field strewn with small crosses. In all these seals the trefoil is prominent, but in the seals of succeeding generations it becomes very small, the long leaves being prominent, until by lapse of time they assumed proportionate dimensions.

It would be idle and unheraldic to endeavour to identify symbols deriving their names from the botanical world, hence it would be useless to define the long leaves in the Bismarck arms as those of the Wegedorn, Christthorn, or White Bramble. This has, however, been done in support of the extraction of the Bismarcks from the Slavonic race—to identify it with *Bij smarku* (Beware of the Bramble), an idea which we must dismiss as entirely erroneous. The legends only recognize the clover leaf, and call the long leaves those of the nettle. In popular tradition these two ideas have become intermingled, as a proverb shows, which was engraven on the blade of a sword of honour presented to Count Bismarck some years ago. This proverb is :—

> Der Wegekraut sollst stehen lah'n—
> Hüt dich, Junge, sind Nesseln d'ran.

Anglicé.[*]

> The bramble thou shouldst let 'a be ;
> The nettle, boy, beneath you 'll see.

The round leaves were here supposed to be bramble (*plantago*) ; the serrated long leaves, leaves of the nettle.

We find the legend of the arms in the third volume of the *Berlin Review* of 1856, afterwards reprinted in Hesekiel's *Wappen Sagen*, Berlin, 1865, as follows :[†]—

[*] From Platt, or Low German.—K. R. H. M.

[†] The reader must excuse the free and somewhat irregular rendering of this legend—*penes me*.—K. R. H. M.

The leaf so green and goodly,
  The wanderer's delight,
In purest gold so shiny,
  The Bismarck's coat bedight—
The cloven leaf lights golden
  All on an azure field,
With nettle leaves so olden,
  Sharp shown upon the shield.
In ancient days departed,
  There was a dainty maid,
By whom the nettle signet
  Was on this shield displayed.
For damsel Gertrude many
  A suitor came to woo,
But her father not with any
  Save her cousin willed to do.
A Wendic chief so princely
  Came down from northern sea ;
A hundred horses with him
  Pranced pricking o'er the lea.
Young Gertrude he demanded,
  But Gertrude, all politely,
Made little courtesy candid—
  Despite his carriage knightly,
She would have naught of he.

The Prince, incensèd highly,
  Upraised his golden wand ;
He called his knaves assembled,
  Around him they did stand.
In angry tones he shouted,—
  " The trefoil bruised shall be ;
Not thus will I be flouted !
  The nettle fain I 'd see.
'Twere merry to be breaking
  The trefoil green or gold,
And havoc to be making
  Amidst these halls so old ! "
And in that self-same hour,
  This Prince of Wendic race
Assaulted Gertrude's bower,
  The trefoil to displace.
The castellan, o'erpowered,
  Sank silent in the moat ;
The chieftain so o'er froward
  His way then onward smote.

Rejoicing in his valour
  The Prince came clanking in,
But Gertrude showed no pallour,
  Despite the battle's din.

" I 'll cull the trefoil golden
  That hath no nettle's sting,
The trefoil quaint and olden—"
  " Thou shalt not do this thing ! "
He to his arms would take her,
  And lovingly embrace :
No courage did forsake her :
  He quickly shouted " Grace ! "
Down in his blood before her,
  He sank in sudden death—
Proud as the race that bore her,
  She stabbed with bated breath ;
And once and twice she smote him,
  And buried deep the steel.
'Twas thus she could devote him
  The nettle's sting to feel—
" Who dares to cull the trefoil
  The nettle's sting shall feel ! "

And since young Gertrude's hour,
  On Bismarck's shield displayed,
The nettle's stinging power
  Round trefoil is arrayed.
With steel of keenest temper,
  Their virtue is upheld,
Since early days of Gertrude,
  Those early days of eld !

According to another and still more simple legend, the
Bismarcks added the oak leaves to their arms on the
occasion of one of their race conquering a Wendic chief,
whose device contained such a leaf, or three such leaves.
We do not lay any stress, and with justice, on the presumed importance of such traditions, so common in the
last century; still we should not like to see them altogether thrown aside as trifling. Every legend contains
some kernel of truth, however small. Thus it does not
seem unimportant that the Bismarcks are continually
represented as combating the heathen Wends. There is
certainly nothing proved by it, but it would never have
arisen had not this family belonged to the followers of
some German prince, who had established himself in the
frontier Marks on the Elbe, and waged unceasing war

thence against the Slavonic tribes existing between that river and the Oder.

Thrice in this century has the dignity of Count been conferred on the Bismarcks of Schönhausen; we now therefore possess Prussian Counts of Bismarck-Bohlen, Würtemberg Counts of Bismarck, the first line of which call themselves Counts of Bismarck-Schierstein, and the second line only Counts von Bismarck; finally we have Prussian Counts of Bismarck-Schönhausen.

The arms of the Prussian Counts of Bismarck-Bohlen are thus given :—The shield is bordered or and quartered, the first and fourth fields azure, displaying a trefoil or surrounded by three oak leaves argent (Bismarck); in the second and third field a griffin gules on a roof tree formed of five stones gules in steps (Bohlen). The Bismarck crest is crowned and surmounted by two buffalo horns emblazoned azure and or crosswise, with a small gold crown between the horns; the helmet trappings are azure and or. The centre (Bohlen) crest is crowned and supported by two uncrowned griffins gules regardant on a trunk of a tree; the helmet trappings are azure and gules. The crowned crest to the left displays three ostrich feathers, the centre one sable, the others white; each ostrich feather bears a diamond argent (perhaps for Schiverni); the helmet trappings gules and argent. Between the shield and crest is the Count's coronet. Supporters, two crowned griffins gules regardant.

The arms of the Würtemberg Counts of Bismarck-Schierstein (called the first or Nassau line, their family estate of Schierstein lying in Nassau) are as follows :— The quartered shield displays, in the first and fourth fields, azure a trefoil or, with three oak leaves argent at the corners; in the second field, gules a lion or passant; in the third, gules a horse argent fresnée. On the crest, coroneted, two buffalo horns of azure and argent crosswise,

BISMARCK'S FATHER.

Karl Wilhelm Ferdinand von Bismarck.

BISMARCK'S FATHER.

(Karl Wilhelm Ferdinand von Bismarck.)

double meaning—one referring to the double trinity of
the trefoils, the other allied to the higher signification of
the Trinity of God.

CHAPTER VI.

THE NEIGHBOURHOOD OF BISMARCK'S BIRTHPLACE.

Genthin.—The Plotho Family.—Jerichow.—Fischbeck.—The Kaiserburg.—
The Emperor Charles IV.—The Elector Joachim Nestor.—Frederick I.—
General Fransecky "to the Front."—Tangermünde.—Town-hall.—Count
Bismarck.—His Uniform, and the South German Deputy.—Departure for
Schönhausen.

[The translator has abridged the following chapters and transferred them to a
place apparently better fitted for them than that they occupy in the German
edition, but nothing of importance is omitted.]

GENTHIN is an ancient place, owing its foundation
during the twelfth century to the noble Lords of Plotho,
whose ancestral mansion, Alten-Plotho, lies close to the
town. At the present time the head of this family, who
is invested with the dignity of Hereditary Chamberlain
of the Duchy of Magdeburg, resides at the Castle of
Parey, on the Elbe. The noble family of Plotho shares
with that of the Gänse of Putlitz the distinction of being
the only race still flourishing, the origin of which can be
traced to the Wendic princes and family chieftains. It
is probable that they were early converted to Christianity,
and thence were enabled to retain some attributes of their
Wendic nobility, and assert some few privileges in the
presence of the Teutonic knightly aristocracy, gradually
thronging forward into the Marks with their feudal
retainers. The Plothos and the Putlitzs hence are called
noblemen (*Edle Herrn, nobiles viri*), at a time when the
designation was usually only applied to dynasties. In

early records they are always named in precedence of the
members of the ancient chivalric races.   They had vassals
of noble blood, and, up to the most recent period, held their
own court at the Manor of Parey.   The features of that
Freiherr von Plotho who so energetically repelled the Imperial Ban, in his capacity as Electoral Brandenburg Ambassador, at the Imperial Diet in Ratisbon, which the Imperial
notary, Doctor April, endeavoured to force upon him against
Frederick the Great, are well known and popular.   The
best portrait of this remarkable personage has been drawn
by Goethe, in his " Fiction and Truth." *   It is not so
generally known that a branch of this Wendic family has
also established itself in Belgium.   The enormous possessions of the Barony of Engelsmünster, in Flanders,
were first alienated from that family amidst the storms of
the French Revolution.

It was on the afternoon of a somewhat chilly June day
that we drove into the green pastures of Jerichow.   The
fragrance of lime blossoms and hay saluted our nostrils.
The eye was gratified by well kept fields, pleasantly alternating with plough-land and meadow ; the heath, with its
thorn bushes, chiefly surrounded by strips of brushwood,
smiled before us.

The first place at which we arrived was Redekin, with
the simple mansion of the Alvensleben family—its tall
poplars, and its neighbouring venerable church with the
bronze figure of Christ.   Next came Jerichow, the small
city which gives its name to two counties.   This pretty
little town has two churches, and welcomed us cheerfully
with its group of fine old elms and fragrant rose trees.
The church at the entrance has nothing remarkable about
it, but the other at the end of the town is very curious, as
one of the earliest specimens of pure Gothic style in these
parts.   This possesses a crypt.

* Goethe's " Fiction and Truth " (*Dichtung und Wahrheit*).—K. R. H. M.

Close behind Jerichow on the left, a landmark, the handsome Kaiser-house of Tangermünde, is visible.

At our next stage, the fine village of Fischbeck, we were already upon ancient Bismarckian soil; we did not, however, drive farther in the direction of Schönhausen, close by, but turned to the left towards the Elbe, on the other bank of which Tangermünde, with its imperial castle, tall towers, walls, and turrets, forming a well preserved piece of mediæval architecture, presented itself to our view in the last golden rays of the evening sun.

We slowly crossed the broad expanse of the Elbe in a ponderous ferry-boat, and went up to the castle, built by the Emperor Charles IV., that acute and politic King of Bohemia, as a metropolis for the great realm which extended from the North Sea and the Baltic as far as Hungary, and in which he designed to found the power of his family—a realm destined to fall to pieces under his sons.

At the castle we did not, of course, find the old lime-tree of justice, at which appeals used to be made from the gate of the old Brandenburg bridge. The gate and the tree have both disappeared, but on entering the castle yard by the massive gate tower, we had the venerable ruins of the ancient pile before us; on the left the tower, on the right the chapel, smothered in festoons of blooming roses. The castle itself, in which the powerful emperor once lived —where the magnificent Elector Joachim Nestor held his joyous wedding feast with the beautiful Princess Elizabeth of Denmark, and where he breathed out the last breath of his noble life, after many bitter disappointments—exists no longer. The sheriff's office, which stands on the site of the castle, was built by King Frederick I. before he was king. His F., with the electoral cap and the Roman numerals III., is still to be seen on the ceilings.

The old Kaiserburg is now inhabited by a retired officer of cavalry, who was then entertaining a visitor, General

von Fransecky, known since the battle of Sadowa as
"Fransecky Vor"—"Fransecky to the front." This hero
of the fight had come thither to inspect the fourth
squadron of the Westphalian Dragoons, lying in garrison
at Tangermünde; hence on this evening the old castle
was full of gay feminine toilettes and brilliant uniforms.
Charles IV., educated at the French court and in Italy,
here at one time instructed the rude squires of the Mark
in his courtly and chivalrous code of manners towards
ladies. The first assemblies in which both sexes intermingled took place at Tangermünde. Until that time
in these regions men and women had sought their
amusements separately, and hence knew nothing of real
society.

The old Emperor would certainly have enjoyed the
pleasant picture of cheerful sociability presented this
evening in the lovely gardens between his chapel and
tower.

Next morning we visited the remarkable town-hall and
the handsome church of the ancient city. Such town-
halls and churches no communities or cities as large as
Tangermünde build at the present day. We are wanting
in that sense of public spirit, and prefer small separate
houses, and devote no proud and extensive structures to
the use of the commonwealth.

The morning sun was shining brightly on the old city,
and the Sunday bells were tolling as we passed back across
the Elbe. A group of children bathing enlivened the
strand below the grey tower. Two officers brought their
fine horses across in the ferry-boat; one of these belonged
to the Westphalian Dragoons, the other wore the yellow
collar and cap-stripe of the Seventh Heavy Militia Cavalry,
the colonel of which is General Count Bismarck. It is
well known that Count Bismarck habitually wears the
uniform of his regiment, and a South German Deputy
to the Diet did not omit to stigmatize the yellow token

of the uniform of the Chancellor of the Diet as very
ominous. The excellent and reverend gentleman saw in
the sulphurous collar of Bismarck a piece of the uniform
of a prince as different from our noble King William as
could possibly be.

On reaching the landing-place, we took a long last
look at Tangermünde, before entering the carriage which
was to convey us to Schönhausen.

CHAPTER VII.

SCHÖNHAUSEN.

ON leaving Fischbeck for Schönhausen there is on the right the Kattenwinkel, or Kattenland. By this we are not reminded of the old Teutonic tribe of the Catte, of whose relations towards the Cherusci we know very little, but of the old and chivalrous race of Katte, established in this region for the last five hundred years. Almost all the villages whose church spires we see or do not see, in the corner between the Havel and the Elbe, belonged or still belong to the family Von Katte.

Among these villages is Wust. In the church of that place are buried the remains of that Katte, whose friendship for Frederick the Great ended in the tragedy of Küstrin.* There is something fantastic, and at the same time touching, in the fact, that as well as the skull of the executed John Hermann von Katte, the periwig trimmed with blue lace, and worn by him, has been

---

* For the most eloquent account of this sad affair, the reader is requested to refer to Mr. Carlyle's " Frederick the Great," Book vii. Chap. 9.—K. R. H. M.

preserved in the family vault at Wust. The Katte family * was very numerous, and in this district there is scarcely a church or family mansion which does not bear its canting heraldic coat of arms. By marriages, also, the azure shield, with the white cat bearing the mouse in its mouth, has spread in all directions. It is impossible to contemplate the armorial bearings of the Kattes without thinking of the beheaded friend of the great Frederick. Just as the cat, in the coat of arms, plays cruelly with the mouse, did the furious King Frederick William play with him. It is a milder trait in the tragedy of Küstrin, that the angry King endeavoured in his peculiar way to comfort John Hermann's father, as well as his grandfather, Field-Marshal Count Wartersleben, for the terrible fate of their son and grandson. Frederick William I. was an angry and almost coarsely-severe monarch, but there was nothing of the Oriental despot about him, and, to do him justice, his native benevolence and Christian conscientiousness must not be overlooked. Oriental despots were not, however, then confined to the Orient. The general character of King Frederick William the Severe bears a favourable contrast with those of the other rulers of his time.

As we drove into Schönhausen, the church bell was ringing ; but it did not give a clear sound, but appeared dull. The bell of the prettiest village church between the Havel and the Elbe is cracked, and will probably soon be recast ; but we cannot deny that the very dulness of its sound, amidst the sunlight and blossoms of the well wooded roadway, had a peculiar effect upon the mind.

* *Katte.* This illustrious family has been historically famous for its liege adherence to the Prussian-Brandenburg house. John Henry von Katte (born 18th Oct., 1681 ; died 31st May, 1741), of Wust, was a Field-Marshal General and Count. His son was the unfortunate friend of Frederick the Crown Prince, beheaded at Küstrin, 6th Nov., 1740. Several others of this family have distinguished themselves, despite the cruelty of the kings, in the Prussian service.—K. R. H. M.

Schönhausen is an ancient place, and, like all this portion of the circle of Jerichow, was originally ecclesiastical property. It formed part of the endowment granted in 946 by Emperor Otto I. to the bishopric of Havelberg, founded by him. This grant of Otto's, in course of time, was considerably divided; Schönhausen and Fischbeck, however, remained attached to the cathedral of Havelberg as maintenance of the bishopric. Until the fifteenth century Schönhausen was an ordinary village, governed by a bailiff. But during the bishopric of John von Schlabrendorf, who occupied the episcopal throne during the peaceful period between 1501 and 1520, the place greatly improved, and made some progress towards becoming a township. In an acknowledgment, still extant, of the year 1547, the receipt runs thus: " Received of the worshipful magistrates and sheriffs of the borough of Schönhausen." The place had therefore become a borough. The bounds of this borough were very considerable, for, besides the forest-land, they comprehended more than 20,000 acres of arable land. Hence it ensued that Schönhausen, down to recent times, always reckoned more inhabitants than the neighbouring township of Jerichow. As, however, there no longer existed any bishops of Havelberg as its protectors, Schönhausen was unable to maintain its rank as a borough, although time has not effaced all similarity in the place to a town or market-place. Schönhausen suffered greatly in the Thirty Years' War, alternately from the Swedes and the Imperial forces; and of forty-eight farms only one remained. In 1642 the manor-house was plundered and burnt; and in 1651 the whole district was visited by a severe inundation. For many years there was no pastor attached to the church, until the Bismarcks summoned, in 1650, the Rev. Adam Winkler from Grosswulkow.

The church and the manor-house are situated close together upon an eminence, and from the churchyard there

is a fine view. This venerable sanctuary was consecrated
on the 7th of November, 1212, and built by Bishop
Siegobodo of Havelberg, at the beginning of his episco-
pate, he being one of the first spiritual shepherds who
busied himself in the establishment of Christianity in this

neighbourhood. Its patron saints were the Virgin and
the Martyr Willebrod. In order to increase the sanctity
of this church, which, from the rarity of churches at that
time, was frequented by the inhabitants of an extensive
district, a rich collection of relics was established there.

Among these were relics of the holy martyr of Thebes, of the martyr Sebastian, of Bishop Constantine, of the Abbot Ægidius, of St. Alban, and others. These were discovered on the repair of the altar in 1712, contained in a sealed casket, together with an original record by Bishop Siegobodo as to the consecration of the church and the deposit of the relics. The church of Schönhausen is the largest, handsomest, and most perfect village church in the whole district—its shape in grand simplicity is that of a tri-naved basilica. Its origin from the Havelberg bishops is also shown by the broad tower transept, the cathedral of Havelberg having been the pattern of all churches in the vicinity. The Landrath August von Bismarck especially promoted the interior decorations of the church; he also, in great measure, restored the manor-house. He presented the handsomely carved pulpit and staircase in the centre, as well as the splendid and richly carved oak dais opposite the pulpit. He also set up the altar and altar-piece. To his parents he erected a memorial with oval portraits; the costume of the pictures is that of the middle of the seventeenth century. His own mural inscription, erected by his son, is at a little distance, but it is far inferior in execution. Under these memorial tablets is placed, in a style of the utmost simplicity, that of the mother of our Minister-President.

The mansion of the Bismarcks is close to the church. It is entered by a gateway with walled railings, having to its left the farm building, and in front of it a tall and handsome lime tree, which, as it were, marks the boundary between the offices and the special courtyard of the mansion. At a few paces from the lime stands a sandstone vase, and we then find ourselves in front of the house where Bismarck was born.

It is a plain, massive, quadrangular building of the last few years of the seventeenth century, the enormous foundation walls of which date from the early castle first inhabited by the Bismarcks : this was ravaged and burnt during the Thirty Years' War. The house is in two stories, with a high roof. On the right a wing is built out, extending as far as a sandstone vase. The park begins on the left with magnificent alleys of chestnuts and limes.

The doorway is as simple as the house, without steps or porch. The shield above it bears on the right the arms of the Bismarcks, and on the left those of the Kattes—the cat with the mouse. The inscription to the right is August von Bismarck, that on the left is Dorothea Sophia Katte, anno 1700.

Round the corner, by a door leading to the garden, the house can be entered through a handsome and spacious garden saloon. The ceiling of this room is decorated with the armorial bearings.

This ground floor leads into a large hall, whence there is a heavy, broad, and dark staircase to the upper rooms. The next room is the comparatively low-ceilinged dining-room, hung with white tapestry; and here we also found the ceiling borders and the two fireplaces richly ornamented with carving. On the side tables stand busts of Frederick William III. and Frederick William IV., the latter as Crown Prince. The furniture is plain.

From the dining-room the door to the left leads into two handsome reception rooms, the one ornamented with oil paintings, the other decorated in the Japanese style. Here are, in the corners, casts of Kiss's Amazon, and Rauch's Walburga riding on the stag.

To the right of the dining-room is situated the sitting-room of Countess Bismarck, tapestried in green. The

pictures and lithographs are of the time of Frederick William III., and over the chimney-piece is the medallion portrait of a woman, probably an antique beauty. The principal object in this room is the portrait of the Minister-President's mother.

Farther on again to the right we enter the bed-chamber; in yonder alcove, now divided from the room by a red curtain, Otto von Bismarck was born, on the 1st of April, 1815. In this alcove his cradle stood, but it is now only occupied by the bed in which his father died.

It is a simple apartment, presenting a comfortable and cosy aspect.

The third door in the background of the green sitting-room leads to the library, a spacious chamber painted red, having in the centre a ponderous and broad table. The books are contained in two book-cases. The collection is not inconsiderable in number, but their arrangement is confused.

It was worth while to cast a glance into the bookshelves, and see what books were studied by Count Bismarck in his youth. In one of the cases we found honest old Zedler's voluminous Universal Lexicon of the Sciences and Arts; next to it the extensive collection

"Theatrum Europæum," still an indispensable companion; a General History of Germany, a Universal History, both written in the pedantic tone of the last century; Gledow's "History of the Empire;" an historical Labyrinth of Time, and Ludwig Gottfried's "Historical Chronicle of the Four Monarchies." Theology was represented by Dr. Martin Luther's German writings. Next to a collection of old travels, stood a Political and News Lexicon, with Busching's "Geography." The other book-case, in its upper shelves, appears dedicated to the Belles Lettres. Voltaire and the Letters of Count von Bussy stood peacefully beside Frederick von Schlegel's works and Leopold Schefer's "Lay Breviary;" next to Basedow's "Introduction" was lying Herschel's "Popular Astronomy."

Turning from the books to the pictures, we find them of special interest, as they chiefly depict members of the family. A couple of portraits of Bismarck's only sister when very young, evidence some remote likeness to the mother.

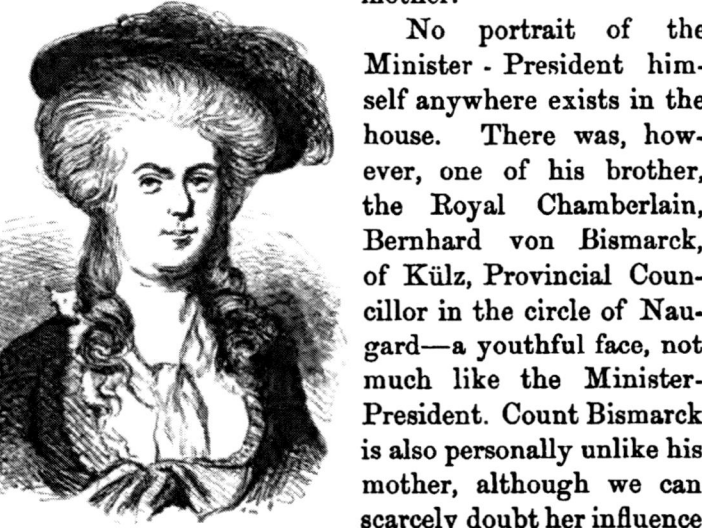

No portrait of the Minister - President himself anywhere exists in the house. There was, however, one of his brother, the Royal Chamberlain, Bernhard von Bismarck, of Külz, Provincial Councillor in the circle of Naugard—a youthful face, not much like the Minister-President. Count Bismarck is also personally unlike his mother, although we can scarcely doubt her influence over his mental qualities. We may mention among the pictures a very interesting one of his maternal grandmother, and also one of his uncle General von Bismarck.

By chance we noticed, half-concealed by the enormous stove, the portrait of a lady. The original had scarcely been a beauty; her features were hard and unformed, though this might partly have been the painter's fault. This picture had its little history.

Madame Bellin, the housekeeper, told us that during the absence of Bismarck's father on a journey, she had found it in a loft, cleaned it, and brought it down to the library. She asked her master on his return whose portrait it was, and learned that it was that of a young

Wappen

Hebt der Väter leuchtende Schilde,
Lasset die Banner im Morgenwind wehn,
Denn bei der Vorzeit mahnendem Bilde
Muss uns die Hoffnung der Zukunft erstehn.

BISMARCK'S ARMORIAL BEARINGS.

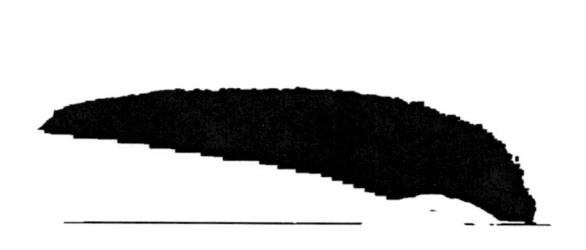

countess who had in his youth been suggested to him as a wife, with a dowry of one hundred thousand thalers.* We could readily understand that Herr von Bismarck found few charms in the picture, but the housekeeper, who was struck with the dowry, exclaimed, "Ah! *gnadiger Herr*, I should have had her if she had possessed a hundred thousand thalers!" Bismarck's father replied, with a smile, "Well, you can have her yourself, if you like her so much."

In those days people had a great deal of respect for a hundred thousand thalers, and such a sum of money was then respectfully called a ton of money. In our times a hundred thousand thalers form no great amount of wealth, although one does not instinctively put one's hand in one's pocket to give the poor possessor a trifle by way of charity. At least, such was the expression of a well-known young nobleman lately, on speaking of the difference in the times. However, the portrait of the young countess with the hundred thousand thalers has hung in the library behind the stove at Schönhausen ever since.

The peculiarity of the paternal mansion of Bismarck consists in its quadrangular form, its thick walls, its massive heavy staircase, the depth and low pitch of its rooms, and the almost extravagant use of stucco on the ceilings, friezes, stoves, and panels. But the whole mansion impresses you with an air of comfort and homely solidity; there is an historical air of noble simplicity throughout the whole of the apartments.

Schönhausen would of course not be a correct dwelling house for an ancient family, if proper ghost stories did not pertain to it; and the ancient structure does not look as if these were deficient. On the contrary, there never was a house more like a haunted house than this cradle of Bismarck's. Those, indeed, who were able to tell of the

* About £13,300 sterling.

F

ghosts which flitted about the mansion are long since
buried, and we were obliged to content ourselves with a
very poor remainder of these traditions; but what is still
preserved was quite sufficient to satisfy the charm of terror
in the ladies, at times guests at the mansion, if not to
arouse terror of a real kind, without any delightful sensation. The library was especially "uncanny;" a faithful
servant, who slept there when the family was from home,
often woke up in the night with a cold breath to disturb
him; he perceived that there was a "something" un-
pleasantly close to him, and his usually fearless spirit was
seized with icy horror. It was by no means so unpleasant
when the "something" evinced its presence in some more
definite manner, as, for instance, when it came tramping
up the oak staircase outside, or banged itself down with
a dull thud. The man who related this was not at all
wanting in courage; he knew that he was quite alone in
the house; he always concluded it to be thieves, but if he
put out his hands they encountered nothing, and if he
went out from the room he found no one there. It is
very easy to laugh at these things, but that is all of no
use; the unexplained always has its terrors until some
false or true solution of the enigma is found.

One night, Bismarck, before he was Minister, occupied
the bedroom in which he was born; he had guests in the
mansion—among others a certain Herr von Dewitz. The
next day a hunting party was to take place, and a servant
had been instructed to awaken his master at an early
hour. Suddenly Bismarck awoke; he heard the door of
the library in the adjacent chamber open, and thought he
perceived soft footsteps. He concluded it was the servant
coming to awaken him. At that moment he heard Herr
von Dewitz exclaim, "Who's there?" He sprang from
the bed, the clock struck twelve, and there was nobody to
be seen. He had felt or heard something, as other persons
had before him, which was susceptible of no explanation.

Another of the Bismarcks had also seen something; if we are not mistaken this was an uncle of the Minister's, the General von Bismarck who died in 1831. He saw, certainly only in a dream, a fleeting white form that beckoned to him; he followed, and it led him down into the cellar, the most ancient part of the building, and there showed him a door in which there was cut an opening in the form of a heart. He thought from the motions of the apparition that it signified to him the existence of a concealed treasure. This was, as already stated, all a dream, but the dream was so vivid, it made such an impression on him, that on the next morning he examined the cellar closely; he found, hidden behind rubbish and lumber, a little door with a heart-shaped opening in it, the existence of which was quite unsuspected by any of the members of the family. The door had now been found, but alas! no treasure was discovered, for the door only concealed a hidden passage leading into the Church.

In the library door there are three deep cracks, commemorating the presence of evil spirits of anything but a ghostly nature; they were French soldiers, who in 1806 pursued the young and lovely lady of the mansion, and endeavoured to break down the door with their bayonets, when the fugitive had locked it behind her. Bismarck's father sheltered his wife from the attentions of the children of the "*grande nation*" in the forest, but his ready money, among which was a considerable sum in louis-d'ors, he buried under the solitary pavilion in the park island. His astonishment was great, when, on his return, he found his treasure disturbed, but not stolen, though the louis-d'ors were scattered about. Not the French, but the dogs, had discovered it, had scratched up the earth, and thrown the gold pieces contemptuously aside.

It does not seem that Schönhausen had ever been in

the possession of the Soldiers of the Holy Virgin—the Order of the Temple; but in the ghostly chronicles of the mansion the Knights Templars play a considerable part. Their long white mantles with the red cross are certainly particularly adapted for this; but it is a sign of the deep impression made by the sudden destruction of the mighty Order, upon the people of these districts, that in all mysterious narratives, all secret subterranean passages, treasure hoards, and similar circumstances, we find the Templars with their long white cloaks occupying a con-

spicuous place. At the same time, there is much avarice mingled with this, for the most extravagant traditions found credence as to the wealth of the Templars. Buried treasures of the Order were suspected everywhere, and the poor Templars were doomed to guard the riches which they had accumulated during their lives, as ghosts, for ever.

From the mansion we passed on to the upper terrace

of the park, and wandered down the cool shady alley of limes, the branches of which bent to the ground, forming a verdant arbour of singular beauty. In this magnificent spot the lord of the mansion often had the table spread for himself and friends. The park is remarkably distinguished for fine rows of trees, both old and new, and the lime tree seems ever to have been the favourite tree of the Bismarcks of Schönhausen.

On the wall, separating the terrace from the park itself, there is growing a very handsome birch tree, which appears to have been self-sown. It has rooted itself deep into the stone, breaking down a portion of the wall, and now grows up amidst ruins and wreaths of roses, like the green flag of a victor.

The park is laid out according to the antique French style, with straight hedges, basins, and statues; but Nature has long since overcome the garden shears of Lenotre.

It is easy to perceive from the lower park itself that the lord of the manor is no longer present, and that the farm is leased. Between the tall noble avenues and picturesque foliage, broad patches planted with vegetables may be observed. This gives a homely, but scarcely a neglected, appearance to the place, as it does not destroy the general beauty of the view.

By an avenue, adorned with really splendid limes, we reach a small bridge, leading across the mantled pool which divides the park from the fields. On this side is the cool shade of the limes; yonder in the sunshine is Indian corn and beetroot. By this bridge stands a statue of Hercules with its hand on its back, cut in sandstone, on the north side of which the Junker Otto Bismarck once fired off his rifle—the marks of which musketry are still visible—and he ever afterwards used to assure his friends that Hercules put his hand there because the shot still pained him! On one thigh, evidently by a later hand, some person has written "Adam." This person, obviously

somewhat wanting in his knowledge of mythology, no
doubt was led to the explanation by the very primitive
style of costume. But so long as the country side
contents itself with such explanations, there is not much
to be said against it. It is somewhat more reprehensible
to decapitate the gods, to provide a whetstone for the
scythe. This fate, however, a somewhat massive Flora
has had to undergo; and there it stands behind a thicket,
apparently mourning the loss of its curly head.

Upon a small artificial island in the park stands a lone-
some pavilion in the style of the Regent, half hidden
by trees and overgrown with moss. The poet might
select it for the scene of the catastrophe of a romance.
We did not cross the wooden bridge, because our friendly
guide warned us against the gnats which for a long time,
in many sorts and sizes, have enjoyed their innocent lives
in that locality.

We did, however, visit two solemn places in the park
—two graves. In a dark shrubbery, grown quite wild,
lies an elder brother of Bismarck, deceased as a child.
The cast-iron cross has evidently been erected over the
grave at a later time.

At the very remotest corner of the park, close by the
sedgy shore, we found the second grave. Here Captain
von Bismarck, a cousin of the Minister, reposes. Above
the last resting-place of the wearied soldier is another
iron cross. This was the favourite spot of the old
gentleman during his lifetime; beneath the trees, on the
banks which now watch over his grave, he used in summer
time to muse every day, over his quiet fishing-rod, or gazing
dreamily across into the blooming meadows beyond the
water. At his express desire he was buried in this spot.

Besides the six-and-twenty farms and subsidiary patches,
there is also at Schönhausen a knight's demesne (*Ritter
gut*), formerly likewise the property of the Bismarcks,
but which had to be sold in time of need. It now belongs

to Dyke Captain Gaertner. It is related that the Minister wished to repurchase it, but Captain Gaertner, who did not wish to part with the property, asked 150,000 thalers more than the value, upon which Bismarck observed, " I would have given 50,000 thalers more than it was worth, but I cannot agree to a larger sum." This is only a popular tale, for the truth of which we cannot vouch.

In taking leave of Schönhausen, we may be allowed to say that, in the general picture of the place, we seem to recognize individual traits of the man there born— or, rather, that the sight of Schönhausen has shown us features which point to cognate and similar facts in the outward appearance of Bismarck. It is difficult to express this in words, but the sentiment remains ; and in this we need not appeal to posterity, as is the custom of authors when they feel assured that they will be unintelligible to their readers, but rather to all those alike familiar with Bismarck and his estate of Schön- hausen.

Be health and blessings ever near
  The mansion old by woods surrounded,
The cradle, so to Prussia dear,
  Of him who Germany refounded.
By strength of thought and weapon's might
He conquered, striving for the right;
Peace to the house and hail the star
That Prussia's glory beams afar !

Helle Jugend

Der Keim verräth die Blüthe schon,
Die Blüthe zeigt die Frucht,
Wir fühlen hier beim ersten Ton
Des ganzen Liedes Wucht.

EARLY YOUTH.

Helle Jugend.

Der Keim verräth die Blüthe schon,
Die Blüthe zeigt die Frucht,
Wir fühlen hier beim erſten Ton
Des ganzen Liedes Wucht.

EARLY YOUTH.

Book the Second.

———•———

YOUTH.

CHAPTER I.

SCHOOL AND COLLEGE DAYS.

Bismarck's Parents.—Brothers and Sisters.—Bismarck Born.—Kniephof, Jarchelin, and Külz.—The Plamann Institute.—The Frederick William Institute.—Residence in Berlin.—Bismarck's Father and Mother.—Letter of Count Bismarck to his Sister.—Confirmation.—Dr. Bonnell.—Severity of the Plamanns.—Holiday Time.—Colonel August Frederick von Bismarck and the Wooden Donkey at Ihna Bridge.—School-life with Dr. Bonnell.—The Cholera of 1831.—The Youthful Character and Appearance of Bismarck.—Early Friends.—Proverbs.—" Far from Sufficient!" quoth Bismarck.

 ARL Wilhelm Ferdinand von Bismarck, of Schönhausen, born on the 13th November, 1771, once belonging to the Body Guard (No. 11 in the old list), who quitted the service as Captain, was married on the 7th of July, 1806, to Louise Wilhelmina Menken, born on the 24th of February, 1790; died the 1st of January, 1839, at Berlin.

Frau von Bismarck was an orphan daughter of the well-known Privy Councillor, Anastatius Ludwig Menken, who had served with distinction under three sovereigns of Prussia and possessed great influence during the first years of the reign of Frederick William III. He was born at Helmstadt on the 2nd of August, 1752, and was a member of a family distinguished for its literary attainments. To a certain extent he was a pupil of the Minister Count Herzberg,* by whose means he was appointed to a post in the Privy Chancery. Frederick the Great held him in great esteem, he having rendered an important service to his sister, the Queen Louise Ulrike, in Stockholm; and he employed him from the year 1782 in the capacity of Secretary to the Cabinet for Foreign Affairs. From 1786 he became Privy Councillor to Frederick William II., and in that office was again entrusted with the administration of foreign affairs, but after the war with France was supplanted by General von Bischofswerder,† and retired into private life. Menken was the only adviser of King Frederick William II., who was recalled and reappointed at the accession of Frederick William III. He was the author of the well-known Cabinet Order issued by Frederick William III., which ensured the young King the confidence of his subjects. Menken was no revolutionist, as Bischofswerder and his partisans asserted, but to a certain extent he agreed with the principles of the first French National Convention. He is portrayed as a gentle, liberal, prudent, and experienced man, but of delicate health; and he died on the 5th August, 1801, in consequence of illness brought on by a life of unintermitting labour. According to the opinion of Stein, Menken was a person of generous

---

* Herzberg, Ewald Fred. (Count von), a distinguished Prussian diplomatist, born at Lotten, near New Stettin, in 1725. He published many most valuable diplomatic, historical, and juridical works, and died on the 27th May, 1795, after having been somewhat harshly treated by those in power.— K. R. H. M.

† Bischofswerder (John Rud. von), General and Minister of Frederick William II., born at Dresden, 1737, of an old Saxon family. He entered the Prussian service, 1760, and was a Major in 1779. The confidence the King, first as Crown Prince, had in him, was unlimited; and he was employed in important diplomatic matters at Szistowe and at Pilnitz. He was ambassador to Paris in 1793. He died in October, 1803.—K. R. H. M.

sentiments, well educated, of fine feeling and benevolent disposition, with noble aims and principles. He desired the good of his native land, which he sought to promote by the diffusion of knowledge, the improvement of the condition of all classes, and the application of philanthropic ideas; but his indisposition for war at an important juncture was adverse to his fame; his too eloquent and humane edict, and his singular gentleness of mind, invested the Government with an appearance of weakness.

His orphan daughter became the mother of Count Bismarck. It is interesting to note that a hundred years before a daughter of the same family, Christine Sybille Menken, deceased in 1750, as the wife of the Imperial Equerry Peter Hohmann von Hohenthal, was the ancestress of the Count von Hohenthal of the elder line.

The brothers and sisters of Count Bismarck were:—

I. Alexander Frederick Ferdinand, born 13th April, 1807; died 13th December, 1809.

II. Louise Johanne, born 3rd November, 1808; died 19th March, 1813.

III. Bernhard, born 24th June, 1810, Royal Chamberlain and Privy Councillor, and Chief Justice of the Circle of Naugard, near Külz and Jarchelin, in Pomerania.

IV. Francis, born 20th June, 1819; died 10th September, 1822.

V. Franziska Angelika Malwina, born the 29th June, 1827; wedded at Schönhausen on the 30th October, 1844, to Ernst Frederick Abraham Henry Charles Oscar von Arnim, of Kröchlendorff, Royal Chamberlain and a member of the Upper House.

The Minister-President himself, Otto Edward Leopold, was born at Schönhausen on the 1st April, 1815. —

His earliest youth, however, was not passed at his ancestral estate in the Alt Mark, but in Pomerania, whither his parents had removed in the year 1816. By the decease of a cousin they had succeeded to the knightly estates of Kniephof, Jarchelin, and Külz, in the circle of Naugard. At Kniephof, where his parents took up their residence, Bismarck passed the first six years of his life, and to Kniephof he returned in his holidays from Berlin, so that this Pomeranian estate of his parents may be regarded as the scene of his earliest sports.

These estates were held in fee from the Dewitz family, in the circle of Pomerania, then known as the Daber and Dewitz circle, and were ceded with the feudal rights to the Colonel August Frederick von Bismarck, the great-grandfather of the Minister-President, on his marriage with Stephanie von Dewitz. After the death of the Colonel, his three sons, Bernd August, Charles Alexander (the Minister's grandfather), and Ernst Frederick (Royal Conservator of Palaces) possessed these estates in common, until, on the partition of 12th August, 1747, they were handed over to Captain Bernd August alone. He bequeathed them to his son, the Deputy of the Daber-Naugard circle, and to Captain August Frederick von Bismarck and his sister Charlotte Henrietta, who was married to Captain Jaroslav Ulrich Frederick von Schwerin. By a deed dated the 7th of August, 1777, August Frederick became the sole possessor, and bequeathed them to Charles William Frederick von Bismarck, the father of the Minister-President.

The knightly estate of Kniephof is about a (German) mile from Naugard to the eastward; its situation is pleasant, being surrounded by woods and meadows, close to the little river Zampel. Even in the last century the beautiful gardens and carp-lake were famous.

Jarchelin, formerly called Grecholin, some quarter of a mile distant from Kniephof, which is incorporated with the parish of the former place. A small stream runs through this village.

Külz is nearer to Naugard; the church there was originally a dependency of Farbezin; formerly it possessed oak and pine forests, and the hamlet of Stowinkel was planted with oaks.

In the year 1838, Captain von Bismarck ceded these estates to his two sons, who farmed them for three years in common, but then divided them so that the elder, Bernhard, retained Külz, while the younger, the Minister-President, took for his share Kniephof and Jarchelin. When, after his father's decease in 1845, the Minister-President took Schönhausen, Jarchelin was surrendered to the elder brother. Kniephof was retained by Count Bismarck until 1868, when, after the purchase of Varzin, it passed into the possession of his eldest nephew, Lieutenant Philip von Bismarck.

As the possessor of Kniephof, the Minister sat till 1868 for the ancient and established fief of the Dukedom Stettin in the Upper Chamber. On its cession the King created him a member of that Chamber for life. In the adjacent estate of Zimmerhausen, belonging to the Von Blanckenburgs, Otto von Bismarck was then and afterwards a frequent guest. The youthful friendship which he then contracted with the present General County Councillor Moritz von Blanckenburg, a well-known leader of the Conservative party in the Chamber of Deputies and at the Diet, remains unshaken to the present day.

About the Easter of 1821, Otto von Bismarck entered the then renowned school of Professor Plamann, in Berlin (Wilhelmstrasse 130), where his only surviving elder brother Bernhard then was. Bismarck remained in this place till 1827, when he left it to pursue his more classical studies at the Frederick William Gymnasium. He was there received into the lower third class—his elder brother having by that time reached the second class.

His parents were accustomed to pass the winter months

in Berlin, and during those times received both their sons at home, so that the boys ever retained feelings of relationship to the home circle, although not always there.

From the year 1827 both brothers became chiefly residents at the Berlin establishment of their parents, and were committed to the care of a faithful servant, Trine Neumann, from Schönhausen, who still lives at the Gesund-Brunnen, at Berlin, though she no longer wears the black and red petticoat of her native spot. Well qualified masters attended, especially during the absence of the parents in the summer time. By their aid they became acquainted with several of the modern languages. Among these tutors, the first was M. Hagens in 1827, then a young Genevese, named Gallot, and in the year 1829, a certain Dr. Winckelmann, unquestionably a clever philologist, but a man of no principle, who vanished one morning with the cash-box, and left his charges behind with Trine Neumann. This occurred at the residence of the parents in Behrenstrasse No. 39; they afterwards resided at No. 52, in the same street, and subsequently on the Dönhofsplatz. At this time Otto von Bismarck laid the foundation of his prowess in English and French, which he ulteriorly brought to perfection.

It is evident that labour, care, or expense were not spared by the parents to foster the talents of these gifted children. This was, indeed, a special duty with their mother, a lady of great education, who combined with many accomplishments the sentimental religious feeling of her period, and had inherited the liberal views of her father. Madame von Bismarck was no doubt a distinguished woman, not only esteemed for her beauty in society, but exercising considerable influence in society. Her activity, which zealously espoused modern ideas, was probably less wanting in insight than in persistency, but

THE CRADLE.

from that very cause operated unfavourably in the management of the estates. The conduct of agriculture suffered under numerous and costly institutions and experiments, reducing the family income to a considerable extent, especially as the brilliant winter establishment in Berlin, and the summer visits to watering places, demanded extensive resources. She evidently sought at a very early age to awaken ambition in her sons; it was particularly her desire that the younger son, Otto, should devote himself to a diplomatic career, for which she considered him especially fitted, while the elder brother was from the first destined for the commission of Provincial Councillor (*Landrath*). Both these aspirations were fulfilled, but not in their mother's lifetime; she had long died when her younger son entered on diplomatic life, but her maternal instinct is honoured by her early perception of the path by which Bismarck was to attain the highest distinction. How often must Bismarck have thought of his mother's heartfelt wish, in his position as Ambassador in Frankfort, Petersburg, and Paris! How frequently his earliest friends must have exclaimed, "Bismarck! had your mother only survived to see this!"

In contradistinction to the wise, ambitious, but somewhat haughty mother, his father, a handsome, personable, and cheerful man, full of humour and wit, rather represented the heart and mind, without very great claims to strong intellect, or even knowledge. Strangely enough, the cultivated and literary Charles Alexander von Bismarck, transformed from a diplomatist into a cavalry officer by the command of the Great Frederick, educated his four sons for the army.

This cavalier, of French sentiments, who subscribed to Parisian journals, still preserved at Schönhausen—a custom not usual with the aristocracy of the Marks—and who lived with great simplicity, but drank wine, and ate off silver

G

plate,—brought up his sons like centaurs, and his greatest
pride was in the excellence of·their horsemanship.

Bismarck's father entered the Body-guard (white and
blue), the commander of which was also a Bismarck, and,
as he often told his sons in later times, "measured out
the corn every morning at four o'clock to the men for five
long years." He loved a country life, grew wearied in
Berlin, especially when he had grown somewhat deaf, but,

with chivalrous devotion to his lady wife, conformed to her
wishes on this point.

Madame von Bismarck, besides esteeming the company of talented persons and scholars, was devoted to
chess, of which she was a complete mistress; but her
husband's amusement was the chase to the end of his
life. How strangely the old gentleman pursued this
pastime we learn from a letter of Bismarck's to his
newly married sister, in the latter part of 1844; very
characteristic of the relations maintained by the son and
brother.

OW you have departed, I have naturally found the house very lonely. I have sate by the stove smoking and contemplating how unnatural and selfish it is in girls who have brothers, and those bachelors, to go and recklessly marry, and act as if they only were in the world to follow their own sweet wills; a selfish principle from which I feel that our family, and myself in proper person, are fortunately free. After perceiving the fruitlessness of these reflections, I arose from the green leather chair in which you used to sit kissing and whispering with Miss and Oscar, and plunged wildly into the elections, which convinced me that five votes were mine for life or death, and two had somewhat lukewarmly supported me; while Krug received four, sixteen to eighteen voted for Arnim, and twelve to fifteen for Alvensleben. I therefore thought it best to retire altogether. Since then I have lived here with father; reading, smoking, walking, helping him to eat lampreys, and joining in a farce called foxhunting. We go out in the pouring rain, or at six degrees of frost, accompanied by Ihle, Bellin, and Charles, surround an old bush in a sportsmanlike way, silent as the grave, as the wind blows through the cover, where we are all fully convinced,—even perhaps my father,—that the only game consists of a few old women gathering faggots—and not another living thing. Then Ihle, Charles, and a couple of hounds, making the strangest and most prodigious noise, particularly Ihle, burst into the thicket, my father standing perfectly stock still, with his rifle just as if he fully expected some beast, until Ihle comes out, shouting " hu! la! la! fuss! hey! hey!" in the queerest

shrieks. Then my father asks me, in the coolest manner, if
I have not seen something ; and I reply, with most natural
air of astonishment, nothing in the world! Then, growling
at the rain, we start for another bush, where Ihle is sure
we shall find, and play the farce over again.   This goes on
for three or four hours, without my father, Ihle, and Fingal
exhibiting the least symptom of being tired. Besides this,
we visit the orangery twice a day, and the sheep-pens once,
consult the four thermometers in the parlour every hour,
mark the weather-glass, and since bright weather has set in
have brought all the clocks so exactly with the sun, that
the clock in the library is only one stroke behind all the
rest.   Charles V. was a silly fellow ! You can understand
that, with such a multitude of things to do, we have no
time to visit parsons ; as they have no votes at the elections,
I did not go at all—impossible.   Bellin has been for these
three days full of a journey to Stendal he made, and about
the coach which he did not catch.   The Elbe is frozen, wind
S.E.E., the last new thermometer from Berlin marks 8°,
(27° Fahr.) barometer rising 28.8 in.   I just mention this
to show you how you might write more homely particulars
to father in your letters, as they amuse him hugely—who
has been to see you and Curts, whom you visit, what you
have had for dinner, how the horses are, and the servants
quarrel, whether the doors crack, and the windows are
tight—in short, trifles, facts ! Mark me, too, that he
detests the name papa—*avis au lecteur !* Antonie wrote
him a very pretty letter on his birthday, and sent him a
green purse, at which papa was deeply moved, and replied
in two pages !   The Rohrs have lately passed through
here without showing themselves ; they baited at the Inn
at Hohen-Göhren for two hours, and sat, wife and children
and all, with ten smoking countrymen, in the taproom !
Bellin declared they were angry with us ; this is very sad
and deeply affects me ! Our father sends best love, and will
soon follow me to Pomerania—he thinks about Christmas.

There is a *café dansant* to-morrow at Genthin; I shall look in, to fire away at the old Landrath, and take my leave of the circle for at least four months. I have seen Miss ———; she has moments when she is exceedingly pretty, but she will lose her complexion very soon. I was in love with her for twenty-four hours. Greet Oscar heartily from me, and farewell, my angel; don't hang up your bride's rank by the tail, and remember me to Curts. If you are not at A. by the eighth—I'll!—but enough of that. Entirely your own "for ever,"

BISMARCK.

Otto von Bismarck, on his sixteenth birthday, as his brother had been before him, was confirmed at Berlin, in the Trinity Church by Schleiermacher, at the Easter of 1830. The same year he went to board with Professor Prévost, the father of Hofrath Prévost, now an official in the Foreign Office under Bismarck; and as the house was very remote from the Frederick William Gymnasium in the Königs Strasse, he quitted it for the Berlin Gymnasium, Zum Grauen Kloster. Bismarck, after a year, passed from Professor Prévost to Dr. Bonnell, afterwards director of the Frederick-Werder Gymnasium, then at the Grauen Kloster, but who had not long before been Bismarck's teacher at the Frederick William. Bismarck remained with him until, at Easter, 1832, he quitted the Kloster after his examination, to study law.

This is an outline of Bismarck's life in his boyhood and school-days; let us endeavour to form some picture of the lad and youth, from the reports of his tutors and contemporaries.

We see Junker Otto leaving his father's house at a very early age, as did his brother. The reasons for this we cannot assign, but no doubt they were well meant, although scarcely wise. Bismarck used subsequently himself to say that his early departure from the paternal

roof was anything but advantageous to him. Perhaps
his mother was afraid he might get too early spoilt;
for with his gay nature and constant friendliness, the
little boy early won all hearts. He was especially spoilt
by his father, and by Lotte Schmeling, his mother's
maid, and his own nurse.

At the boarding-school of Plamann in Berlin, whither
he was next brought, he did not get on at all well. This
then very renowned institution had adopted the thorough
system of old Jahn, and carried out the theory of
" hardening up," then fashionable, by starving, exposure,
and so forth—not without carrying it to extremes in
practice. Bismarck, who had always submitted meekly to
all his masters, could not, in later days, refrain from
complaining bitterly of the severity with which he was
treated in this institution. He was very miserable there,
and longed for home so much, that when they were
out walking, he could not help weeping whenever he
saw a plough at work. The masters were especially
obnoxious to him on account of the strictness with which
they insisted on gymnastics and athletic sports, from the
hatred of the French they methodically preached, and
by the tough German usage they exercised towards the
little scion of nobility. In his paternal house, Bismarck
had not been educated in class-hatred, as it is called; on
the contrary, his mother was very liberal, and had no
sympathy with the nobility. Marriages between nobles
and citizens were then much more unfrequent; Madame
von Bismarck had very likely encountered some slights
from the proud families of the Alt Mark and of Pomerania,
and caste feeling could scarcely have been felt by Bismarck
in his childhood. It was not any want of sympathy with
his school-fellows, but the democratic doctrines of some of
the masters, which roused the Junker in the bosom of the
proud lad. We shall see that in later years it was the
incapacity of two masters at the Graue Kloster which

caused them to handle him ungently, because of his noble birth, and thus impelled him to resistance.

It is easy to understand that Otto von Bismarck, as long as he stayed at the hateful Plamann Institute, and at the Gymnasium, longed ardently for the holidays, for these times are the bright stars in the heaven of every schoolboy.

And how was the holiday journey performed in those days from Berlin to Kniephof in the Circle Naugard? The stage coach of Nagler—then the pride of Prussia—set off in the evening from Berlin, and arrived at Stettin at noon the next day. There were not over good roads at that time from Berlin to the capital of Pomerania. From

Stettin young Bismarck proceeded, with horses sent by his parents, to Gollnow, where his grandfather was born, and where proverbially there was a fire once a fortnight. In Gollnow he slept at the house of an aged widow named Dalmer, who held some relation to the family. This aged lady used to tell the eager lad stories of his great grandfather the Colonel von Bismarck, who fell at Czaslau, and

who once lay in garrison at Gollnow with his regiment of
dragoons—the Schulenburg Regiment, afterwards the
Anspach Bayreuth. After almost a century, the memory
of the famous warrior and huntsman remained alive.
.Stories were told of the Colonel's fine dogs and horses.
When he gave a banquet, not only did the sound of
trumpet accompany each toast, but the dragoons fired off
volleys in the hall, to heighten the noise. Then the
Colonel would march with the whole mess, preceded by
the band and followed by the whole regiment, to the
bridge of Ihna, where the Wooden Donkey stood. This

terrible instrument of punishment—riding the Donkey
was like riding the rail—was then cast into the Ihna,
amidst execrations and applause. "All offenders are forgiven, and the Donkey shall die!" But the applause of
the dragoons could not have been very sincere, for they
knew very well that the Provost would set up the Donkey

in all its terrors the very next morning; therefore they only huzzaed to please their facetious Colonel.

This is a picture of garrison life under King Frederick William I. There still exists a hunting register belonging to this old worthy, which reports that the old soldier in one year had shot a hundred stags—an unlikely event nowadays. One of the first sportsmen of the present day—H.R.H. Prince Frederick Charles of Prussia—shot three hundred head of game between the 18th of September, 1848, and the 18th of September, 1868, pronounced "worthy of fire." A correspondence of the old Colonel's is still extant, which evinces a highly eccentric stanchness; in this his cousin, the cunning diplomatist Von Dewitz, afterwards Ambassador to Vienna, is severely enough handled. It was doubtless from these statements of the acute colonel of cavalry that the Great Frederick did not allow his son, Charles Alexander, to accompany him to Vienna in the Embassy, but ordered him to become a cornet, with some very unflattering expressions concerning the diplomatist.

The next day young Otto von Bismarck used to leave Gollnow, and thus on the third day he reached Kniephof, where for three weeks he led a glorious life, troubled only by a few holiday tasks. Among the most pleasant events of holiday time were visits to Zimmerhausen, to the Blanckenburgs, which possessed an additional charm from a sort of cheese-cake prepared in this locality.

From Plamann's school, Bismarck passed to the Frederick William Gymnasium; and here he immediately attracted the attention of a master, with whom he was afterwards to be more closely associated, and of whom mention will afterwards be made in this work. This gentleman (the Director, Dr. Bonnell) relates:—" My attention was drawn to Bismarck on the very day of his entry, on which occasion the new boys sat in the schoolroom on rows of benches in order that the masters could overlook the new comers with attention, during the inauguration. Otto von Bismarck sat—as I still distinctly remember, and often have related—with visible eagerness, a clear and pleasant boyish face and bright eyes, in a gay and lightsome mood among his comrades, so that it caused me to think, 'That's a nice boy; I'll keep my eye upon him.' He became my pupil first when he entered the upper third. I was transferred at Michaelmas, 1829, from the Berlin Gymnasium to the Graue Kloster, to which Bismarck also came in the following year. He became an inmate of my house at Easter, 1831, where he behaved himself in my modest household, then numbering only my wife and my infant son, in a friendly and confiding manner. In every respect he was most charming; he seldom quitted us of an evening; if I was sometimes absent, he conversed in a friendly and innocent manner with my wife, and evinced a strong inclination for domestic life. He won our hearts and we met his advances with affection and care—so that his father, when he quitted us, declared that his son had never been so happy as with us."

Bismarck to this day has preserved the most grateful intimacy with Dr. Bonnell and his wife; even as Minister-President he loved to cast a passing glance at the window of the small chamber he had occupied in Königsgraben No. 18, while he resided with Dr. Bonnell. The window is now built up. The powerful minister and great statesman ever remained the friendly and kindly Otto von Bismarck towards his old teacher. He sought his counsel in the selection of a tutor for his sons, and afterwards sent them to the Werder Gymnasium, that still flourishes under the thoroughly excellent guidance of Bonnell.

Among the favourite masters of Bismarck at the Frederick William Gymnasium, he distinguished Professor Siebenhaar, an excellent man, who subsequently unfortunately died by his own hand. He found himself

welcomed at the Graue Kloster by Koepke with great
friendship—his youth alone prevented his being placed in
the first class. Besides Bonnell, he here found a great
friend in Dr. Wendt; Bollermann, however, and the
mathematician Fischer, raised the Junker in him in an
unwise manner. He also got into many disputes with
the French Professor, and learnt English in an incredibly

short space of time, in order not to be submitted to the
test of the French Professor; as it was allowed to the
pupils to choose either English or French for a prize
theme.

As a pupil, in general, Bismarck's conduct preserved
him almost entirely from punishment, and seldom was he
amenable to censure. He exhibited such powers of understanding, and his talents were so considerable, that he was
able to perform his required tasks without great exertion.
He even at that time exhibited a marked preference for

historical studies—especially that of his native Brandenburg, Prussia, and Germany. He laid the foundations of
his eminent historical attainments, afterwards so formidable to his opponents in parliamentary discussion, in
these youthful years. The style of his Latin essays was
always clear and elegant, although perhaps not, in a
grammatical sense, always correct. The decision on his
prize essay of Easter, 1832, was, *Oratio est lucida ac
latina, sed non satis castigata.* (The language is clear and
Latin, but not sufficiently polished.)

On his departure for the University, Bismarck was not
seventeen years of age, and possessed none of the broad
imposing presence he later attained ; his stature was thin
and graceful. His countenance possessed the brightness
of youthful liberality, and his eyes beamed with goodness.
His eldest son Herbert now recalls in his likeness the
vivid image of his father in those last days of his pupilage. Bismarck has inherited his tall stature from his
father, who, with his fine presence and cultured manners,
had been a personage of most aristocratic appearance. But
in general the elder son, Bernhard, was more like his father
than the younger brother.

When the cholera broke out in Berlin, in 1831, in the
general cholera mania, Bismarck was desired by his father
to return home so soon as the first case had declared itself
in that city. Like a true schoolboy, it was utterly impossible for him to receive the news too soon. He hired
a horse, and several times rode to the " Frederick's field,"
from which district the cholera was expected. He, however, fell with the horse by the new Guard House, and
was carried into his dwelling with a sprained leg. To his
greatest annoyance he was now obliged to remain for a
considerable time in bed, and endure the approach of the
cholera to Berlin, before he could leave. But he never
lost his gaiety and good humour on this account. Bonnell,
as might be expected, was greatly alarmed, when, on re-

turning home, he learnt that Bismarck had tumbled from
the horse and had been carried to his room; but he was
soon comforted by the good temper with which the patient
recounted the particulars of the accident.

Bismarck awaited his convalescence with patient resignation, and when he was finally able to enter upon his
journey to Kniephof, an event took place owing to the

strange cholera measures caused by the cholera mania.
Travellers by stage, for instance, might not alight at such
places as Bernau or Werneuchen on any account but
the coaches drove side by side until their doors touched,
and then the exchanges were effected, while the local guard
paraded with spears in a manner almost Falstaffian. In
another place, Bismarck was allowed to alight, but he could
enter no house; there was a table spread in the open street,
where tea and bread and butter were provided for travellers,

and the latter breakfasted, while the inhabitants retired to
look upon them in abject terror.   When Bismarck called
to a waitress to pay her, she fled shrieking, and he was
obliged to leave the price of his breakfast on the table.
The saddest case was that of a lady traveller, who was
proceeding as governess to Count Borck's mansion, in Stargard.   This poor girl dreaded travelling, and got into the
condition which so outwardly resembles an attack of
cholera.   The doctors of Stargard were in an uproar, so the
poor governess was put into quarantine in the town gaol.
Bismarck himself went into quarantine, and was first locked
up in the police office at Naugard, and afterwards at his
native place.   His mother, it should be mentioned, had
taken every precaution then in fashion, and had engaged
a retired military surgeon, named Geppert, who had seen
much of the cholera during his residence in Russia, as a
cholera doctor, for her immediate service.   With this doctor
Bismarck was used to hold arguments, for though his conversation was rude and desultory, he could tell the story
of his voyages in a practical and animated manner.   Madame
von Bismarck would have been very angry had she had
an idea of the carelessness with which her son observed
the severe quarantine rules.   However, despite all the pains
which the wise lady took, cholera showed itself on her
estate, while all the neighbours were free from it.   At
Jarchelin Mill two boys had bathed against the regulations;
they had eaten fruit and drank water—they were sacrificed
to the disease.   It can be easily understood what a nuisance
the quarantine, even in its mildest form, must have been
for Bismarck, who never believed in the infectious nature
of cholera.   In later times, when the two brothers farmed
the estates, there was a case of cholera in Külz; no one
dared to enter the house; the two Bismarcks went in, and
declared that they themselves would not quit it until they
were properly relieved.   This shamed every one, and proper medical aid was obtained.

As a boy and youth Bismarck was not usually very animated. There was rather a quiet and observant carriage in him, especially evinced by the "blank" eyes, as they were once very aptly called by a lady; these qualities were soon accompanied by determination and endurance in no insignificant degree. He was obliging and thoughtful in social intercourse, and soon acquired the reputation of being "good company," without having transgressed in the ways so common among social persons. He never allowed himself to be approached without politeness, and severely censured intruders. His mental qualifications very early showed themselves to be considerable; memory and comprehensiveness aided him remarkably in his study of modern languages. He exhibited a love for "dumb" animals even as a child; he went to much expense in fine horses and dogs; his magnificent Danish dog, so faithful to him, long continued a distinguished personage in the whole neighbourhood of Kniephof. Riding and hunting were his favourite pastimes. He has always been an intrepid and elegant horseman, without being exactly a "riding-master." To this he added the accomplishment of swimming; he was a good fencer and dancer, but averse to athletic sports. The gymnastic ground of the Plamann Institution had caused him to regard that branch of culture with profound dislike. As a boy and youth he had grown tall, but he was slim and thin; his frame did not develop itself laterally until a later time; his face was pale, but his health was always good, and he was, from his youth up, a hearty eater. A certain proportion of daring was to be noticed in his carriage, but expressed in a kindly way; his whole gait was frank and free, but with some reticence. Thus we do not find that he retained many friends of his boyhood and pupilage, a time usually so rife in friendships for most men. But such friendships as he did form, continued for life. Among Bismarck's friends of the Gymnasium period, were, besides

Moritz von Blanckenburg, Oscar von Arnim, afterwards his brother-in-law, William von Schenk, afterwards the possessor of Schloss Mansfeld and Member of the Chamber of Deputies, and Hans von Dewitz of Gross Milzow in Mecklenburg. At the University he added to these Count Kayserlingk of Courland, the American Lothropp Motley,* Oldekop of Hanover, afterwards Councillor of War, and Lauenstein, subsequently pastor of Altenwerder on the Elbe.

In conclusion, we should not omit to say that he from youth preserved a proper attitude towards his domestics; they almost all loved him, although his demands were heavy on them at times. Afterwards, while administering the Pomeranian estates with his brother, he censured one of his junior inspectors very severely. The inspector sought to turn aside the reproaches by pleading his own dislike to farming, that he had been forced to it, and so forth.

"I have long attested myself," the young man concluded.

"Far from sufficient!" replied Bismarck, drily.

This reply brought the inspector to his senses; since that time he has become an excellent agriculturist, and to this day thinks gratefully of Bismarck's "Far from sufficient!"

This "Far from sufficient!" is associated in the Alt Mark with the name of Bismarck from olden time; in the country speech of the district it is proverbial.

"Noch lange nicht genug! (Far from sufficient!) quoth Bismarck."

"Ueber und über! (Over and over!) quoth Schulenburg."

"Grade aus! (Straight forward!) quoth Itzenplitz (Lüderitz?)."

"Meinetwegen! (I care not!) quoth Alvensleben."

It would be interesting to trace the origin of these

---

* Now (1869) American Ambassador to St. James's.

peasant proverbs. The Alvenslebens since early times were reputed " mild ;" they are the *Gens Valeria* (*Valerius Poblicola*) of the Alt Mark. The Schulenburgs are " severe," the *Gens Marcia* (*Marcius Rex*) of that country ; and certainly we can perceive some affinity between these qualities and the proverbs ; but what may the " Noch lange nicht genug! sagt Bismarck!" mean? Perhaps the energetic striving, the essential characteristic of the whole family, in a greater or lesser degree : an element of progress which ever, in their own and others' action, exclaims, " Far from sufficient!"

CHAPTER II.

UNIVERSITY AND MILITARY LIFE.

1832—1844.

Göttingen.—The Danish Dog and the Professor.—Duels.—Berlin.—Appointed Examiner.—Anecdotes of his Legal Life.—Bismarck and his Boots.— Meeting with Prince, now King, William.—Helene von Kessel.—Aix la Chapelle.—Greifswald.—Undertaking the Pomeranian Estates.—Kniephof. —"Mad Bismarck."—His Studies.—Marriage of his Sister.—Letters to her. —Norderney.—Saves his Servant Hildebrand's Life.—"The Golden Dog." —A Dinner Party at the Blanckenburgs.—Von Blanckenburg.—Major, now General, Von Roon.—Dr. Beutner.

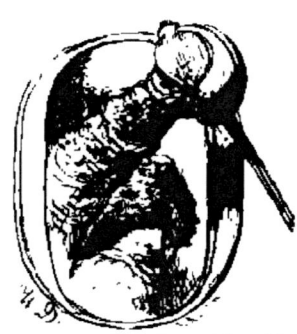 TTO von Bismarck was anxious to enter himself at Heidelberg, but his mother objected to it, because she was afraid that at this University her son would contract the habit, to her detestable, of drinking beer; and she therefore chose, at the advice of a relative, —the Geh. Finanzrath Kerl, who was a great authority with her in matters of learning— the University of Göttingen, where Kerl had himself studied. Bismarck agreed to the change; he longed for the joys of academic freedom, the more delightful to him from the strictness with which his education had hitherto been conducted, as well as from his little knowledge of student life. In Berlin student life was somewhat tame, obtruding itself nowhere; and Bismarck had also been withheld from all contact with it. He

entered into possession of his new liberty with enthusiasm, not easily comprehensible to the students of the present day. With the entire recklessness of a sturdy constitution he plunged into its every enjoyment.

Even before entering at Göttingen he had fought his first duel at Berlin. His opponent was a brave lad of the Hebrew persuasion, named Wolf. It is true he fought, but, like the ancient Parthians, he fought flying. The arrangements must have been somewhat unscientific, in fact quite out of form, for Bismarck was wounded in the leg, while he cut off his Jewish opponent's spectacles!

In the didactic epic "Bismarckias," by Dr. G. Schwetschle, of which several editions have appeared at Halle, containing many a good joke, the following aptly alludes to the present period of the hero's life:—

> From his boot soles now is shaken
> All the school dust: higher wavelets
> Bear the ship of the aspirant;
> Weighed on deck is every anchor,
> And spread out is every canvass,
> While the youthful flag of freedom,
> Gaily fluttering in the breezes,
> Bears: " Nitimur in vetitum !"
>
> Jolly days of wild enjoyment!
> Votaries now gay assemble
> Of the nine Castalian sisters;
> Crowd together in new temples;
> Crowd aroun l the fragrant altars
> Of old Bacchus and Gambrinus:
> And the neophyte so gaily
> Brings the liquid sacrifices.
>
> While the battle-loving Mavors
> Opes the clanging doors of combat;
> Dost thou hear the clash of weapons?
> Dost thou mark the shouts of contest?
> Ha! how gleam the flashing sword-blades;
> With the tierce and carte resounding:
> As the hewer hews so fiercely,
> Hews, and his fellow fighter heweth !
>
> E'en then sped a slender red line
> (A red line of blood and iron),
> Through the life of our young hero

Göttingen, Berlin, and Greifswald
Echo deeds of noble daring,
Done in years that now have fleeted ;
"Days departed, days all silent,"
As old Ossian once out-carolled.*

When Bismarck came to Göttingen, as we have said, he had not the remotest notion of student life; its customs were all unknown to him, nor did he learn any-

thing of them immediately, as he there found no friend of any degree of intimacy. By a certain Herr von Drenck-

* It is again necessary to explain that the translation is as close as the translator can make, without violating sense and metre. The reader will find the original of this, and other interjected poems in the Appendices.—K. R. H. M.

hahn, whom he had formerly seen for a short time, he was introduced to a circle of Mecklenburgers, who belonged to no academical body, but passed a tolerably jolly life. With these he travelled into the Harz, and on his return it was agreed that the glories of real student life should be opened to him. Bismarck gave his fellow travellers a breakfast in celebration of the journey, and here matters went on somewhat madly. At length somebody threw a bottle out of the window. Next morning the Dominus de Bismarck was cited to the Deanery and, obedient to his academical superiors, he set forth on the way. He came in a tall hat, a gay Berlin dressing-gown, and riding boots, accompanied by his enormous dog. The Dean stared at this fantastic garb, and only dared to pass the huge creature when Bismarck had called him in. On account of this illegal dog, his fortunate possessor was at once fined five thalers—then came a painful investigation into the bottle-throwing matter. The formal official was not satisfied with the simple explanation of Bismarck, that the bottle had been thrown out of the window; it must have flown out. He was determined to know how this had happened, and was not content until the culprit had clearly shown him how he had held the bottle, and by proper muscular action had given it the necessary impetus. Somewhat annoyed by this inquiry, he set forth on his way home, and was greatly incensed at the laughter with which he was encountered by four young students of the corps of Hanover—although it was impossible not to laugh at his dress. "Are you laughing at me?" inquired Bismarck of the foremost of the party, and received as a reply, "Hm! that you must very well see!" In his inexperience Bismarck hardly knew how to proceed; he felt that he was in the right way to encounter a duel, but he knew nothing of the proper form. He was afraid of exposing himself, when suddenly—happy thought!—the "dumme Junger" (foolish fellow) occurred especially fond of Beethoven. After Kayserlingk, an American named Lothropp Motley became his companion. This gentleman won himself fame as the author of a History of the Rise of the Dutch Republic, and other works, was sent as United States Ambassador to Vienna, and is now Ambassador to Great Britain.

When Bismarck became sworn, after his examination about Easter, 1835, in the capacity of Auscultator (Examiner) he again occupied apartments in the Behrenstrasse, jointly with his brother Bernhard, who, about that time, after having served four years in the Dragoon Regiment of Guards, exchanged the sword for the pen, passed his examination in the following year, and became Referendary in the government at Potsdam. During Bismarck's service as clerk in the City Police, he exhibited his sense of humour by many pranks, of which we could give an account were we able to vouch for their authenticity—these are, however, so numerous, that we are sure many are ascribed to Bismarck, properly the acts of others. The following anecdote we know to be genuine. The Auscultator was taking the protocol of a true Berliner, who finally so tried the patience of Bismarck by his impudence, that he jumped up, and exclaimed, "Sir, behave better, or I'll have you kicked out!" The magistrate present patted the zealous official in a friendly way upon the shoulder, and said quietly, "Herr Auscultator, the kicking out is *my* business." They proceeded in taking evidence, but very soon Bismarck again sprang to his feet, thundering out, "Sir, behave yourself better, or the magistrate shall kick you out!" The face of the Court may be imagined.

Bismarck had a great deal to do in divorce cases, which were then treated in a manner in Prussia—with a thoughtlessness still sadly remembered, although long since receiving a more solemn and worthier attention. The young jurist was deeply impressed by a lady with whom he had to arrange a divorce, when she decisively refused to attest it. She had determined otherwise. Bismarck, who had never met with such a refusal, was disconcerted, and at last went and consulted with the senior jurist, and requested his aid. Arrogantly shrugging his shoulders at the inexperience of his young colleague, he entered into the matter, and endeavoured with all his wisdom and authority to induce the poor woman to consent to the divorce.. She, however, continued her refusal; the matter ended without any result. Bismarck never forgot this circumstance..

To the more amusing events of that time belongs the history of how Bismarck taught a boot-maker in the Kronenstrasse punctuality. This man, after many express promises, had neglected him on several occasions. When this again occurred, the shoemaker was roused at six o'clock the next morning by a messenger with the simple question: "Are Herr von Bismarck's boots ready yet?" When the maker said, "No," he retired, but in ten minutes another arrived. Loud rang the bell. "Are Herr von Bismarck's boots ready yet?" "No;" and so it went on every ten minutes until the boots were ready in the evening. The shoemaker no doubt never disappointed him again.

To the social circles, in which the brothers Bernhard and Otto von Bismarck then moved, there belonged the intimately related house of Madame General von Kessel. She was a sister of Bismarck's mother, and resided in Berlin, possessing many daughters. Here he found pleasant and amiable society, and the affection of a relative. Another house he was very fond of visiting was that of his cousin, the Count von Bismarck-Bohlen, who was also accustomed to pass the winter in Berlin with his family. During the winter of 1835–6, Bismarck was also introduced to the Court festivities, and took part in the usual amusements.

fore he went to Aachen (Aix la Chapelle) to the Crown Court. Count Arnim-Boytzenburg was at that time President; he possessed a great reputation, and Bismarck hoped that he should be able to effect a conjunction with this rising star, and follow in his course. He was received by the Arnim family with great kindness, and at first was very industrious; but he soon was carried into the vortex of society which existed during the season at the celebrated baths of the Imperial city. He associated much with Englishmen, Frenchmen, and Belgians, and in their company made several excursions to Belgium, France, and the Rhine province. He was especially the favourite of the English, as they were delighted to find in him an amiable gentleman, possessing a perfect mastery over their language. These connections, however, got him into many scrapes.

He, in consequence, quitted " het ryk van Aaken " (the realm of Aachen), and, in the autumn of 1837, had himself transferred to the Crown Office at Potsdam. About the same time, in 1838, he entered the Jäger Guard, to fulfil his military duties. But the merry mess-room life did not last long, and in the same year he exchanged into the second battalion of Jäger, at Greifswald, hoping to attend the lectures of the Agricultural Academy of Eldena.

To such studies he was compelled by the sad state into which the administration of the paternal estates in Pomerania had fallen, and which threatened total ruin. On this account the sons proposed to their father to grant them the Pomeranian estates, as the only way in which the estates could be saved. His parents acceded to the proposition, and retired to Schönhausen, under the faithful care of Bellin, to there pass the evening of their lives. His father continued to reside there until 1845; but his mother, long an invalid, sought better medical attendance in Berlin, and died in that city on the 1st of November, 1839.

At first, the elder brother, Bernhard von Bismarck, undertook the sole administration of the estates, Otto remaining until the end of his year of service, until Easter, 1839, at Greifswald, but he soon perceived that it was impossible to combine military service with agricultural studies. He soon fell into wild student ways again, there being nothing better to do in that place.

In the summer of 1839 Bismarck entered on the administration of the Pomeranian estates, and carried it on, in conjunction with his brother, until the summer of 1841. At this time the elder brother was elected Landrath of the circle of Naugard, married, and settled in the chief town. By this the common household of Kniephof was broken up; and they divided the estates in such a manner that the elder brother retained Külz, the younger receiving Kniephof and Jarchelin.

The younger brother had already desired to divide the estates, as he spent more than his elder brother, and the income of the common treasury therefore fell short. Until his marriage, Bernhard would not consent to this, the brotherly affection between them having always been very sincere.

Bismarck became Deputy to the circle in his brother's place, and in that capacity conducted the management of Naugard, and was chosen representative in the Provincial Pomeranian Diet; but, after the first session, wearied by the unimportant duties assigned to him, he resigned his functions; his place was filled by his brother.

When Bismarck, at the age of twenty-three, in the most pressing circumstances, without credit or capital, undertook the conduct of the wasted estates, he evinced prudence and activity, and, as long as bitter want pressed upon him, he found solace in agricultural activity; but when, by his means, the estates began to rise in value, and everything went on smoothly, and he was able to rely upon able subordinates, the administration gave him less satisfaction, and he felt the circle in which he moved too contracted for him. In his youthful fancy, he had formed a certain ideal of a country Junker; hence he had no carriage, performed all his journeys on horseback, and astonished the neighbourhood by riding six to ten miles* to evening assemblies in Polzin. Despite of his wild life and actions, he felt a continually increasing sense of loneliness; and the same Bismarck who gave himself to jolly carouses among the officers of the neighbouring garrisons, sank, when alone, into the bitterest and most desolate state of reflection. He suffered from that disgust of life common to the boldest officers at certain times, and which has been called " first lieutenant's melancholy." The less real pleasure he had in his wild career, the madder it became; and he earned himself a fearful reputation among the elder ladies and gentlemen, who predicted the moral and pecuniary ruin of " Mad Bismarck."

The mansion of Kniephof is pleasantly situated, but was built in a very simple style by its first possessor, the brave Cavalry Colonel Frederick August, who lay in garrison at that time at Gollnow, hard by, and who personally superintended its construction. The whole arrangements of the dwelling—little changed to this day—are of the sober simplicity of the era of Frederick William I. The then Major von Bismarck had purchased these estates chiefly to gratify his passion for the chase, for game then abounded on it, especially deer, very few of which remained when his grandson, Otto, came to reside there.

Kniephof did not then behold stag huntings with horses and mastiffs, as in the previous century. But strange scenes occurred when the youthful owner, tortured by dark thoughts, dashed restlessly, to kill time, through the fields, sometimes in solitude, and sometimes in the company of gay companions and guests; so that Kniephof

* In English miles about eighteen and thirty.—K. R. H. M.

became a Kneiphof far and wide in the land.* Strange
stories were current about their nocturnal carouses, at
which none could equal "Mad Bismarck" in emptying
the great beaker filled with porter and champagne. Tales
of a wild character were whispered in the circles of
shuddering ladies—the power of imagination being rife in
dear old Pomerania. At each mad adventure, each wild
burst of humour, a dozen myths started up, sometimes of
a comical, sometimes a terrible character, until the little
mansion of Kniephof˙or "Kneiphof" was looked upon as
haunted. But the ghosts must have had tolerably strong
nerves, for the guests, slumbering with nightcaps of porter
and ˙champagne, were often roused by pistol-shots, the
bullets whistling over their heads, and the lime from their
ceilings tumbling into their faces.

And yet the guests at this time relate that they were
" miserably" bored at Bismarck's nocturnal political discussions with his intimate friends, Dewitz of Mesow and Bülow
of Hoffelde—so different in character, but so inseparable
from him. Young gentlemen in those days were not so
accustomed to political discussions as the youth of our time,
and political parties were then nearly unknown. It should
be stated, however, that Otto von Bismarck, despite his wild
life, stood in high consideration, and he was heard with
avidity, though the affair might be "miserably" tedious.
"He made an impression on all of us—and I think at
that time he was somewhat of a liberal!" a companion of
those days told us, who complained of being "wretchedly
bored" amongst the rest. The estimation in which Bismarck was held was in nowise confined to youth; grave
men of position, in a greater or less degree, felt that from
this fermenting mass would be formed an excellent and

---

* This requires explanation, the pun not being susceptible of translation.
The derivation of Kniephof is uncertain; *Knie* is, however, *Knee*, and it might
have come from its being granted for knee-service. *Kneipe* is a *pot-house*:
Hof a court.—K. R. H. M.

strong wine.   Many of the electors desired to nominate
him for the Landrath, but Bismarck, decidedly enough,
refused this.

And then there came a day, on which the furious revelry
of "Kneiphof" was silent; the old mansion, as if by enchantment, grew quiet and respectable, so that the world
was first astonished and then whispered, "A lady will
become mistress of Kniephof!"

But no lady appeared at Kniephof—it was a mistake,
perhaps a disappointment.   It was then said, "Bismarck
is going to India!"   He did not go, though, perhaps, he
for a time desired to do so.

For the rest, it must be said that Bismarck fought
chivalrously with the demons around him.   He read
much, and continually received parcels of books from his
bookseller, chiefly historical works, but also theological
and philosophical works.   Spinoza he studied deeply.   The
melancholy he had contracted by the events which befel him
on the Rhine, he strove to dissipate by travelling.   About
this time he visited France and England; he even resumed
the position of Referendarius under the Crown at Potsdam,
and was very industrious.   His friends, among whom were
Baron Senfft von Pilsach, afterwards Chief President of
Pomerania, and his brother, considering him remarkably
adapted for the service of the State, although at that time
he assumed a very surly attitude in reference to the
bureaucracy.   It was probably about this time, at a party,
where his President somewhat slighted him, as he was
inferior to him as an official, that he begged the President
in a friendly way to consider that in society Herr von Bismarck was as good as Herr von Anybody Else—which
scarcely pleased the President.   Another of his chiefs once
pretended not to notice the presence of Bismarck, went to
the window and began drumming with his fingers, where-
upon Bismarck went to the window and stood beside him,
drumming the Dessau March.   It was very likely the

same official who allowed Bismarck to wait in the ante-chamber for an hour, and received the answer to his short question, "What do you want?"—"I came here to beg for leave of absence, and now demand leave to resign." To about this time may be referred a report of Bismarck's as to certain expropriations, which attained much celebrity. He might have been appointed Landrath in Posen or Prussia Proper, had he been willing to go. In this report Bismarck freely and faithfully spoke his opinion as to the injustice of many expropriations, and his friends still quote the classical phrase, "You could not pay it me in cash, if you were to turn the park of my father into a carp lake, or the grave of my deceased aunt into an eel swamp!"

He decided in the end to go to Schönhausen, and become Landrath in the original seat of his race. His father was ready to resign Schönhausen to him, but this plan also failed. In the autumn of 1844, on the 30th of October, he had the delight, after his return from a longer journey, to betroth his only sister Malwin, to whom he was ever affectionately attached, to the friend of his youth, the Landrath of Angermünde, Oscar von Arnim. The affection of the brother and sister, people proverbially compared to that of a bridegroom to a bride.

After the death of his father, which took place in November, 1845, the sons so divided the property, that the elder retained Külz and received Jarchelin, the younger retaining Kniephof and adding to it Schönhausen. From that time Bismarck resided in Schönhausen, became Dyke Captain there, and afterwards Knight's Deputy in the circle of Jerichow in the Saxon Provincial Diet at Merseburg. In that capacity he attended the first meeting of the United Diets in 1847, on which occasion he first attracted the notice of the public to himself in more extended circles.

We shall now give some letters written by Bismarck to his sister at this troubled time, as they afford an insight into his peculiarities. We called this a troubled time, as the management of Kniephof and Jarchelin afforded him no satisfaction, for we find him continually flitting about between Pomerania, Schönhausen, and Berlin. In Berlin itself he changed his residence very often. On the morning of such removal he used to say abruptly to his servant, "Bring all my things to No. so-and-so, in so-and-so Street; I shall be there by bed-time." The things were placed on tables, chairs, and sofa, spread out; for Bismarck loved, as he said, to hold a review of his worldly possessions.

We must add that the disquiet he then suffered had a particular reason, and we shall find some allusions to this in his letters.

I.

Mademoiselle,—I have just received your boots from Glaser, and while they are being packed up I write to say that I am fairly amused here, and hope you enjoy your quadrille as much. I was pleasantly surprised to hear you danced with ———. If the boots are not properly made I am sorry, for you did not write anything to me on the subject, so I had them made like the old ones. To-morrow I go with Arnim to Schönhausen, where we propose to have a hunting-party. Father has given permission to us to kill a stag, but it is almost a pity at the present time of year. It has been freezing since yesterday. Among you Samoyeds the snow ought to be as high as the house. There are no news here—all is mourning—the King of Sweden also is dead. I feel ever more how alone I am in the world. To your quadrille you will probably only see ——— from here. I have been able to excite jealousy. Take care that ice is brought in at Kniephof, and as much as possible, or you will have to drink luke-warm champagne in summer. Greet every one, especially father.

Berlin, Wednesday, 1844.   B.

II.

Dear Maldewine,—Only because it is yourself, I will depart from one of my principles, by writing a letter of congratulation *purement pour féliciter*. I cannot come myself to your birthday, because my viceroy is not here to relieve me; but I would risk the assertion, that according to your incredulous bridegroom's view, you would be convinced that I came to you on business, and not for your own sake. Looking at it carefully, I don't know what I can wish you, for you can remain as you are; but I could wish that you had two more sisters-in-law; one who is gone, and one who will not arrive. Good bye, my heart—greet my father, Arnim, Antonie, &c.; in about a fortnight I hope to see you. Count the days till then, and kiss

Your affectionate Brother,
BISMARCK.

Kniephof, 27th June, 1844.

III.

Dear Little One,—Being too much engaged in packing to attend the Landwehr drill, I will only just write a couple of lines, as I shall have no time to do so after this, just now. Very shortly after the wool-market I represented our vagabond of a Landrath, have had many fires, many sessions in the burning heats, and much travelling through sandy bramble moors, so that I am completely tired of playing the Landrath, and so are my horses. I am hardly at rest for a week, and now I must go serve my country as a soldier! You see* "how men of merit are sought after, the undeserver may," etc. I am sorry to say I have had to buy another horse, as mine is not adapted for evolutions; however, I must try it, with Grosvenor for a reserve. The latter pulls the carriage like an old coach

---

* This passage is written by Bismarck in English. I have put inverted commas.—K. R. H. M.

horse; I must therefore pay for it, you can tell Oscar (as soon as the rape harvest is current), which I had firmly resolved not to do—if he did not draw well. [Here a blot.] Forgive the preceding Arabic; I have not a moment's time to write this billet over again, for I must set out in an hour, and much packing has yet to be done. We shall remain for fourteen days in garrison at Crüssow, by Stargard, afterwards near Fiddichow and Bahn, opposite Schwedt. If you write to me, address me at Stargard, Poste Restante; I shall make no apologies for my long silence, and, if the case arise, regard you in the same way. Good bye—-my portmanteau is yawning at me in expectation of being packed, and it looks very blue and white and military all around me.

When we reach Fiddichow, Oscar can visit me at Bahn. I will let him know.   Your faithful Brother,

BISMARCK.

Kniephof, the 21st.

IV.

Norderney, 9th Sept., 1844.

Darling Little One,—A fortnight ago I intended to write to you, without being able, amidst the throng of business and pleasure, to do so. If you are curious to know the nature of the business, I am really unable, with the sparseness of my time and paper, to give you a complete picture, as its series and nature, according to the change of ebb and flood, every day produces the most manifold variety. Bathing, for instance, only takes place at flood tide, the waves being then strongest; this happens between six in the morning and six in the evening, every day one hour later, and is enjoyed with the advantages of a breezy, rainy, summer morning, sometimes in God's beautiful nature with the glorious impressions of land and water, sometimes in my landlord's *Mousse Omne Fimmen* bed, five feet long, with the delightful ideas inspired by a seaweed mattress. In the same way, the *table d'hôte* changes its times between

one and five o'clock, its component parts varying between
shell-fish, beans, and mutton on the odd days, and soles,
peas, and veal on the even days of the month, in which
case sweet porridge with fruit sauce accompanies the
former, and currant pudding the latter. That the eye
may not envy the palate, a lady from Denmark sits beside
me, whose appearance fills me with sorrow and longings
for home, for she reminds me of the pepper at Kniephof,
when it is very thin. Her mind must be heavenly, or Fate
was very much unjust to her, for she offers me, in a sweet
voice, two helpings from every dish before her. Opposite
sits the old minister ———, one of those beings we only
behold in dreams, when we are somnolently ill ; a fat frog
without legs, who opens his mouth before every morsel
like a carpet-bag, right up to his shoulders, so that I am
obliged to hold on to the table for giddiness. My other
neighbour is a Russian officer ; a good fellow, built like a
bootjack, with a long slender body, and short crooked
legs. Most of the people have left, and our dinner company has melted from two to three hundred down to
twelve or fifteen. My holiday at the baths is now
over, and I shall leave by the next steamboat, expected
the day after to-morrow (the 11th) for Heligoland, and
then by Hamburg to Schönhausen. I cannot, however,
fix the day of my arrival, because it is uncertain that the
steamer will arrive the day after to-morrow ; the notices
say so, but they often retard the later passages if there
are not sufficient passengers to bear the expense. The
Bremen steamships have long since stopped, and I do not
like travelling by land, the roads being so bad that it is
only possible to reach Hanover by the third day, and the
post coaches are abominable. If, therefore, the steamer
does not come the day after to-morrow, I propose to go by
sailing vessel to Heligoland ; thence there is a twice-a-
week boat to Hamburg, but I do not know on what days.
Father wrote me word that you would go to Berlin on the

15th; if I therefore find, on reaching Hamburg, that I cannot reach you per steamer by the 15th, I shall try and get the Potsdam boat, and go direct to Berlin, to talk about art and industrial matters with you. If you receive this letter in time, which, considering the slowness of the post here, I scarcely think you will, you might send me a couple of lines to Hamburg—Old Stadt London Hotel—to say whether father has changed his travelling plans. The bathing here pleases me, and I should not mind stopping a few days longer. The shore is splendid,—very flat, even, soft sand, without any stones, and a surf such as I have neither seen in the Baltic, nor at Dieppe. Even when I am only knee-high in the water, a wave comes as high as a house (but the houses here are not so high as the palace at Berlin), turns me over ten times, and throws me on the sand some twenty paces off—a simple amusement which I daily enjoy, *con amore*, as long as the medical men advise. I have made great friends with the lake; every day I sail for some hours, fish, and shoot at seals. I only killed one of the last; such a gentle dog's face, with large, handsome eyes; I was really sorry. A fortnight ago we had heavy storms; some twenty ships, of all nations, came ashore here, and for several days the shore was covered with innumerable fragments of wreck, utensils, goods in casks, bodies, clothes, and papers. I have, myself, had some sample of what a storm is. With a piscatorial friend, Tonke Hams, I had sailed in four hours to the island of Wangeroge; on our return we were tossed about for twenty-four hours in the little boat, and in the first hour had not a dry thread on us, although I lay in an apology for a cabin; fortunately, we were well provided with ham and port wine, or the voyage would have been very distressing. Hearty greetings to father, and thanks for his letter; the same to Antonie and Arnim. Farewell, my treasure, my heart.   Your loving Brother,

BISMARCK.

V.

Madame,—It is only with great difficulty that I withstand my desire to fill a whole letter with agricultural
complaints, about night-frosts, sick cattle, bad rape and
bad roads, dead lambs, hungry sheep, scarcity of straw,
fodder, money, potatoes, and manure; in addition to that,
John outside is, as continually as badly, whistling a
wretched Scottische, and I have not the cruelty to forbid
him, as music may perhaps soothe his despair in love.
The ideal of his dreams, at her parents' desire, has lately
refused him, and married a frame-maker. Just my case,
except the frame-maker, who is rasping away in the
bosom of the future. I *must*, the Devil take me! get
married, I can again see, plainly; since, after my father's
departure I feel lonely and forsaken, and this mild, damp
weather makes me melancholy, and longingly prone to
love. I cannot help it, in the end I must marry————;
everybody will have it so, and nothing seems more
natural, as we have both remained behind. She is somewhat cold to me, but that is the way with them all; it is
pretty not to be able to change one's affections like one's
shirt, however seldom the last event may occur. That on
the 1st I bore the visit of several ladies with polite
urbanity, our father will have informed you. When I
came from Angermünde, I was cut off from Kniephof by
the floods of the Hampel, and as no one would let me
have horses, I was obliged to remain for the night at
Naugard, with many merchants and other travellers who
also awaited the subsidence of the waters. Afterwards
the bridges over the Hampel were carried away, so that
Knobelsdorf and I, the Regents of two mighty Circles,
were surrounded here on a little patch by the waters, and
there was an anarchical interregnum from Schievelbein to
Damm. About one o'clock one of my waggons with
three casks of spirits was carried away by the flood, and
in my little river the Hampel, I pride myself to say, a

man driving a pitch-cart was carried away by the flood and drowned.* Besides this, several houses in Gollnow fell in, a criminal in the gaol hanged himself for being flogged, and my neighbour, the proprietor —— in ——, shot himself on account of the want of fodder; three widows and an infant mourn in tearless sorrow, besides the bloody coffin of the suicide. An eventful time! It is to be expected that several of our acquaintance will quit the scene, as this year, with its bad harvest, low prices, and the long winter, is difficult to be encountered by embarrassed proprietors. To-morrow I expect Bernhard to return, and am glad to be quit of the District business, very agreeable in summer, but very unpleasant during this weather and rain. Then I shall, should Oscar not write otherwise, come to Kröchelndorf and thence to you.

I have nothing new to tell you from hence, except that I am still satisfied with Bellin—the thermometer now at 10 P.M. marks + 10° (50° Fahr.). Odin still continues lame of his right fore paw, and enjoys the society of his Rebecca with touching affection all day, and I was obliged to chain her up for domestic misbehaviour. Good night, *m'amie, je t'embrasse.* Thine, &c., &c.,   BISMARCK.

Kniephof, 9th April, 1845.

VI.

Most dear Creusa,—I have not taken the smallest key with me, and can assure you from experience that it never leads to the slightest result to look for keys; for which reason, in such circumstances—very rare with me, with my love of order—I at once turn to the locksmith to have a new one made. With important ones, such as safes, one has the choice of altering the wards and all the keys in use. I can see that I shall soon end my letter; not from

---

* It is obvious that this pride arose from the smallness of the river, not the loss of the man and horse.—K. R. H. M.

malice, because you only wrote a page to me—it would
be terrible to think that you would consider me so
wretchedly revengeful; but from sleepiness. I have been
riding and walking all day in the sun—saw a dance in
Plathe yesterday, and drank a good deal of Montebello;
the one gives me bile, the other the cramp. Add to this,
in swallowing, a painful swelling of the uvula, a slight
headache, cramped legs, and sun-burn, and you can understand that neither my thoughts of you, my angel, nor the
melancholy howling of a shepherd dog, locked up for too
great a passion for hunting, can keep me longer awake. I
will only tell you that the Kränzchen (club) is not very
much visited; a very pretty little Miss ——, sister of ——,
was there, and that most of the young and old ladies are
lying in childbed, except Frau von ——, the little one
who wore the light blue satin; and that I go to-morrow
to an æsthetic tea in ——. Sleep well, my idolized one—
it is eleven o'clock.

BISMARCK.

K., 27th April, 1845.

VII.

Ma Sœur,—Je t'écris pour t'annoncer that I shall be
with you at Angermünde at the latest by the 3rd March,
if you do not write to me before that you will not have
me. I think then, after I have enjoyed a sight of you
for three or four days, to carry off your husband to attend
a meeting of the Society for the Improvement of the
Working Classes, on the 7th March, at Potsdam. My
journey, previously intended, has been delayed by all sorts
of Dyke suits, and Game cases, so that I shall leave here
by the 28th at earliest. I am to be invested here with
the important office of Dyke Captain, and I have also
considerable chance of being elected to the Saxon (not the
Dresden) Diet. The acceptance of the first office would
be decisive as to the settlement of my residence—that is,
here! There is no salary, but the administration of the

position is of importance to Schönhausen and the other estates, inasmuch as it very much depends upon this whether we may occasionally get under water again or no. On the other hand, my friend ——, who is determined to send me to East Prussia, pushes me hard to accept the office there of H. M. Commissioner for Improvements. Bernhard urges me, contrary to my expectation, to go to Prussia. I should like to know what he thinks himself about it. He declares that by taste and education I am made for Government service, and must enter it, sooner or later. Greet Oscar, Detlev, Miss ——, and the other children heartily, from your devoted Brother

Schönhausen 25th February, 1846.   BISMARCK.

VIII.

Dear Arnimen,—I have within the few last days been obliged to write so many letters, that I have only left by me one sheet, stained with coffee, which I will not, however, deprive you of. My existence here has not been the most agreeable. To make inventories is tedious, particularly when the rascally valuer has left one three times in the lurch for nothing, and one has to wait in vain for several days. Besides this, I have lost a considerable amount of corn by hail, on the 17th, and finally I am suffering from a very annoying cough, although I have drank no wine since Angermünde, and have taken every precaution against catching cold, cannot complain of want of appetite, and sleep like a badger. At the same time every one laughs at me for my healthy looks, when I declare I am suffering from the chest. To-morrow, at noon, I will visit Redekin, the next day go to Magdeburg, and then, after a day or two's sojourn, throw myself immediately into your arms. I cannot tell you of any further news here, except that the grass was fourteen days in advance, in comparison with Angermünde, and the crops, take them altogether, very middling. The results of the inundation are very annoyingly visible, I am sorry to say, in the garden. Besides the many trees I took during the winter from the plantation as useless, it now appears that all the other acacias and the ashes are dried up, so that little remains; seventeen of the limes at the lower end of the great avenue are either dead or appear dying visibly. I shall have those showing a leaf anywhere, topped, and see whether this operation will save them. In fruit trees, and especially plums, there has been a considerable loss. In the fields, and more particularly in the meadows, there are many places in which the grass has not grown, because the upper vegetative soil has been washed away. The Bellins and the rest of the Schönhausers send their respects; the former suffer much from to-day's heat. Sultan not less. Thermometer 21° (68° Fahr.) in the shade. Many greetings to Oscar.

Your consumptive Brother,

BISMARCK.

Schönhausen, 22nd July, 1846.

In the course of this year Bismarck obtained his first decoration, for many years the only one which graced his breast, but which he wears to this day beside the stars of the highest Orders of Christendom. In the summer of 1842, he was on duty as Cavalry Officer with the Stargard Landwehr Squadron of Uhlans, in exercise at Lippehne, in the Neumark, and one afternoon was standing with other officers on the bridge over the lake, when his groom Hildebrand, the son of the forester on his estate, rode one of the horses to water and for a bath in the lake, close by the bridge. Suddenly the horse lost footing, and as the terrified horseman clung tight to the bridle, it fell, and Hildebrand disappeared in the water. A terrible cry of horror resounded; Bismarck threw off his sword in an instant, tore off his uniform, and dashed headlong into the lake to save his servant. By great good fortune he

seized him, but the man clung to him so fast in his death
agony, that he had to dive before he could loose himself
from him. The crowd stood in horror on the shore;
master and servant were both given up for lost—bubbles
rose to the surface, but the powerful swimmer had succeeded in releasing himself from the deadly embrace of
the drowning man; he rose to the surface, raising his
servant with him. He also brought him safely to land,
of course in an inanimate condition; but Hildebrand
soon recovered, and the following day was well. This
little town, some of the inhabitants of which had witnessed the brave rescue, was in great commotion; they
expressed their feelings by the Superintendent meeting the
noble rescuer in full official dress, and wishing him happiness for the mercy of the Almighty. Hence he obtained
the simple medalion " for rescue from danger," the well-
known Prussian Safety Medal, which may be seen beside
so many exalted stars on the breast of the Minister-President. Bismarck is proud of this mark of honour, and
when on one occasion a noble diplomatist, perhaps not
without a tinge of satire, asked him the meaning of this
modest decoration, then his only one, he at once replied:
" I am in the habit sometimes of saving a man's life!"
The diplomatist abased his eyes before the stern look
which accompanied the lightly spoken words of Bismarck.

In the spring of 1843, Lieutenant von Bismarck sought
and obtained permission from the Landwehr Battalion of
Stargard to enter the 4th Uhlans (now the 1st Pomeranian
Regiment, Uhlans, No. 4), then in garrison at Treptow
and Greiffenberg, and do some months' duty. Bismarck
certainly aimed, when he entered this regiment, to serve
as an officer in the active army, and to become acquainted
with the regular routine of duty, although he did not
say so, and allowed the officers of Uhlans to believe that
he had only been induced by their agreeable society to

join them. It is true he lived with them as a comrade, and often entertained them, almost every Saturday, as his guests at Kniephof; but they had frequently been his guests before, and afterwards they became so constantly. The Regimental Commandant, at that time, of the 4th Uhlans, was Lieutenant-Colonel von Plehwe, who fell in a duel as General, a person well known in many circles, and of a very distinguished character. Plehwe was one of the few important men, without an idea of what there was "in" the wild Landwehr Lieutenant, who joined his regiment in so strange a manner, for he did not know how to deal with Bismarck in any way. Half-way between Treptow, where the staff of the regiment was quartered, and Greiffenberg, where Bismarck lay, was a rendezvous known as "The Golden Dog" (*Zum Goldenen Mops*); to this place the severe Regimental Commandant was accustomed to summon the officers of Greiffenberg when he wanted to treat them to—compliments, or rather the very opposite to compliments. Oh! how often did Lieutenant von Bismarck ride to "The Golden Dog" upon his Caleb!

Caleb was Bismarck's favourite charger; a dark chestnut, not very handsome, but a good hunter; the warmer the work the more furious his pace. Caleb has carried his master at such speed impossible to relate without being supposed guilty of fabulation; but these rides were nevertheless true, according to the most credible witnesses. It was Caleb who bore Bismarck on that wild ride when the stirrup flew up to the epaulet. How it happened, who can tell?—but the fact is sure.

Although Von Plehwe may have summoned Lieutenant von Bismarck a few times too often to "The Golden Dog," although he may have been commanded to appear in full regimentals on more occasions than was necessary, Bismarck even now tells his former comrades in the 4th Uhlans, "I spent a very pleasant time with you!" He still chuckles with satisfaction at the little practical joke when, in company with other officers, he seated himself, smoking a cigar, on the bench before the Burgomaster of Treptow's house. This official was an enemy of tobacco, and officers were even then forbidden to smoke in the streets. It was in vain that the Burgomaster, who in other things was a very excellent man, informed them that it was no hotel, but the Burgomaster's house; Bismarck remained immovable, until the severe Commandant appeared in full uniform, and raised the tobacco blockade.

During the Christmas holidays of 1844, there was a dinner-party at the house of the youthful Frau von Blanckenburg, at Cardemin in Pomerania. This pious and intellectual lady—born a Von Thadden-Triglaff—had great influence over Bismarck, and had confirmed the ancient family friendship between the Blanckenburgs and the Bismarcks. After dinner four gentlemen sat in the Red Saloon under the lamp, who were to meet again after many years, although in different positions, but still fighting on the same side. Next to the host, the retired Examiner, Moritz von Blanckenburg, sat Otto von Bismarck, then in the same official position; beside the latter, Major von Roon, whose cradle was also in Pomerania; and, last, Dr. Theodor Beutner, since 1855 editor in chief of the "New Prussian Gazette," popularly known as the *Kreuzzeitung*, from the cross on the title-leaf.

CHAPTER III.

BETROTHAL AND MARRIAGE.

1847.

Falls in Love.—Johanna von Putkammer.—Marriage.—Meets King Frederick William IV.—Birth of his First Child.—Schönhausen and Kniephof with a New Mistress.

 N the society and at the house of his friend and neighbour, Moritz von Blanckenburg, Bismarck had often seen a friend of his noble hostess, who greatly interested him. But he first became more intimately acquainted with Fräulein Johanna von Putkammer on a trip which both of them made in company with the Blanckenburgs. Bismarck soon became aware of the affection he felt for the young lady, but he naturally found many obstacles in learning—as may be readily understood—whether his affection was returned by her. This would easily explain the inquietude of his behaviour, for even when assured of his attachment being returned, there were still many difficulties to be surmounted.

We have already mentioned the reputation which "Mad Bismarck" had won for himself among the elder ladies and gentlemen in Pomerania. The consternation and horror may easily be imagined, in which the quiet Christian house of Herr von Putkammer was plunged, on the receipt of a letter in which Bismarck directly and frankly asked for the hand of his daughter. But how much greater must have been his horror when the gentle daughter of the house, in a modest but firm manner, acknowledged her affection! "It seemed as if I had been felled with an axe!" old Herr von Putkammer said, in describing his feelings at that time, in a drastic tone. Even the story of the wolf, which always devours the meekest lambs, did not console him. However, he was far removed from playing the tyrant father, and he gave his consent, although with a heavy heart—a consent he has never had reason to regret. Her mother, of a more spirited nature, protested until Bismarck appeared in person at Reinfeld, and before her eyes clasped his bride to his heart. With a flood of passionate tears, she then consented to their union, and from that moment became the warmest and most zealous friend of the man to whom she gave her beloved daughter after so severe a struggle. Under the motto "All right," * Bismarck announces the fact to his sister, his "Arnimen."

Between this betrothal and his marriage falls Bismarck's first appearance at the first United Diet.

On the 28th of July, 1847, Otto von Bismarck-Schönhausen married Johanna Frederica Charlotte Dorothea Eleonore von Putkammer, born on the 11th of April, 1824, the only daughter of Herr Henry Ernst Jacob von Putkammer, of Kartlum, and the Lady Luitgarde, born Von Glasenapp of Reinfeld.

On the journey which Bismarck took after the wedding with his young wife through Switzerland and Italy, he accidentally met his King Frederick William IV., at Venice. He was at once commanded to attend at the royal dinner-table, and his royal master conversed with him for a long time in a gracious manner, particularly concerning German politics, a conversation not, perhaps, without its influence on the subsequent and very sudden

* So in Bismarck's letter.—K. R. H. M.

appointment of Bismarck to the post of Ambassador to the Federation; but it unquestionably laid the foundation for the favour with which King Frederick William IV. always regarded Bismarck. For the rest, he was so unprepared to meet his King and master at Venice, that he had not even had time to take with him a court suit, and was obliged to appear before his sovereign in borrowed clothes, which, considering his stature, must have fitted him very badly.

Bismarck now set up his domestic hearth at the old stone mansion of Schönhausen. There, where his cradle once stood, in the following years stood that of his eldest child, his daughter Marie; and though his actual residence in Schönhausen only lasted a few years, he took with him his domestic happiness thence to Berlin, Frankfurt, and St. Petersburg. Nominally Schönhausen continued to be his residence, until he became Minister-President; and though he now prefers to live on his Pomeranian estates to those in the Alt Mark, during his days of retirement, this does not occur from any want of affection for his old home, but from a feeling of delicacy towards his father-in-law, now a venerable man almost eighty years of age, but still fresh and hale, who lives in the vicinity of Varzin, and also because he finds in Pomerania three things for which he would seek in

K

vain at Schönhausen. The forest is not at Schönhausen close round the house, as at Varzin, for at Schönhausen he has an hour's ride to reach the wood, and the forest he loves as an old friend. The game about Schönhausen is also almost entirely destroyed, and the heavy wheat soil there is either flat and hard, or cloddy, and therefore little fitted for riding. Bismarck, as he ever was, remains a great horseman and a zealous sportsman.

The marriage of Bismarck has been blessed with three children—Mary Elizabeth Johanna, born the 21st August, 1848, at Schönhausen; Nicolas Ferdinand Herbert, born the 28th December, 1849, at Berlin; William Otto Albert, born the 1st August, 1852, at Frankfurt-on-the-Maine.

Amidst the severe battles of a time so rife in immeasurable contradictions, Bismarck commenced his family life in a simple but substantial manner, as befitting a nobleman of the Alt Mark or Pomerania; and so he has been able to maintain himself even at the elevation at which God the Almighty has placed him for the good of his native country. That he may ever maintain it is the aspiration of every patriot, for in him the fountain ever freshly runs, whence he draws continual renovation for the service of his King and country.

Book the Third.

———•———

LEARNING THE BUSINESS.

Der

Ehrn. Wanderschaft

6ter Theil.

Der Meister wird geboren,
Doch seine Meisterschaft
Er kann sie nur gewinnen
Ganz und dauerhaft,
Wenn er sich seinem Werke
Mit Leib und Seele weiht —
Noch brauchte jeder Meister
Lehr und Wanderzeit.

LEARNING THE BUSINESS.

Der Lehr- und Wanderjahre
Oder Theil.

Der Meister wird geboren,
Doch seine Meisterschaft
Er kann sie nur gewinnen
Ganz und dauerhaft,
Wenn er sich seinem Werke
Mit Leib und Seele weiht —
Noch brauchte jeder Meister
Lehr und Wanderzeit.

LEARNING THE BUSINESS.

Der

Ehre Wanderjahre

Erster Theil.

Der Meister wird geboren,
Doch seine Meisterschaft
Er kann sie nur gewinnen
Ganz und dauerhaft,
Wenn er sich seinem Werke
Mit Leib und Seele weiht —
Noch brauchte jeder Meister
Lehr und Wanderzeit.

LEARNING THE BUSINESS.

CHAPTER I.

INTRODUCTORY.

"UT SCIAT REGNARE."

Bismarck's Policy.—Its Gradual Growth and Political Character.—Contrast with Lucchesini.—Bismarck's Open Honesty.—Vassal and Liege.—Liberalism a Danger.—Democracy a Danger.—The Relative Positions of Prussia and Austria in the Federation.—Gerlach's Ideal Conservatism.

ISMARCK has now to be politically tested, and amidst all the strange eventualities in the remarkable history of Prussia, we perceive, first as a counsellor, then as an actor, and finally as a guide, that the one man emerges, a man ever the same, yet ever appearing to change. Otto von Bismarck is best to be compared to a tree, which continues the same, although gaining in height and strength by growth; whose lofty top, with its wide-spreading leaves, alters its appearance at each new spring, to a greater or lesser degree; it remains the same, even if the wind bends the trunk, despite its toughest power of resistance, slightly aside; an imperfect twig may be broken off by the storm, or a heavy rain-fall may bare one of the deep roots, and abandon the growing power a prize to the effects of the breeze and the sun.

The altered appearance which Bismarck at different times has presented, has blinded many eyes; many thought he had grown into another man, as he presented himself ever stronger, mightier, and of greater stature! Of course, he has long since become too great, too strong, and too mighty for his opponents, and some have found, in a manner not so entirely agreeable, the influence of the wide-spreading tree with its potent shadow.

There have certainly been alterations in the man, but none of them inconsistent with the growth of the tree. The simile may not be accurate, but it indicates the truth. Bismarck has himself pointed out the changes which he has undergone very much better by the modest sentence, " I have learnt something!" Perhaps he did not always learn the best, but he has learnt more than many who now turn maliciously from him, because they could not keep step with him; some others, also, because they would not.

We owe to Guizot the expression of the same thought, so moderately phrased by Bismarck, in the pointed French remark, "*L'homme absurde seul ne change pas!*" The word, however, is somewhat suspicious in the mouth of the French statesman, for its utterance is *pro domo*, as an excuse for various political apostasies.

Now, in Bismarck there is no trace of apostasy throughout his political life, and perhaps in no statesman can an enduring political principle be more easily discovered, and followed into detail—if we only adhere to facts, and do not allow ourselves to be diverted by absurd misinterpretations of his words, the diatribes of political opposition, or the hollow declamation of foolish party babblers.

This is the more easy, as Bismarck is precisely the opposite of one of his predecessors in the Foreign Office of Prussia. The cunning of the Marquis of Lucchesini,* a predecessor of Bismarck, had become so well known, so proverbial, that none of his negotiations ever led to anything, because whoever was representing the other side always commenced with the conviction that Lucchesini would, in the end, outwit him. A certain degree of confidence, however inconsiderable, is necessary on both sides, if political arrangements are to end in results. Bismarck, on the other hand, is a thoroughly honest politician—honest to such a degree, that his political adversary is sometimes puzzled, and suspects some snare in his very openness. Bismarck is a thoroughly honest man, who scorns every intentional deception on the part of his opponents.

We are well aware that this assertion will be met in many circles with scornful contradiction; but it is nevertheless true, and we will demonstrate the proposition. But they also err, who may perhaps believe that we are of opinion that we have, in this, said something flattering to the Minister-President; we merely acknowledge that this

---

* Lucchesini, Girolamo, Marchese, was born at Lucca in 1752 of a patrician family, and presented by the Abbé Fontana to King Frederick II., by whom he was appointed librarian and reader with the title of Chamberlain. He was sent to Rome in 1787 to obtain certain ratifications from the Pope, and thence to Warsaw, where he succeeded in 1790 in bringing Poland and Prussia into a treaty of amity. He attended the congress of Reichenbach as Minister Plenipotentiary in 1791. In 1792 he went to Warsaw and destroyed the very treaty he had himself negotiated between Prussia and Poland. Hence the above strictures on him. He was Ambassador to Vienna in 1793, but was generally with the King. In September, 1802, he was sent to Paris as Ambassador Extraordinary, and followed Napoleon to Milan. He was present at the battle of Jena, and signed the truce at Charlottenburg with Napoleon. This not being sanctioned by the King, he resigned. He then became Chamberlain to Napoleon's sister, the Duchess of Lucca, and died the 19th October, 1825, at Florence. He was the author of some political works on the Rhenish Confederation and the like. He seems to have been a shifty and unprincipled politician. His younger brother, Cesare Lucchesini, was a distinguished author and antiquary.—K. R. H. M.

honesty has been implanted in the nature of Bismarck by
the Almighty, that it could not but develope itself and
become a sustaining principle ; but such acknowledgment
does not constitute flattery.

Bismarck rode into the political lists in 1847 as a
courageous, sensible, and honourable man, and has held
his place in the arena for more than twenty years as a
loyal champion of the King, both in single combat and
general battle.   He has made mistakes in his innumerable
contests, but he has learnt from them, has gallantly paid
in person, and never concealed or denied his colours or
insignia.

Even the most furious opponents of these colours and
insignia cannot deny this.

We have not used the simile of the knightly tournament
unadvisedly, for the whole political faith of Bismarck is
founded on a chivalric idea, in the deep immovable conviction of his personal position towards the Prussian
sovereignty.   The ultimate foundation of Bismarck's
political action consists in his personal position as an
Alt Mark vassal and nobleman to his liege lord, the
Margrave of Brandenburg, the King of Prussia.   It will
be understood that this position is the ultimate, but not
precisely the only one ; it is only the least, but also the
inmost circle, whence the other principles around him
have evolved themselves, according to his consciousness.
As the liegeman stood in personal relation to his lord, so
the deputy stood to the King, and the relation to the
Regent was analogous to the relation of the Minister-
President and Chancellor of the Diet to the King and
Chief of the North German Federation.   From this strong
consciousness of the moral connection of his own person
with that of the sovereign, his liege, Bismarck's whole
political acts arise and may be discerned.

King William is, however, aware of the construction
which Bismarck places upon their inter-relations, and in

this, on the one hand, lies the strength, on the other the weakness, of the position held by Bismarck, as chief counsellor of the King.   This hint may here suffice.

And if we now contemplate, from this point of view, the whole political life of Bismarck—his speeches, his letters, his despatches and ordinances, the result of his exertions everywhere, from the beginning until now—what do we find?   The same loyal Brandenburg states-man, who, in chivalrous and liege faith, has grown greater in courage and self-sacrifice ; learning more how to per-form his functions as year by year has passed away ; with greater self-possession and good-humour before the throne of his monarch ; before that throne, in his conception, the bulwark of Prussia and Germany, and defended by him with equal zeal against inward detractors and outward foes.

At the first United Diet, in the year 1847, he was impressed with the idea that liberalism might endanger the throne of his liege ; it was not a perfect conviction, but the daring phrase roused him ; he supposed he saw danger, and he instantly showed a firm front to it.

At that time he was but little acquainted with the use of parliamentary weapons ; his opponents were far more experienced in eloquence than himself, and he stood, as it were, almost alone before a multitude ; for those of his own opinions, with the exception of the two Manteuffels, perhaps, were still less experienced speakers than he ; but the bravery with which he encountered the word "liberal" deserved all praise.   The bold attitude with which he entered the arena revealed to his opponents that the unknown Dyke Captain from the banks of the Elbe was not a man to be undervalued by them ; this they did not do ; and the fierce irony with which they, with more or less talent, overwhelmed him, betrayed the fact that in this Junker the Crown had found a mighty defender.

When the second United Diet took place, the enemy of

the kingdom was no longer liberalism, but democracy, and Bismarck met this foe with the most unhesitating conviction.   But the nobleman who honours in the King of Prussia his liege lord, is by no means the Aga, or Pasha, of an Oriental Sultan, blindly obedient and adoring.   The manly words of Bismarck were a rebuke, not only to the low, but the high.

In 1849-51 Bismarck occupied a position in the Diet, as one of the chief leaders of the Conservative party against democracy.   He entered into the strife with ardour, both at Berlin and Erfurt; wherever he saw the sovereignty of Prussia assailed, he sprang to the breach with decision.   He seemed to have a fine intuition for everything hostile to his beloved sovereignty.

When Ambassador at Frankfurt to the Federation, he at once recognized the impending ruin of Prussia to consist in the false position she there occupied, and he arrived at the conviction that the jealousy of Austria would strive to retain Prussia in this position, and not only that, but would employ itself in active measures, by which it should end in the final destruction of Germany. He therefore resolved upon opposition to Austria.   This was not a very easy task; the compact between Prussia and Austria had descended to him from his fathers as a sacred tradition.   He would readily have held out his hand, he would have desired earnestly to remain true to tradition; nor did he remit in attempts and offers, until he knew that there was a change coming over the policy of Austria not tending to the good of Prussia and Germany.   He then changed with military precision. The vassal approached with full front before the throne of his liege, even against Austria.   He did not do it secretly, but openly and honestly; every one might be able to tell how it fared with him everywhere.   He defined his position in writing from Frankfurt, from St. Petersburgh, from Paris, both by his own hand and by that of others.

And when, in 1862, he entered upon the conflict inherited by him from the new era, the result of the thorny
fight, at the head of the government, it was the mighti-
ness of the kingdom, the position of his liege lord, for

which he fought for years with body and soul against
the pretentions of the parliamentary spirit, with glorious
devotion and tough Brandenburg tenacity.

The interior defence of the Prussian monarchy, in its
inherent integrity, the rehabilitation of the liberty of

Germany, so important for its own safety, and a dignified attitude towards foreign nations, constitute the unity of the policy of Bismarck.

Liberalism, democracy, the inimical jealousy of Austria, the envy of foreign nations, with its train of parliamentary spirit and specialisms—such are the enemies of the Prussian sovereignty; and Bismarck has, with equal courage and firmness, with as much insight as success, fought openly and honestly against these. And if all outward symptoms do not deceive us, he is now powerfully preparing against another great foe of real sovereignty — that is bureaucracy, still lying armed to the teeth behind the Table of Green Cloth as its stronghold.

In these different contests it is quite possible that Bismarck may often have erred; he may not immediately have found the right weapons, and he may also not have employed them in the proper localities. It is certain there is much to blame, much to deplore; but accept him in all that is great and real, then most persons will voluntarily bow before the man, who, for twenty years, has fought so great a battle, with visor down, without false deceit or any kind of malice. Nor has the man earned his hard victories without having had to pay for them.

Bismarck has not destroyed the enemies of the Prussian monarchy; this is in the power of no man—nor perhaps was it within the sphere of his intentions; but he has subdued them, and in greater or lesser proportion made them serviceable to the interests of the Crown.

One of the chief difficulties in his political action is, on the one hand to discipline these elements which so very unwillingly serve the Prussian monarchy, and on the other to spare the perfectly intelligible sensitiveness of ancient fidelity, and to conquer the readily understood want of confidence of his own old coadjutors in the gay ranks of his new allies. He is thus met with the idealistic conservatism of Gerlach, whose organ was the "Neue

Preussische Zeitung" for so many years. Gerlach's principal service consisted in the actual formation of a political conservative party in Prussia — an idealism long revered by Bismarck, but certainly not to be contained within its own bounds when opposed to those demands which are made on a guiding statesman by the hard necessities of daily life. The old conservative party of Prussia has made great sacrifices, and is making them daily ; but she makes them to the glorious kingdom of Prussia, and it is a high honour to be the regnant party when a Bismarck is the King's first councillor. And, indeed, is it possible for the conservative party to be otherwise than the reigning party in Prussia ?

The tried Prussian patriotism of the conservatives will not allow itself to be disconnected by details from the great statesman who has emerged from their ranks ; they know that Bismarck not only is frequently compelled to pour his new wine into old bottles, but also to pour his old wine into new bottles. The good is not always the enemy of the better, but sometimes the bridge to the best and highest. The lightning does not pursue the course where it finds the best conductor, but that in which the sum of conduction is the most powerful. Bismarck's real policy consists in forcing parties unwilling to do so, to work and strive for the monarchy. In royal Prussia no party can any longer exist with the object of weakening the royal power. There will always continue to be a number of those whose efforts are more or less openly directed to such an end ; but no party dare, as such, to acknowledge such an aim.

If we, then, see the unity of Bismarck's policy to consist in the defence of the sovereignty, it might almost seem as if this policy were of a negative character ; but this is only apparent, for such a defence leads to positive creations, although at first sight they may appear as mighty beginnings — such as the North German Confederation—and are not all so evident to the eye, as may be seen on the map of the kingdom · of Prussia since 1866.

We shall now accompany Bismarck to the Assembly of the Three Estates of the first United Diet, then from battle-field to battle-field at Berlin, at Erfurt, and at Frankfurt, until those of Königgrätz and Nicolsburg, and still farther, for the great contest is not yet fought out—the last victory is not won. The statesman whom God will yet awaken to enter upon the inheritance of Bismarck, and continue his work, will find new and mighty armour, the creation of King William and Bismarck, in which to encounter the enemy with the ancient Prussian war-cry, *Mit Gott für König und Vaterland!* " With God for King and Country ! "

CHAPTER II.

THE ASSEMBLY OF THE THREE ESTATES.

1847.

The February Constitution.—Merseburg.—First Appearance of Bismarck in the White Saloon.—Von Saucken.—Bismarck's First Speech.—Conservatives and Liberals.—The First of June.—Jewish Emancipation.—Illusions Destroyed.

WHEN King Frederick William IV. issued the February manifesto, in 1847,* and summoned the United Diet with the Chambers, he thought in his royal great-heartedness to have accorded to his people a free gift of his affection and his confidence, and to have anticipated many wishes; but close behind the rejoicings which welcomed the patent of February, there lay the bitterest disenchantment for the noble King.

The honourable old royalists of Prussia, who had been educated and had grown up in the honest Prussian absolutism of Frederick William III., first looked with suspicion at this new royal gift; they could not at all understand why their own King of Prussia should have thought it necessary to summon a Parliament somewhat on the model of England, and they foresaw all sorts of evils in the future, as they thoughtfully shook their grey and honoured heads. To these men, who at that time were still very numerous, and whose influence was considerable, succeeded those who certainly felt that the abuses of bureaucracy were no longer curable by patriarchal

* This Constitution is given in the Appendix, being an important state document—K. R. H. M.

absolutism, but who still thought that the King, by this measure, had conceded the very utmost possible in that direction. They saw in the patent the last fortress of the monarchy which must be held against liberalism at any cost. In opposition to these royalists, the host of liberals unfolded their gay banner in different columns. They only could see in the February patent the starting point of a further movement, which, founded on the patent, might transform the absolute state into a modern constitutional monarchy. There existed even individuals who perceived that the patent would prove an obstacle to their revolutionary tendencies, and desired to refuse its acceptance.

We will not criticise these parties, but it is certain that none of them regarded the patent in the spirit of the royal donor—unless perhaps some who had understood that the King, basing his action on the existing Provincial Assemblies, proposed in a similar manner to erect a peculiar Prussian Representative Monarchy. They beheld the February patent to be no final measure, but the beginning of States Government, which could only develope itself under specially favourable circumstances, and in course of time.

Bismarck was one of the men who, although without absolutely expressing the opinion, regarded the patent as the starting point of a new order of things, in common with the liberals, but not in the sense of a constitutional monarchy, but comprehended it, as the King did, as a step towards a peculiar and specifically Prussian State Government.

The Saxon Provincial Diet at Merseburg had chosen the Dyke Captain and First Lieutenant von Brauchitsch of Scharteuke, in the Circle of Jerichow, as Deputy at the United Diet, and had selected Dyke Captain von Bismarck of Schönhausen as his representative. As Herr von Brauchitsch was very ill, his representative was summoned.

Bismarck appeared in the White Saloon of the Royal Palace at Cölln on the Spree, where the Three Estates' Assembly held its Sessions, as a representative of the Knight's Estate of Jerichow, and a vassal and chivalric servitor of the King. He was at that time, however, as liberal as most of his associates; liberalism then floated in the air and was inhaled; it was impossible to avoid it. Against many abuses it was also justifiable; hence its mighty influence.

A conservative party, in the sense in which we wish it to be understood, did not then exist; nor did the general confusion of opinions at the time allow of the formation of true parties. It is true that Bismarck met many men in the White Saloon, whose opinions were well known to him; of these were his brother, the Landrath, his cousins, the Counts von Bismarck-Bohlen and von Bismarck-Briest, his future father-in-law, Herr von Putkammer, von Thadden, von Wedell, and many others—but unfortunately these gentlemen in general, as Herr von Thadden once bluntly said of himself, were not even bad orators, but no orators at all. Nor could the two Freiherrs von Manteuffel contend in eloquence with the brilliant rhetoricians of the liberals, such as Freiherr von Vincke, Camphausen, Mevissen, Beckerath, and others.

Very few persons now exist who can read those speeches of the First United Diet, once so celebrated, without a melancholy or satirical smile: those were the blossom-days of liberal phraseology, causing an enthusiasm of which we cannot now form any adequate idea.

They acted with such an influence upon Bismarck, but he was soon sobered, when he attained the conviction that these great speakers, moved by their construction of the patent of February, advocated an end not contemplated by the spirit of the patent. To him it did not seem honest to contend for modern constitutionalism upon the judicial merits of the February patent, against its sense and spirit.

An inimical inspiration acted on him in liberal phraseology, and the more magnificent the oratory, the more repugnant it became to him, especially where he saw untruth clearly in view. He employed some time in making it evident to himself that the liberal idea was the very fact under the government of which men, otherwise of great honour, in the very best of faith, brought forward matters in themselves quite false; and the deepest want of confidence then made itself master of his mind. He began to understand how dangerous a power so intangible might become to the sovereignty.

At the sitting of the Three Estates on the 17th May, the Deputy von Saucken made one of those wordy enthusiastic speeches at that time so popular, and declared that the Prussian people had risen in the year 1813 for the sole end of obtaining a constitution. . This had previously been asserted by Beckerath and others on several occasions.

After the liberal speaker had descended amidst the plaudits of the Assembly, the Deputy Bismarck, for the first time, appeared upon the tribune. His stature was great, his plentiful hair was cut short, his healthily ruddy countenance was fringed by a strong blond beard, his shining eyes were somewhat prominent, *à fleur de tête*, as the French idiom has it—such was his aspect. He gazed upon the Assembly for a moment, and then spoke simply, but with some hesitation, in a strong, sometimes shrill, with not altogether pleasing emphasis :—"For me it is difficult—after a speech replete with such noble enthusiasm—to address you, in order to bring before you a plain re-statement." He then glanced at some length at the real merits of a previous vote, and continued in the following words :—

" To discuss the remaining points of the speech, I prefer to choose a time when it will be necessary to enter upon

questions of policy; at present I am compelled to contradict what is stated from this tribune, as well as what is so
loudly and so frequently asserted outside this hall, in
reference to the necessity for a constitution, as if the movements of our nation in 1813 should be ascribed to other

Bismarck in 1847—1848.

causes and motives than those of the tyranny exercised by
the foreigner in our land."

Here the speaker was assailed with such loud marks of
disapprobation, hisses, and outcries, that he could no
longer make himself intelligible. He quietly drew a news-

I. 2

paper from his pocket—it was the "Spenersche Zeitung"
—and read it, leaning in an easy attitude, until the Pre-
sident-Marshal had restored order; he then concluded, still
interrupted by hisses, with these words :—"In my opinion
it is doing sorry service to the national honour, to conclude that ill-treatment and humiliation suffered by
Prussia at the hands of a foreign ruler, would not be
enough to rouse Prussian blood, and cause all other
feelings to be absorbed by the hatred of foreigners."

Amidst great commotion Bismarck left the tribune, ten
or twelve voices being clamorous to be heard.

It is not intelligible to us at the present day, how the
casual statement of a simple opinion, which, even had it been
untrue, need have offended no one, could raise such a storm.
Nor had Bismarck personally offended any one, but he had
protested against liberalism, and at once the mamelukes of
this most evil despot pounced upon him—upon this unfortunate member of the chivalry of the province of
Saxony. The elder gentlemen were especially offended,
who had voluntarily taken the field in 1813, and had now
attributed the motive they thought then actuated them,
and perhaps they really entertained, to the nation. It was
curious, too, that they flatly denied the right of criticism
to this member, on the ground that he was not in existence in those great days. When, with loud clamour,
these gentlemen had given vent to their moral indignation,
Bismarck again ascended the tribune; but the anger of
the liberals was so great that the Marshal had to use all
his authority to protect him during his speech.

Bismarck now spoke fluently, in the manner since so
familiar to us, but coldly and sarcastically : "I can
certainly not deny that I did not as yet exist in those
days, and I am truly sorry not to have been permitted
to take part in that movement; my regret for this is
certainly diminished by the explanations I have received
just now upon the movements of that epoch. I always

thought the servitude against which the sword was then used was a foreign servitude; I now learn that it lay at home. For this correction I am not by any means grateful!"

The hisses of the liberals were now met by many voices with "Hear, hear!" From this moment the hatred of the press was concentrated upon Bismarck; being without exception in the hands of the liberals, it governed public opinion entirely, and it assailed Bismarck even more unscrupulously and unconscientiously than it had attacked Von Thadden and Von Manteuffel. As contradiction was impossible, the world probably thought Bismarck was still one of the wild Junkers, who, armed to the teeth in steel, considered village tyranny and dissoluteness to be the best kind of constitution, and in deep political ignorance was still standing at about the mental mark of Dietrich von Quitzow,* or at the most of one of the Junkers of the time of Frederick I. The liberal press certainly succeeded in producing a caricature of Bismarck, composed of a kind of black bogy and a ridiculous bugbear; the latter they were speedily obliged to drop, but the bogy they have the more firmly retained, and frightened political babies with it until very recent days.

No one has any idea at the present time how the liberal press of those days assailed men who were obnoxious to them. In the year 1849, two gentlemen were introduced to each other in society; as ordinarily happens, they mistook their several names on a hurried introduction. The elder gentleman spoke in an intellectual, remarkable, exhaustive, and instructive manner concerning the affairs of Hungary, whence he had recently returned, and showed himself to be a person of thought, information, and

* An account of this family has been given at p. 10 in a note. Those who wish to pursue further details may consult Klöden's history, published in 1828.—K. R. H. M.

politeness. His interlocutor for a long time could not believe that this was Herr von Thadden-Triglaff; the ridiculous caricature the liberal press had sent broadcast into society of this eminent and singular man was so firmly fixed in his convictions.

We have laid some emphasis on this point, as it forms an explanation of the obstinate suspicion with which, for many after years, Bismarck was regarded by a section of the public. It is also plainly evident that the young politician often defended himself against this "world of scorn" with equal and biting scorn, and covered himself with the shield of contempt against mockery he did not deserve. He was continually assailed, sometimes in the rudest manner, and sometimes with poisonous acumen; and he could not have been Bismarck had he borne it with patience.

Thus it befel that he soon found himself in full battle array against liberalism, and his speeches at the time show that he took a serious view of the matter. He gave utterance to his convictions and opinions in conformity with his natural fearless nature; he adhered closely to the matter at issue, but the form in which he did so was that of the most cutting attack, whetted in general by a cloud of contempt for his opponent, or of bitter ridicule.

In the debate of the Three Estates of the 1st of June, 1847, known as the Periodicity Debate, Bismarck spoke as follows :—

"I will not take the trouble to examine the solidity of the various grounds of right, on which each of us presumes himself to stand; but, I believe, it has become certain, from the debate and from everything which I have gathered from the discussion of the question, that a different construction and interpretation of the older estates legislation was possible and practically existent— not among laymen only, but also among weighty jurists—

and that it would be very doubtful what a court of justice, if such a question were before it, would decree concerning it. Under such circumstances, the declaration would, according to general principles of law, afford a solution. This declaration has become implicit upon us, implicit by the patent of the 3rd of February of this year; by this the King has declared that the general promises of former laws have been no other than those fulfilled by the present law. It appears that this declaration has been regarded by a portion of this Assembly as inaccurate, but such is a fate to which every declaration is equally subject. Every declaration is considered by those whose opinions it does not confirm, to be wrong, or the previous conviction could not have been sincere. The question really is, in whom the right resides to issue an authentic and legally binding declaration. In my opinion, the King alone; and this conviction, I believe, lies in the conscience of the people. For when yesterday an Hon. Deputy from Königsberg asserted that there was a dull dissatisfaction among the people on the proclamation of the patent of the 3rd of February, I must reply, on the contrary, that I do not find the majority of the Prussian nation represented in the meetings which take place in the Böttchershöfchen.—(Murmurs.) In inarticulate sounds I really cannot discover any refutation of what I have said, nor do I find it in the goose-quills of the newspaper correspondents; no! not even in a fraction of the population of some of the large provincial towns. It is difficult to ascertain public opinion; I think I find it in some of the middle provinces, and it is the old Prussian conviction that a royal word is worth more than all the constructions and quirks applied to the letter of the law. (Some voices: Bravo!). Yesterday a parallel was drawn between the method employed by the English people in 1688, after the abdication of James II., for the preservation of its rights, and that by which the Prussian nation should now attain a similar end. There is always something suspicious in parallels with foreign countries. Russia had been held up to us as a model of religious toleration; the French and Danish exchequers have been recommended as examples of proper finances. To return to the year 1688 in England, I must really beg this august assembly, and especially an honourable deputy from Silesia, to pardon me if I again speak of a circumstance which I did not personally perceive. The English people was then in a different position to that of the Prussian people now; a century of revolution and civil war had invested it with the right to dispose of a crown, and bind up with it conditions accepted by William of Orange. On the other hand, the Prussian sovereigns were in possession of a crown, not by grace of the people, but by God's grace; an actually unconditional crown, some of the rights of which they voluntarily conceded to the people— an example rare in history. I will leave the question of right, and proceed to that concerning the utility and desirability of asking or suggesting any change in the legislation as it actually now exists. I adhere to the conviction, which I assume to be that of the majority of the Assembly, that periodicity is necessary to a real vitality of this Assembly; but it is another matter whether we should seek this by way of petition. Since the emanation of the patent of the 3rd of February, I do not believe that it would be consonant with the royal pleasure, or that it is inherent with the position of ourselves as estates, to approach His Majesty already with a petition for an amendment of it. At any rate let us allow the grass of this summer to grow over it. The King has repeatedly said, that he did not wish to be coerced and driven; but I ask the Assembly what should we be doing otherwise than coercing and driving him, if we already approached the throne with requests for changes in the legislation? To the gravity of this

view I ask permission of the Assembly to add another
reason. It is certainly well known how many sad predictions have been made by the opponents of our polity
connected with the fact that the Government would find
itself forced by the estates into a position which it would
not have willingly taken up. But although I do not
assume the Government would allow itself to be coerced, I
still think that it is in the interests of the Government to
avoid the slightest trace of unwillingness as to concessions,
and that it is in all our interests not to concede to the
enemies of Prussia the delight of witnessing the fact that,
by a petition—a vote—presented by us as the representatives of sixteen millions of subjects, we should throw a
shade of unwillingness upon such a concession. It has
been said that His Majesty the King and the Commissioner of the Diet have themselves pointed out this path.
For *myself*, I could not otherwise understand this than
that, as the King has done, so also the Commissioner of
the Diet indicated this as the legal way we should pursue
in case we found ourselves aggrieved; but that it would
be acceptable to His Majesty the King and the Government that we should make use of this right, I have not
been able to perceive. If, however, we did so, it would be
believed that urgent grounds existed for it—that there
was immediate danger in the future; but of this I cannot
convince myself. The next session of the Assembly is
assured; the Crown, also, is thereby in the advantageous
position, that within four years, or even a shorter period,
it can with perfect voluntariness, and without asking, take
the initiative as to that which is now desired. Now, I
ask, is not the edifice of our State firmer towards foreign
countries?—will not the feeling of satisfaction be greater
at home, if the continuation of our national polity be
inaugurated by the initiative of the Crown, than by
petition from ourselves? Should the Crown not find it
good to take the initiative, no time is lost. The third

Diet will not follow so rapidly upon the second, that the King would have no time to reply to a petition presented under such circumstances by the second. Yesterday a deputy from Prussia—I think from the circle of Neustadt—uttered a speech which I could only comprehend as meaning that it was our interest to pull up the flower of confidence as a weed preventing us from seeing the bare ground, and cast it out. I say with pride that I cannot agree with such an opinion. If I look back for ten years, and compare that which was written and said in the year 1837 with that which is proclaimed from the steps of the throne to the whole nation, I believe we have great reason to have confidence in the intentions of His Majesty. In this confidence I beg to recommend this august assembly to adopt the amendment of the Hon. Deputy from West-phalia—not that of the Hon. Deputy from the county of Mark—but that of Herr von Lilien."

This speech is certainly a Prussian-Royalist confession of faith as opposed to the constitutional doctrine, and was so accepted at times with cheers, at other times with murmurs, and, finally, with a flood of personal opposition.

The political side of Bismarck's attitude is clear enough from this speech. We will signalize another aspect of it by the following passages from a speech delivered by Bismarck on the occasion of that debate known as the Jews' Debate, on the 15th of June.

"On ascending this place to-day, it is with greater hesitation than usual, as I am sensible that by what I am about to utter, some few remarks of the speakers of yesterday, of no very flattering tone, will have in a certain sense to be reviewed. I must openly confess that I am attached to a certain tendency, yesterday characterized by the Hon. Deputy from Crefeld as dark and mediæval; this tendency which again dares to oppose the freer development of Christianity in the way the Deputy from Crefeld regards as the only true one. Nor can I further deny that I belong to that great mass, which, as was remarked by the Hon. Deputy from Posen, stands in opposition to the more intelligent portion of the nation, and, if my memory do not betray me, was held in considerable scorn by that intelligent section—the great mass that still clings to the convictions imbibed at the breast,—the great mass to which a Christianity superior to the State is too elevated. If I find myself in the line of fire of such sharp sarcasms without a murmur, I believe I may throw myself upon the indulgence of the Hon. Assembly, if I confess, with the same frankness which distinguished my opponents, that yesterday, at times of inattention, it did not quite appear certain to me whether I was in an assembly for which the law had provided, in reference to its election, the condition of communion with some one of the Christian churches. I will pass at once to the question itself. Most of the speakers have spoken less upon the bill than upon emancipation in general. I will follow their example. I am no enemy to the Jews, and if they are enemies to me, I forgive them. Under certain circumstances I even love them. I would grant them every right, save that of holding superior official posts in Christian countries.

" We have heard from the Minister of Finance, and from other gentlemen on the ministerial bench, sentiments as to the definition of a Christian State, to which I almost entirely subscribe ; but, on the other hand, we were yesterday told that Christian supremacy is an idle fiction, an invention of recent State philosophers. I am of opinion that the idea of Christian supremacy is as ancient as the ci-devant Holy Roman Empire—as ancient as the great family of European states ; that it is, in fact, the very soil in which these states have taken root, and that every state which wishes to have its existence enduring, if it desires to point to any justification for that existence, when called in question, must be constituted on a religious basis. For me, the words ' by the grace of God ' affixed by Christian rulers to their names form no empty sound; but I see in the phrase the acknowledgment that princes desire to sway the sceptres entrusted to them by the Almighty, according to God's will on earth. I, however, can only recognize as the will of God that which is contained in the Christian Gospels, and I believe I am within my right when I call such a State Christian, whose problem is to realize and verify the doctrine of Christianity. That our State does not in all ways succeed in this, the Hon. Deputy from the county of Mark yesterday demonstrated in a parallel he drew between the truths of the Gospel and the paragraphs of national jurisprudence, in a way rather clever than consonant with my religious feelings. But although the solution of the problem is not always successful, I am still convinced that the aim of the State is the realization of Christian doctrine; however, I do *not* think we shall approach this aim more closely with the aid of the Jews. If the religious basis of the State be acknowledged, I am sure that among ourselves the basis can only be that of Christianity. If we withdraw from the State this religious basis, our State becomes nothing more than a fortuitous aggregation of rights, a sort of bulwark against the universal war of each against all, such as an elder philosophy instituted. Its legislation then would no longer recreate itself from the original fountain of eternal truth, but only from the vague and mutable ideas of humanity taking shape only from the conceptions formed in the brains of those who occupy the apex. How such states could deny the right of the practical application of such ideas—as, for instance, those of the communists on the immorality of property, the high moral value of theft, as an experiment for the rehabilitation of the native rights of man—is not clear to me; for these very ideas are entertained by their advocates as humane, and, indeed, as constituting the very flower of humanitarianism. Therefore, gentlemen, let us not diminish the

Christianity of the people by showing that it is superfluous to the legislature; let us not deprive the people of the belief that our legislation is derived from the fountain of Christianity, and that the State seeks to promote the realization of Christianity, though that end may not always be attained.

 * * * * * *

"Besides this, several speakers, as in almost every question, have referred to the examples of England and France as models worthy of imitation. This question is of much less consequence there, because the Jews are so much less numerous than here. But I would recommend to the gentlemen who are so fond of seeking their ideas beyond the Vosges, a guide line distinguishing the English and the French. That consists in the proud feeling of national honour, which does not so easily and commonly seek for models worthy of imitation and wonderful patterns, as we do here, in foreign lands."

It will be understood that this speech was much criticised; but it became a regular armoury for his opponents; it was taken for granted that Bismarck himself had stated that he stood in "the dark ages," that he had "imbibed reactionary ideas with his mother's milk," and other similar things, although he was only ridiculing the ideas of his opponents; there was seldom an opportunity lost, when he was twitted with "the dark ages" and the "prejudices imbibed at the breast." Bismarck possessed humour enough to laugh at this pitiful trick, and once exclaimed very well: "Deputy Krause rode in the lists against me on a horse, in front the dark ages, behind mother's milk!" What a picture Herr Krause, the Burgomaster of Elbing (if we are not misinformed), would make upon such a fabulous steed!

Bismarck left the United Diet with a thorn in his breast. He had lost many of the youthful illusions he had carried thither; the Prussia he found in the White

Saloon was as remote as heaven from the Prussia he had hitherto believed in, and his patriotic heart was sorrowful. He perceived that the sovereignty of Prussia was about to encounter severe contests ; that his duty lay with the monarch's idea, and that his native land must be rescued from the insolent pretensions of the modern parliamentary spirit, from the most dangerous of all paper governments. In short, he arrived with hazy, but somewhat liberal, views, and he returned a politician thoroughly acquainted with his duty and his work, which consisted in aiding the King to restore the Estates' Monarchy. It was a gift, but he received it with a sigh. His youth was at an end.

Bismarck has ever remained true to his patriotic duties, everywhere in earnestness, and at no time has he withdrawn his hand from the plough ; he went bravely on, when so many cast their weapons away and fled.

CHAPTER III.

THE DAYS OF MARCH.

1848.

Rest at Home.—Contemplation.—The Revolution in Paris, February, 1848.—
Progress of the Revolutionary Spirit.—The March Days of Berlin.—The
Citizen Guard.—Opening of the Second Session of the United Diet, 2nd
April, 1848.—Prince Solms-Hohen-Solms-Lich.—Fr. Foerster.—" Eagle's
Wings and Bodelswings."—Prince Felix Lichnowsky.—The Debate on the
Address.—Speech of Bismarck.—Revolution at the Portal of the White
Saloon.—*Vaticinium Lehninense.*—The Kreuzzeitung Letter of Bismarck
on Organization of Labour.—Bismarck at Stolpe on the Baltic.—The
Winter of Discontent.—Manteuffel.

In a previous section we have already recorded that, shortly after the close of the First United Diet, on the 28th of July, 1847, Herr Otto von Bismarck celebrated his wedding at Reinfeld, in Pomerania, with Fraulein Johanna von Putkammer, and then entered upon a journey with his youthful wife by way of Dresden, Prague, Vienna, and Salzburg, to Italy, meeting his sovereign, Frederick William IV., at Venice, and finally, returning through Switzerland and the Rhine-Province, fixed his residence at the ancient hearth of his ancestors at Schönhausen.

It was a short but happy time of rest, passed in rural retirement. The ancient family traits of the Bismarcks, after a silent activity in field and forest, became more strongly marked in him than in many other branches of his race, and his wife also retained a charming reminiscence of these peaceful days in Schönhausen. She still preserves grateful recollections of that happy

COUNTESS VON BISMARCK-SCHÖNHAUSEN.

when a want of presence of mind and irresolute counsels, and at times crass cowardice, rather than ill-will or treason, in almost every direction, lamed or broke down the power of resistance.

He saw, sinking and destroyed, bulwarks and dykes he had held to be unassailable; his heart palpitated with patriotic ardour and manly sorrow, but he lost neither courage nor clear insight, like a true dykesman. It had hitherto been his office to protect the Elbe dykes against the floods, and in a similar character it was his duty to act against the floods of revolution. Nor has the valiant man unfaithfully acquitted himself of his severe duty.

The March-days of Berlin pressed hard upon the heart of the sturdy March-squire, and there ensued a long series of days of grief; for he felt as a personal insult everything spoken, written, or enacted against his royal master. He passed as in a feverish dream through the streets of the capital of his King, filled with threatening forms.* He saw flags displayed and colours fluttering unknown to him; Polish standards, tricolours of black, red, and gold, but nowhere the ancient honoured flag of Prussia. Even on the palace of his deceased lord and king the three colours flaunted, ever the battle standard of the enemies of Prussia, never those of the ancient German realm. In place of the

---

* A short anecdote of the venerable Alexander von Humboldt, as illustrative of the popular spirit, deserves preservation here. During the eventful days of March, when barricades were the order of the day, a mob came rushing into the Oranienburger Strasse, where Humboldt resided. Materials for a barricade were required, and every door was besieged for the purpose. One of these opened, and a venerable-looking man presented himself and begged the excited mass not to disturb him. Such a request was not to be borne by the sovereign people, and he was asked menacingly who he was, that he should use such language. "I am Alexander von Humboldt," was the quiet reply. In a moment every hat was off, and with reverent greetings the multitude swept forward and left the scholar and philosopher at peace. It is only right to record such a fact, as it may serve to show that the fierce revolutionists at least knew how to restrain themselves, even in the midst of their enthusiastic fury. I give the anecdote on the authority of the admirable German newspaper *Hermann*, of the 11th September, 1869.—K. R. H. M.

M

proud regiments of Guards, he only beheld citizen soldiers watching in a half ludicrous, half dispirited manner. Men had ceased to speak; all the world speechified and de-

claimed; vain folly and ignominious treason grasped each other with dirty hands in an alliance against royalty, and those who ought to have been defending the crown, and indeed desired to do so, found themselves caught in the spider-webs of liberal doctrines; trammelled themselves in the sere bonds of political theories, scornfully rent asunder by the rude hands of revolution.

· It was sufficient to bring the burning tear to Bismarck's eye, and his soul struggled in unspeakable torment; but he manfully wrestled insult and vexation down. With a pale but impassible countenance he took his place on the 2nd of April, 1848, in the first session of the Second United Diet.

The White Saloon still existed, but the bright days were gone in which Vincke had sought to polish diamonds with diamond-dust; true, the same men were present, but it was a vastly different assembly. In those former days, certain of victory and intoxicated with power, this assembly now meditated suicide; it could scarcely be quick enough in transferring its legislative functions to the new creation, the first-born of Revolution, standing impatiently watching at the door.

The President was still the Marshal of the Guild of Nobles, the Serene Prince of Solms-Hohen-Solms-Lich; but the Royal Commissioner was no longer the Freiherr von Bodelschwingh-Velmede; his place was occupied by the new Minister of State, Ludolf Camphausen—one of the chiefs of the Rhine-land liberal party.

Some weeks before, a liberal, F. Foerster, at the volunteer anniversary, had saluted the Minister von Bodelschwingh with the compliment that time did not fly with *Eagle's wings* but *Bodelswings*; but this very Bodelschwingh, the most faithful subject of the King, was now despised by the revolutionary party as an obscure reactionary. There was reason for laughter, had not the crisis been so terribly grave.

Camphausen read the well-known Royal Decree of Proposition, after betraying, in his introductory oration, that liberalism no longer felt itself entirely secure; in fact these liberal ministers, such as Hansemann, Auerswald, Schwerin, and Bornemann, were not the men able to steer the royal vessel with safety during this severe westerly storm.

Prince Felix Lichnowsky moved the replicatory address. The Marshal declared the proposition to be carried unanimously, as he perceived the majority to be of his opinion

"It is not unanimous. I protest against it!" exclaimed Herr von Thadden-Trieglaff.

"Carried by an almost unanimous majority!" proclaimed the Marshal.

The next proceeding was to frame the address at once, and to accept the plenum at the same session. Most unseemly and discreditable haste!

Upon this the Deputy von Bismarck-Schönhausen rose and said :—

"It is my opinion that we owe to the dignity, ever upheld in this Assembly, due discretion in the conduct of all its deliberations ; that we owe it to all the simplest rules of expediency—especially on an occasion when we meet for the last time—by no means to deviate from our fixed customs. Heretofore every law, however simple, has been referred to a committee, which has considered it with deliberation, and submitted it on the following day to the Chamber. I believe at so serious a moment as this, that on the expression of the sentiments of this Assembly, still having the honour to represent the Prussian people, it is a sufficiently important procedure not to admit of such a hasty consideration of the address,—so far removed from the rules of expediency according to my individual feelings."

Bismarck spoke with more than usual hesitation; his features appeared sharper than usual to his friends, his countenance was pale, his white teeth were more visible and prominent, his manner was stolid; he presented the appearance of a man combating a critical hour.

Yes—to him it was indeed a critical hour. He was unable to arrest the progress of events, but he was determined to do his duty. The tumult of the streets might rage, the whirlpool of thronging events might carry away with them men usually of the utmost courage; but Bismarck was not to be carried away as well. He was unable to stem the rapidity with which the address was draughted, considered, and accepted. Milde and company pressed forward, and the Second United Diet could not be in sufficient hurry to transfer its functions to the convention to be assembled for the consolidation of the constitution.

It is impossible to pursue the progress of this session without pain; it passed over the ruins and fragments of all the royal hopes which but a few months before had existed in all their pride and glory, and appeared so instinct with happiness and founded on such secure grounds.

In this debate on the address it would have been impossible for Bismarck to speak, had not his political opponents, Von Saucken-Tarputschen and Milde, with much difficulty obtained a hearing for him; so madly was the Assembly determined upon self-destruction.

Revolution was knocking at the portals of the White Saloon.

Bismarck, however, said :—

"I am one of the few who would vote against the address, and I have only requested permission to speak, in order to explain this disapproval, and to declare to you that I accept the address, in the sense of a programme of the future, at once; but for the sole reason that I am powerless to do otherwise. (Laughter.) Not voluntarily, but by stress of circumstances; for I have not changed my opinions during these six months; I would rather believe that this ministry is the only one able to conduct us from our actual position into an orderly and constitutional condition, and for that reason I shall give it my inconsiderable support in every case within my power. But the cause of my voting against the address consists in the expressions of joy and gratitude made use of for the events of recent days; the past is buried, and I mourn it with greater pain than many among you, because no human power can reawaken it—when the Crown itself has scattered ashes upon the coffin. But if I accept this from the force of circumstances, I cannot retire from my functions in this Diet with the lie in my mouth that I shall give thanks and rejoice at what I must in any sense hold to be an erroneous path. If it be indeed possible to attain to a united German Fatherland by the new path now pursued, to arrive at a happy or even legally well ordered condition of things, the moment will have come when I can tender my thanks to the originator of the new state of things; but at present this is beyond my power."

This was the earnest language of a true statesman, and it was not without its impression even then. When Bismarck ended, no one dared to laugh. He accepted the situation because he had no other course open to him; but he could not return thanks for that which appeared likely to militate against his reverence for his King. He knew that the past was beyond recall, now that the Crown had itself cast ashes upon its coffin—nor, indeed, was it at all within the thoughts of Bismarck ever to reawaken the past. He could mourn over the past, and this with considerable affliction; but he began to arm himself for the future; that future he resolved to conquer for the monarchy.

Such were the events of the 2nd of April, 1848.

The immediate necessity was to strive against revolution, which continued to advance with bloody feet and shameless countenance. First, conferences were held with friends and allies of equal rank and similar opinions; arrangements were made in all directions. He exhibited a restless activity, at first apparently without any hope, and which seemed to lead to no results for weeks, though it were destined in the end to bear fruit. Such was the policy pursued by the faithful royalist in the terrible spring and summer of 1848, passed by him alternately at Schönhausen, Berlin, Potsdam, Reinfeld, and (on the occasion of the presence of the Prince of Prussia) at Stettin.

Bismarck was one of those who laboured most assiduously and successfully towards the erection of a barrier against revolution even at the twelfth hour. A royal or conservative party could not be conjured up out of the earth, but the elements for such a party, existing in great multitude, were assembled in clubs, united by ties, gradually organized, and finally disciplined.

Nor did Bismarck ever falter in courage, for he trusted in the Divine mercy and the Kingdom of Prussia, but not in the well-known prophecy of Lehnin, as the liberal historian, Adolf Schmidt, asserted,[*] no matter whether the

* "Preussen's Deutsche Politik." "Prussia's German Policy," 3rd edition, Leipzig, 1867, p. 236.

librarian La Croze in 1607 really saw a copy of this document in the hands of a Von Schönhausen at Berlin or no. The Herr von Schönhausen in question could scarcely have been a Bismarck, as Professor Schmidt would seem to infer, and our Bismarck was, in any case, sufficiently informed to know for what purpose the so-called *Vaticinium Lehninense* had been forged, and possessed other sources whence to draw confidence and trust. The revolution had to be combated by clubs and by the press—both so dangerous to the monarchy. No one was more active in the organization of these than Bismarck; he entered with confidence on the ground whither events had driven him. Thus arose the Prussian clubs, the patriotic societies, and many others, and at last the club which bore as its motto " Mit Gott für König und Vaterland" (With God for King and Country). The *New Prussian Gazette*, with Bismarck's aid, was founded, as well as many smaller periodicals. There was also the *New Prussian Sunday News*, which, sent in thousands to the smaller towns and provinces, became a powerful weapon.

Bismarck at the same time kept a vigilant eye upon the " Vereinbarungs" Society in Berlin, and the Parliament at Frankfurt, but he never joined the meetings in the Church of St. Paul, nor the Academy of Music, nor those in the Concert Room of the Royal Theatre in Berlin. We do not know whether it would then have been possible for him to have succeeded in getting elected for Berlin or Frankfurt; at any rate, he never thought of doing so, for he was firmly convinced that nothing stable would be created in either place.

We will here give a highly characteristic example of the manner in which Bismarck so powerfully and openly attacked the malicious and silly aspersions upon the Junkers, then the order of the day, showing with what acuteness and ability he could encounter the hollow declamations of unconscientious sophists. At the end of

August he published the following address, in the form then greatly in vogue, of a *communiqué* :—

"The Deputy for the Belgard Circle, Herr Jänsch, asserted in the debate of the 16th instant that the Pomeranian labourers only obtained from 2¼ to 4 silbergroschen per day, and in addition to this had to give 190 days' labour for nothing. If so, the 52 Sundays being subtracted, the earnings of a labourer in the other 123 days, calculated at an average of 3¼ sgr., would represent 13$ 9 sgr. 9 pf.* That no man can live upon that every one must see—even Herr Jänsch, if he takes the trouble to think farther about it. I should therefore have characterized the statement of this gentleman as a deliberate lie in his official capacity as a national representative, had not the demand for a uniform wage of 6 sgr. proved that Herr Jänsch has either not been able, or not had leisure, to make himself acquainted with the condition of the most numerous class of the electors he represents. For with a wage of 6 sgr. the Pomeranian labourer would be worse off than he is now. The labourers on the estate of Kniephof, Circle Stargard, for the last eight years, during my residence at that place, were living under the following conditions, which are the same, with very slight differences, common to the whole district—indeed, I could prove that in other places, such as Zimmerhausen and Trieglaff, they are even better off. The daily wage certainly is, in summer, 4 sgr. per man, 3 sgr. per woman, and in winter 1 sgr. less in each case ; and they have to give 156 man's days' work and 26 woman's days' work in the year without pay. But each working family received from the proprietor the following advantages free :—

"1. House, consisting of parlour, bedroom, kitchen, cellar, and loft, stabling for their cattle of every kind, and the necessary barn accommodation, which is all maintained by the proprietor.

* About £2 sterling per annum.—K. R. H. M.

" 2. Three morgen (acres) plough-land, one for winter corn, one for summer, one for potatoes, for which the labourer finds the seed, but the estate furnishes the appointments, inclusive of manure; add to this one-half morgen (acre) of garden ground, near the house, and one-half morgen (acre) for flax; the whole profit of this superficies belongs to the labourer.

" 3. Pasture for two cows, six sheep, and two geese with their broods; hay for one cow during the winter.

" 4. Firing, consisting of turf, and the right of gathering wood through three morgen of forest.

" 5. Corn from the proprietor's land, five scheffel (sacks) rye, one of barley.

" 6. On an average each labourer gets fifteen scheffel (sacks) corn of each kind for threshing.

" 7. Medical attendance and medicines free.

" 8. If the husband dies the widow receives, until her children are grown up, dwelling-room, one morgen of potatoes, one-half morgen of garden, one-quarter morgen of flax, and one cow, which feeds and pastures with the proprietor's herd, without any kind of return on her part.

" Every day-labourer—those who have not grown-up daughters—keeps one servant girl, with wages of, say 10 thalers (£1 10s.) per annum, who, on account of the labourer, performs services to the proprietor, which the labourer's wife never does, but takes care of the children, and cooks.

" The pay in cash, which such a family, with servant, according to the foregoing tariff, after deducting the produce, much of which remains for sale, is ascertained, according to the number of children able to assist in the work, to be about 34 to 50 thalers per annum.* A family without children receives, after deducting the 190 non-paid days (including 60 days for threshing) and the 52 Sundays = 242

* £5 2s. to £7 10s.—K. R. H. M.

days (inclusive of market days and the like), annually, in cash-paid days for man and maid—some of these days being semi-labour days, and so justifying the apparent difference —52 days at 4 sgr., 178 days at 3 sgr., and 150 days at 2 sgr., in all 34 thalers 22 sgr. If this be added to the above-named produce, it will not be astonishing that the Pomeranian labourers would not be disposed to exchange their present condition for the poor 6 sgr. per day which Herr Jänsch in his ignorance would obtain for them.* I will not boast, but only state, as a matter of fact, that the greater number of the proprietors have hitherto voluntarily adopted the usual practice of supporting the inhabitants during calamity, cattle murrain, and years of famine— many to a degree of which the babbling philanthropists who declaim against the Junkers have no idea whatever. In the past year of famine, in which the Deputy Master Butcher Jänsch made a disturbance in Belgard, which, if I mistake not, obtained some notice from the Court of Justice, the large class of proprietors he has attacked by erroneous or fictitious statements made great sacrifices to give the inhabitants of their estates no reason to increase the class of the dissatisfied, at the head of whom Deputy Herr Jänsch now fights to attain tumultuary laurels. I have added this personal remark in order to draw the attention of Herr Jänsch to the rest of the article, and thus afford him the opportunity of learning something of the condition of the class he asserts himself to represent; a condition of which he ought to have known, before he talked about them in the National Assembly.

"Schönhausen, the 21st August, 1848."   " BISMARCK."

The then Deputy for Belgard has never attempted to obtain any advantage by a reply !

* We should think not. 6 sgr. per day at 213 days = 46. 18 = £7 within a fraction.—K. R. H. M.

Immediately after the days of March, Bismarck, impelled by his Prussian heart, addressed a letter to His Majesty; not a political letter, full of counsels and plans, but an outpouring of the feelings produced by the moment. Throughout the whole of that summer this letter lay upon King Frederick William's writing table, as a precious token of unchangeable Prussian fidelity. During that summer, so fraught with weighty events, Bismarck was often called to Sans Souci, and the King took his advice in many important affairs.

Stolpe, on the Baltic, was the residence of Bismarck for some weeks of the summer. An incident of his life is furnished by a spectator. After one of the concerts denominated "Navy Concerts"—for in those days an opinion was entertained that a fleet could be built by means of beer-drinking, concert-pence, and such similar "miserabilities" of good intentions—Bismarck, drawing himself up to his full height, majestically addressed one of the gentlemen who had been active in the concert, greeting him as an acquaintance, and added: "You have taken pains to make the work somewhat hotter for us!" It was one of the hottest days of the year. An anxious smile played upon his lips, but bright daring spoke in the firm contour of the bearded face. His hat alone bore the Prussian colours. It was indeed refreshing to see such a man in those days.

And when the "winter of discontent" came for democracy, when the question of saving the construction of a ministry was prominent, it was Bismarck who took the initiative concerning the introduction of the elder Von Manteuffel, his partisan at the United Diet, and thus drew the eyes of the people upon the man who promptly restored order. He had discovered the right man for the situation as it then existed.

CHAPTER IV.

CONSERVATIVE LEADERSHIP.

1849—1851.

The Second Chamber.—The Sword and the Throne.—Acceptance of the
Frankfurt Project.—The New Electoral Law.—Bismarck's Speeches.—The
King and the Stag.—Birth of Herbert von Bismarck.—"What does this
Broken Glass Cost?"—The Kreuzzeitung Letters.—The Prussian Nobility.
—"I am Proud to be a Prussian Junker!"—Close of the Session.

IMMEDIATELY after the publication of the December constitution of 1848, Bismarck was, in the same month,
elected in Brandenburg the representative of West-Havelland, as a member of the Second Chamber.

The Diet was
opened on the 26th
of February, 1849;
and Bismarck was
among the first
members to repair
to the solemnity in
the White Saloon.
How many remin-
iscences were as-
sociated in Bis-
marck's mind with
the White Saloon!
How many more
were to arise! Memorials and landmarks still remain!

Without any special object, most probably, Bismarck took the same seat in the Assembly he had formerly occupied as representative of the Knight's Estate of Jerichow, in the United Diet; and here he held, as it were, as member for the electoral metropolis of Brandenburg, a sort of court. It was at least something of a court, for not only was he received by his former associates, such as Count Arnim-Boytzenburg, the minister Von Manteuffel, and many others, but his opponents also addressed him—those who had been his opponents, and were to become so again. Among these were Auerswald, Vincke, and Grabow; at that time they all stood with Bismarck on the right, in the terrible crisis of the country. Bismarck received them with the perfect confidence of a great-hearted gentleman, in that gracious manner of which he was so perfect a master, but which he could, at any moment, for the sake of a joke, frankly and freely abandon, without in the least imperilling his position. On that day his face remained serious, despite the anecdote related by Freiherr von Vincke, who recounted in a humorous way that on alighting from his carriage he had been hissed at the palace gate by the Berlin mob, while plaudits were made to Temmes and D'Esters. Bismarck did not allow himself any illusions as to the difficulty of the position, although the royalists were in ecstasies at the result of the elections. Parties were at the time about equal in numbers, if those were counted to the royalist side that had not formally sided with the democrats. It was a very beggarly account, and yet this was to be regarded, after the events of the spring, as a considerable gain—a gain greatly to be ascribed to the endeavours of Bismarck and his immediate friends.

A conservative deputy from Pomerania, addressing the member for West-Havelland, said: " We have conquered ! "

" Not so ! " replied Bismarck, coolly. " We have not

parliamentary debates; ere long the Almighty, who is the arbiter of battles, will throw the dice and so determine the controversy."

The Second Chamber adopted the Frankfurt Imperial Constitution by a vote of 179 against 159. Bismarck spoke energetically against it, because it bore the broad impress of national sovereignty, this being evident, as the Emperor retained nothing more than a right of a veto of suspension. The Radicals, he said, would approach the new Emperor with the imperial arms, and ask,—

"Think you that this eagle is given you merely as a present?"

"The Frankfurt crown," he continued, "may be very brilliant, but the gold, which lends truth to its splendour, must be added by melting into its composition the Prussian crown; and I cannot believe that this recasting is possible by means of the proposed constitution."

The course of the discussions in the Second Chamber gradually showed an increase in the power of the democrats, and they would render a monarchical government impossible. They insisted on the abolition of the state of siege in Berlin, as this materially impeded their projects; and when they had finally succeeded in effecting this, the Government could do no otherwise than dissolve the Second Chamber and prorogue the First. It seemed at one time that this dissolution would be the signal for another insurrection, but the democratic mob was taken aback when the Government showed the necessary severity. It was a terrible exaggeration for a Paris newspaper to announce, "*Le canon gronde à Berlin.*" One volley in the Dönhofsplatz, and then, "Arms—to the right," and a cavalry charge in the Leipziger Strasse, were enough thoroughly to deprive the democrats of all taste for another rising.

Bismarck was then residing at Wilhelmstrasse, No. 71; in the summer he went to Pomerania, and thence, in

August, proceeded to Brandenburg for the election, and finally to Berlin.

The new electoral law for the Second Chamber, and a decree summoning both Chambers for the 7th of August, had already been published, on the 30th of May. This new Chamber, which had grown clearer as to the position of parties, was employed with the revision of the Customs Constitution and with the German policy of Prussia—in fact, with the plans for union proposed by Herr von Radowitz.

Bismarck, who now appeared more and more as one of the leaders of the conservative party, declared against the projects of union and the triple alliance, because it was founded at the cost of Prussia's specific interests, and, if successful, would, in the end, ruin her. On the 6th of September, 1849, Bismarck spoke as follows :—

" I am of opinion that the motive principles of the year 1848 were far more social than national. National action would have confined itself to a few, but prominent, persons, in more contracted circles, if the ground had not been shaken under our feet, drawing in the social element, by false representations as to the ambition of the proletariat to acquire the property of others. The envy the poor had of the rich was excited in proportion to the continued feeding of a spirit of license from high quarters, which destroyed the moral elements of resistance in the minds of men. I do not believe that these evils would be averted by democratic concessions, or by projects of German unity; the seat of the disease is deeper; but I deny that any desire has ever existed in the Prussian people towards a national regeneration on the model of the theories of Frankfurt. The policy of Frederick the Great has been frequently alluded to ; and it has even been identified with the proposition for union. I rather am of opinion that Frederick II. would have turned to the most prominent peculiarity of Prussian nationality,

N

to her warlike element, and not without a result. He
would have known that to-day, as in the era of our
fathers, the sound of the trumpet which called to the
standard of the father of the country, has lost no charm
for the Prussian ear, whether the question concern the
defence of the frontier or the fame and greatness of
Prussia. He would have had the alternative, after the
rupture with Frankfurt, to ally himself with our ancient
ally, Austria, and then assume the brilliant part enacted
by the Emperor of Russia, in alliance with Austria, to
destroy the common enemy—Revolution ; or he would
have been free, with the same justification he possessed
for the conquest of Silesia, after declining the Frankfurt
imperial crown, to decide what the nature of the German
constitution should be, at the risk of casting the sword .
into the balance. This would have been a national
Prussian policy! In this way Prussia, in union with
Austria or alone, would have been able to arrive at the
proper position that would have endowed Germany with
the power it should possess in Europe. The plan of a
constitutional union, however, destroys the Prussian
specific character."

We must draw especial attention to the reply which
Bismarck made to the argument of Herr von Radowitz,
that the Frankfurt Assembly had shielded Prussia against
some dangers.

"I am not in the least aware," said Bismarck, "of
such a thing. I only know that the 38th Prussian
Regiment, on the 18th of September, 1848, preserved us
from that which the Frankfurt Parliament, with its predecessor, had conjured up. The specific character of
Prussia actually accomplished this. This was the remains
of the heretic Prussiadom which had survived the Revolution; the Prussian army, the Prussian treasury, the
fruits of Prussian administration accumulated through
many years, and the animated reaction exerted by King

and people on each other in Prussia. It consisted in
the attachment of the Prussian population to the established dynasty; it consisted in the old Prussian virtues
of honour, fidelity, obedience, and bravery, which inspire
every Prussian soldier from the backbone—from the officers
to the youngest recruit. The army has no enthusiasm for
the tricolour; in it, as in the rest of the people, will be
found no longing for national regeneration. The name
of Prussia is all-sufficient for it. These hosts follow the
banner of black and white, and not the tricolour: under
the black and white they joyfully die for their country.
The tricolour has been, since the 18th March, recognized
as the attribute of their opponents. The accents of the
Prussian National Anthem, the strains of the Dessau
and Hohenfriedberg March, are well known and beloved
among them: but I have never yet heard a Prussian
soldier sing, 'What is the German fatherland?' The
nation whence this army has sprung, and of which the
army is the truest representative, in the happy and
accurate words of the President of the First Chamber,
Rudolf von Auerswald, does not need to see the Prussian
monarchy melt away in the filthy ferment of South
German immorality. We are Prussians, and Prussians
we desire to remain. I know that in these words I utter
the creed of the Prussian army, the creed of the majority
of my fellow-countrymen, and I hope to God that we
shall continue Prussians, when this bit of paper is forgotten like the withered leaf of autumn!"

This love for the Prussian army, this enthusiasm for it,
is a red line which runs through the whole political life of
Bismarck. In it he recognizes the especial representative
of the Prussian nation, the pillar of the State; and this
was quite in the style of Frederick; for did not the great
monarch say, "that the sky did not rest more firmly
on the shoulders of Atlas, than the Prussian State on the
regiments of the army." The German policy of Herr

von Radowitz had no more conscious and energetic opponent than Herr von Bismarck, unless in the excellent General von Rauch, the Royal Adjutant-General, a remarkable and highly gifted statesman, who opposed him on every opportunity in his powerful way, even in the royal presence. Radowitz, on one occasion, in his emphatic style, conjured the King, like Cæsar, to cross the Rubicon. General von Rauch replied, with a twang of the Berlin dialect, " I do not know that fellow Cæsar, nor that fellow the Rubicon, but the man cannot be a true Prussian who counsels His Majesty thus ! " Herr von Radowitz, it is known, was not a born Prussian.

As to the revision of the constitution, Herr von Bismarck and his associates strove actively to endow it with such a shape that it would be possible for the King actually to govern with it. Much was accomplished, but " Far from sufficient ! " said Bismarck. Nor was it the fault of Bismarck that much more was not done.

He was particularly zealous against the power of granting taxation by the Diet. " The centre of gravity, the whole power of the State, departs from the Crown to the Chambers, or their majorities, and nothing then will remain to the Crown but the power of carrying out the votes of the majority. It is true the Government can dissolve the Chambers, and proceed to new elections, but the new Chambers might choose to pursue the way of the old, and thus the conflict would become insoluble and eternal; there is no way of avoiding this. This would be overturning the Prussian State Prerogative, he perceived, the effects of which very easily would be of a more enduring nature than those of the so-called March Revolution ! "

The orator of 1849 seemed to have a perception of the conflicts which the Premier of 1862 would have to pass through : he then did not see how he should emerge from such a state of things, but in 1866 he found the way the *via triumphalis*.

Bismarck had been forced to accept constitutionalism, but he did not unconditionally do so: it was at least to be a Prussian constitution, or modelled on Prussian, principles, not directly inimical to the Kingship.

Prussia, said he, must be distinguishable from other countries. The downfall of German States kept tolerable pace with the concessions made by their Governments to the people. A reference to England was a mistake. "Give us everything English that we do not possess; give us English piety, and English respect for the law; give the entire English constitution, but with this the entire relations of the English landlords, English wealth, and English common sense—then it will be possible to govern in a similar manner. The Prussian Crown must not be forced into the powerless position of the English Crown, which appears more like an elegant ornament at the apex of the edifice of the State. In ours I recognize the supporting pillar."

England, he added, had given itself the leading principles of the constitution of 1688, only after having been, for more than a century, under the curatorship of an omnipotent aristocracy, consisting of a very few families. Parliamentary Reform had now, it was true, broken the power of the aristocracy, but it was yet to be seen whether it would endure like the influence of the aristocracy. "We are deficient in the very class which controls politics in England, the class of wealthy and thence conservative gentlemen, independent of material interests, whose whole education is directed to becoming statesmen."

Bismarck's words were no longer hesitating, as at the United Diet, although there was always some slight impediment until his language began to flow more readily. But, as now, we perceive in his speeches that he had always to contend with the too rapidly advancing flood of thought. In his outward appearance his aspect was the picture of manly perfection; the tall, strong-boned frame was erect, but light and unconstrained; his attitude was somewhat daring, but the blue-grey eye glanced forth earnestly and sharply, when it was not animated with the light of sincere friendship. It was not the contemplative eye of the thinker, but the straightforward look of the man of action.

In the last days of autumn, Bismarck was commanded to the royal hunting-parties at Letzlingen, as he afterwards always continued to be, if not too far away. Frederick William IV. treated him with especial favour on this occasion; it was also with peculiar pleasure that he hunted on the moors and among the forests, centuries

before the proud heritage of his race; a heritage his ancestors had surrendered only under the influence of affection for their princes, and reverence for their liege lord. These old Bismarckian preserves are the richest in Prussia: the red deer and bucks are counted by thousands, and the royal hunts, which take place every winter since the restoration of the mansion of Letzlingen by Frederick William IV., at the beginning of his reign, are among the best in Europe. Frederick William IV., although

familiar with the chase, was not at all times a keen
sportsman. Once he leaned his gun against a tree, drew
a volume of Shakspeare from his pocket, seated himself on a stump, and was so absorbed in the poetry, that
he never noticed that an inquisitive stag, who wished
to know what the King was reading, crept up behind him
and looked into the book over his shoulder. This pretty
scene was witnessed by several sportsmen, and among
these Bismarck, from a distance.

In this winter of 1849-50 Bismarck established his
family in Berlin, although he retained his seat at Schönhausen ; his household lived on the first floor on Dorotheen
Strasse, No. 37; here his second child and eldest son
Herbert was born.

He was christened on the 13th February, 1850, by the
well known and so highly esteemed preacher Gossner. In
the spring of 1868 the heirs of Gossner, with other manu-
scripts, presented the letter of Bismarck, in which he
asked Gossner to christen his son, to a bazaar for mis-
sionary purposes. A cousin of the Minister-President—
General Count Bismarck-Bohlen, the Commandant of
Berlin—purchased the letter, and presented it to Count
Herbert. This letter is as follows :—

Berlin, 11th February, 1850.

Reverend Sir,—Although I have not the honour to be
personally known to you, I venture to hope, as we have
friends in common, that you will not refuse to baptize my
first-born son ; and I beg respectfully to ask whether it
will be agreeable to your engagements to perform this
holy office on the day after to-morrow, Wednesday, the 13th
current, at about half-past eleven, at my residence, Dorotheen Strasse, No. 37, and for this purpose would honour
me with a visit. In case of your consent, I trust you will
make an appointment for to-morrow afternoon or evening,

when I can visit you and make the further necessary arrangements.

With great respect, reverend sir, I remain faithfully,

Von Bismarck-Schönhausen, M. Sec. Ch.

Among the friends who about that time visited Bismarck's hospitable though simple household in the Dorotheen Strasse (afterwards in the Behrenstrasse, No. 60), we may name Von Savigny, André, and Von Kleist-Retzow.

Bismarck's life in those days was almost entirely absorbed by politics: sessions of the Chambers, commissions, committees, clubs, and appointments of all kinds occupied him, and politics formed the theme of the conversations he held in the evening in the beer saloon of Schwarz (corner of Friedichs and Leipziger Strassen), when he went in to drink a glass of Grünthaler beer. This beer saloon—it is still existent, although in another locality and under other management—was a principal centre of the conservatives; it was jestingly said, that even the landlord's little dog was so conservative that he barked at every democrat.

At another establishment, not that of Schwarz, Bismarck had a little adventure. He had just taken a seat, when a particularly offensive expression was used at the next table concerning a member of the Royal Family. Bismarck immediately rose to his full height, turned to the speaker, and thundered forth:—"Out of the house! If you are not off when I have drunk this beer, I will break this glass on your head!" At this there ensued a fierce commotion, and threatening outcries resounded in all directions. Without the slightest notice Bismarck finished his draught, and then brought it down upon the offender's pate with such effect that the glass flew into fragments, and the man fell down, howling with anguish. There was a deep silence, during which Bismarck's voice was heard to say, in the quietest tone, as if nothing whatever had taken place :—" Waiter, what is to pay for this broken glass?" At this exclamations were heard, but not against Bismarck, every one rejoiced and cried :—" That was right! That is the proper thing to do! The wretch richly deserved it!" This deed had its intended effect, and Bismarck went on his way unmolested.

There was something indescribably commanding in his firm countenance, with its close beard, and the cold glance which lay in his eyes, in his form and whole bearing, at this time. This a certain Herr Nelke (Pink) or Stengel

(Stalk)—we are not certain of the name—one day learnt to his cost. Bismarck was returning from Potsdam with the venerable and worthy Lieutenant-Colonel von Wolden, who is still remembered in certain circles. In the coupé a silly bagman or something of that kind was making a violent political speech, and at last ventured to ridicule and libel the grizzly Lieutenant-Colonel to his face. Bismarck looked at the man, who was continuing his insults, for a time, until the train stopped at the station in Berlin. Bismarck paced along the platform at his full height, and advanced in the firmest attitude to the chattering gentleman, so that he involuntarily receded a step with alarm. Silently Bismarck approached and drove him to the wall, and then simply asked him,—

" What is your name ? "

" Nelke, my name is Nelke ! " stammered the person addressed, with a pale and anxious face.

" Then take care, you Nelke (Pink), you—or I shall have to pluck you ! "

He then turned and left the poor Pink in a crushed state—but richer by a golden lesson—leaning against the wall.

Bismarck wore a long yellowish-grey overcoat, which to this day is called in his house the " dyke coat," as he was accustomed to put it on when he visited the dyke, for which purpose it had done long and faithful service. In Fritz Reuter's " Journey to Constantinople " the Commerce Councillor Schwofel says :—" In all Eisenach there are only three white hats ; His Royal Highness wears one when he is there ; Mr. O'Kelly wears the second ; and I wear the third. Certainly there are plenty more white hats in the place, but these are the most important." We might say here that Berlin in those days only contained three yellow overcoats ; Bismarck wore one of these ; the immortal Baron von Hertefeld wore the second, until he died, the last of his memorable race, as Hereditary Grand Huntsman, at Cleve, in 1867 ; and the author of this book the third. There might be many more yellow coats in Berlin, but these were the most important.

Bismarck very often, as did many members of the conservative party, visited the office of the *New Prussian Gazette*, in the Dessauer Strasse, No. 5, to learn the news. He was one of those, however, who always brought more than he carried away. Bismarck is an admirable narrator, especially of anecdotes, which he used to point with epigrammatic skill ; the under current of little traits of malice are generally invested with a dose of good humour, so that the subject of the stories were obliged to laugh themselves. The Napoleonist Duc de Persigny would no doubt have laughed had he heard Bismarck in those days. Fialin de Persigny at that time was entrusted with a political mission in Berlin, which he no doubt carried through to the greatest satisfaction of the higher powers ; but he exhibited such *disinvolture* in the circles of the court society, and so naïve an admiration for female beauty, that a number of tales passed current at his expense. Bismarck's mode of narration was only tinged with good humour in the majority of cases, not in all ;

he could be exceedingly peppery, and could give vent to severe sarcasms, and shoot off arrows which pierced through and through.

He was, however, not only a teller of anecdotes in the editorial room of the *New Prussian Gazette* ; he supported the paper he had contributed to found with original articles. These were mostly written at the great round table where so many distinguished men have taken their seats, from Von Radowitz and Bethmann-Hollweg to Count Arnim, Pernice, Stahl, Von Gerlach, and Huber ; and he wrote in his peculiar, firm, but high and compact style. Sometimes he rushed into the room with hasty greeting, and stood at the high desk, retaining his hat and gloves in his left hand, and threw some lines swiftly on to paper. " Put the national motto to these," he would exclaim to the editor-in-chief, and ran off with another salutation. He was always full of life and activity.

After the close of this session, on the 25th of February, 1850, he returned for a short time to Schönhausen, and in the following April we discover. him again in Erfurt, at the Union Parliament. He had, as we know, been opposed from the very beginning to these attempts at union; they were not, in his firm opinion, fraught with any fortunate omen to Prussia. The very next few months proved that his acute insight and his Prussian patriotism had not erred. We need not therefore be astonished that he gave vent to his patriotic sorrow at the Erfurt project, and the humiliations contemplated to Prussia thereby, in unmeasured language. He closed one of his speeches of that time with the following sentences :—

"It has been a painful feeling for me to see here Prussians, and not nominal Prussians only, who advocate this constitution, who have defended it with ardour. It would have been a humiliating feeling to me, and so it would have been to thousands and thousands of my fellow-countrymen, to see the representatives of princes whom I honour in their own sphere, but who are not my liege-lords, clothed with supreme power; a feeling the bitterness of which could not be diminished by seeing the seats we occupy decked with colours—never those of the German empire—but which for two years have been the colours of rebellion, and of the barricades, colours worn in my native land by the democrat alone, except when in sorrowful obedience by the soldier. Gentlemen! If you make no more concessions than are contained in this constitution to the Prussian—ancient Prussian spirit—call it obstinate Prussian feeling if you choose—I do not believe it will be realized ; and if you endeavour to force this constitution on this Prussian spirit, you will find it to be a Bucephalus, who bears his accustomed lord and rider with daring joy, but who will cast the unwelcome Sunday rider with his black-red-gold harness to the earth. I find one comfort against these eventualities in the firm conviction that no long time will elapse ere the parties to this constitution will stand, as, in the fable of Lafontaine, the two doctors stood by the patient whose corpse they were abandoning. The one said, ' He is dead, I said so from the beginning ! ' — the other, ' Had he followed my advice, he would have been alive now.' "

The further debates of the Erfurt Parliament gave him leisure enough, but this leisure brought no vigour with it, for the impression of a great political blunder sat heavy on the souls of Bismarck and his political partisans.

Bismarck wished to reinvigorate himself by a thorough hunting party ; he conferred with the Privy Councillor Oppermann, one of the "mighty hunters" of Prussia ; this gentleman joined him with enthusiasm, and they communicated through the Oberforstmeister von Wedell, in Schleusingen, to obtain a woodcock foray with the famous shot Oberförsters Klingner. Bismarck and Oppermann left Erfurt one morning together. At the first stage the travellers refreshed themselves, at Arnstadt, as keen sportsmen, thinking nothing of the caddish opinions of the day, by a plentiful breakfast at eight o'clock, of delicate groundlings, and drank 1811 Bocksbeutel therewith. At the succeeding stations they whetted their appetites with trout, and drank beer with them, as the nectar of 1811 would allow no other wines to attract the palate.   On their arrival in Schleusingen at 3 P.M., they had more trout and beer, then an interview and arrangements with the Oberförster, and in the evening more trout, which Oppermann ate with wine sauce, Bismarck remaining true to beer, despite of urgent dissuasions. At night, about 12 o'clock, the Oberförster made his appearance with a keeper, to take the gentlemen off to the forest. Bismarck, however, was in a very lamentable plight; the mixture of fish and beer did not suit his constitution, and he was in a feverish state. He was advised to have some peppermint and stop in bed, but it was in vain; the keen sportsman was not afraid of stomach-ache; he was soon dressed, and away they went. Oppermann fired and killed a bird, but Bismarck returned home with nothing. He had put up two woodcocks, but at the decisive moment he fired both times at the wrong instant. The keeper showed him another woodcock, but Bismarck was unfit for any further exertion; he returned to Schleusingen and went to bed. By eleven o'clock the mischief was ended by some strong grog, and the sportsmen then went by the express coach over the hills, and arrived very merrily in Erfurt by the evening. Bismarck, however, has never taken beer upon trout since.

During his stay in Erfurt, Dr. Stahl was presented with an album by his admirers. On its eleventh page, the album (which was afterwards printed) contains the following inscription:—

"Our watchword therefore is not 'A United State at any price,' but, 'The independence of the Prussian Crown at every price.'

"BISMARCK-SCHÖNHAUSEN,
"Deputy for Brandenburg."

"Erfurt, 24th April, 1850."

This expression, if we are not mistaken, was a quotation from a speech made by Stahl, at that time in Erfurt. Evidently it came from Bismarck's inmost soul.

After his return from Erfurt, Bismarck dedicated some weeks to his business in Schönhausen, and then travelled into Pomerania with his family. It is this journey of which such humorous mention is made in the two following letters to his sister.

BISMARCK TO FRAU VON ARNIM.

Schönhausen, 28th June, 1850.

I write you a solemn letter of congratulation on the occasion (I think) of your twenty-fourth birthday. (I won't tell anybody of this.) You are now really a major, or, rather, would have been so, had you not had the misfortune to belong to the female sex, whose limbs,

in the eyes of jurists, can never emerge from minority—not even when they are the mothers of the lustiest of Jacks. Why this apparent injustice is a very wise arrangement I will instruct you, when, I hope some fortnight hence, I have you *à la portée de la voix humaine* before

me. Johanna—who at the present time is in the arms of Lieutenant Morpheus—will have written to you what is in prospect for me. The boy bellowing in a major key, the girl in minor, two singing nurse-girls, wet napkins and milk bottles, myself in the character of an affectionate Paterfamilias. I resisted a long time, but as all the mothers and aunts were unanimous that poor little Molly could only be cured by sea-water and air, I should, if I resisted any longer, have my avarice and my paternal barbarity paraded before me on the occasion of every cold the child will catch till it is seventy, with the words: "Don't you see! Ah! if the poor child could but have gone to the seaside!" The little being is suffering from the eyes, which are tearful and sticky. Perhaps this arises from the salt baths, perhaps from eye teeth. Johanna is dreadfully excited about it, and for her satisfaction I have sent to-day for Dr. Bünger, at Stendal, who is the Fanninger of the Alt Mark. We take it for granted that you will be at home next month, and do not contemplate an excursion yourselves, in which event we would defer our visit until our return. But we write in order to settle time and place. I have very unwillingly decided to abandon my country laziness here, but now that it is settled, I see rose-coloured hues in the affair, and am heartily delighted to seek you in the cavern, which I only know to be situated some ten feet above the earth, and hope to seize the herring myself in the depths of the Baltic. Johanna is still asleep, or she would certainly send many greetings. For reasons of health I now rise at six o'clock. Hoping soon to see you, I invoke God's blessing on you and yours, for this year and all those to come.

THE SAME TO THE SAME.

Schönhausen, 8th July, 1850.

Yesterday a letter arrived from Oscar, according to which he will also be in Berlin to-morrow, but will not return until Thursday. I am very sorry your horses will be kept at work for two days together, but Oscar will not be able to set out on Wednesday, and it would be inconvenient for us to remain a day and a half in Berlin without any business whatever, or any other motive. The children and servants, Oscar, Johanna, and I could not go in one carriage. I therefore remain, and my principal reason for writing to you is in relation to my former letter, according to which we should reach Angermünde on Wednesday and find horses at Gerswalde, unless you have arranged it yourselves differently—in which case Oscar will let me know,

and it will be all right. I do not wish to propose any other
route, or it will bring the horses into confusion, from the
little time before us. This journey I perceive will give me
an introduction to the new Lunatic Asylum, or at least
the Second Chamber, for life. I already see myself on the
platform at Genthin with the children; then both of us
in the carriage with all sort of infantine requirements,
businesses at which one turns up one's nose—Johanna does
not like to give the boy the breast, and he roars himself
blue—then come official crowds, the inn, with both
howlers in the Stettin railway-yard—at Angermünde
we shall have to wait an hour for the horses, and pack
ourselves up again. How shall we get from Kröchlendorf
to Külz? If we have to remain a night in Stettin it
will be horrible. Last year I had to undergo all this
with Marie and her screaming. Yesterday I got so
despairing as to all these things that I positively determined to give the whole journey up, and so went to
bed, determined at least to coach it right through or stop
somewhere. But what do we not do for domestic peace?
" The young cousins ought to know each other, and who
can tell when Johanna will see you again?" In the night
she attacked me with the boy in her arms, and with the
arts that lost us Paradise she naturally succeeded, and
everything remains as before. But I feel that I am
myself the victim of a terrible wrong; next year I shall
be forced to travel about with three cradles, nurses, sheets,
and all the rest. I wake at six o'clock in a mild rage, and
can sleep no more, from the pictures of travel which my
fancy paints me in the blackest hues—down to the picnics
in the sandhills of Stolpmünde. And even were one's
expenses paid! But to throw away the ruins of a once
brilliant fortune by travelling about with suckling children !
I am very unhappy !

Therefore, on Wednesday we reach Gerswalde. Perhaps I had in the end better have gone by way of Passow,

and you would not have had to send so far to Prenzlau as to G. However, it is a *fait accompli ;* and the misery of choice is succeeded by the rest of resignation. Johanna greets you and packs. We shall send some of our things per freight ; Johanna is therefore in some anxiety about her toilette, in case you Boitzenbürgers have company.

The period till the latter autumn of 1850 was very instructive to Bismarck as a politician ; he continued to observe—we should, had not his Prussian heart been in the task, have said with scientific attention and curiosity—the effort made by Radowitz to save the Union ; he was astonished at the dexterity of this statesman, but he also saw clearly that all this dexterity would fail, for want of real pressure. Bismarck learnt that it was as impossible to create a German Unity as any other form of state, if one is wanting in courage or power to exert a sufficient pressure upon that which opposes. While Austria opposed, union was not possible without war, nor did Bismarck forget this truth.

The triple alliance collapsed, war was forbidden by the political facts of the time—the union was abandoned, Herr von Radowitz resigned, and Herr von Manteuffel, who then entered upon his office as Minister of Foreign Affairs, went to Olmütz.

What a terrible outcry was raised as to this visit to Olmütz at the time, and how greatly Herr von Manteuffel was censured on the subject ! Prussian feeling was deeply wounded, and was worthy of much respect ; it was a severe transposition—but from Erfurt to Olmütz was a necessity, if it were not resolved to break the opposition of Austria by the sword. Herr von Manteuffel, however, who entered upon this severe task in patriotic devotion to his country, certainly did not deserve the flood of abuse which was heaped upon his head for many years. He, at least, had not led Prussia to Erfurt.

On the 3rd December, 1850, Bismarck in a long speech defended the policy of the Ministry respecting the negotiations at Olmütz. He emphasized the community of interests existing between Prussia and Austria in reference to revolution, on the community of action of both States in German affairs. He censured war, by which Prussia would have set her existence upon the hazard of the die, in view of the threatening attitude abroad, and would have done so, not for herself, but for the lurking democracy. It will be understood that much of the so-called disgrace of Olmütz was cast upon Bismarck, and he was bitterly censured until the year 1866 for having defended those negotiations.

In the course of the session Bismarck had an opportunity of pronouncing a brilliant defence of the Prussian nobility, then assailed with unequalled license and malice. His words were these :—

" You ought not to undervalue in these latter days the services of that class, whether as officers of the army, or in such positions where landed property enables it to fight against anarchy and for the salvation of Prussia. The nobility of Prussia has in these affairs been spinning no silk, take it as a whole ; it will be remembered that its immediate ancestry conquered the Westphalian Land Tax in the Rhine Province, and that its grandfathers paid for the Patow Promemoria with their blood in Silesia. In like manner, you will find the sons of this class ever among the truest servants of the country. It is true the Prussian nobility have had their Jena ; in common with the political associates of those who now attack it, they have had their Second United Diet. If, however, I survey their history as a great whole, I believe there exist no reasons for such attacks as we hear in this place, and I do not think it necessary to despair of discovering within this class worthy members of a Prussian peerage."

o 2

To the continually reiterated taunt concerning Junkerdom and the Junker party, he fearlessly replied :—

" I am proud to be a Prussian Junker, and feel honoured
by the appellation. Whigs and Tories were terms which
once also had a very mean signification; and be assured,
gentlemen, that we shall on our part bring Junkerdom to
be regarded with honour and respect."

We here take leave of Bismarck's activity as a conservative party leader in the Second Chamber. This volcanic
earth in the Hardenberg Palace, on the Dönhoffsplatz, he
only re-entered eleven years afterwards as a Minister,
although in the winter of 1851-2 he several times came
from Frankfurt to Berlin, and also appeared in the
Chamber.

ON THE VOYAGE OF LIFE.

Der Lehr und Wanderjahre

anderer Theil.

Solch Wandern ist nicht eitel Lust,
Oft giebt's ein hartes Drängen,
Du bleibt bewußt und unbewußt,
Bald hier, bald dort was hängen.

CHAPTER I.

ON THE VOYAGE OF LIFE.

1851—1859.

Ambassador.—Interview with the King.—Lieut.-General von Rochow.—Anecdotes.—Frankfurt.—Reception of the Prince of Prussia.—Society at Frankfurt.—The King's Birthday.—Position of Prussia.—Correspondence.

 T some resting-place on a journey into Pomerania which Bismarck undertook in the early spring of 1851, he heard from several persons of his appointment as Ambassador to the Diet in Frankfurt-on-the-Maine, where the Diet was just then re-assembling. That this was not true he knew, but that he was very likely intended for the post he considered far from impossible. He thought deeply over the matter; the reflection was a novel one, but by no means unwelcome; to him a parliamentary career had become the less pleasing the longer he had followed it,—he was not vain enough for that: his manly self-confidence, however, was considerable, and perhaps he thought of his mother's

predictions.   On his return to Berlin, after minute self-examination, he determined to accept the position of Ambassador to the Diet, should it be offered him.

We do not know whether the idea of entrusting Bismarck with this office — unquestionably the most important which Prussia at that time had to fill—first occurred to Frederick William IV. himself, or whether it was the thought of the Minister von Manteuffel; at any rate it was founded on the assumption that Bismarck would be a *persona grata* to Austria, as it was then Prussia's problem to treat of German politics with the best under-

standing towards Austria.   It was the custom of Frederick William IV., who more than proved how dear everything that concerned Germany was to his heart, to select his Ambassador to the Diet with the utmost care ; and the delicate circumstances of the time rendered the necessity for caution all the greater. Yet, it will be said, on this occasion his choice fell upon a man who had hitherto never served in diplomatic matters. We certainly know from the mouth of a Minister of State, on very confidential terms with the King, that the latter "was much attached to Bismarck, and expected great things at his hands."

Bismarck paid a visit to Herr von Manteuffel; the latter soon told him that His Majesty the King desired to speak with him, and then, without any circumlocution, asked him in what his views concerning the ambassadorship consisted. The cautious Minister was not a little surprised when Bismarck, in so many words, declared himself prepared to undertake it. He was evidently not without hesitation at so rapid a decision, desiring him, however, to wait upon His Majesty the King without delay.

Bismarck was received by his King, at Sans Souci, with that favour and grace which he ever evinced towards him; but the King was even perhaps more astonished than his Prime Minister, when Bismarck frankly and honestly declared—"If your Majesty is desirous of trying the experiment, I am ready to fulfil your wishes!"

Frederick William IV. perhaps thought there was a certain degree of temerity in the rapid decision of Bismarck, and drew his attention to the significance and difficulty of the position.

"Your Majesty can surely try me," replied Bismarck; "if it prove a failure, I can be recalled in six months, or even sooner than that!"

Despite all the doubts and hesitation which arose in his mind, the King remained firm to his intention, and in May, 1851, Bismarck was appointed to the post of First Secretary of the Embassy to the Diet, with the title of Privy Councillor.

He immediately departed for his post. He here found himself on new, and, to him, entirely strange ground, and his duty was certainly not rendered easy for him. Lieut.-

General Theodor Rochus von Rochow, who was to introduce him to his new position, kept him at a distance from
actual business, with the well-known and intelligible
jealousy which most men entertain towards their successors
in office. Herr von Gruner was a liberal and an opponent
of Bismarck's, but the other German representatives felt
a sort of virtuous shudder at the famous reactionary
Junker. Perhaps the Presiding Deputy, Count von Thun-
Hohenstein, who thought to see in Bismarck the thorough
partisan of Austria, was the only person who bid him welcome, at the same time with the intention of causing him
to see what marked influence Austria possessed. This was
a rather strong diplomatic blunder, for Bismarck knew
precisely how to take and retain his proper position.

A pretty anecdote was related at the time, for which
certainly we cannot absolutely vouch, but if not true, it
might have been. Bismarck one day paid the Presiding
Deputy a visit. Count Thun received him with a sort of
brusque familiarity, went on coolly smoking his cigar, and
did not even ask Bismarck to take a chair. The latter
simply took out his cigar-case, pulled out a cigar, and said,
in an easy tone, " May I beg a light, Excellency !" Excellency, astonished to the greatest degree, supplied the
desired light. Bismarck got a good blaze up, and then
took the unoffered seat in the coolest way in the world,
and led the way to a conversation.

Bismarck never allowed any liberties with himself, but
still less would he tolerate them when they were offered
to him as the representative of his Sovereign.

In the August of the same year he received the rank
of Ambassador. The Councillors at the Embassy consisted
of the Legations—Rath Otto Wentzel, and as Attachés,
the Count Lynar, and Count Theodor of Stolberg-Werni-
gerode.

General von Rochow continued his jealous behaviour
to the end. On the day of his departure he pretended

to send Bismarck the current papers in a green portfolio ; but Bismarck found it empty. Bismarck immediately went to the station, which Rochow had not expected, and was accordingly much embarrassed. In the choicest expressions, Bismarck thanked him for all the delicate kindnesses he had experienced from him, and added, that he presumed to ascribe it to the friendship that Rochow had entertained for his deceased father. These few moments could scarcely have been very pleasant to the poor General.

During this first visit to Frankfurt, Bismarck resided with his friend Count Lynar (who subsequently died at

Paris), in the house of M. Krug, a merchant, in the Hoch Strasse, whose wife was a native of Berlin. He was unable to work much at the Bills of the Bund, and

General von Rochow, famous for his wit, jested not a little at Bismarck's late habits of rising, although he was far more industrious than was generally apparent, being engaged in an active correspondence with his political friends in Berlin, especially with the Actual Privy Councillor, Freiherr von Manteuffel II. Before dinner he usually rode out, and, in order to feel his ground, visited the neighbouring Courts of Darmstadt, Biebrich, and Karlsruhe, where his old friend Von Savigny was then Prussian Envoy. An acute, sometimes a severe, judge of character, as well as an observer of passing events; Bismarck had, at the desire, or, at any rate, with the consent of Rochow, undertaken an immediate part in the press. The articles contributed or suggested by him created much attention; they possessed wit and point, often destroying the arguments of his opponents; this became his peculiar province. At other times, as a new man in diplomacy, he assisted at the discussions in the society of Herr von Rochow, in order to become familiar with the course of business and the exterior formalities of diplomacy.

On the 11th of July, 1851, the then Prince of Prussia (now King) visited Frankfurt, and was received by the body corporate of the Bund, and the general staff. The Prince was graciously inclined towards Bismarck, but made some observations during his passage to the terminus to Herr von Rochow, on the anomaly of this militia lieutenant—for Bismarck had appeared in uniform, being a Deputy of the Bund. General von Rochow, however, who was wise enough not to undervalue Bismarck's importance, although he did not always testify the liveliest friendship towards him, replied, "The selection is worthy, novel, and vigorous; your Royal Highness will certainly find all your requirements fulfilled."

The Prince could reply nothing to this, and, in fact, he certainly entertained the most favourable opinion of this still somewhat youthful champion of the justice and the honour of Prussia.

" I believe," General von Rochow said at the time, " he only wished him to have possessed grey hair and a few additional years ; but it is questionable whether the plans of the Prince would be much nearer their fulfilment for those."

This is all very characteristic, considering the relation destined at a future time to subsist between King William

and Bismarck. Personal goodwill in the highest degree he entertained for him, but want of confidence in his youth and inexperience.

The Prince of Prussia frequently alluded to this view, but Rochow found means of quieting his fears. Otherwise he was fond of having Bismarck about him, conversed with him freely, drove about, and soon went to the theatre with him. The Prince exhibited real friendship for Bismarck, and, on the occasion of the birth of a son, in the following year (2nd August, 1852), became its sponsor. Bismarck's younger son is named William after his royal godfather, although his usual name has continued to be "Bill." General von Rochow also, on his return to his post at St. Petersburg, freely stated his anticipation of great things from the talents and decision of character of his successor at Frankfurt.

When Bismarck became Envoy to the Bund, on the 18th August, 1851, he rented a villa of the younger Rothschild of Naples, distant some quarter of an hour from the city gate on the Bockenheimer Chaussée, close to the frontier of Hesse; the same dwelling previously inhabited by the Archduke John in his official capacity as Imperial Curator. In the garden, as upon the flight of steps, the most magnificent flowers were arranged; it is said there were more than one thousand camellias. Bismarck's house, after the arrival of Madame von Bismarck with her children, became the most prominently hospitable house in Frankfurt.

He soon became intimate with the Austrian Ambassador. Count Thun was a noble cavalier, and his very handsome wife, born a Countess Lamberg, knew how to invest his house with great attractions. Bismarck also managed to keep on terms with Count Thun's successor, the well-known Freiherr Prokesch von Osten, whose hatred of Prussia was so little a secret that his nomination to the office was regarded as a demonstration against Prussia; and this Bismarck did without in the least lowering the dignity of Prussia—a problem somewhat difficult, considering the reputation of this entirely Eastern diplomatist. Of a much more friendly character were his relations to Count Rechberg, who replaced Prokesch.

The other representatives with whom Bismarck came into more intimate contact were, Von Scherff, who represented the King of the Netherlands as Grandduke of Luxemburg, Von Fritsch (Grandduke of Saxony), Von

Bülow (King of Denmark as Duke of Holstein and Lauenburg), Von Oertzen (Mecklenburg), and Von Eisendecher
(Oldenburg). Bismarck farmed some sporting in conjunction with the English Ambassador, Sir Alexander Malet.

Besides enjoying the society of the diplomatists, Bismarck liked to mingle with the Prussian and foreign
higher military officers; to his dinners, soirées, and balls,
he also invited musicians, authors, and artists—a fact not
of very frequent occurrence among the chief diplomatists
in Frankfurt, and one which created some notice. His
intercourse with these circles was principally conducted by
the highly esteemed artist Professor Becker, who, with his
wife and handsome daughters, belonged to the most intimate society of his house. The excellent portrait of Bismarck which hangs in the room of the Countess at Berlin,
is by Professor Becker.

Still more remarkable than this intercourse with painters
and sculptors were certain domestic festivals, of which the

In the Diet itself, Bismarck was successful in establishing such an order of business, to some extent limiting the arbitrary action of the President, and finally led to some method in the debates of the Diet. It might even be said that he soon attained a leading power in the Diet, and thereby worked blessings for Prussia; but even all this could not alter the unfortunate position of Prussian Germany, founded as it was upon the principles of the Diet and the Zollverein. Had Austria given its goodwill, all this might have been effected, but in the teeth of its ill-will, the whole negotiations could only terminate in ruin or in a rupture.

The position of Prussia consisted in the fact, that the constitution of the Diet had only become possible through the policy of Prince Metternich. This policy, which advocated a probable segregation of Austria from Germany, and at least left Prussia free room to act in North Germany, ever moved in the most limited grooves. As Prince Schwarzenberg adopted a policy diametrically opposed to this, which consciously and deliberately determined upon the humiliation of Prussia, in order afterwards to destroy it, and violated every form with the uttermost carelessness, the conflict could only be a matter of time.

Bismarck was therefore necessarily made an antagonist of Austria by the Schwarzenberg policy, continued by Count Buol Schauenstein; and opposition against the anti-Prussian policy of the Vienna Cabinet became the watchword for his political activity. This was soon very apparent, nor did he conceal it the less, as his vigorous patriotism impelled him to bring his opposition actually to bear; his frankness also rendered any equivocation impossible. In such a course he could hardly depend upon any co-operation from the King and the Prime Minister, Von Manteuffel, who both hoped, discouraged by the failure of the Union negotiations, that Austria might still revert to the earlier pro-Prussian policy of Prince Metternich. Bismarck himself, although he could scarcely hope this, ardently desired it. A position worthy of the Prussian kingdom in Germany was that for which he had to strive—a position it ought to occupy, if it were to worthily maintain its place in Europe; and desired to secure to the German people those advantages, to be resigned by no people unless at the peril of political death. Bismarck was determined to devote his life to aiding the Prussian Crown in the attainment of this position. He would rather have gone hand-in-hand with Austria; if this were an impossibility, then without Austria; but should it prove necessary, then antagonism to Austria. It must not be overlooked how, in the sequel, Bismarck in every political struggle attempted to accomplish it in union with Austria, in which he was sometimes successful, and how, when it was impossible, he continued the effort without Austria, and finally in opposition to Austria. It were superfluous here to pursue Bismarck's political career in the details of his German policy.

The following correspondence (rearranged by the translator in their proper chronological order) passed during these years.

Frankfurt, 18th May, '51.

Frankfurt is wretchedly wearisome; I am so spoilt with having so much affection about me, and a great deal to do; and I now first perceive how unthankful I have been towards many people in Berlin—for I will not take you and yours into the question. Even the coolness of fellow-countrymen and party associates I had in Berlin is an intimate connection compared with the relations one makes here; being, in fact, nothing more than mutual suspicious espionage. If one had anything indeed to detect or to conceal! The people here worry themselves about the merest trifles; and these diplomatists, with their important

nothings, already appear more ridiculous to me than a
Deputy of the Second Chamber in his full-blown dignity.
Unless outward events take place—and those we clever
members of the Diet can neither guide nor predetermine—
I now know accurately what we shall have done in one,
two, or five years, and could bring it about in twenty-four
hours, if the others would for a single day be reasonable
and truthful.   I never doubted that they all made soup
with water; but such a simple, thin water-gruel, in which
you can't see a globule of fat, astonishes me!   Send me
Justice X. or Herr von Parsky hither from the toll-gate,
when they are washed and combed, and I will lord it in
diplomacy with them.   I am making enormous progress
in the art of saying nothing in a great many words.   I
write reports of many sheets, which read as tersely and
roundly as leading articles; and if Manteuffel can say what
there is in them, after he has read them, he can do more
than I can.

Each of us pretends to believe of his neighbour that he
is full of thoughts and plans, if he would only tell; and at
the same time we none of us know an atom more of what
is going to happen to Germany than of next year's snow.
Nobody, not even the most malicious sceptic of a democrat, believes what quackery and self-importance there is
in this diplomatizing.   Well, I have railed long enough,
and now I will tell you that I am very well.   Yesterday I
was in Mainz: the neighbourhood is lovely.   The rye is
in full ear, although it is infamously cold all night and in
the mornings.   Excursions by railroad are the best here.
One can reach Heidelberg, Baden-Baden, Odenwald, Homburg, Soden, Wiesbaden, Bingen, Rüdesheim, and Niederwald comfortably in one day, stop five or six hours, and
return here in the evening.   Until now I have not gone
much about, but shall do so, that I may take you about
when you come.   Rochow started yesterday for Warsaw—
he went off at nine o'clock in the evening; the day after

to-morrow he will be there, and probably back in a week.
As to politics and people, I cannot write much, as most of
the letters are opened here. When they know your
address on mine, and your handwriting on your letters,
they will very likely find out they have no time to read
family letters.

Frankfurt, 3rd July, 1851.

The day before yesterday I thankfully received your
letter and the news that you were all well. But do not
forget, when you write to me, that the letters are not only
read by myself, but by all sorts of postal spies ; and do not
inveigh against certain persons in them, for that is all set
down to the husband—to my account ; besides, you do the
people injustice. As to my appointment or non-appoint-
ment, I know no more than was told me at my departure :
all other things are possibilities and conjectures. What is
irregular in the matter is the silence of the Government
towards me, as it would be as well to let me know for certain, and indeed officially, whether I am to live here or in
Pomerania with wife and child next month. Be prudent
in all you say to people, then, without exception—not
only against ——, particularly in opinions of persons,
for you cannot conceive what one has to endure if one once
becomes an object of observation ; be assured that whatever you say in the —— or the bathing-machine is
served up with sauce either here or at Sans-Souci.
Forgive me for scolding you so, but after your last letter
I must take up the diplomatic hedge-knife. If ——
and others could sow distrust in our diplomatic camp, they
would thereby attain one of the chief ends of their letter
robberies. I went the day before yesterday to Wiesbaden
to ——, and, with a mixture of sadness and wisdom,
we went to see the scene of former folly. Would it
might please God to fill this vessel with his clear and
strong wine, in which formerly the champagne of twenty-

one years of youth foamed uselessly, and left nothing but loathing behind. Where now are ———— and Miss ————? How many are buried with whom I then flirted, drank, and diced? How many transformations have taken place in my views of the world in these fourteen years, among which I have ever looked upon the actually Present as the True?. How little are some things to me that then appeared great? How much is venerable to me now, that I then ridiculed? How much foliage may bud, grow green, give shadow, rustle, and worthlessly fade within the next fourteen years, till 1865, if we live to see it? I cannot understand how a man who considers his own nature, and yet knows nothing of God, and will know nothing, can endure his existence from contempt and wearisomeness. I know not how I could formerly support it; were I to live as then, without God, without you, without my children! I should not, indeed, know whether I had not better abandon life like a dirty shirt; and yet most of my acquaintances are in that state, and live on! If I ask of an individual, what object he has in living on, in labouring and growing angry, in intriguing and spying, I obtain no answer. Do not conclude from this *tirade* that my mood is dark; on the contrary, I feel like a person who looks, on a fine September morning, on the yellowing foliage; I am healthy and cheerful, but I feel some melancholy, some longing for home, a desire for forests, ocean, wilderness, for you and my children, mingled with the impressions of sunset and of Beethoven. Instead of which I have to pay dreary visits to ———— and read endless ciphers about German steam corvettes and cannon-balls, rusting and eating up money in Bremerhaven. I should like to have a horse, but I could not ride alone—it is too wearisome; and the society with whom one rides is also wearisome. And now I must go to Rochow, and to all sorts of -ins and -offs, who are here with the Archduchess Olga.

Frankfurt, 8th July, 1851.

Yesterday and to-day I have been anxious to write to you, but in the whirl of business could not get so far until the evening late, on my return from a walk during which I blew away the dust of business with the summer night's breeze, moonlight, and the rustle of poplar foliage. On Saturday afternoon I went with Rochow and Lynar to Rüdesheim. I there took a boat, went out on the Rhine, and swam in the moonlight, eyes and nose only above the tepid water, to the Rat Tower, near Bingen, where the bad bishop met his end. There is something strangely dreamy to lie in the water on a still night, slowly driven by the stream, seeing the heavens, with moon and stars, above, and on either hand the wood-capped mountains and city spires in the moonlight, without hearing anything but one's own gentle splashing. I should like to swim like that every night. I then drank some very decent wine, and sat for a long time smoking with Lynar on the balcony, the Rhine below us. My small Testament and the starry night led to some conversation on Christianity; and I shook earnestly at the Rousseau-like virtue of his soul, only reducing him to silence. As a child he has been ill-treated by nurses and tutors, without really knowing his parents, and has emerged from his youth with similar ideas, founded on a similar education, to my own, but bears them with more content than ever has been my case. Next day we went in the steamer to Coblenz, breakfasted there for an hour, and returned in the same way to Frankfurt, where we arrived in the evening. I undertook the journey with the object of visiting old Metternich, at Johannisberg, at his invitation; but the Rhine delighted me so much, that I preferred a trip to Coblenz, and postponed the visit. We saw the river, on our immediate journey to the Alps, in the finest weather; on this fresh summer morning, and after the dusty weariness of Frankfurt, it rises much in my esteem.

I look forward with real delight to spending a couple of days with you, at Rüdesheim; the place is so calm and rural, the people pleasant, and nothing dear. We would then take a small rowing boat, and go quietly down, climb the Niederwald, and this and the other castle, and return by the steamer. One can leave here in the morning early, stay eight hours at Rüdesheim, Bingen, Rheinstein, and so forth, and return hither by the evening. My appointment here seems now to be certain.

Frankfurt, 13th Aug., 1851.

I worked very hard to-day and yesterday about the King's journey, and a multitude of petty details concerning the minor Courts, and I am now in hourly expectation of a tiresome ambassadorial visit; so that this letter must be very short, and yet serve as a love token. Who has started this nonsense about St. Petersburg? I heard the very first of it from your letters. Will you not go to Nicolai? I should not think one winter there at all disagreeable; but I am tired of these separations, and the climate might not suit you and the babies. I yesterday took a long and solitary walk into the mountains, deep into the wonderful night. I had been at work from eight o'clock till five, then dined, and luxuriated in the fresh evening mountain air of the Taunus, after leaving this dusty hole, by half an hour's railway to Soden, some two miles behind me. The King passes through here on the 19th, and returns, by way of Ischl and Prague, to Berlin about the 7th of September. I shall meet him at Coblenz, as I have much to say to ———. If he brings my appointment, as I expect, I shall immediately hire quarters, and then we can talk of your coming.

Frankfurt, 23rd August, 1851.

In the midst of my business post time has arrived, and I will rather write you a hasty note than not at all. Since

Monday I have been still going on. First, there was a great State dinner here to the Emperor of Austria—twenty thousand thalers' worth of uniforms at table; then I went to Mainz to receive the King; he was very gracious to me, for the first time after a long interval harmless and merry. Next came a grand supper, then work with Manteuffel till two; then a cigar with dear old Stolberg; at half-past six parade, and a great theatrical representation. I went on as far as Darmstadt; there we dined. The King then went to Baden, and after three weary hours I reached this place in the evening with ———. On Wednesday I was summoned from my bed to the Duke of Nassau at Bieberich, and there dined. Late in the evening I returned, to be waked very early next morning by the President G. and I., who took possession of me and led me off to Heidelberg, where I remained the night, and enjoyed some delightful hours with them at Castle Wolfsbrunn and Neckarsteinsach, and last night returned from this excess. G. was pleasanter than ever, did not dispute, grew enthusiastic, poetical, and generous. At the Castle we saw a sunset the day before yesterday like that one at Rigi. We breakfasted up there, walked to Wolfsbrunn, where I drank some beer at the same table I did with you; then boated up the Neckar to Steinach, and parted in the evening at Heidelberg. G. goes to-day to Coblenz, I. to Italy.

Bismarck was so often summoned to Berlin during his residence at Frankfurt, that it would be wearisome to relate all these journeys here. In one year, we do not exactly remember which, he travelled between Berlin and Frankfurt no less than 2,600 miles. His counsel was often required by the highest authority, and very often Bismarck was very nearly becoming a Minister, even then; nor was it the powerful influence of both sides which conclusively prevented his entry into the Ministry, but his own aversion to become a Minister so soon. He declared

to an acquaintance in those days that he would prefer to
be first an ambassador for ten years, and then a Minister
for ten years more, that he might close his days as a
country nobleman thereafter in peace. King Frederick
William IV., who regarded it as necessary for Bismarck's
political education that he should go to Vienna, entrusted
him in the May of 1852 with an important mission
thither; but above this was his desire to restore a complete understanding between Austria and Prussia. We
already know that in this Bismarck was likely to become
wrecked upon the Schwarzenberg policy. In a personal
sense, however, on following the Imperial Court into Hungary, Bismarck received very pleasing impressions, as to
which he speaks in the following letters to his wife :—

Halle, the 7th January, 1852.

I have never, as well as I can recollect, ever written to
you from hence, and I hope that it will not happen again.
I have really been thinking whether, after all, yesterday was
not Friday, on which I set out; it was certainly a *dies
nefastus* (N. N. will tell you what this means). In Giessen
I got a room as cold as ice, with three windows that
wouldn't shut; a bed too short and too narrow; it was
dirty, with bugs; infamous coffee—never knew it so bad.
At Guntershausen ladies came into the first class; there
was an end of smoking. A high lady of commerce (N. N.
will tell you what that is), with two lady's maids; sable
furs; they spoke alternately with a Russian and English
accent in German, French very well, a little English, but
in my opinion they came from the Reezen Alley in Berlin,
and one of the lady's maids was her mother, or elder lady
of commerce (N. N., &c.). Between Guntershausen and
Gerstungen a tube in the engine burst, so gently! The
water all ran away; so there we sat for an hour and a half
in the open—very pretty neighbourhood, and a warm sunlight. I got into the second class to smoke, and fell into

the hands of a Berlinese Chamber and Privy Council colleague, who had been drinking Homburg waters for a fortnight, and asked me a lot of questions before a number of
Jews coming from the fair, until, in despair, I took refuge
with the princess from the Reezen Alley. By this stoppage we reached Halle three hours too late; the Berlin
train was gone a long time. Here I must sleep, and travel
with the luggage train at half-past one to arrive at two.
In the station yard there are two hotels; by accident I'm
in the wrong one; a gend'arme walked up and down
the saloon, and seemed very thoughtful about my beard,
while I ate a tough beefsteak. I am very unhappy, but
will finish my bit of goose, drink some port wine, and then
to bed.

Berlin, 1st May, 1852.

I have just returned from an infinitely tedious dinner
at Le Coq's, where I sat between L. G. and the younger
M.—two persons widely different in nature. I tried in
vain to settle some dispute about what is now agitating
the King and the Chamber. The one was dry, wise, and
practical; the other delightful, enthusiastic, and theoretical; he might really have forgotten the world and its
government, in his own views about them, but the air of
the Chambers has stimulated this impractical direction
in him, and in this gymnastic exercise of soul and
tongue he forgets, or holds cheap, what is necessary to be
done. There is really something quite demoralizing in
the atmosphere of the Chambers—the best people grow
vain without perceiving it, and get accustomed to the
tribune as to a toilet-table, by means of which they
exhibit themselves to the public. Forgive this political
avalanche.

Berlin, 3rd May, 1852.

I am really tired of being here, and long for the day
of departure. Chamber intrigues I find terribly shallow

and undignified; if one lives always amongst them, one
deceives oneself, and they seem wonders. When I come
straightforwardly from Frankfurt, I feel like a sober man
who has suddenly fallen amongst tipplers. I wish they
would send me to Constantinople; it would not be necessary to be returning here every minute.

Vienna, 11th June, 1852.

" 'Sg'fällt mer hier gar net " (I don't like this place at
all) as Schrenck says, although it was so pleasant with
you, anno '47; but I not only miss you, but I find myself
not wanted, and that is worse than I can make plain to
your unpolitical mind. If I were here, as I was there, for
amusement, I could not grumble: all those whom I have
become acquainted with are remarkably charming people,
and the town is rather hot with narrow streets, but still
a splendid town. In business, however, there prevails
great *nonchalance;* either the people don't want to arrange
with us, or they think we look upon it as more important
than appears to them. I fear that the opportunity of
coming to an understanding is gone, which will prove a
bad result for us; for it was thought that a very great
step towards reconciliation was taken in sending me, and
they will not soon send another here so desirous of
coming to an understanding, and who at the time can
deal so freely. Forgive me for writing politics to you,
but when the heart is full, &c. I am really drying up
in this mishmash, and I am afraid I shall begin to take
an interest in it. I have just come from the opera with
old Westmoreland; Don Giovanni, played by a good
Italian Opera troop, in hearing which I felt the wretched-
ness of the Frankfurt theatre doubly. Yesterday I went
to Schönbrunn, and thought of our romantic moonlight
expedition, as I looked at the tall hedges and the white
statues in the green thickets, peeped also at the private
garden which we first got into—quite forbidden ground--

so, that the Jäger sentinel, who was at his post, would not allow its even being looked into.

Ofen, 23rd June, '52.

I have just come from the steamboat, and do not know how to employ the interval until Hildebrand follows with my luggage, better than in giving you some account of this very eastward but very beautiful world. The Emperor graciously assigned me quarters in his palace, and I am seated at an open window in a spacious vaulted hall, listening to the evening bells of Pesth. The view is charming. The castle stands high; beneath me flows the Danube, spanned by the suspension bridge; beyond is Pesth, and in the far distance is an endless plain melting away into the purple twilight. Next to Pesth, on the left, I see the upper course of the Danube; far, very far off from me, viz., on the right bank, the river is fringed by the town of Ofen; behind this are mountains, blue, and bluer, and then tinged with brownish-red in the evening, heaven glowing behind them. In the midst of the two cities the broad sheet of water lies, like Linz, broken only by the suspension bridge and a woody island. The passage hither, at least from Gran to Pesth, would have delighted you. Think of the Odenwald and the Taunus brought close together, and the interval filled with the waters of the Danube. The shady side of the voyage was the sunny side, for the sun burnt us as if Tokay were to grow on the ship, and the number of travellers was very great; but only fancy, not a single Englishman amongst them—they can hardly have discovered Hungary as yet. Otherwise these were queer folks—from every oriental and occidental nation—greasy and washed. My chief travelling companion was a very delightful General, with whom I sat for the most part on the paddle-box and smoked. I am getting somewhat impatient as to where Hildebrand can be; I am lying in the window, half enthusiastic at the moonlight, half waiting for him, as for one's beloved—for I feel a marvellous disposition for a clean shirt. If you could be here for a moment, and could see the silvery stream of the Danube, the dark mountains on a pale red ground, and the lights twinkling up from Pesth, Vienna would sink in your estimation as compared with Buda-Pesth, as the Hungarian calls it; you see I am also an enthusiast for nature. I will now calm my excited blood with a cup of tea, as Hildebrand has really arrived, and then soon go to bed.

Last night I only had four hours' sleep, and the Court is very early here. The young Duke rises at five; I should then be a very bad courtier if I thought of sleeping longer. Therefore, with a glance at a gigantic tea-urn, and a seductive dish containing ices, amongst other things, as I see, I waft you a good-night from afar. What can that song be which has haunted me all day long?

> " Over the blue mountain, over the white sea foam,
> Come, thou beloved one, come to thy lonely home ! "

I cannot tell who it was who sang this to me in "Old lang syne."

The 24th June.—After a good night's rest, although upon a flinty bed, I wish you a good morning. The entire landscape before me swims in bright burning sunshine, so that I cannot look out without being dazzled. Until it is time to begin my visits, I am sitting here alone at breakfast, and smoking in a very spacious apartment, four rooms—all vaulted massively—two about the size of our dining-room, thick walls like Schönhausen, giant walnut-wood cabinets, furniture of blue silk, on the floor a number of yard-wide black stains, that a more excited imagination than mine would take for blood, but which I, décidément, declare to be ink. An incredibly unskilful writer must have lived here, or another Luther must several times have thrown very large inkstands at the Adversary. A very obliging old servant in a bright yellow livery shares the duties of the household with Hildebrand; indeed they are all very obliging. In honour of the King's representative, the steamer yesterday hoisted the great Prussian standard, and, thanks to the telegraph, a royal carriage was in waiting at the landing-place. Don't tell N. N., or he will write articles about it. Below, on long rafts, are floating the queerest brown broad-hatted and broad-breeched figures along the Danube. I am sorry that I am not an artist; I should like to have introduced you to these wild faces, with heavy moustaches and long hair, flashing black eyes, and their picturesque draperies, as I beheld them yesterday. I must now make an end and begin my visits. I do not know when you will receive these lines; perhaps I shall send a courier to-morrow or next day to Berlin, who can take them with him.

Evening.—I have not had any opportunity as yet of forwarding this. The lights again are twinkling up from Pesth; towards the horizon, near the Theiss, there is lightning; above us the heavens are full of stars. I have been in uniform the greater part of the day, in private audience; I handed my credentials to the youthful ruler of this land, and have been agreeably impressed. After dinner the whole Court made an excursion into the mountains, to the " pretty shepherdess;" who is long since dead; some centuries ago King Matthew Corvinus loved her. Thence there is a prospect of Ofen, its mountains and plains, over woody Neckar-like rocks. A national feast had brought thousands forth, thronging around the Emperor, who mingled freely with them, with re-sounding *eljen evviva* they danced Csardas, waltzed, sang, played music, climbed the trees, and crowded round the Court. Upon a grass slope there was a supper-table laid out for some twenty people—only on one side, the other being left free for a view of the forest, castle, city, and country; above us were tall beeches with climbing Hungarians on the branches; behind us dense crowds of people thronged together and pushing each other about; in the distance wind instruments mingled with song, wild gipsy music. Illuminations, moonshine, and the rosy twilight, torches flitting through the forest—the whole might have figured unchanged as a great scene of effect in a romantic opera. Next to me sat the venerable Archbishop of Gran, the Primate of Hungary, in a black silk talar with a red cape; on the other a very charming and elegant cavalry general. You see that the picture was a variegated one, rich in contrasts. Then we drove home in the moonshine by torchlight. Tell Frau von V. that her brother was a most delightful man, as I could not but expect from her two sisters whom I already knew. I had just received a telegraphic despatch from Berlin; it contained only four letters—*Nein* (No!). A word full of significance. I was told to-day of the storm of the castle three years ago by the insurgents; at this the brave General Hentzi and the whole garrison, after a wonderfully courageous resistance, were cut down. The black stains upon my floor are partly the result of fire, and where I am writing bursting grenades were then dancing, and the fight went on over smoking ruins. It has only been restored a few weeks ago, before the arrival of the Emperor. It is very quiet and peaceful up here now. I hear nothing but the ticking of a clock, and the sound of distant carriage-wheels below. May angels watch over thee—a bearskin-capped grenadier does so with me—I can see six inches of his bayonet at a couple of arms' length from me above the window-sill, and the reflection of a foot. He stands on the terrace by the Danube, and is probably thinking of his Nanny.

Szolnok, 27th June, 1852.

In your atlases you will find a map of Hungary, and on this a river Theiss, and, if you follow up the source

EDWARD'S ONLY LOVER
FANNY ELSSLER

towards Szegedin, a place named Szolnok. Yesterday I
went by railway from Pesth to Alberti-Josa, where a
Prince W. lies in garrison. He is married to a Princess
M. I paid him a visit in order to inform —— of the
state of his health. This place lies on the edge of the
Hungarian steppes between the Danube and the Theiss,
which I desired to see by way of a joke. I was not
allowed to ride without an escort, as the district is over-
run by cavalry robber bands, here called Betyars, and is
therefore unsafe. After a comfortable breakfast under the
shade of a Schönhausen lime, I got upon a low waggon
with sacks of straw and three horses; the Uhlans loaded
their carbines, mounted, and away we went at full gallop.
Hildebrand and a Hungarian servant occupied the front
seat, and our coachman was a dark brown peasant, with a
moustache, a broad-brimmed hat, long hair shining with
fat, a shirt only reaching to the stomach, leaving a broad
band of dark brown skin visible, to where the white
trousers begin, each leg of which would make a woman's
gown, and reach to the knee, where boots and spurs complete the costume. Only think of firm grass plat, as level
as a table, on which nothing can be seen for miles towards
the horizon, except the tall naked beams of the wells dug
for the half-wild horses and oxen, thousands of whitey-
brown oxen, with long horns, as timorous as deer, rough,
disreputable-looking horses, watched by half-naked shepherds on horseback, with lances; endless herds of swine,
among which you see a donkey carrying the fur-cloak
(*bunda*) of the herdsman, and sometimes himself; huge
swarms of bustards, hares, rabbits, and other small deer;
near a salt-water pool, wild geese, ducks, and lapwings;
such were the objects we flew by, and which flew by us
during our three hours' journey of seven miles to Ketskemet, with a slight halt at a csarda (inn). Ketskemet is
a village, the streets of which, if the inhabitants are left
out, reminds one of the small end of Schönhausen. It has,

Q

however, forty-five thousand inhabitants, unpaved streets, low houses, closed on the eastern side against the sun, with huge cattle-yards. A foreign ambassador was such an unusual sight there—and my Magyar servant rattled out the "excellency" to such a degree—that I immediately obtained a guard of honour, the village authorities announced themselves, and a change of horses was required. I spent the evening with a delightful set of officers, who insisted upon my taking an additional escort, and entertained me with a number of robber stories. In the very neighbourhood into which I was going the worst robber nests exist; on the Theiss, the morasses and wilds render their destruction almost impossible. They are splendidly horsed and armed, these Betyars; they attack travellers and farms in bands of fifteen or twenty strong, and next day are twenty miles away. They are polite to respectable people. I had left the greater part of my ready money with Prince W., and only had some linen with me, and really felt a desire to make the nearer acquaintance of these mounted brigands, in their great fur dresses, with double-barrelled guns and pistols in their girdles. Their captains wear black masks, and sometimes belong to the small country gentry. Some days ago the gens d'armes had a skirmish with them, and some were killed; two robbers, however, were caught, and shot, with all the honours, in Ketskemet. We don't hear of such things in our tiresome districts. About the time you woke this morning, you little thought that I was flying over the steppes of Cumania, in the neighbourhood of Felegyhaza and Csonygrad, with Hildebrand at full gallop, a delightful sunburnt Uhlan officer by my side, loaded pistols lying in the hay before us, and a squadron of Uhlans with ready carbines in their hands wildly dashing after us. Three swift horses drew us, called Rosa, Csillak (star), and Betyar (vagabond). The driver unintermittingly called them by name, in a piteous tone, until he got his whip handle well

over their heads, and with a cry of *"mega! mega!"* (hold on!)
the gallop changed into a wild career. A delightful sensation! We saw no robbers; as my light-brown lieutenant
told me, they knew before daylight that I was travelling
under protection; certainly some of them were among
those worthy-looking and dignified peasants who gazed
seriously at us at the stations, in their sleeveless sheepskin
cloaks reaching to the ground, and greeted us with an
honourable "*istem adiamek*" (praised be God)! The sun's
heat was scorching all day—I am as red as a crab in the
face. We made eighteen miles in twelve hours, to which
must be reckoned two or three hours, if not more, in
putting-to and waiting, as the twelve horses I required
had first to be caught for myself and escort. A third of
the distance was shifting sands and downs, like those of
Stolpmünde.

At five I reached this place, the streets of which are
animated by a gay crowd of Hungarians, Slowaks, and
Wallachians, who fill my chamber with a din of the
wildest and maddest gipsy melodies. (Szolnok is a village
of some six thousand inhabitants, but there is a railway
and steam-boat station on the Theiss.) At times they
sing through the nose, with gaping mouths, in a weak
minor discord, histories of black eyes, and of the brave
death of some robber, in sounds that remind one of the
wind howling Lettish songs down the chimney. The
women are generally well grown, a few remarkably handsome; they all have raven hair, bound in tresses behind
with red ribbons. The married women wear either bright
green and red cloths, or red velvet caps on their heads;
about their shoulders and bosoms a handsome yellow silk
shawl; black or pure blue short gowns, and red Turkey
leather shoes, reaching up under the petticoats. Their
faces have a yellowish brown hue, with lustrous black eyes;
a group of these women present a play of colours that
would please you; every colour is as distinctly expressed as

possible. Since my arrival at five I have been swimming in the Theiss, while expecting dinner. I have seen Csardas danced; it vexes me that I cannot draw, to bring these fairy-tale forms on paper for you. I then had *paprika, stürl* (fish), and *tick* for dinner, drank a good deal of Hungarian, and now shall go to bed, if the gipsy music will let me sleep. ˙ Good night! *Istem adiamek.*

———

Pesth, the 28th.

Again I see the mountains of Ofen, this time from the Pesth side, from below. From the plains I have just left, the dim outlines of blue Carpathian ridges, distant some twelve or fifteen miles, are in some places, when the air is very clear, barely distinguishable. To the south and east the plain was fathomless; in the first direction it stretches far away into Turkey, in the second towards Siebenbürgen. The heat to-day was again scorching, and has peeled all the skin from my face. A heat-storm is now raging, driving so fiercely over the steppes, that the houses tremble. I swam in the Danube, saw the magnificent suspension-bridge from beneath, paid visits, heard very good gipsy music on the parade, and shall soon go to bed. The parts on the edge of the Pusta, where it is beginning to be cultivated, remind me of Pomerania, in the neighbourhoods of Rommelow, Romahn, and Coseger. The gipsies have greyish-black complexions. Their costume is fabulous; the children quite naked, except a string of glass pearls about their necks. Two women had handsome, regular features, and were cleaner and more ornamented than the men. When the Hungarians want a dance over again, they shout in a surprised tone, " *Hody wol? Hody?* " (" What was it? What?"), and look at each other interrogatively, as if they had not understood, although they know the music by heart. It is, indeed, a singular people, but pleases me very well.

It was just as well I had the escort of Uhlans. At about the same time I left Ketskemet for the south, sixty-three waggons went off in a northerly direction towards Körös. Two hours later they were stopped and plundered. A colonel, who was by accident driving before this waggon-train, had some shots sent after him, as he would not halt. One horse was shot through the neck, but not enough to bring it down, and as he returned the fire, with his two servants, flying at full gallop, they preferred to be satisfied with the other travellers. They did no other harm to any one, and only plundered some individuals, or rather ransomed them, for they do not take all a person has, but only in proportion to property, and according to their own needs; for instance, they will quietly receive forty florins out of a thousand, without touching the remainder. Thieves with whom one can talk!

Vienna, the 30th.

Here I am again at the "Roman Emperor." While you were looking from the Castle of Coblenz on the Rhine in attendance on our King and Lord, I was looking from the Castle of Ofen upon the Danube, and had an after-dinner conversation with the young Emperor upon the Prussian military system; and, oddly enough, on the same afternoon on which you visited Ehrenbreitstein and Stolzenfels, I took a drive through the Citadel above the palace, and into the forest district of Ofen. The view from the first is admirable. It reminds one of Prague, only there is more background and distance, therefore rather resembles Ehrenbreitstein, and the Danube is grander than the Moldau. I reached here last night, per the Pesth train, about half-past six.

Bismarck, as usual, was invited to the Royal hunting party in the autumn, as we perceive by the following letter to his wife :—

Blankenburg. 1st Nov., 1852.

A very unusual early rising, caused by the circumstance that my room is a passage for some Court servants still asleep, gives me time for these lines. Our Queen is also here, and is just being awakened by soft music of horns. I have not had such good sport in Letzlingen this time as three years ago ; it was on Friday. Only three stags, *voilà tout;* one of them I hope will reach you. Eat the wild boar devoutly, and pickle some of it. His Majesty shot it with his own gracious hand. Otherwise, things went off very well ; and, as I found N. N. there, I need not go to Berlin, and hope to reach you by the evening after to-morrow, of which please inform ——, as well as that his appointment for Berlin at our Court may be regarded as certain.   B.

The band is still playing very well from the Freischütz, —" *Ob auch die Wolke sie Verhülle* " (If the cloud still doth surround her); very apt in this doubtful weather.

In the following year he received many visits from the Duke of Schleswig-Holstein-Sonderburg-Augustenburg, for whom he was engaged at the time, at the instance of the King's Government, in obtaining a pecuniary settlement of the Duke's claims with Denmark. Bismarck was able, with great difficulty, to extract from very unwilling Denmark a handsome compensation. At this the Duke was so rejoiced, that he devoted himself and followers, with the entire gratitude of the House of Augustenburg, to the policy of Bismarck, as is well known.

In the summer of 1853 Bismarck first visited Ostend and Holland, then Westphalia and Nordeney. He then had a mission to Hanover, of which he rendered an account at Potsdam. In the autumn he spent a considerable time with his family in Switzerland, at Villeneuve, on the Lake of Geneva, and thence visited Upper Italy, especially Aosta and Genoa. In October he was summoned to Potsdam by His Majesty the King; was present at the hunting parties of Letzlingen, and then returned for the winter to Frankfurt; some time, however, he spent in Berlin.

During the summer trip, which Bismarck made alone, he wrote the following letters to his wife :—

Ostend, 19th August, 1853.

Up to the present time, besides the one of to-day, I have taken three baths, with which I have been well pleased; there is a strong sea and soft bottom. Most people bathe close under the pier forming the parade, ladies and gentlemen all together; the first in very unbecoming long gowns of dark woollen, the last in a tricot, being jacket and trousers in one piece, so that the arms above and the legs beneath are almost free. Only the consciousness of possessing a perfectly well-proportioned form can allow one of us to produce himself in ladies' society thus.

Brussels, 21st August, 1853.

I have left Ostend with sorrow, and really wish myself back again : I found an old sweetheart of mine there, and as unchanged and charming as on our first acquaintance. I really feel the sorrow of separation deeply at this moment, and look forward impatiently to the instant when I shall cast myself on her heaving bosom at Nordeney. I can hardly understand why people cannot always live by the sea, and why I have been cajoled into passing two days in this parallelogrammatic stone heap, to see bull fights, Waterloo, and pompous processions. If I had not to keep that most unlucky appointment with N. N., I should stay several weeks longer in Ostend, and give N. N. up. I shall only remain till noon to-morrow, and then start, or early the next morning for,

Antwerp, Rotterdam, and Amsterdam; thence by steamer to Harlingen, and through Friesland to Nordeney. I am afraid N. N. will soon disturb me there, and if I once get to Bremen with him, I hardly know whether I ever shall accomplish the tiresome journey to N. again, but shall make my way by Hanover, Hamm, Kassel, and Frankfurt to the place you inhabit. If you write to me, direct to Nordeney.

Amsterdam, 24th August, 1853.

In Brussels and Antwerp I have never had a quiet minute on account of feasts and sightseeing. I have passed a detestable night on a campstool, in a crowded boat from Antwerp, starting at one in the morning. By an angular labyrinth of arms of the Scheldt and Maas, and the Rhine, I reached Rotterdam early, about eleven, and about four arrived here. That is a singular town : many streets are like Venice, some with water right up to the walls, others like canals with a towing path, and with narrow walks planted with limes before the houses. The latter have fantastic gables, strange and smoky, almost ghostly—the chimneys like men standing on their heads and stretching out their legs. That which does not savour of Venice is the busy life, and the massive handsome shops—one window close to the other, and more magnificently than I remember those of Paris or London. When I listen to the bells, and, with a long clay pipe in my mouth, look through the forest of masts, across the canals into the twilight towards the roman-tically confused gables and chimneys, all the Dutch ghost stories of my childhood come back to me, of Dolph Heylinger, and Rip van Winkle, and the Flying Dutch-man. To-morrow morning I go by steamer to Harlingen on the Zuyder Zee, and to-morrow evening I hope to be in Nordeney, the farthest point from you I propose to touch ; and then the time will not be far off when I hope to encounter you unexpectedly on a glacier. I have nothing from Berlin since I left Ostend, and therefore conclude that the storms are all laid, and the waters returned into the old bed—the pleasantest event that could happen for us. I am very glad I have seen Holland ; from Rotterdam to this place, there is one continual verdant and level meadow, upon which there are many bushes, much grazing cattle, and some old cities cut out of picture books : no arable land anywhere.

Norderney, 27th Aug. 1853.

Last evening I arrived here on a stout Dutch sloop, amidst thunder, lightning, and rain—have, after an abstinence of a week, taken another glorious sea-bath, and am sitting in a fishing hut with a feeling of great loneliness and longing for you—partly heightened by the clamour of mine host's children, partly by the piping scream of the storm against the roof and flagstaff. It is really tiresome here, and that suits me, as I have a long piece of work to finish. I wrote to you last from Amsterdam, previously from Brussels. Since then I have seen a charming little country—West Friesland ; quite flat, but so bushy green, hedgy, every farm-house surrounded by its little wood, that one seems to envy the peaceful independence reigning there. —— will probably ascribe this satisfaction to the circumstance that, as at Linz and Gmünden, all the girls are pictures of beauty, only taller and more slender, fair, colours like milk and roses, and a very becoming helmet-like golden head-dress.

In the spring of 1854 we find Bismarck at Potsdam, in the summer at Munich and Stuttgart. On the 28th of June he wrote to his sister from Frankfurt, thus :—

I should have liked under all circumstances to have brought you my good wishes in person, particularly as I know my roving wife is with you. But unfortunately we seem too important to ourselves here, to deprive confused Europe of the light of our wisdom. Whoever speaks of holidays now is regarded as a traitor to the world-important problem of the Germanic Confederation. I long deeply for the country, the forest and laziness, with the *obligato* addition of affectionate wives and well conducted clean children. If I hear one of these hopefuls crying in the street, my heart is filled with parental feelings, and educational maxims. How do our descendants agree, and are mine good? I have been obliged to write these few lines at three intervals, because N. N. and N. N. East and West disturbed me during the time, and Z. is just announced : he won't go for an hour, so I say farewell. I want to go fishing with the Englishman to-day, but it rains too much, so instead I am a victim of visitors. Farewell and live long. Your faithful Brother.

Bismarck then accompanied the King, who grew continually more attached to him, to the island of Rügen ; by Pomerania, Berlin, and Baden he returned to Frankfurt.

During the summer of 1855 he visited the Exhibition at Paris, residing with the Prussian Ambassador, Count Hatzfeld, and was introduced to the Emperor of the French. Afterwards he went to Stuttgard and Munich, and then visited the King and Queen at Stolzenfels. The year 1856 was comparatively quiet, and he passed his summer at Stolpmünde.

Reinfeld, in Pomerania, 11th Sept., 1856.

The Diet will, I think, in November, devote its sessions to the Holstein question with greater goodwill than results.

Outwardly all the governments will appear united in this matter. Austria will, however, secretly remain an adherent of the Danes; its press will teem with German phrases, and Prussia will be saddled with the error of inaction. The centre of gravity of the affair actually does not lie at Frankfurt, but in the question whether Denmark is secure from the assaults of one or more of the extra German States. If she be, then she will look upon the decision of the Diet as a sufficient settlement.

From Courland Bismarck returned to Berlin and Potsdam, and thence went to Baden; afterwards he was at Hohendorf in East Prussia, and Reinfeld in Pomerania. These were certainly years of apprenticeship, but still more years of journey. In the following years he was frequently summoned to the Prince of Prussia in Baden-Baden; he then went to Stolpmünde, and remained in Berlin throughout October and November. During these years the following letters were written to Frau von Arnim, the two last containing some notices of the Ministry of the so-called "new era"—Bismarck speaking in a very intelligible way as to his own position.

BISMARCK TO FRAU VON ARNIM.

Reinfeld, 15th Oct., 1856.

It looks as if I never was to reach Kröchlendorf. Harry will no doubt have told you how I intended to do so. I should already have been with you, but last week my poor little Marie was seized with some kind of chicken-pox, and so I could not well leave Johanna until the symptoms were declared. She is still as variegated as a trout, but decidedly better. I wanted to set off to-day for Passow direct, but yesterday had a letter from ———, by which he lets me know that he wants to see me by the 18th at ———. As a diplomatist I cannot refuse to meet our trustiest companion, and one of the Olympian deities of our Frankfurt Pantheon. If I receive no letter from Berlin in between, I hope to rest in your sororial arms by the 19th. Should I be able to get away from —————— on the evening of the 18th, I shall leave by the early train from Stettin. If I cannot do this, I still hope to reach Stettin by the twelve o'clock train, if the postillions can be got to a trot. But do not wait dinner for me.

———————

THE SAME TO THE SAME.

Frankfurt, 26th Nov., 1856.

· Bernhard will have told you by what unexpected chain of infantine disease and royal mandates I have been deranged in my chronological calculations, and how ——————, who has claims upon my ideas of the service, also abridged my lecture, so that it happened, a few hours before we were about to set out for Kröchlendorf, all together, that I had to announce to the male as well as the female Bernhard that I could only escort them as far as Passow. At that frontier of the Uckermark I met ——————, and in Angermünde we were joined by ——————, so that I was gradually prepared, by ministerial conferences and three hours of smokelessness, for my Berlin strait-waistcoat. It seemed as if I was never to get to Kröchlendorf. I had plenty of time and desire to do so, after the terminations of the Berlin marriage festivities, and only after a conference with —————— did I decide first to go to Reinfeld, and, on my return, to you, in order to stop a week with him there; because he only got his holiday in October, and our arrangement was that I should come hither with him about the 15th, and return to Berlin about the 22nd. On the 11th my child was taken ill, at first severely; then I had to attend to official parade. Then I was summoned to His Majesty at Berlin, where, on the 25th of October, I found myself early enough. And now I am here, have only seen the sun twice in the last month, and every day I say to myself that it is impossible in November to live without wife and children. From sheer ennui I give dinner parties. In the evening one rout succeeds another, and I shall soon begin to gamble if Johanna and the children do not occupy this vacuum. She thought of starting from Reinfeld on Saturday the 22nd, but on the 20th wrote me a plaintive letter about cold and snow, which I received on the 23rd. Since then I have no idea whether she is on the other side of the Gollenberg or this side of the Randow. I begged her generally to inform you of her confinement in Berlin beforehand, and to let you know from Cöslin by telegraph when she would actually arrive there. The last time I lived in —— very fairly, but it appeared to me this youthful undertaking must either not have taken place, or already been "over." If Johanna should by accident be in Berlin, greet her from me. Perhaps I shall get there by Saturday. I am summoned to the Upper Chamber, but the contents do not assure me whether His Majesty wishes me to be there *myself* personally, or only desires to see his most humble servant *en bloc*. In the latter case I should not consider myself called to leave my important business, and the stove in the red study, to sit up to the neck in snow at Halle, and next heighten the effect of the White Saloon by a flying costume under the rubric of " People, nobility, detectives, and priests." I expect an answer from Berlin about this, as to whether I am wanted as an ornament or a coadjutor. In the latter case I should reach Berlin early on Saturday. I should be very glad on that occasion to see you, as some recompense for Kröchlendorf; otherwise, I am glad to remain away from Berlin, and receive my own folks here.

———

TO FRAU VON ARNIM.

Frankfurt (without date).

While I was forced to hear an almost incredibly long speech by a highly esteemed colleague on the anarchical condition of things in Upper Lippe, I thought how I could use the time, and the most prominent want of my heart seemed to be a desire to pour forth fraternal feelings. A very highly respectable but slightly amusing company surrounds me, at a green-covered circular table, some twenty feet in diameter, in the ground floor of the Prince of Tour and Taxis' palace, with a view of the garden. The average appearance of these folks is somewhat like that of N. N. and Z. in Berlin—they have quite a Federal Diet cut!

I go out shooting pretty regularly, when a single individual shoots some six to fifteen hares and a few pheasants —very seldom a roe or a fox—and a head of red deer is sometimes seen in the far distance. Time for this I have been able to spare from being far more lazy, as my industry in Berlin led to no results.

N. N. is by no means as charming as he used to be; he listens to all kinds of lying stories, and allows himself to be persuaded that I am anxious for his heritage, although I am glad to be left where I am. I am getting accustomed, in the consciousness of yawning innocence, to submit to all symptoms of coldness, and permit a spirit of entire indolence to possess me, after having, I flatter myself, gradually brought the Diet to a knowledge of its piercing nihilism. The well-known song of Heine, "*O Bund, du Hund, du bist nicht gesund*" (O! Diet, you dog, you are not well), will soon be unanimously adopted by resolution as the national anthem of the Germans.

Nobody troubles themselves about the East here. The Russians or the Turks may put what they like in the newspapers; nobody believes either in land or sea fights, and doubts the existence of Sinope, Kalafat, and Schefketel.

Darmstadt has at last stopped reading—and I fall, full of emotion, into your arms, and wish you a pleasant feast. Many greetings to Oscar.

Your faithful Brother,

B.

TO THE SAME.

From Paris, Hotel de Douvres, April, 1857.

I have five stoves, and am freezing—five clocks, and never know how late it is—eleven great looking-glasses, and my necktie is always awry. I shall probably have to remain here until Tuesday evening, although I am anxious to be at home. Since November I have not emerged from this Bohemianism—since November, and I have not had a sensation of regular and lasting domesticity since you went last summer with Johanna to Schwalbach. Now they want to summon me to Berlin about the salt tax; if I had the time, I could not take part in this debate. I cannot, according to my conviction, vote for the Government; but, if I vote for the Opposition, it is hardly proper to ask for leave of absence on such an account; and, considering the rumours as to my eventual entry into the Ministry, of which Johanna, on account of your statements, writes despairingly, one could think I had some ideas of joining in the swindle. Hearty greetings to Oscar.

B.

In the spring of 1857 we again find Bismarck in Paris, and it was then that he had his first special political conference with the Emperor Napoleon. In the summer he made a journey to the North—went to Denmark and Sweden, ending by field sports in Courland; on his return he found his family at Stolpmünde.

While on this journey he wrote the following letter to his wife :—

Copenhagen, 6th August, 1857.

This morning at seven I safely arrived here, after a very pleasant passage; mild air, a red moon, the chalk cliffs lighted by tar-barrels; two storms at sea, and a little wind; what more can one want? The night prevented my sleeping, and when the rain drove me from the deck about two o'clock, it was so hot and reeking of humanity below, that about three I went on deck with cloak and cigar. I have now taken a sea-bath, eaten some lobster, and about half-past one I must attend at the Court—so now I will sleep a couple of hours.

Räsbyholm, 9th August, 1857.

You will have already received the few lines I wrote directly I reached Copenhagen. Since then I have been occupied for two days with museums and politics, yesterday was ferried over to Malmö, and driven some eight miles to the north-eastward, and am at the above-named place, in a white castle situated very high on a peninsula surrounded by a large lake. Through the window and the thicket of ivy, that admit of some view of the water and hills beyond, I perceive that the sun is shining and flies are buzzing. Behind me sits ———; he is reading and dozing; broad Swedish is spoken under the window, and from the kitchen I can hear a pestle grinding away like a saw. That is all I can tell you of the present. Yesterday we stalked roebucks, one was killed, but I did not shoot; we got thoroughly drenched; then we took hot wine, and slept soundly for nine hours. Roebucks are more plentiful than I have ever seen anywhere, and the neighbourhood is prettier than I thought. Magnificent beech forests, and walnut trees the size of a man's body, in the garden. We have just visited the pheasantry; after dinner we are going on the lake, and may perhaps shoot a duck, unless we fear to disturb the Sunday rest of this lovely solitude by a shot; to-morrow we are to have a regular day, next day we return to Copenhagen, and from there to N. N., and a stag hunt on Wednesday; Thursday by Copenhagen to Helsingborg, some twenty miles into Sweden. We shall seek woodcocks and moorfowl in the wilderness; we shall lodge in farm-houses; our provisions we take with us. This will last for about a week, and then I hardly know what I shall do; either proceed by way of Jönkeping, at the south end of Lake Wetter, and so to Stockholm, or by Götheborg and Lake Wener, or to Christiania, abandoning Stockholm, or perhaps *viá* Memel to Courland. This depends on a letter I expect from —— in Copenhagen.

———

Tomsjönas, 16th Aug., 1857.

I again employ the quiet of Sunday to give you some sign of life, although I do not yet know on what day we shall find an opportunity of reaching the post from this wilderness. For some fifteen miles have I driven into the depths of the woods to reach this place, and before me lie some twenty-five miles ere we shall get to cultivated provinces. There is no town, no village, far or near—only isolated settlers and plank-huts, with a little barley and potatoes, strewn irregularly between dead trees, rocks, and thickets, over a few rods of ploughed land. Think of the wildest region near Viartlum,* for some hundred of square miles, tall heather, varied by short grass and moorland, beset with birch, juniper, pines, beech, oaks, and alders, sometimes unpassably thick and sometimes very sparse, the whole sown with innumerable stones to the size of houses, smelling of wild rosemary and firs; and between them strangely formed lakes, surrounded by sand and forest—and you will see Smaland; where I now am. Really the land of my dreams, not to be reached by despatches, colleagues, and N. N., but unhappily also for you; I should like to have a hunting-box on one of these quiet lakes, and people it for a few months with all the dear ones I now fancy are assembled at Reinfeld. It would be impossible to winter it out here, particularly amidst the dirt of the rain. Yesterday we started about five, and hunted in the burning heat, up hill and down dale, through bog and bush, until eleven; but found nothing at all. It is very tiring to walk through moors

* One of the Putkammer estates in Pomerania.—K. R. H. M.

R

and impassable thickets of juniper, over great stones and underwood. We slept in a hay barn till two, drank a great deal of milk, and continued the chase till sunset, killing twenty-five woodcocks and two snipes.   We then dined at the lodge—a wonderful structure of wood—on a peninsula by the lake.   My room, with its three stools, two tables, and bedstead, presents the same uniform tint of rough pine planks, as does the whole house and its walls.   The bed is very hard, but after all this exertion one sleeps without rocking.   From my window I see a knoll with birch trees, whose branches rustle in the breeze; between these the mirror of the lake, and beyond it fir forests.   Beside the house is a tent for huntsman, driver, servants, and peasants; then the carriage-house and a little dog of a village of some eighteen or twenty huts on both sides of a little street, and from each of these a tired beater is looking out.   I propose to remain in this oasis till Wednesday or Thursday, then leave for another expedition on the shore, and return this day week to Copenhagen, on account of miserable politics.   What next, I do not know as yet.

The 17th.—This morning early six wolves have been here and have torn up a poor bullock; we found their fresh traces, but personally we did not see them.   From four in the morning till eight in the evening we have been in motion, have shot four woodcocks, slept for two hours on mown heather, and now, dog-tired, to bed.

The 19th.—It is impossible to send a letter to the post from here, without sending a messenger twelve miles; I shall therefore take this to the coast myself to-morrow.   Yesterday, when the dog pointed, and I was looking more at him than at the ground I was treading on, I fell and hurt my left shin.   Yesterday we had a very tired day's sport, long and rocky; it produced me a woodcock; but has tamed me so completely, that to-day I am sitting at home with bandages, so that I should be ready to travel to-morrow and shoot the next day.   I really am astonished at myself for stopping at home alone in such charming weather, and can scarcely refrain from the abominable wish that the others will shoot nothing. It is a little too late in the year, the birds are shy, or sport would be more plentiful. We shot through a charming place yesterday; great lakes, with islands and shores, mountain torrents, over rocks, plains for miles without houses or plough-land; everything just as God created it, forest, field, heath, morass, and lake. I shall certainly return hither some day.

Two gentlemen of the Danish Chambers are already back; it was too hot for them, and they have gone to sleep. It is about half-past five; the others will only arrive about eight. I have been amusing myself all day in learning Danish from the doctor who applied the bandages. We brought him with us from Copenhagen, for there are no doctors here. Since a report has been spread of the presence of a physician in the woods, every day some twenty or thirty inhabitants of the huts come streaming in to take his advice. On Sunday evening we gave a very amusing dance to the inhabitants of the five square miles of forest; the music was played and sung by turns. Then they heard of the "wise man," and now cripples of twenty years' standing come and hope to be cured by him.

————

Königsberg, 12th Sept., 1857.

I found to my great joy your four letters at Polangen (which, by the bye, is not in Prussia but Russia), and find from them that you and the children are well. I got on very well; the Courlanders were all touchingly kind to me, in a way seldom found by a foreigner. Besides several roebucks and stags, I shot five elks, one a very fine stag, measuring roughly six feet eight, without his colossal head. He fell like a hare, but as he was still alive, I mercifully gave him my second barrel; scarcely had I done so ere a second came up, still taller, so close to me that

Engel, my loader, had to jump behind a tree to avoid
being run over. I was obliged to look at him in a
friendly way, as I had no other shot. I cannot get rid of
this disappointment, and must complain to you about it.
I shot at another—no doubt he will be found—but one I
missed entirely. I might, therefore, have killed three
more. The night before last we left Dondangen, and in
twenty-nine hours made forty miles without a road,
through the forest and desert to Memel, in an open carriage, over stock and stone ; we were obliged to hold on,
so that we should not be thrown out. After three hours'
sleep at Memel, we started this morning in the steamboat
for this place, whence we leave for Berlin to-night and
arrive to-morrow. " We " means Behr and myself. I
cannot stop in Hohendorf ; I ought to have been in Berlin
to-morrow, my furlough being up. I should, however,
have been obliged to give up my best sport at Dondangen,
with the enormous stags, or, as they call them there, *bolls ;*
nor should I have seen how the axle of a great waggon
broke under the enormous creature. On Monday the
Emperor arrives at Berlin, therefore I am obliged to be
there " some days " before. I hope to return from Berlin
to Hohendorf and Reinfeld ; but if the King goes to
Frankfurt, this is unlikely.

Frankfurt, 19th December, 1857.

Your true sisterly heart has offered in so friendly a
manner to look after Christmas exigencies, that I will not
apologize if I now allow you to carry out the seductions of
Gerson and other rascals once more, and ask you *sans
phrase* to make the following purchases for Johanna:—

1. Jewelry : she wishes to have an opal heart, like yours,
and " the mind of man his kingdom is." I am willing to
pay some two hundred *thalers* for it. If for that price it
is possible to obtain a pair of earrings, each consisting of
one clear brilliant, I should think it more tasteful. You

have some like it, but they are much dearer, and should you think the opal heart preferable, I will try later to find a pair of fitting earrings founded upon pearls.

2. One dress, at about 100 *thalers*—not more. She wants to see herself "very light and bright," *à deux passes, moirée antique*, or something of that kind: she requires ten *rods*—about twenty ells.

3. Should you discover a valuable and pretty gilt fan, rustling a great deal, buy it also. Ten *thalers* are quite enough. I can't bear the things.

4. A large warm rug to lay over the feet in the carriage, with designs of tigers, glass eyes in their heads; might be a fox or hippopotamus—any ferocious animal. I have seen one at ——'s, of very soft wool; won't cost ten *thalers*. If you want to remain a charming sister, buy me all this, and send at once by *express luggage train;* address, Hofrath —— Prussian Embassy.

I have so much to write about Holstein, Mainz, the Bridge of Kehl, and all sorts of things in Berlin, that I have been obliged to decline two capital days of sport, to-day and to-morrow, after red deer. Johanna and the children are well, and the former would send love if she knew I wrote; but do not let her know anything about it, . my heart, and so farewell. Greetings to Oscar. The money I will send through Fritz, the receiver, by the new year.

Frankfurt o. t. M., 2nd April, 1859.

I quite agree with you that our position in the Zollverein is blundered. I go further than this, being firmly convinced that we must give notice to the whole of the Zollverein, as soon as the term has arrived. The reasons for this conviction are far too stratified to be developed here, and they are too closely connected to be named one by one. We must terminate the treaty in view of the danger of remaining alone with Dessau and Sondershausen. It is, however, not to be *desired*

that this last should be the case, or that such a state
of things should long subsist; therefore we must render
it agreeable—if possible, an unavoidable necessity—to
the other states of the Zollverein, during the period yet
to run, that after proper notice has been given they should
seek adherence to *our* conditions.   One portion of this
system would be to allow them to draw higher nett
revenues than they could obtain by frontier customs
without Prussia.   Another thing is that they must not be
allowed to think that the continuance of a Zollverein with
Prussia is impossible in fact; this would, however, be the
case if, besides the twenty-eight governments, some fifty
class corporations, guided by particular interests should
be able to exercise a *liberum veto*.   If the Prussian
Chambers begin with this, the equality vertigo of the
German governments will not allow the rest to remain
behind; they will desire to make themselves also of importance.

In order to avoid these rocks in a Zollverein to be re-
constituted by Prussia, after 1865, for the exercise of
corporation electoral rights, I think we shall have to
adopt one feature of the Union project of 1849, and erect
a sort of Customs Parliament, with conditions for *itio in
partes*, if the others demand it.   The Governments will
object gravely to such a course; but if we are daring and
consequent we could effect much.   The idea expressed
in your letter, to make the Prussian Chambers a means,
by their representation of all German taxpayers, to found
a hegemony, is from the same point of view.   The most
powerful aids of our foreign policy might consist in the
Chambers and the Press.   In the present state of things,
which may be confirmed by the vote, the Zollverein
policy, the evil of the Verein for Prussia, would render
the necessity for the termination a matter for the most
circumstantial and closest debate, that a recognition of it
should take place; your letter ought to appear as an

article in the *Kreuzzeitung*, instead of lying upon my table here. The German Custom policy should be broadly and unreservedly discussed from the Prussian stand-point by the Chambers and the Press—then the flagging attention of Germany would be drawn to it, and our Chambers would become a power for Prussia in Germany. I should like to see the Zollverein and the Bund, with Prussia's relations to both, subjected to the scalpel of the acutest criticism in our Chambers. This would only be an advantage to the King, his Ministers, and their policy, presuming them to know their business. At the same time, I could wish, as the result of such a discussion, that the proposition should be *adopted* by a small majority. For the Zollverein desires at the present moment rather to fetter the German governments to their flesh-pots, than for them to win the sympathies of their subjects. The latter are powerless, as, so far as they are concerned, a powerful, business-like, and honourable debate would do the same, as the chance of the results of a vote.

Frankfort, 12th Nov., 1858.

Your letter was an unexpected pleasure ; the address looked just like one of Johanna's, and I wondered how she could have got to the Uckermark. I have not been able to answer before : business, a cold, hunting, has partly taken up all my time, nor did I quite know what to write to you about the new phenomenon in the political heaven, that I could not have written as well about the comet. An interesting phenomenon wholly unexpected by me, the object and nature of which is yet unknown to me. The orbit of the comet our astronomers are pretty well able to calculate, but it would be difficult for them to do the same by this new political septasterism. Johanna reached here safely with the children this morning ; God be praised, they are well, but not in good spirits. She is upset by all the political

terrors they have filled her with in Pomerania and Berlin,
and I try in vain to render her more lighthearted. The
natural distress of the lady of a house also influences her,
when it becomes doubtful whether one remains in a new
house set up with care and expense. She came hither
with the idea that I was about to take my leave. I do
not know whether my resignation will be forced on me
without my own will, or whether I must seek it for
decency's sake. Before I do it voluntarily, I shall wait
to see what the ministerial colours are.

If the Upper Chamber retain their feelings for the
conservative party, and sincerely strive for a good understanding and peace *at home*, they may rely upon a healthy
state in our *foreign* affairs, and that is of great importance
to me, for "we had fallen, and did not know how." That
is what I especially felt. I think that the Prince has
been especially placed at the head to secure a guarantee
against party government, and against any concessions to
the Left. If I am mistaken in this, or if they wish to
dispose of me as an office seeker, I shall retire behind the
cannon of Schönhausen, and observe how Prussia can be
governed by majorities of the Left, and also endeavour to
do my duty in the Upper Chamber. Change is the soul
of life, and I shall feel myself ten years younger if I find
myself in the same attitude as in 1848-9. Should I not
find the parts of gentleman and diplomatist consistent,
the pleasure or the burden of fulfilling a prominent
position will not cause me to err for a moment in my
choice. I have enough to live upon according to my
wants, and if God keeps my wife and children healthy, as
they have been, I say "*vogue la galère*," no matter what
water we swim in. It will be very unimportant to *me*,
after thirty years, whether I play the diplomatist or the
country Junker; and hitherto the prospect of an honest
contest, without being confined by any official tram-
mels — particularly in political swimming-baths — has

almost as much charm for me as the prospect of a *régime* of truffles, dispatches, and grand crosses. "After nine, all is over," says the player. I cannot tell you more than these personal opinions—the enigma stands before me unsolved. I have one great satisfaction here at the Diet. All those gentlemen who six months ago demanded my recall as a necessity for German unity, now tremble at the thought of losing me. To ———— the phantom of 1848 is a terror; and they are all like pigeons who see the hawk—afraid of democracy, barricades, Parliament, and . . . ———— sinks into my arms touchingly, and says, with a cramped shake of the hand, "We are again forced into *one* field." The French naturally, but the English also, look upon us as firebrands, and the Russians fear that the Emperor will be led astray by our plans of reform. I say to every one naturally, "Only be calm, and all will come right;" and they answer, "Yes, if you were going to stay, then we should have a guarantee, but . ." If he doesn't feel Frankfurt singing in his ears, he has no ear-drums. In a week he has been degraded from a worthy liberal conservative in the imaginations of his eventual colleagues, to a scarlet tiger—helper's helper of Kinkel and D'Ester. The Bamberg diplomatist talks of a continental assurance against Prussian firebrandism, growls of a tri-Imperial alliance against us—a new Olmütz with effectual operations. In short, the political world is getting less tiresome. My children cry, "Pietsch comes!" in the joy at my having a servant of that name at Schönhausen; and it would seem that the arrival of this Pietsch and the comet are not without significance. Heartily farewell, my very dear one, and greet Oscar. He must not hang down his head—it's all gammon.

———

Frankfurt, 10th Dec., 1858.

You had rightly guessed, in your letter to Johanna, that your kindness would be asked for a Christmas commission. I should like to give Johanna a bracelet. The kind of thing flitting before me is broad, smooth, mailed, bending, made of chessboard-patterned little four-cornered gold pieces—*without* jewels—pure gold, as far as two hundred *thalers* will go. If you find something that pleases you better, I have every confidence in your taste. The exact thing in the fashion is not, *therefore*, pleasing to me—such things last longer than the fashion. Be so good, and have it directed to "Privy Councillor ———, Prussian Embassy," with an enclosed letter for *me*, or the old gentleman may think it a delicate attention for *himself*.

Johanna will have written you as to the child complaints we have had, and how I have suffered from colds and coughs. I do not know whether much or little sleep, diet or excess, housekeeping or hunting, improves or hurts, but I turn from one to the other, from ideas of health. As to my transfer or recall, all is still again; for a time, Petersburg seemed very certain, and I had grown so accustomed to the idea, that I felt quite disappointed when the rumour went forth that I was to remain here. There will be some bad political weather here, which I should be very glad to weather out in bear-furs, with caviar and elk-shooting. Our new Cabinet is still looked upon abroad with suspicion; Austria alone, with cunning calculation, gives it a meed of praise; while ———, behind his hand, warns us; and so do his colleagues, at all the Courts. The cat won't let the mice alone. But, in the end, the Ministers must show a policy; merely cursing the Kreuzzeitung will not last for ever. I shall hardly come to Berlin in the winter; it would be very agreeable if you would visit us here before I am " put out in the cold " on the Neva.

———————

St. Petersburg, 12th May, 1859.

I have become convinced, by the experience of the eight years of my official life in Frankfurt, that the settlement by the Diet, made in those days, form a pressing, and, in critical times, a vitally dangerous fetter for Prussia, without giving, in return, such equivalents, enjoyed by Austria, under an unequally large mass of free self-action. The two greater Powers do not attain an equal measurement from the Princes and Governments of the smaller States ; the construction of the object and the law of the Diet is modified according to the requirements of Austrian policy. I need not, considering your knowledge, enter upon more circumstantial arguments respecting the history of the policy of the Diet since 1850, and hence confine myself by naming the paragraphs concerning the restoration of the Diet, the question of the German Navy, Customs disputes, the laws respecting commerce, the press, and the Constitution, the Diet fortresses of Rastatt and Mainz, and the questions of Neuenburg and the East. *We have always found ourselves face to face with the same compact majority, with the same demand for concessions from Prussia.* In the Eastern question, the power of Austria has ever proved so superior to ours, that even the identity of the wishes and aspirations of the Diet governments, with the efforts of Prussia, have presented for her an ever-receding obstacle. With scarcely any exception, our associates in the Diet have given us to understand, or have even openly declared, that they were unable to maintain the Diet with us, should Austria pursue her own course ; although it is unquestionable that federal law and real German interests were side by side with our peace policy ; this, at least, was then the opinion of almost all the Princes. Would the latter have ever brought their own interests and wishes as a sacrifice to the wants, or even the safety, of Prussia ? Certainly not : for their attachment to Austria is founded on outbalancing false interests, which prescribe to both a coalition against Prussia, a repression of all further development of the influence and power of Prussia, as a foundation for their common policy. A

development of federal relations, under Austrian leadership, is the natural end of the policy of the German
Princes and their Ministers; according to their opinions,
this can only be accomplished at the expense of Prussia,
and is necessarily directed against Prussia, so long as
Prussia will not confine herself to the useful problem of
providing for her equally entitled associates in the Diet
an assurance against the preponderance of Austria, and is
willing to bear the disproportion of her duties towards
her rights in the Diet, being resigned to the wishes of the
majority with untiring complacency. This tendency of
the policy of the Central States will reappear with the
constancy of the magnetic needle after every evanescent
variation, because it represents no arbitrary product of
individual events or persons, but is, in fact, a natural and
necessary result of federal relations for the smaller States.
There are no existing means by which we can maintain
the actual federal treaties in an intimate manner.

Since our associates in the Diet, some years ago, began,
under the guidance of Austria, to bring to light, from the
hitherto neglected arsenal of the constitution of the Diet,
the principles that would give prominence to their system
—since it has been endeavoured, in a partial way, to stifle
the policy of Prussia by propositions which could only
possess one signification in the sense of their proposers, in
so far as they apply to the unanimity of Prussia and
Austria—we have been obliged to endure the stress of
the situation that the Diet and its whole historical development has forced upon us. We could say to ourselves, that in peaceful and orderly times we could weaken
the evil in its results by skilful treatment, but we should
be powerless to effect a cure; it is only too natural that in
dangerous times, such as the present, the other side, in
possession of all the advantages of the Diet settlement,
should willingly confess that much has taken place of an
improper nature, but should at the same time declare, in

the " general interests," that the present juncture is
highly inapplicable for the discussion of past matters and
" internal " disputes. But such an opportunity, if we do
not make use of it at once, may not so speedily recur ;
and in the future we shall be forced to our normal
resignation, which allows of no changes in the condition
of things in orderly times.

His Royal Highness the Prince Regent has taken up
a position commanding the unqualified approval of all
those who are entitled to form any judgment of Prussian
politics, and who thence have not allowed themselves to
be disturbed by party feeling. Some of our associates in
the Diet seek to blind us, by thoughtless and fanatical
efforts, as to this attitude. If the statesmen of Bamberg
are so frivolously ready to follow the first war outcry of
an uncritical and mutable public opinion, if it does not
take place probably quite without a comforting after-
thought of the easiness with which a small state can
change its colours in case of need ; but if, in order to
send a power like Prussia under fire, they desire to make
use of the treaties of the Diet ; if it be supposed that we
shall substitute property and blood for political wisdom,
and the thirst for action on the part of governments, to
whom our defence is absolutely necessary for their
existence ; if these States think they are to dictate the
guiding impulse, and regard *theories concerning the rights
of the Diet* as means to such an end, then *with such recognition all Prussian political autonomy would be over ;* then, in
my opinion, it would be time for us to remember that the
guides, who imagine we should follow them, serve other
interests than those of Prussia, and that they understand
the interests of Germany they talk so much about as non-
identical with the interests of Prussia, if we decline to
accede to their desires.

Perhaps I am going too far when I express it as my
opinion, that we should seize every justifiable opportunity,

presented by our associates in the Diet, to arrive at the revision of our mutual relations, necessary to Prussia, by which she can exist in defined relations to the smaller German States. I think we should willingly take up the gauntlet, and regard it as no misfortune, but as real progress, a crisis leading to improvement, if a majority at Frankfurt should decide upon such a vote, which we could look upon as a transgression of competency, an arbitrary change in the object of the confederation, a violation of its treaties. *The more unmistakable this violation the better.* We shall not easily find conditions of such a favourable nature in Austria, France, and Russia, by which we can alter our own position towards Germany for the better. Our allies are on the high road towards giving us perfectly justifiable motives for such a course, without our stimulating their insolence. Even the *Kreuzzeitung*, as I see by the number of last Sunday, is becoming somewhat startled at the thought that a Frankfurt majority could immediately dispose of the Prussian army. *Not in this newspaper alone* have I hitherto perceived with sorrow how Austria has established an autocracy over the German press by the skilfully laid net of her influence, and how well she knows to use the weapon. Without this, so-called public opinion could scarcely have risen to this height; I designate it so-called, for the real mass of the population is never inclined for war, unless the demonstrable suffering of real oppression has aroused it. To such a pitch has it risen, that even under the cloak of general German opinion, any Prussian newspaper can hardly declare itself in favour of Prussian patriotism. General Twiddle-twaddle plays a great part in this, nor must we omit the Zwanzigers (cash) that never fail Austria for this aim. Most newspaper correspondents write for their bread and cheese, most newspapers look to their incomes, and an experienced reader may easily see, by our newspapers and others, whether they have received, or speedily anticipate, or wish by threatening pantomime to force, a subsidy from Austria.

I think we should produce an admirable revulsion in public opinion if we were to sound the chords of independent Prussian policy in the press, in opposition to the exaggerations of our German allies. Perhaps things may happen at Frankfurt which may give us full reason to do so.

Under these circumstances the wisdom of our military precautions might be extended in other directions, and impart significance to our attitude; then Prussian self-respect would speak perhaps with a more conclusive tone than the Diet. *I should only then care to see the word "German" in place of "Prussian" inscribed upon our standard, when we should have become more intimately and effectually bound up with our German fellow-countrymen than we have hitherto been;* the word loses its charm in proximity to the ideas of the Diet.

I fear that your Excellency will interrupt me in this epistolary digression into the field of my former activity, with the cry, "*Ne sutor ultra crepidam;*" nor was it my intention to hold an official oration; I desired only to present the testimony of an experienced person against the Diet. *I see in our position in the Diet, a defect of Prussia, which we shall have sooner or later to heal, ferro et igni,* unless we adopt in time, and at a proper season of the year, measures for a cure. Were the Confederation abolished this very day, without substituting something in its place, I believe that this negative acquisition would soon form better and more natural relations between Prussia and her German neighbours, than have hitherto existed. BISMARCK.

TO A PRUSSIAN DIPLOMATIST.

Petersburg, 1st July, 1859.

I thank you for your letter, and hope you will not allow the first to be the last. Among the matters which in-

A BALL AT BISMARCK'S.

thousand Prussians, for whom one has to be police, advocate, judge, assistant, and councillor—every day there are twenty to fifty signatures, without passports. I am still, as it were, in camp, with a few beds, towels, and caps, bought in a hurry; without cook and kitchen, as all utensils are wanting—and, in all this heat, without summer clothing! My house is large enough, and handsomely situated on the Newa; three great saloons, two of them larger than those at Seufferheld's; I have had the Chancery placed in one, with a good flooring, looking-glass doors, and silver chandeliers. All that I have as yet received from Frankfurt are my weapons, unfortunately packed under some crown chandeliers in such a way that three guns were quite broken to pieces, and the barrels ruined. I wonder what wiseacre packed them! If the rest of the things have been packed so, I may perhaps congratulate myself if they have been lost. The insurance is small, if the plate is with it; the premium high, because the fool has insured against "war risk!"

———

Hohendorf, 3rd February, 1860.

I still hear with pleasure, and with a sort of longing for home, all intelligence concerning the state of things and persons at Frankfurt; and, when I read the papers, I often feel a desire to hurry into the midst of battle at the sessions. The campaign over the war constitution was capital. Let them proceed openly and daringly to urge our demands; they are too just not finally to be, although slowly, recognized. The Sovereign States, by grace of the Rhenish Confederation and the Diet, cannot rely upon their particularity for any duration against the stream of events. As in my recovery, there may occur a time of standing-still and relapse occasionally; but it still will go forward, when we courageously *dare* and are not ashamed of our daring any more, but openly proclaim in the Diet, in the press, and, above all, in our

Chambers, that which we desire to represent in Germany, and what the Federation has hitherto been for Prussia—an Alp and a noose about our necks, with the end of it in the hands of the enemy, that only waits the proper moment to run it tight.   But enough of politics.

I hope soon to be in trim for my journey—am perhaps already so.   My wife and the physicians conjure me to go south—to Heidelberg or Switzerland.   I long for Petersburg, that I may at last live quietly in my own house.

Petersburg, 16th June, 1860.

We are pretty well at present, and I am much better than if I were in Germany without being wanted.   Rest and the comforts of domestic life are doing their best.   It is 24° in the shade,* but always cool nights.   Business proceeds, thanks to so delightful a Minister as Gortschakoff, without annoyance—in short, *cela va bien, pourvu que cela dure.*   Our relations here are excellent, no matter what the newspapers may fable about it.

The Augsburger people and Company are still afraid lest I should become Minister, and think they can prevent it by abusing me and my Franco-Russian ideas.   It is a great honour to be dreaded by the enemies of Prussia.   My political flirtations in the spring, at the Court, and with the Ministry, have, furthermore, been so accurately sifted that they are well aware of what the state of the case is, and how I am believed to find precisely in the national aspirations powers of resistance and strength.   If I *am* written down a devil, it is a Teutonic one, and no Gallic fiend.   ——'s lie factory might attack me much more to the purpose on other grounds than on Buonapartism, if they wish to make an impression at our Court, as among the Augsburgers.

St. Petersburg, 22nd August, 1860.

I am quite excluded from home politics, for with the

* 74° Fahr.—K. R. H. M.

exception of newspapers, I only receive official statements, which do not give me the ground-work of things. According to these, we have promised nothing definite at Teplitz, but have made our support of Austria dependent upon that *practical* demonstration of her good-will towards us in German politics; when this has been done, she may reckon on our gratitude. I should be very content with this; and if we only see the Vienna soap in a lather, we should be glad to return the service. Certainly the indirect accounts we receive from other courts sound otherwise. According to these, if true, though we have not concluded any guarantee treaty, we have, at any rate, bound ourselves verbally to assist Austria, under all circumstances, should she. be *attacked* by *France* in Italy. Should Austria find it necessary to act on the offensive, our consent would be requisite, if our co-operation is to be anticipated. This version appears more unprejudiced than it would, in fact, be. Austria having security that we should fight for Venice, she will know how to provoke the *attack* of France—it has been asserted that since Teplitz, Austria has come out boldly and defiantly in Italy. Viennese politics, since the Garibaldian expedition, desire to make things in Italy as bad as they can be, in order that if Napoleon himself should find it necessary to declare against the Italian Revolution, movements should commence on all sides and former conditions be assimilatively restored. This reckoning with and upon Napoleon may be very deceptive, and it would seem as if, since Teplitz, it has been given up, and there were hopes of attaining results by *opposing* Napoleon. The restless, passionate character of Austrian politics endangers peace in both ways. What will the Chamber say to Teplitz—to the organization of the army? All sensible men will naturally agree with Government as to the latter. But the influence . of foreign politics can first be estimated, when it is known *what the meaning of Teplitz really is.* A well informed but somewhat Buonapartist correspondent writes to me from Berlin, "We were prettily taken in at Teplitz by Viennese good-humour; sold, for nothing, not even a mess of pottage." God grant that he errs in this! In speaking of the Buonapartists, it occurs to me that some kind of general rumours reach me, that the press, *National Verein, Magdeburger, Ostpreussische Zeitung*, carry on a systematic war of calumny against me. I am said to have openly supported Russo-French pretensions respecting a cession of the Rhine province on the condition of compensation nearer home; I am a second Borries, and so on. I will pay a thousand Fredericks-d'or to the person who will prove to me that any such Russo-French propositions have ever been brought to my knowledge by any one. In the whole period of my German residence I never advised anything else than that we should rely on our *own* strength, and in the case of war, upon the aid of the national forces of Germany. These foolish geese of the German press do not see that in attacking me they are losing the better part of their own efforts. I am informed that the fountain-head of these attacks was the Court of Coburg, in a writer who has personal spite against me. Were I an Austrian statesman, or a German Prince and Austrian reactionist, like the Duke of Meiningen, our *Kreuzzeitung* would have protected me as it has him; the mendacity of these assaults is unknown to some of our political friends. As I am, however, an old member of their party, entertaining particular ideas upon certain points, well known to him to his misfortune, I may be slandered to their hearts' content. I hear of the whole affair principally from the *officious* advocacy of the *Elberfeld Zeitung*, which is sent to me. There is nothing like inquisitors among themselves, and friends, who long have partaken of the same cup, are more unjust than foes. I am satisfied. One ought not to rely on men, and I am thankful for every breath which draws me inward.

Stolpmünde, 18th Sept., 1861.

In reference to the Conservative programme, I fully subscribe to your observations. The *negative* construction prevailing throughout of the propositions should have been avoided from the first. A political party can never stand, much less conquer position and adherents, by a mere languid defensive policy. Every party professes to abhor the dirt of the German Republic, and the Opposition now forming give themselves honest trouble not to have it—that is, the dirt. A figure of speech so much wider than the requirements of the time, either means nothing, or conceals what people do not desire to say. I myself am in doubt whether the authors of the programme do not really stand at the pure Würzburg point of view. Among our best friends, we have so many doctrinaires who ask from Prussia an identical duty of protecting foreign princes and countries as she protects her own subjects. The system of the solidarity of the conservative interests of all countries, is a dangerous fiction as long as the fullest and most honest reciprocity does not exist between the rulers of all countries. Were Prussia to carry it out in isolation, it would become Quixotism, which would only weaken our King and his Government in the solution of the most important question, viz., that defence of Prussia confided to the Crown of Prussia by the Almighty, against injustice coming from within or without. We are gradually making the whole unhistorical, ungodly, and illegal sovereignty swindle of *those* German princes who use the confederation as a pedestal whence to play at being European powers, into the nurse child of the Conservative party of Prussia. Internally our Prussian *Government* is liberal; abroad it is legitimist. We respect foreign crown rights with greater constancy than we do our own, and become enthusiastic about those lesser sovereignties created by Napoleon and sanctioned by Metternich, to blindness against all the

perils with which the independence of Prussia and
Germany is threatened in the future, as long as the
nonsense of the *present* Confederation endures, which is
nothing more than a hothouse of dangerous and revolutionary efforts. I could have wished that, instead of
vague expressions against the German Republic, it had
been openly stated in the programme what we desire to
see changed and restored in Germany, whether by justly
directed efforts towards alterations in the constitution of
the Confederation, such as definite associations like the
Customs Union, and the Military Treaty of Coburg.
We have the double task of giving evidence that the
existing Confederation is not our *ideal*, but that we
purpose to attempt the necessary alterations openly in a
legal way, and that we do not intend to go *beyond* these
in confirming security and prosperity. To us the
necessity of a firmer consolidation of our defensive powers
is as patent as that of daily bread; we require a new
and plastic system of customs, and a number of institutions in common, to defend material interests against the
evils resulting from the unnatural interior configuration
of German frontiers. There should be no doubt as to the
sincerity and earnestness with which we ask for these
objects. Nor do I see, moreover, *why we should recoil so
prudishly from the idea of popular representation, whether in
the Diet, or in any customs, or associative parliament.* Surely
we cannot combat an institution as revolutionary which
is legally established in every German State, and which
we Conservatives even would not wish to see abolished,
even in Prussia. In national matters we have hitherto
regarded very moderate concessions as valuable. A
thoroughly conservative national representation might be
created, and yet receive the gratitude of the liberals.

I am interrupted by the sounds of packing. In case
you still have an opportunity of conferring with our friends
on the subject, I enclose you the sketch I read to you, with

the request, however, that it shall not become public, as I am unaware whether the King would like that this hasty memorandum of the conversation I had with His Majesty, and which I committed to writing at his command, should become known, as I hear several discussions have taken place about it.

Berlin, the 2nd Oct., 1861.

In Koblenz and here I have been active for German politics, and in the present state of things not quite without results. I wrote about the 19th of last month from Stolpmünde to your residence here, and enclosed in my letter the draft of the short sketch I had presented to the King. I am to carry this matter into greater detail. If, therefore, the letter and enclosure, as I hope, has reached your hands, I beg of you to send it me to Reinfeld, that I may work it up more completely there. I am really home-sick for my household on the English Quay, with the tranquil view of the Neva ice. On the 13th, it will be necessary to meet at Königsberg.

Berlin, the 16th May, 1864.

I can understand your hesitation against the address, which, however, in my opinion, at the present time seizes the diplomatic position with useful pressure. I may certainly be mistaken in this, for the longer I act in political affairs the less is my confidence in human calculation; and if you feel an inward opposition to it, I speak the less of it, as I would rather be able to declare with a good conscience that the Government has not inspired the idea mirrored in it. The actual state of things, however, is such, that it appears very necessary to let loose all the dogs willing to give tongue (forgive this sporting simile) against Denmark at the Conference; the general cry of the pack will effect a conviction on the part of alien Powers that the subjection of the Duchies to Denmark is an impossibility, and the

latter will be obliged to consider projects which the Prussian Government cannot present to them. Among alien
Powers in this last category I class the Holsteiners themselves, together with the *Augustenburg*, and all the eternally
ignoble down to Königsau. The Duchies have hitherto
played the part of the birthday child in the German family,
and have accustomed themselves to think that we are
willing to bring every sacrifice to the altar of their particular interests, and are willing to risk the existence of
Prussia for every individual German in the north of
Schleswig. The address will especially counteract this
frenzy; I do not fear that it will have so strong an effect
as to bring us into any difficulty. If Prussian ambition
were to rise to such a height among the nation, so that
the Government, instead of stimulating, would have to
moderate the feeling, I should not at all regret such
a condition.

You will perceive from this how I comprehend the
matter from a human point of view. As to the rest, my
impression of gratitude for God's assistance till now rises
into a conviction that the Lord knows how to turn even
our errors to our benefit. I daily observe this with salu-
tary humility.

To clear up the situation I will conclude by saying
that to me Prussian annexation is *not* the chief and necessary end, but probably the most agreeable result.

With hearty salutation to your honoured household, I
am yours,

BISMARCK.

That Bismarck not only followed the German policy of
Austria, but also her whole political action, with the lynx
eyes of an opponent, is a matter of course, and he soon
perceived on what a dangerous error this was based.
Relying upon the apparent power which Prince Schwarzenberg's daring moves, and Radetzky's victories over Sar-

dinia had obtained, Austria desired to attain to a European hegemony for herself by diplomatic trickery. By amity with France she wished to keep Italy down; by amity with England to overawe Turkey; by the alliance of both, as well as by the pressure she thought to exert over Prussia and the other German States, to humble and lame Russia, in whom she saw the sole antagonist of her visionary hegemony. This plan, however, which explains the attitude of Austria during the Eastern war, was condemned to failure, as the massive power of Russia, under the most favourable circumstances, could only be transitorily shaken by the temporary alliance of England and France; was condemned, as France certainly did not remain quiet in the west, out of pure friendship for Austria, after measuring swords with Russia in the East; was condemned because England scarcely would do anything for Austria after attaining her ends in the East; finally, it was most certainly condemned, as Austria undervalued the power of Prussia to an almost incomprehensible degree. Bismarck foresaw this failure, and, in his opinion, Prussia ought to make use of the crisis which had arrived to save herself and Germany from Austria. Hence at Berlin he continually urged the uttermost possible increase in the strength of the army. Nor were his warnings neglected, but, to his deep sorrow, circumstances took such a form that when the crisis actually came Prussia made no use of the situation. When the Italian war broke out, when Prussia did not declare against Austria, the Ministry thought the presence of Bismarck in Frankfurt had become an impossibility, and he was recalled. It was reserved for Bismarck himself, eight years afterwards, to carry through his German policy, by which Prussia was alone to accomplish her proper position, although at that time it was in alliance with France. Bismarck, in 1858, left the scene of his activity in Frankfurt with a heavy heart. He was convinced it was only there, where he was so accurately acquainted with the

ground, that he could render his King and country important services. He departed with patriotic indignation at
the contempt which Austria openly showed towards
Prussia, but he also knew that a time of retribution would
arrive.

His position at Frankfurt gave Bismarck an advantage
not lightly esteemed by the statesman. Frankfurt lies like
a great hotel on the road into which the great European
travelling guild especially loves to call in the summer
time. Not only did the representative of Prussia entertain princely guests, related or friendly to the Royal
House of Prussia, but gradually became acquainted with
a great number of the ministers and diplomatists of all
European States. Among the princely personages whom
he received in Frankfurt, and to whom he afterwards paid
his respects in the watering places close at hand, we
should especially name the Grand-Duchess Helena of
Russia, a born Princess of Würtemberg and widow of
the Grand-Duke Michael Paulowitsch, a lady of extraordinary abilities, and well informed in political matters,
whose influence is said to be very great, and that not alone
in Russia.

Among the states-
men whose acquaint-
ance Bismarck made
upon the Rhine, we
must first name the
venerable Prince
Metternich, to
whom he paid a
visit, shortly after
his arrival in Frank-
furt in the summer
of 1851, at the
Castle of Johannis-
berg. He had many conversations with the man who

had so long conducted the policy of Austria, in more than one respect, in so masterly a manner, and, in contradistinction to Schwarzenberg, had ever evinced a statesmanlike amenity towards Prussia, and continued to do this in a very distinct manner.

Metternich and Bismarck seated together at the Johannisberg! The one venerable with age, who had been everything; the other a man who was to become everything. The representative of the past, and the representative of the future; the past had been allotted to Austria, the future was to be the heritage of Prussia. The present and the Johannisberg constituted the neutral ground where the last remains of Austrian good-will towards Prussia, and the last fragments of traditional reverence for Austria in Bismarck's patriotic heart, were to meet. The two statesmen parted from each other with mutual respect.

CHAPTER II.

BISMARCK ON THE NEVA.

1859—1862.

Ambassador to St. Petersburg.—Illness.—Journey.—Hunting.—The Coronation of William I.

WE have already stated that Bismarck would have preferred to remain at Frankfurt, because he hoped to be useful to Prussia; and he personally complained to the Prince Regent of his transference. The Prince Regent, on the other hand, demonstrated to him that such an official position in St. Petersburg was one of the first in the

diplomacy of Prussia, and that he ought to regard his
mission there as a distinction. It was, perhaps, fortunate
for Bismarck that thus placed in a remote position from
the party spirit of those days, he was able as from an
observatory to watch the course of political events, both
inwardly and outwardly, and allow his views to assume
distinctness, his plans to ripen. To his many journeys
was also due the preservation of personal interests. The
peculiar good-will with which he was received by the
Czar, and especially by the Empress-Mother at that time,
he knew how to preserve, at the same time winning the
respect of the Russian statesmen. Of his life in these
days, his letters, which we shall presently communicate,
addressed to his wife and sister, afford us most characteristic traits. From this time forward, sadly enough,
several attacks of indisposition appear, which dull the
picture of manly strength and health we have hitherto
beheld in him. In March he set forward on his journey
to St. Petersburg, and assumed his new office on his
birthday, the 1st of April, 1859; in May he went to
Moscow, but upon his return he became seriously ill, and
suffered greatly from a rheumatic attack in the left leg,
which was very painful to him.

He there placed himself in the hands of his physicians.
One evening a blister was applied to the calf of the leg,
and Bismarck went to sleep, but soon awoke in raging
tortures, which increased to such a degree that he tore
away the blister, and with it some portion of the flesh.
Perhaps in the end this proved his salvation, but such
remarkable symptoms of illness appeared that it was
necessary for him to ask permission for leave of absence
in Berlin. The Emperor was terrified at the alteration in
Bismarck, when he came to present his letters of recall.
After a miserable journey Bismarck arrived in Berlin, but
in a pitiable state. He remained there at the Hotel
d'Angleterre in a hopeless condition ; the physicians

treated him with iodine, without, however, any result, and in this condition he was found by his wife, whom he summoned from Pomerania. Madame von Bismarck, in everything touching her husband, possesses the greatest energy and affection; herself instructed in the healing art, she had all the iodine bottles thrown away, and devoted herself to the sick bed. From this time the condition of Bismarck visibly improved, and although much still remained ere he could regard himself as fully convalescent, he was at any rate enabled to seek further health and strength at Wiesbaden and Nauheim. The cure, however, was very incomplete, and it cost him a great effort to perform the duty of receiving the Emperor Alexander at Warsaw, and attending him to Berlin. After this he sought retirement for a while with his family at Reinfeld, whence he proposed to return to his post in St. Petersburg in November.

Reinfeld has been so often mentioned in these pages, and that spot of ground has so much significance for Bismarck, that some few notes concerning it cannot be unwelcome to the reader. Reinfeld lies in the undulating hill country slanting from the Baltic land ridge towards the Eastern Ocean, close to the left bank of the Stolpe, in a very pleasant part of Pomerania. The mansion of Reinfeld presents that peculiar type of Christian amiability,* which, in its unaffectation, produces so pleasant an effect on the visitor. There is nothing artificial about it. In the courtyard no oaths are heard, but in place of these the venerable Herr von Putkammer raises his velvet skull-cap, and from his lips come the peaceful words, "Let us all return our thanks unto the Lord," &c., when at harvest home the reapers enter with the corn-wreath of increase.

Bismarck had often fled to these fragrant Hinder Pomerania thorn-thickets for rest and refreshment in the

---

* See Wangemann's "Ringen und Regen," ("Strife and Activity,") on the Ost See Shore.

summer time from busy official life and the social saloon
of office. Hitherward he bent his steps cheerfully from
Berlin and Paris, from Frankfurt and St. Petersburg.
Here, with heartfelt contentment, he greeted his ancient
friend, the forest; and in the neighbourhood of Reinfeld
there are many select localities remaining as proofs of his
never-resting spirit of enterprise—as green trophies of his
creative power. Frau von Bismarck, too, had grown up
in Reinfeld. There she lived, at the service of all, with
words of comfort and active aid, as well as with medical
counsel, prudent enough to amaze many an experienced
physician. Nor has Frau von Bismarck denied herself
such a sphere of helpful activity in her town life. Like a
true woman, she has forgotten her own sorrows to take
care of the humblest persons around her, and thus she
has ever been a true helpmate for her consort in heavy
labours and in dark hours. Frau von Bismarck possesses
a fine ear for music. Her passionate performance has
often delighted and soothed her husband amidst his cares,
when the storms of life assailed him, and the waves ran
high. How often has he sat still at night and listened to
her melody, receiving the mighty influence of music into
his heart of hearts!

On his journey from Reinfeld to St. Petersburg, in the
November of 1859, Bismarck was taken dangerously ill
at the house of his friend Alexander von Below, a
Member of the Upper House, at Hohendorf in Prussia,
beyond Elbing. The next station on the Eastern Railroad is Güldenboden (Goldbottom), which gives some
conclusion as to the prolificacy of the Hohendorf district
and agricultural system. After his illness there was a long
period of reconvalescence, but Bismarck was comforted
by having all his dear ones at hand. Herr von Below
and his excellent sister, Mademoiselle Jeannette von
Below, evinced princely hospitality. Besides Bismarck,
his wife and children, his father and mother-in-law, Herr

and Frau von Putkammer, remained for weeks at Hohen-dorf, together with Miss Fatio, the friendly home-spirit of the Bismarck family, and the boy's tutor, Candidate Braune, now preacher at Strausberg-on-the-Barnim.

On the recovery of his health, Bismarck went, in March, 1860, to Berlin, where he took part in the Sessions of the Upper House; in May he returned to Hohendorf, whence he conducted his family to St. Petersburg. They started for Königsberg on the 30th May, slept at Marienpol on the 31st, at Wilkomierz on the 1st June, on the 2nd at Dünaburg, on the 3rd at Regitza, and on the morning of the 5th the travellers arrived in St. Petersburg. The railway was not completed at the time, so that some portion of the journey between the frontier and Dünaburg was performed in carriages.

Bismarck had hired the house of Countess Stenbock, on the English Quay, with a fine view of the Neva, the quarter of Wassili Ostrov, and the Nicholas Bridge. When Bismarck had his family about him, he felt at home on the Neva. He also took a special master, in order to learn the Russian language; and it is said to have very much pleased and astonished the Emperor Alexander when Bismarck first answered him in Russian. It is no trifling task to learn Russian; we know persons who have frequently attempted to do so, but have always abandoned the task in despair. Bismarck was much in society, at the Court of the witty Archduchess Helena. There was no lack of sporting parties; he hunted the elk, the bear, and the wolf. At Varzin, as at Berlin, may be seen many trophies of his skill from the North. These bear-hunts were very contributive to his conva-lescence, and he warded off many a cold on these expeditions, in the bitter weather. Bismarck, who was always a friend to dumb animals, had much amusement in some young cubs he kept in the house, until they grew into the ornaments of the Zoological Gardens at

Frankfurt and Cologne, at a later age. Mischka (such is the Russian name of the young bear) often made his appearance, as did the foxes at Kniephof, to the great amusement of the guests, at the dinner table; and walked about among the plates and glasses on the cloth, nipped the servant in the calf of the leg, or slid about on the slide in the dining-room.

During this Petersburg time, Bismarck was able to devote himself more fully to the education of his children. Every Saturday they appeared before their father with their exercise books, and reported what progress they had made during the week. Then followed a short examination, which evinced his minute accuracy in scholastic teaching, and even the tutor who was present learned something —the method of education. In later years Bismarck has been unable to spare time for such examinations, the duties of his office having entirely absorbed him.

Among the gentlemen who then frequented the house of Bismarck, we will mention the then Royal Prussian Commissioner, Freiherr von Loën (now General); Captain von Erkert (now Colonel); the historian Legation Councillor von Schloezer; the Prince von Croy and his old friend, Count von Kaiserling; Baron Nolde; and Count Yxkull. In the aristocratic circles of Russian society Bismarck was very greatly prized and esteemed, and this not alone on account of the favour accorded to him and his wife by the Imperial family. The Chancellor, Prince Gortschakoff, at all times regarded him with the greatest interest, and stood in continued and agreeable relations with him. Bismarck's sporting skill and fortune became almost proverbial in the Court circles of Petersburg. From an authentic, although Suabian, source, the following anecdote was related to us, how Bismarck and seven others went a bear-hunting :—" On their return, one of the seven was asked, ' How did things go?' and he replied, ' Very

T

ill for us, father. The first bear trotted in ; the Prussian
fired, and down fell the bear. Then came the second, and I
fired, missed, and Bismarck shot him dead at my very
feet. Then came the third bear ; Colonel M. fired twice and
missed twice ; then the Prussian knocked him over with

one barrel. So Bismarck shot all three, and we could get
no more. It went very ill for us, father ! ' " Bismarck, in
his Russian hunting-coat, high boots, and big brown juff's
leather cloak, was a magically imposing sight.

The following year, 1861, Bismarck spent the most of
the summer in Pomerania, and part of it in Baden-
Baden, where he was considerably consulted by King
William in political affairs. In the large coronation
painting by Menzel, he forms a conspicuous and sig-
nificative object. From Königsberg he returned to his
post at Petersburg.

His outward appearance had much changed : he looked
much more like what we see him now. His once rich hair

has grown somewhat thin, which makes the forehead very prominent; his enormous beard had disappeared in Frankfurt; the features are very marked, but a humorous smile still plays about his lips; his eyes retain their fire, and his firm bearing is still preserved. In his letters the old hearty spirit still is evident in all its freshness, nor is good-humour wanting; but sometimes there is a feeling of mournfulness, which, although slightly toned, still shows that  he had not come unwounded from the fierce contest.

The following letters belong to this period of his career :—

BISMARCK TO HIS WIFE.

Pskow, 28th March, 1859.

Russia lengthened herself out under our wheels, and at each station the versts gave birth to young; but we have now run into the haven of the railway. From Königsberg we travelled for ninety-six hours without intermission; at Kowno we slept four hours, and three in Egypt (a station near Dünaberg), I think, the day before yesterday. I am now very well, but my skin is still burning, as I was outside almost all night, and we changed from 1 to 12 degrees of cold, R. The snow was so deep that we literally remained sticking with six to eight horses, and had to descend. The slippery hills were worse, particularly in going down; it took us an hour to go twenty paces; the horses fell down four times, and all eight got the harness complicated together. Add to this night and

T 2

wind—a real winter journey. It was impossible to sleep
in consequence of the cold; yet it was better to be in the
air. Sleep I shall recover. The Niemen was free; but
the Wilna, a river you scarcely would know, as broad as
the Maine—the stream like a torrent, with blocks of ice.
The Düna was only fordable at one place, where we were able
to cross, with four hours' waiting and three hours' labour.
The whole region resembles Hither Pomerania, without
villages, chiefly like the district of Bütow and Bohren;
some good forests, but the majority like the coast of New-
Kolpizlow. Many birch woods, morasses for miles, the
road straight as a line; a post-station at from every 14 to
22 versts, like Hornskrug, very well arranged, everything
to be had, and plenty of warmth—everybody very civil,
and the service punctual. Beyond Dünaberg there was a
want of horses; at one station near Kowno we waited
three hours, and then only obtained tired animals. Where
the road was good they went excellently—at half-mile
pace, with our heavy, ponderous carriage; but through the
heavy parts they could not draw, skilful fellows as the
postilions were. The common class of man pleases me at
first sight. It is now six—we have just dined. Opposite
to me, as I write on the table-cloth, ———— is sitting,
meditatively smoking.

BISMARCK TO HIS SISTER.

Petersburg, 19/31 March, 1859.

Since early the day before yesterday, I have been
warmly and drily lodged here, in the Hotel Demidoff; but
I did not get here without great exertion. Scarcely had
I left Königsberg, eight days ago, than a lively snow
storm began, and since then I have not seen the natural
colour of the earth's surface. At Insterburg we began only
to make a mile an hour with couriers' horses. At Wir-
ballen I found a mail-post carriage, the interior of which
proved too narrow for my stature; I therefore changed

places with Engel, and made the whole journey on the outer seat, open in front: a narrow bench, with an acute-angled back, so that it was impossible to sleep at night, without reckoning the temperature, which reached 1,2.° In this condition I remained from Wednesday morning early until Monday evening, and, except during the first and last nights of railroad, I have only slept once for three hours, and once for two hours on the post-station sofa. The skin of my face peeled off when I arrived. The journey was so long, in consequence of the deep snow, which had newly fallen, and the want of a sledge-road; several times we were obliged to get out and walk, eight horses being unable to drag the carriage forward. The Düna was frozen, but about half a mile further up there was free water, by which we passed; the Wilna drifted with ice, the Niemen was open. Horses, however, were scarce, as each post required eight and ten instead of the usual three and four. I have never had less than six, although the carriage was not heavy. The guard, postilions, and outriders did their utmost, so that I set my face against horse-slaughtering. The icy hills were the greatest obstacle; the four hindmost horses, on one occasion, all tumbled over into a tangle—but the outriders on the right of the two foremost never stumbled—and hardly had they arisen than they went forward, in full career, with the fully-laden carriage, down hill and over bridges, at the top of their wind, amidst shouting and whipcord. They fell, only at step; but had they stumbled amidst the verst-long gallops on any declivity, we should have been the real —— of Prince ———! Well! it is over, and I enjoy the fun of having passed through it. The Neva here is like granite; but since yesterday there has been sunshine and thaw. It is well known that the town is handsome; but were I to abandon myself to the sentiment of wonder, it would arise from the extraordinary animation of the streets; despite their width, it requires good drivers to wind their way at a proper pace, carriages are so numerous ; the sledges disappeared yesterday. My commissions were completed the day before yesterday ; my address for ———— was written down the Chancery, as I had arrived unexpectedly.

1st April.—On writing this date, it occurs to me that to-day is my birthday, the first I ever spent amidst a rattling frost—for that has again set in—and, for twelve years, without Johanna. Yesterday I had a long audience of the Empress-Mother, and was delighted with the aristocratic nobility of the venerable lady. To-day I saw the Czar ; so that on my birthday I enter upon my new functions. The day before yesterday the Emperor shot two bears. Unfortunately, it is now all over with Petz ; he will not allow himself to be attacked, or rarely. The new snow has been, as it were, swept away by three days of thaw ; the whole country is said to be free. Business is just beginning. Loving letters to-day from Johanna and the children.

————

BISMARCK TO HIS WIFE.

Moscow, 6th June, 1859.

I will try to give you a sign of life, at least hence, while I am awaiting the samovar (tea urn), and behind me a young Russian, red-shirted, is troubling himself with entirely fruitless attempts to heat the stove ; he sneezes and sighs, but it won't burn. After having recently complained so much of the scorching heat, I woke up this morning, between Twer and here, and thought I was dreaming when I saw the country, with its fresh verdure, covered, far and near, with snow! I never wonder at anything now ; so, when I had satisfied myself that there was no doubt about it, I turned quickly on the other side to sleep and roll on, although the play of colours, green and white, was not without their charm in the redness of the dawn. I do not know whether it has melted away at Twer, but *here* it is gone, and cold drizzling rain is rattling on the green leads of the roofs. Green, truly, is the body-colour of the Russian. I slept some forty miles out of the hundred to this place; but the other sixty miles showed me nothing but every shade of green. I did not notice cities and villages, or even houses, excepting at the stations; thickset woods and birches cover morass and hill; some fine grass crop between, and long meadows. Thus it is for ten—twenty—forty miles. I do not remember to have noticed the bramble, and no sand; but lonely cows or horses grazing raised an idea that men were not far off. Moscow, from above, looks like a sown field—the soldiers green, the cupolas green, and I do not doubt that the eggs before me were laid by green hens. You probably know why I am here; I have asked myself, and immediately received the reply that change is the soul of life. The truth of this profound remark becomes remarkably intelligible, after living ten weeks in a sunny hotel apartment, with the aspect of paving-stones. Besides, the joys of changing apparel, when they repeat themselves frequently, become somewhat deadened; I therefore determined to deny them to myself, gave all the papers to ———, to Engel my keys, declared that I would return in a week to the Stenbock house, and drove to the Moscow terminus. This occurred yesterday at noon, and at eight this morning I descended at the Hotel de France. I will now visit a pleasant friend of earlier days, living some twenty versts off in the country; to-morrow evening I shall be here again; Wednesday and Thursday I shall devote to the Kremlin and such matters; and Friday or Saturday shall sleep in the beds which Engel will purchase in the meantime. To harness slowly, and drive rapidly, lies in the character of this people; I ordered the carriage two hours ago; to every enquiry I have had put at ten minutes' interval, for the last hour and a half, the reply is, "Directly!" with stolid, friendly quietness; and so it remains. You know my pattern-like patience in waiting, but everything has its bounds: presently we shall dash along, so that carriage and horses will break down in these bad roads, and we shall end our journey on foot. In the interval I have had three glasses of tea, destroyed several eggs, and the requirements of fuel have been so fully answered that I feel a desire for fresh air. Had I a looking-glass, I should shave from very impatience. This city is very spacious, and very strange, with its churches with green roofs and innumerable cupolas; far different from Amsterdam, although both are the most original cities I have ever seen. The amount of luggage brought here in the coupée no German conductor could divine. No Russian travels without two pillows, children in baskets, and masses of provisions of every kind. From politeness, I was complimented with a sleeping coupée, where I was worse situated than in my arm-chair. I am really astonished at making a journey under such circumstances.

Archangelski, late in the evening.

A year ago this very day I never even dreamt that I should be sitting here. On the river by which Moscow stands, some three miles away, amidst spacious gardens, lies a mansion in the Italian style. In front there is a broad, terraced, sloping lawn, surrounded by hedges like those of Schönbrunn, to the river side, and to the left of it a pavilion, in the six rooms of which I wander alone. On the other side of the water is a broad moonlit plain; here, grass-plats, hedges, and orangeries. The wind howls, and the flame flickers in the stove; old pictures look in a ghostly manner at me from the walls, and white marble statues from without. I return to-morrow, with my host, to Moscow; the day after to-morrow, by way of St. Petersburg, to Berlin. I shall remain, if it be the will of God, until Friday, to " see what is to be seen." My pen is very bad. I shall go to bed, though it looks broad and cold. Good night. God be with you, and all those sheltered by Rienfeld!

The 7th.—Despite the broad cold bed, I slept well—had a capital fire made up, and am looking over the steaming tea-urn out to the somewhat clearer, but still grayish, horizon, and into the entirely green surroundings of my pavilion. It is a pleasant spot of earth, and I have the comfortable feeling that I am beyond the reach of tele-graphs. My servant, like a true Russian, has, as I per-ceive, slept in my antechamber on a silken divan, and this would seem to be a domestic arrangement, servants not being provided with special sleeping accommodation. My pavilion has an orangery, now empty, attached to it, about 150 feet long, at the least—the winter inhabitants of which are at present planted out in the hedges in stately grandeur. The whole with its appurtenances is something like a very magnified ———— with rococo ap-pendices in the way of furniture, hedges, terraces, and statues. I am now going out walking.

Moscow, 8th June.—The city, as a city, is certainly the handsomest and most original in existence; the environs are friendly, neither pretty nor ugly; but the prospect above from the Kremlin, over the surrounding houses, with green roofs, gardens, churches, towers of the most extraordinary shapes and colours—most of them green, red, or bright blue, usually crowned by a gigantic golden ball, many with five or more on a church, unquestionably a thousand towers—something so curiously beautiful, as it appears in the setting sun, cannot be seen elsewhere. The weather is again clear, and I should remain here some days longer, had there not arisen rumours of a great battle in Italy which may lead to diplomatic work; so I will make haste to be at my post. The house in which I write is very remarkable, as being one of the few remaining from

1812, with ancient thick walls like those of Schönhausen, of Oriental architecture—great Moorish courts.

BISMARCK TO HIS WIFE.

Peterhof, 28th June, 1859.

By the preceding date, you can see I am again up. I drove here early, to take leave of the Empress-Mother, who sails to-morrow. Her charming sincerity has truly for me something of a character of maternity, and I can explain myself to her as if I had known her from a child. She conversed with me to-day for a long time on many subjects; she was lying in a *chaise-longue*, dressed in black, knitting at a white and red woollen shawl with long needles, on the balcony looking to the country. I could have listened to her deep voice and honest laugh and scolding for many an hour longer, I felt so at home. I had only come for two hours in undress; but as she finally said she did not wish to say farewell, but that I must have a great deal to do, I assured her nothing at all, and then she said, "You had better remain till to-morrow, when I leave." I accepted the invitation joyfully as a command, for here it is delightful, and in Petersburg so stony. Only imagine the heights of Oliva and Zoppot all laid out as parks, with a dozen palaces having terraces, fountains, and lakes between, with shady walks and lawns down to the sea-line, blue sky, and warm sun with white clouds, and beyond the green ocean of foliage, the real blue sea with ships and seagulls. I have not enjoyed anything so much for a long time. In a few hours the Emperor and Gortschakow will be here, and then some business will penetrate the idyll; but, God be thanked, the world seems more peaceful despite our mobilization, and I need make myself less anxious at certain conclusions. I am sorry for the Austrian soldiers; how can they be commanded, that they are always beaten? On the twenty-fourth again. It is a lesson for the ministers, which, in their stupidity, they will still not take to heart. I should fear France rather than Austria from the moment we took up arms.

28th, Evening.—After a drive for three hours in an open carriage through the gardens, and having seen all their beauties *seriatim*, I am drinking tea and looking at the golden evening sky and green woods. The Imperial family desired last night to be alone, for which I cannot blame them, and as a reconvalescent I sought solitude, and quite enough of it for this trip. I smoke my cigar in peace, drink excellent tea, and through the smoke of both gaze at a sunset of rare magnificence. The enclosed jasmine I send you as a proof that it really does grow in the open air and blossoms here. On the other hand, I must confess that I was shown the common chestnut in espalier as a rare plant, wrapped up in the winter. But there are very fine oaks, ashes, limes, poplars, and birches as thick as oaks.

BISMARCK TO HIS SISTER.

Peterhof, 29th June, 1859.

I wished to send you my good wishes in a pair of slippers by the steamer of the 25th, so that you would have received them this very day, but I could not even do it the week before, I lay so exhausted on my back. Since January in Berlin I have never been quite well, and anxiety, climate, and colds increased my originally unimportant rheumatism to such a pitch some ten days since, that I could not breathe without very great pain. The complaint, rheumatico-gastric-nervous, had settled in the liver, and was attacked by large cupping-glasses like saucers, and cantharides and mustard everywhere, until I succeeded, after having been half won for a better world, in convincing the physicians that my nerves, by eight years of uninterrupted anxiety and continual excitement, had been weakened, and that more tapping of blood would

lead to typhus or idiocy. A week ago yesterday was the
worst, but my good constitution soon came to my rescue,
after moderate quantities of canary were ordered. I came
hither yesterday—my first trip—to take leave of the
Empress-Mother, who is goodness itself towards me, and
at her desire I have remained here till her departure,
which takes place to-day about noon, to enjoy myself
with green and sea and country air after all my sufferings.
Do not write to Johanna about these details of sickness ;
I will tell her myself; I have till now only told her of
ordinary witchcraft. As soon as I am at rest I will write
especially to Oscar ; I was deeply touched by his long
letter, and should have replied long since, but before my
illness I was for a week in the neighbourhood of Moscow,
and the conduct of much business is doubly difficult by
the presence of the Court and Ministers in Zarskoe-Selo.
I hope to obtain my furlough in the first third of July,
and shall then go to Berlin, and I hope by Kröchlendorf
to Pomerania.

BISMARCK TO HIS WIFE.

Petersburg, 2nd July, 1859.

Half an hour ago a courier awakened me with tidings
of war and peace. Our politics are sliding more and more
into the Austrian groove, and if we fire one shot on the
Rhine the Italo-Austrian war is over ; and in place of it
we shall see a Prusso-French war, in which Austria, after
we have taken the load from her shoulders, will assist, or
assist so far as her own interests are concerned. That we
should play a very victorious part is scarcely to be conceded. Be it as God wills! it is here below always a question of time ; nations and men, folly and wisdom, war and
peace, they come like waves and so depart, while the ocean
remains! On this earth there is nothing but hypocrisy
and jugglery, and whether this mask of flesh is to be torn
off by fever or a cartridge, it must fall at last, and then the

difference between a Prussian and an Austrian, if of the same stature, will be so small that it will be difficult to distinguish between them. Fools and wise men, as skeletons, look very much like one another; specific patriotism we thus lose, but it would be desperate if we carried it into eternity.

BISMARCK TO HIS WIFE.

Saturday, Petersburg.

Until half-past three this morning I was engaged in writing. The sun then rose, and I went to bed, and have been at the ink-bottle from before nine again; in half an hour the steamer starts; —— is behind me. For three days together I have been obliged to go to Zarskoe-Selo, always taking up the whole day. I dined with the Emperor recently, in the clothes of four different people, not being prepared for dress; I must have looked very odd. Here people are very good to me; but in Berlin, Austria and all our dear allies are intriguing to get me away; and yet I am such a well-behaved person! Be it as God wills! I had as lief live in the country as not.

BISMARCK TO HIS SISTER.

Berlin, 14th Sept., 1859.

Forgive me for not answering your letter as yet. I thought I should be able to stay a few days longer at Rein-feld, but was yesterday suddenly telegraphed for. Formerly it took twenty-eight hours to reach here, but since the railway has been opened it takes thirty-two, and one has to get up at four o'clock. I have just arrived here at six o'clock, have satisfied my appetite, and now propose to sleep. I am to receive the Regent very early to-morrow morning at the station; thence probably to Potsdam, to receive letters and commissions; to-morrow evening off to Warsaw. I shall very likely return with the Emperor to Breslau, and thence come back here; perhaps we shall then be able to see each other for one day at last. A fourteen-seated carriage arrives at Tauroggen for me to-day: how long it will remain there Heaven knows—this vagabondizing in the autumn chills ending in the goal of winter is far from amusing.

_____

BISMARCK TO HIS SISTER.

Berlin, 24th Sept., 1859.

After I learnt from ———— that you had passed through Berlin, and had probably reached Kröchlendorf again, I made enormous exertions to be free by six to-morrow morning, and reach Stettin to-morrow night by way of Kröchlendorf. After having talked myself hoarse with mechanics and statesmen, I have become almost idiotic with anxiety, hunger, and business. I now at eleven o'clock do not know how to write either a short or simple letter to ———— on the business of the day; to rise to-morrow at half-past five, and commit some financial and legal matters to paper. _Je suis au bout de mes forces_ and must sleep, painful as it is to me to be compelled to dispense with my intended surprise for you to-morrow. I have already torn up two letters to Baden I had commenced. I cannot keep my thoughts fixed to the political cothurnus, and must defer my journey to Stettin till to-morrow night. There I shall sleep. The day after to-morrow I have to meet Bernhard at Freienwalde; he will accompany me as far as Labes, where the trains join; at night I shall sleep at Reddentin, and early on the 27th I start for Reinfeld, or Johanna will scratch my eyes out. It is her father's birthday, and horses are already ordered. If I thought this letter would reach you in time, I should try to persuade you to go to Reinfeld at the same time, but you would be worn out with the journey. I have greatly recovered, particularly during the fortnight at Baden. My left leg is still weak and swollen from walking, my nerves not yet recovered from the iodine. I still

sleep badly, and after the many people and things I have
seen and spoken to to-day, I am tired and angry; I do
not know what at, but I have very different ideas to those
of six weeks ago, when I cared little for living longer, and
the people who then saw me here say that they did not
believe to have had that pleasure to-day. Every Prussian
ambassador dies or goes mad, says ———, with a look which
vouches for the truth of his words. Other people, however, do the same. I hope to remain a fortnight at
Reinfeld, and then leave for the North. It is possible
that I may be called back here after the Regent's return,
and my journey may be delayed by that of the Emperor.
In any case it will be a winter journey; in Petersburg
there is already snow and two degrees of frost. I cannot
even wish for another post, as according to medical advice
I am to be lazy—and that is only possible at Petersburg—
unless I desire to resign altogether. I shall wrap myself
in bear-skins and be snowed up, and see what remains of
me and mine next May in the thaw. If there are too
few I shall return to agriculture and close with politics, as
Gischberg does in his fourth picture. It would be very
pleasant, however, if we could see each other before the
winter sleep; should I return in a fortnight this would
be easy, otherwise we must seek other means, visit Danzig
or the Gollenberg together.

BISMARCK TO HIS WIFE.

Lazienki, 17th Oct., 1859.

So far have they got me! Early this morning I sought
in the first Polish station for the ticket-office to take my
place as far as here, when suddenly a benevolent Fate, in
the shape of a white-bearded Russian General, seized me;
this angel is named P., and before I recovered consciousness,
my pass was recovered from the police, my luggage from
the custom-house officer, and I was transplanted from the
luggage train to the express, seated in one of the Imperial

saloon carriages, over a cigar, with this agreeable gentleman, and, after a good dinner at Petorkan, arrrived at the
station here, where I was parted from Alexander and
luggage by the golden throng. My carriage was ready,
and my questions, shouted in various languages, as to where
I was to stay, were lost in the carriage roll, with which
two fine horses galloped me into the night. For some half
an hour I was rolling in mad haste through the darkness,
and now I am sitting here in uniform with my orders on,
which we all donned at the last station. Tea is beside
me, a mirror before me, and I know no more than that I
am in the Pavilion of Stanislaus August in Lazienki, but
not where it is situated, and I live in hopes that Alexander
will soon find traces of me in more comfortable attire. By
the noise there should be tall trees or a fountain in front
of the windows; except many people in Court liveries, I do
not discover any one. The Emperor reaches Breslau early
on the 23rd, remains there a week, and then, after two
days, I shall be with you.

THE SAME TO THE SAME.

Lazienki, 19th Oct., 1859.

I can only tell you in so many words that I am well.
Yesterday I was the whole day *en grandeur*; breakfasted
with the Emperor, then an audience, was very graciously
and kindly received; dinner with H. I. M.; theatre in the
evening, a very good ballet, and the boxes filled with handsome ladies. I have slept excellently; tea is on the table,
and when I have taken it I am going to drive out. The
Emperor reaches Breslau early on the 23rd; on the morning of the 25th we shall probably start for Berlin. The
tea I mentioned consisted not only of tea, but of coffee,
six eggs, three kinds of meat, biscuits, and a bottle of
Bordeaux; and from the breach I made this morning you
would see that the journey has not hurt me. The wind
is rushing over the Vistula, and rages among the chestnuts

and limes surrounding me, ⸴whirling the yellow leaves against the windows; but here inside, with double windows, tea, and thoughts of you and the children, I smoke my cigar in great comfort. Unfortunately all comfort in this world has its bounds, and I am only awaiting the end of the breakfast of those in the antechamber (I hear Alexander's voice calling out loudly for a corkscrew!) to jump into the carriage, and first drive to several castles and mansions, and then into the city.

THE SAME TO THE SAME.

Lazienki, 21st Oct., 1859.

I shall only just give you a sign of life this morning, for I have slept too long. Yesterday there was a grand dinner, a water and forest illumination which transcended everything I had ever seen of the kind, and a ballet with mazurka. Whatever can be done is done, and for gay people this is Abraham's bosom. I should enjoy this more had I any news of you. You have, no doubt, in the uncertainty of my journey, not ventured to write to me here, or the letter is delayed. To-morrow about nine we go to Skianiawicze, where there is to be a hunting party in the park; in the evening on to Breslau. With God's assistance this day week I shall be in Reinfeld, and shall, I hope, find you and the little ones in good health, and ready to travel. I long for the moment when we shall sit quietly at the tea-table in our winter quarters, be the Neva as frozen as it may.

THE SAME TO THE SAME.

Skianiawicze, 22nd Oct., 9 P.M.

For five hours I have shot deer, hunted four hares, rode for three hours—everything went off well. We are just getting into the coupé for Breslau, where we shall be early to-morrow.

U

Peterhof, 1st/13th July, 1860.

As in former times, during the sessions of the Diet, I
can find no pleasanter employment for a leisure moment than
to write you a line as to the state of my health. Under the
impression that at eight o'clock a steamer left for Petersburg,
I remained at table till half-past six—just long enough to
be detained till ten. The plan is altered to-day; instead
of eight, they start at half-past six and ten. But it is
very pleasant here. There is charming weather to-day;
a fine view of the green and the sea from a well-arranged
corner room of the palace; music in honour of the birthday of the Empress-Mother; and a good carriage, in which
I shall take a drive for an hour. Peterhof is the jewel of
this neighbourhood, and delightful also for a west European,
both as a park and landscape—something like the neighbourhood of Danzig and Zoppot, of which you naturally
know nothing, nor of Rügen; the latter is in the same
style, but prettier. My health is unexpectedly good since
I have lived in my own house. Your kindness in Berlin
to some extent replaced this want; but the green hotel
saloon, and the provisional character of my existence, still
somewhat oppresses my memory. I feel like an old pen-
sioner who has done with the business of this world, or
like a formerly ambitious soldier, who has reached the
haven of a comfortable command; and I feel that I could
travel towards my end through long contented years.
Till twelve I am employed with the Carlsbaders, walking,
breakfast, dressing; from then till five official life gives me
just enough regular work to feel that I am not superfluous
in the world. Dinner I enjoy perfectly, particularly such
things as I ought not to eat. From eight to ten I ride,
also *par ordonnance du médecin,* and then read the newspapers and despatches—enjoying some peaches the while
—till twelve. I shall be able to endure this for a long

time, provided I succeed in retaining the position of an observant natural philosopher in our politics. Yesterday Johanna made her first appearance in society. As I had to be in bed by twelve, and no one comes till eleven, it did not last long. My health is a welcome excuse for keeping out of all company. I dined here to-day. Such are the only irregularities that have taken place since my first reception at Court. The Emperor was very hearty on seeing me again, embraced me, and evinced an unquestionably sincere pleasure at my return. Johanna finds the life far pleasanter than she expected. Some slight cold somewhat upset her a few days since, but thank God all is right again, as with your Marie.

THE SAME TO THE SAME.

Zarskoe-Selo, 4th Oct., 1860.

I must be withdrawn from the clock-work of business, and by imperial command obtain an hour of leisure, to take thought and write to you. My daily life is taken up from the hour of breakfast until four without rest—work of all kinds, on paper and among men. I then ride till six; but after dinner, by order of the physician, I approach the ink-bottle with caution, and only under extreme necessity. On the other hand, I read everything which has arrived in despatches and newspapers, and retire to rest about midnight, generally in good spirits, and in a contemplative mood as to the singular demands the Prussian in Russia makes upon his ambassador. Before sinking to sleep, I think of the best of sisters; but to write to this angel is only possible when I am sent for to an audience at one, and I have to take the railway for that purpose about nine. I thus have two hours remaining, during which I am quartered in the vacant rooms of the handsomest of all grandmothers, the Princess ———, where I write to you and smoke paper cigars until a visit or breakfast disturbs me. I look from the table, down hill, over birches and planes, where red and yellow are already predominating over green leaves. Behind them are the grass-green roofs of the village, over which, to the left, a church stands, with five golden towers in the shape of onions; and the whole is framed in on the horizon by the endless bushes, meadows, and forest plains, behind whose brown-greyish blue shadows a telescope would show the Isaac's Church in Petersburg. A characteristic landscape, but under the cold grey sky more than autumnal—at any rate, a very northern autumn landscape. Yesterday the young Archduke Paul was born, and in a week the long-delayed journey to Warsaw will be commenced. I hope to remain here; at least, I have written that I did not consider the custom of a reception on the frontier necessary, and should only come if specially commanded. I feel, thank God, much better than in the spring; but I do not trust in my health so entirely, and the Court life there, with diurnal balls until three o'clock, and all its restlessness, will be a severe trial even for people in perfect health. After my many journeys since the beginning of 1859, the feeling of really living anywhere with my own family is so beneficial that I am loath to tear myself away from domesticity. I should like to remain, like the badger, in my lair, at least until summer returns. Johanna and the children, thank God, are well, although Bill gave us some anxiety for a time, as Johanna will have informed you. The tutor and Josephine, the nurse, are, however, in bed. Quite without sickness we never are, and the doctor is a daily guest. God grant that all sufferings are at an end in your house! The Chamberlain is just announced, and I do not know whether I shall be able to finish these lines here, or the day after to-morrow in Petersburg, when the Eagle sails, having many despatches to write till then.

Petersburg, the 12th Oct.—On taking up my letter-case, among my preparations for departure I found the foregoing, of which I was guilty at Zarskoe-Selo, and will not withhold it from you. Since then I have been ordered to go to Warsaw, and obey with somewhat of a heavy heart, after having somewhat evasively declined an invitation of the Emperor's to that place. I am well enough for business, but not for pleasure. When you read this, probably on Wednesday, I shall, if God will, already be in Berlin. On Thursday I leave for Warsaw, and thence, by way of Wilna, hither. I shall not therefore have the pleasure of seeing you, unless by chance you should be in Berlin. I hope to do so next summer. The sea voyage will not be comfortable, but the land journey is too monotonous.

THE SAME TO THE SAME.

Petersburg, 9th Dec., 1860.

I take it for granted that you are already in Berlin, as I do not know what you could do in the long evenings at Kröchlendorf, although they are not so long as here, where lights are now brought punctually at 3 o'clock, to see to read and write. On some of our foggy days it is hardly possible, despite of the double windows and distance from the cold, to enter upon such pursuits after noon. But I cannot say that my evenings or nights are too long; my anger at the swift progress of time is as great in the evening when I go to bed, or in the morning when I rise. I have just now a great deal to do; we are not at all social—my means do not permit it. I catch cold in 'other people's houses, and generally an ambassador with 30,000 thalers salary is condemned to great economy. I receive visitors at dinner, *i.e.*, I give them according to *fortune de pot*, but no evening parties. Evening parties, theatres, and so forth, are interdicted by the mourning carriages; coachmen, jägers, are all dressed in black. I have been out hunting once, but found the wolves wiser than the huntsmen; I was glad, however, to be able to do so once more. The cold is not very intense; three, five, seven, seldom eleven degrees of frost; there has been good sledging for some weeks.

I am in the midst of Christmas plagues, and find nothing for Johanna that is not too dear. Please buy her some twelve or twenty pearls at Friedberg's, suitable for her necklace, *i.e.*, for the largest; say about 300 thalers. I should also like some picture-books, in Schneider's Library; if you are unable to get them, ask ——— to do so. I should like "Düsseldorf Magazines" of last year, "Düsseldorf Art Albums" of last and this year, München *Fliegender Blätter* of last year, and München *Bilderbogen* of this year and the last; also Kladderdatsch Almanack, and such nonsense.

Please get all this as soon as you can, and send it me by the aid of Harry with the next despatch-bag—also the pearls, so that they may be here by Christmas; a courier will probably start before then. Put a few boxes of confections with them, but not too many, for the children are in a customary state of digestion without them.

The death of old Bellin makes a breach at Schönhausen, and puts me into some doubt as to my arrangements there. I do not know whether the widow will remain in the mansion, or whether she will prefer her little cottage —the ice-house—which the old man arranged for her. The garden I shall have to resign to the farmer, but will reserve a right of resumption by a notice from year to year, should I return thither. The accounts I must give to my attorney; I do not know any one there.

THE SAME TO THE SAME.

Petersburg, 26/14 March, 1861.

I first congratulate you on my birthday; this disinterested step, however, is not the only reason of the unusual appearance of an autograph letter from me. You know that on the 11th April the basis of my domestic bliss was born; it is not, however, as well known to you that I signified my delight at the return of this day last year by the present of a pair of earrings, brilliants, purchased of Wagner Unter den Linden, and that they have recently disappeared from the possession of the charming owner, and have probably been stolen. In order to soften the sorrow of this loss, I should be glad to receive by the 11th—there is sure to be a courier or some other traveller before that time—a pair of similar decorations of the conjugal earshells. Wagner will know about what they were and cost; if possible I should like them similar; a simple setting like your own, and they may be a little dearer than those of last year. The equality of my budget cannot be maintained, whether the deficit be a hundred thalers more or less. I must await the restoration of my finances, when I take wife and children to Pomerania, and send the horses to grass in Ingermanland in the summer. Experience alone can tell how great the saving will be by such an operation. Should it prove insufficient, I shall next year leave my very pleasant house, and put myself on a Saxo-Bavaro-Würtemberg footing, until my salary is raised, or the leisure of private life is restored me. Otherwise I have grown friendly with the existence here, do not find the winter so bad as I thought, and require no change in my position, until, if it be God's will, I can sit down in peace at Schönhausen or Reinfeld, to have my coffin made without undue haste. The ambition to be a minister dies away nowadays from a multitude of causes, not all fitted for epistolary communication; in Paris or in London I should live less pleasantly than here, and have no more to say; and a removal is half a death. The protection of two hundred thousand vagabondizing Prussians, one-third of whom live in Russia, and two-thirds of whom visit it annually, gives me enough to do not to get bored. My wife and children endure the climate very well; there is a certain number of people with whom I associate; now and then I shoot a bear or an elk, the latter some two hundred versts hence; there is charming sledging; high society—whose daily visits are without the slightest advantage for the royal service—I avoid, because I cannot sleep if I go to bed so late. It is impossible to appear much before eleven; most people come after twelve, and about two go to a second soirée of supper-eating folks. This I am unable yet to endure, and perhaps never shall again, and I am not angry at it, as the ennui of a rout is more intense here than anywhere else, because one has too few circumstances of life and interests in common. Johanna goes out often, and answers without annoyance all questions about my health, as the necessary manure on the unfertile soil of conversation. I wish Johanna, for economical reasons, would go to Germany as soon as possible, but she will not! I mean to Pomerania, and I would follow her as soon and for as long as I can get leave of absence. I will take the waters somewhere, and then above all take a sea-bath, to get rid again of this intolerable tenderness of skin. There is nothing heard from and seen of ————; couriers seem to have left off travelling. For months I have had no express despatches from the Ministry, and what come by post are tiresome. Farewell, dear heart; greet Oscar. The Neva still bears carriages of every kind, although we have had a thaw for weeks, so that no sledges can pass in the city, and carriages are daily broken in the deep fissures in the ice which covers the pavements; it is like driving over a frozen ploughed field. You, no doubt, have green leaves about you.

BISMARCK TO OSCAR VON ARNIM.

Reinfeld, 16th Aug., 1861.

I have just received the news of the terrible misfortune which has befallen you and Malwine. My first thought was to come to you instanter, but I had over-estimated my strength. The cure has commenced, and the thought to break it off suddenly was so definitely contradicted, that I determined to let Johanna travel alone. Such a blow is beyond the power of human consolation; and yet it is a natural desire to be near those whom one loves, in sorrow, and to join in their lamentations. It is all we can do. A greater sorrow could scarcely have befallen you — to lose so charming and joyfully growing child in this way, and with it to bury all the hopes which were to become the joys of your old age. As to this, mourning cannot depart from you as long as you live in this world. This I feel with you in deeply painful sympathy. We are without counsel, and helpless in the mighty hand of God—insofar as He will not help us—and can do nothing but bow in humility under His behest. He can take away from us all that He gave us, and leave us entirely desolate; and our mourning over this would be the more bitter the more we rise against the Omnipotent will in anger and opposition. Do not mingle bitterness and murmuring with your just sorrow, but remember that you still have a son and daughter left you, and that you must regard yourself as blest with them, and even with the feeling of having possessed a beloved child for fifteen years, in comparison with the many who have never had children and known paternal joys. I will not burthen you with weak grounds for comfort, but assure you in these lines that as a friend and brother I feel your sorrow as my own, and am cut to the heart by it. How do all the little cares and troubles which beset our daily lives vanish beside the iron advent of real misfortunes! And I feel the recollections of all complaints and desires, by which I have forgotten how many blessings God gives us, and how much danger surrounds us without touching us, as so many reproofs. We should not depend on this world, and come to regard it as our home. Another twenty or thirty years, under the most favourable circumstances, and we shall both have

passed from the sorrows of this world; our children will
have arrived at our present position, and will find with
astonishment that the life so freshly begun is going down
hill. Were it all over with us so, it would not be worth
while dressing and undressing. Do not you remember the
words of a Stolpmünder fellow-traveller? The thought
that death is but the passage to another life may perhaps
diminish your sorrow but little, but you might believe
that your beloved son would have been a faithful and true
companion for the time you have yet to live here, and
would have continued your memory. The circle of those
whom we love grows narrower, and receives no increase
until we have grandchildren. At our years we make no
new connections which can replace those who have died
away. Let us therefore hold each other closer in affection,
until death parts us also, as your son is now parted from
us. Who can tell how soon! Will you not come with
Malle to Stolpmünde, and live quietly with us for a few
weeks or days? In any case I shall come in three or four
weeks to you to Kröchlendorf, or wherever you may be.
I greet my beloved Malle from my heart. May God
grant her, as also yourself, strength to endure and patient
resignation!

BISMARCK TO HIS SISTER.

Petersburg, 17/5 Jan., 1862.

I wished last night to go shooting some fifteen miles
hence on the road to ——, where some wild quadrupeds,
already purchased by me, are awaiting me. I therefore
wrote in great haste all that to-day's courier was to take
with him. Brotherly love in this case, however, would
have suffered. Then it grew so cold again that the
nocturnal sledging would have put my nose in a dilemma,
and the chase would have been cruel for the beaters. I
therefore gave it up, and won a little time to write you a
few loving words—especially to thank you for your

excellent purchases and letters. The dress is everywhere admired; and in the little brooch also your good taste has evinced itself. Christmas, with God's grace, has passed away from us in quietness and content, and Marie is making satisfactory progress. It would, therefore, be unthankful to complain of the cold, which has remained fixed at 18° to 28° with a persistency remarkable even for Russia, which would give 22° to 32° for the little hills to the south-west, where I usually shoot. For fourteen days the temperature has never been less than 18°. Usually, it is seldom longer than thirty hours consecutively over 20°. The houses are so frozen that no fires are of any use. To-day it is 24° at the window in the sun; a bright sun and blue sky. You write in your last letter of imprudent words spoken by ———, in Berlin. Tact he has not, and never will have; but that he is intentionally my enemy I do not consider. Nor does anything take place here that everybody might not know. If I were disposed to continue my career, it might perhaps be the very best thing if a great deal were heard to my disadvantage, for then I should, at least, get back to Frankfurt; or if I were very idle and pretensious for eight years, that would do. This is far too late a thing for me; I shall therefore continue to do my duty. Since my illness I have become so mentally weak, that the energy for exciting circumstances is deficient. Three years ago, I might still have been a useful minister, but now I regard myself, mentally, as a sick circus-rider. I must remain in the service some years, if ever I am to see it. In three years the Kniephof lease will be out, in four years that of Schönhausen; until then I should not know exactly where to live, if I resigned. The present revision of posts leaves me out in the cold. I have a superstitious dread of expressing any wish about it, and afterwards to regret it by experience. I should go to Paris or London without sorrow, without joy, or remain here, as God and His Majesty please; the cabbage will

grow no fatter for our policy, nor for me, whichever
should happen. Johanna wishes for Paris, because she
thinks the climate would suit the children better. Sickness happens everywhere, and so does misfortune; with
God's help, one gets over them, or one bends in resignation to His will; locality has nothing to do with it. To
———— I concede any post; he has the material. I
should be ungrateful to God and man, were I to declare
I am badly off here, and anxious for a change; but for
the Ministry I have an absolute fear, as against a cold
bath. I would rather go to one of those vacant posts, or
back to Frankfurt, even to Berne, where I lived very
well. If I am to leave here, I should like to hear of it
soon. On the 1/13 February I must declare whether I
retain my house, must, *en cas que si*, stipulate for buildings
and repairs; expensive horses and other matters would
have to be purchased, which requires months here, and
causes a loss or saving of thousands. To move in winter
is scarcely possible. After some interruptions, I read my
letter again, and it makes a melancholy impression; unjustly so, for I am neither discontented nor tired of life,
and, after careful consideration, have discovered no wish
unfulfilled, except that it should be 10° less cold, and that
I should have paid some fifty visits which press upon me.
Modest wishes! I hear that I am expected in the winter
to the Diet. I do not think of coming to Berlin without
special orders from the King, unless in summer, upon leave.
Johanna and the children will, I think, go to Germany in
about four months. I shall follow, if God will, in some
four or six weeks, and shall return about as much sooner.
By reason of the cold, the children have not been out of
the house for nearly three weeks. All Russian mothers
observe this rule, so soon as it is more than 10°; it must
therefore be a matter of experience, although I go to 15°,
but no farther. Despite this want of air, they look very
well, notwithstanding matters of diet—which is constitu-

tional—and their Christmas feastings. Marie has become a sensible little person, but is still quite a child, which I am glad to see. By my side lies Varnhagen's Diary. I cannot understand the expenditure of moral indignation with which this needy mirror of the times, from 1836 to 1845, has been condemned. There are vulgarities enough in it, but people conversed in that manner in those days, and worse; it is drawn from life. V. is vain and malicious, but who is not? It is merely a question how life has ripened the nature of one or another with wormholes, sunshine or wet weather, bitter, sweet, or rotten. During the whole time at my command there has been humbug of all sorts; so I have written away up to two o'clock, and at three the messenger must be on the railway.

THE SAME TO THE SAME.

Petersburg. the 7th March, 1862.

I make use of an English courier to send you a greeting of a few lines; a groan at all the illness with which God afflicts us. We have had scarcely a day all this winter on which we were all well in the house. Johanna has a cough just now, which quite exhausts her, so that she must not go out; Bill is in bed with fever, pains in body and throat—the physician cannot tell us yet what will come of it; our new governess scarcely hopes to see Germany again. She has been lying prostrate for weeks, daily weaker and more helpless; the doctor thinks probably galloping consumption will be the end of it. I am only well when out shooting; directly I enter a ball-room or a theatre I catch cold, and neither eat nor sleep. As soon as the climate is milder I shall send them, stock, block, and barrel, to Reinfeld. The indifference with which I contemplate a transfer is much diminished by these facts: I should scarcely have the courage to face next winter here. Johanna will scarcely be persuaded to allow me to return hither by myself. If I am not transferred I shall

perhaps seek a longer leave of absence. I have recently
had a letter from ———— ; he believes he is intended to be
sent here, but would rather go to Paris; he thinks me
intended for London, and I have somewhat familiarized
myself with the thought. Letters from the Prince
spoke of ————'s resignation and my succession; I do
not think this is the intention, but should decline were it
so. Independently of political exigencies, I do not feel
myself well enough for so much excitement and labour.
This feeling also causes me some thought, if I were
offered Paris, London is quieter; were it not for climate
and my children's health, I should doubtless prefer
to remain here. Berne is also a fixed idea of mine;
tiresome places in pretty neighbourhoods suit old people,
but there is no sporting there, as I do not care for
climbing after chamois.

CHAPTER III.

BISMARCK ON THE SEINE.

1862.

The Premiership Ahead.—Ambassador to Paris.—Unveiling of the Branden-
burg Statue.—Uncertainty.—Delivers his Credentials to Napoleon III.—
Description of the Embassy House at Paris, and of Prussia House,
London.—Journey to the South of France.—Trouville.—Bordeaux.—
Bayonne.—San Sebastian.—Biarritz.—Luchon.—Toulouse.—End of his
Journeyman Days.

WE have arrived at the last section in Bismarck's political
apprenticeship and journeymanship—to his embassy in
Paris. This only comprises a period of a few weeks, but
it has become very important, by reason of the distinguished acquaintances that Bismarck then made, by the
more accurate knowledge he then obtained of French
relations, which grew more extensive subsequently, on his
later journeys to the waters of Biarritz. We know from
one of the letters already given that Bismarck had already
received an intimation at St. Petersburg that his King
intended to appoint him Minister-President, and put him
at the head of the Government. This intimation was
probably not the only one; the relations between the King
and himself had for a long time been very intimate. The
events of those days are too near to us to admit of the
veil being entirely drawn aside; probably it was King
William's intention to have appointed him Minister-President in the spring of 1862 at once. We do not know what

hindered the appointment at that time ; the result showed that it was a fortunate circumstance in several respects that Bismarck was first Ambassador in Paris before becoming head of the Government. Whether Bismarck had misgivings about assuming so great a responsibility, who can tell? He would have ripely tested himself, but certainly he would not have hesitated for an instant to respond to the call of his King with patriotic zeal, for he saw the reorganization of the army threatened by the liberal opposition, and in that for him was the sole hope of obtaining for Prussia at the right hour her just position, and the future of Germany. He certainly knew that severe struggles were before him, but he also knew they had to be fought through—that Parliamentarianism should be rendered innoxious to the kingdom of Prussia, and that the black-and-white standard should float from unassaulted battlements.

On the 23rd of May, 1862, Bismarck was appointed Ambassador to Paris, and set out thither. He had previously remained a few weeks at Berlin, where it is certain several conferences took place as to his acceptance

of the office of Minister-President ; a passage in a letter to his wife below alludes to this.

On the 17th of May, the statue of the Count of Brandenburg was dedicated on the Leipziger Platz, in the presence of King William. At that time, as it may be said, the Ministry of Bismarck was in the air. Bismarck was present. When the cover of the statue had fallen, amidst the strains of the Hohenfriedberg March, H. R. H.

BISMARCK AS CHANCELLOR.

BISMARCK AS CHANCELLOR.

the Prince Carl advanced to him, and shook him by the hand, with a " Good morning, Bismarck ! "

" Salute the new Minister-President ! " said a member of the former Ministry of Manteuffel, in a very animated manner, to a representative of the new era.

The acclamations for the King, and the trumpet-call of the trumpeters of the Cuirassiers, accompanied the prophecy.

The three following letters to his wife show that he felt himself painfully oppressed by the uncertainty of his then position :—

Berlin, 17th May, 1862.

Our future is still as obscure as in Petersburg. Berlin is more in the foreground. I do nothing for or against it, but shall drink a good drop when I have my credentials to Paris in my pocket. Nothing at all is said about London just now, but things may change again. I go to the dedication of Brandenburg, and then to ————, at ————, to dinner. I have not been able to detach myself all day from Ministerial conversations, and do not find these gentlemen at all more united than their predecessors.

Berlin, 23rd May, 1862.

From the newspapers you will already have seen that I am appointed to Paris. I am very glad of it, but the shadow remains in the background. I was already as good as taken prisoner for the Ministry. I shall start for Paris as soon as I can get loose, to-morrow or next day ; but I cannot direct our " uncertain " things to that place as yet, for I cannot but expect that in a few months or weeks they may recall me and keep me here. I do not come to you first, as I wish to take possession. in Paris first; perhaps they will find another Minister-President, when I am out of their sight. I will not go to Schön-hausen for the same reason, that I may not again be

X

seized. Yesterday I rode about for four hours in a major's uniform, and received my credentials for Paris in the saddle. The roan mare is here, and has been my joy and refreshment in the Thiergarten; I shall take her with me. The bears went off to Frankfurt yesterday. I have my hands full in order to render my journey possible.

***

BISMARCK TO HIS WIFE.

Berlin, 25th May, 1862.

You write very seldom, and no doubt have more time for it than I have. Since I have been here I have not had time to sleep one night through. Yesterday I went out about eight o'clock in the morning, came home five times to change my dress in a hurry; at eight again I went to Potsdam to Prince Frederick Charles, and returned at eleven. Now, at four, I have my first free moment, and use it for heaping fiery coals upon your black head. I think of leaving to-morrow—at latest on Tuesday—for Paris; whether for long God only knows—perhaps only for months or weeks. They have all conspired to keep me here, and I shall be very glad when I have found a point of rest on the Seine, and a porter at the door who will let nobody see me for some days. I do not know, indeed, whether to send our furniture to Paris at all, for it is possible that I may be recalled before they arrived. I am rather seeking a Hegira than a new dwelling-place. I have been obliged to be very firm, to get rid of the hotel life of waiting here. I am ready for everything that God sends, and only regret that I am separated from you, without being able to say when we shall meet again. If I find a prospect of remaining in Paris till the winter, I think you will soon follow me, and we will settle, if it be only for a short time. The course of June will decide whether I return hither before the end of the session of the Diet, or remain in Paris longer, and long enough to send for you. I shall do what I can

towards the latter result, and in any case I should like you
to come to Paris, were it only for a short time, and without

a regular residence,
in order that you
might see it. Yester-
day there was a grand
military dinner, where
I appeared as a major.
First there was a
parade. The mare is
my daily delight in
the Thiergarten, but
not quiet enough for
military service.

As to his residence in Paris, the following letters give
the best account :

BISMARCK TO HIS WIFE.

Paris, 31st May, 1862.

Just a few lines amidst the throng of business, to tell
you I am well; but I feel somewhat lonely with the
prospect of green, with dull rainy weather, the humming
of bees, and twittering of sparrows. To-morrow I have a
grand audience. It is annoying that I have to buy linen
—napkins, tablecloths, and sheets. Do not have the
"uncertain" things sent as yet from Petersburg; those
for Schönhausen and Reinfeld send to Stettin, both to
Bernhard's exporter, D. Witte's successor, to whom I have
written. Those for Reinfeld go by ship from Stettin to
Stolpmünde. My stay here is not certain, until the
Ministry has another President in place of Hohenlohe,
and London is filled up. Farewell! I greet you heartily.
Pray write. ———————

THE SAME TO THE SAME.

Paris, 1st June, 1862.

To-day I was received by the Emperor, and delivered
my credentials. He received me in a friendly manner,

looks well, has become somewhat stronger, but by no means fat and aged, as he is caricatured. The Empress is still one of the handsomest women I know, despite Petersburg; she has even grown handsomer within these five years. The whole affair was official and solemn. I was fetched in an Imperial carriage by the Master of the Ceremonies, and shall probably soon have a private audience. I am anxious for work, because I do not know what to do. To-day I dined alone; the young gentlemen were out. The whole evening there was rain, and I was alone at home. To whom could I go? I am more lonely in the midst of great Paris than you are at Reinfeld, and sit here like a rat in an empty house. My only amusement was to send away the cook for cheating me in the accounts. You know how narrowly I look after such things; but —— was a child in this respect. I shall dine for the present at a café. How long this is to last, God knows! In from eight to ten days I shall probably receive a telegraphic summons to Berlin, and then dance and song is over. If my opponents only knew what a benefit they would confer upon me personally by their victory, and how sincerely I wish them success, —— would then, perhaps, from malice, do all he could to bring me to Berlin. You cannot detest the Wilhelmstrasse more than I do, and if I am not convinced that it *must* be, I will not go. To leave the King in a dilemma during illness, I regard as cowardice and infidelity. If it is not to be, God will raise up, for those who seek, some —— who will consent to be a saucepan-lid. If it is to be, then forward! as our coachmen said when they took the reins. Next summer we shall then probably live at Schönhausen. *Hurero!* I shall get into my canopy bed, as broad as it is long—the only living being in the whole house, for I do not think anybody lives in the parterre.

BISMARCK TO HIS SISTER.

Paris, 16th June, 1862.

If all has happened according to the programme, you will to-day have reached Landeck, where I wish you happy and healthy days. On the completion of your twenty-ninth year I hope to present myself with good wishes, although I do not accurately know in how short a time the post goes between here and Landeck. The barometer is always at changeable, as during the past year, and will long continue so, whether I live here or in Berlin. There is rest in the grave—at least I hope so. Since my departure from Berlin I have not heard a word from anybody about the Ministerial question. ————'s leave of absence is out, and he does not again enter on his duties; this I knew before. The end of June I wait quietly for; if I do not then know what is to become of me, I will urgently ask for certainty, so as to settle myself here. If I seem likely to remain here till January, I think I shall fetch Johanna in September, although a domestic establishment of four months is very provisional and uncomfortable. In packing and unpacking a small fortune is broken up in glass and china. Besides my wife and children, the mare is what I chiefly want. I have tried some hired horses, but I would rather never ride again. The house is well situated, but is dark, damp, and cold. The sunny side is spoilt with staircases and *non-valeurs*; everything lies to the north, and smells musty and cloacic. There is not a single piece of furniture one can sit upon, nor a single corner in which one can sit; three-quarters of the house is shut up as " state rooms," covered up, and, without a great change in arrangements, not suitable for daily use. The nurses would live on the third-floor, the children on the second. The principal staircase (first-floor) only leads to a bed-chamber, with a large bed, also an old-fashioned saloon (style of 1818) next to it, many staircases and anterooms. Actual living room is on the ground-floor, northwards towards the garden, where I warm myself, when the sun shines, for some hours, at most three times a week.   You will see it in the margin : 1. Dressing-room, spongy and uninhabitable, damp; 2. Study, dark, stinking ; 3. Reception-room ; 4. A view from the house to the garden, with bookcases ; 5. Dining-room ; 6. My bed-room ; 7. Office ; 8. Garden, where the lines are, Quai D'Orsay and the Seine ; 9 and 10. Chancery; 11. Hall ; 12. Stair-case.   Add to this, on the first-floor one bedroom, and no more, and all the domestic offices two stories high ; narrow, dark, steep stairs, which I cannot mount upright, on account of the breadth of my shoulders, and without crinoline.   The principal staircase only goes to the first-floor, but there are three ladder stairs at both ends to the upper rooms.   Hatzfeld and Pourtales existed thus their whole time, but died over it in the prime of life ; and if I stay in the house, I shall die sooner than I wish.   I would not live in it for nothing, on account of the smell.

Please send Johanna the address where you had such good cakes (baum kuchen) made two years ago, for the birthday.   I promised one to the Archduchess Marie. Or rather, send me the address, and I will order the cake by letter from here, and will enclose a letter for ————, which the confectioner can send with the thing by ship from Stettin.   I am somewhat afraid if we stay here that Johanna will be but little pleased.   In a few days I am to go to Fontainebleau.   The Empress is a little stronger, and thus handsomer than ever, and always very delightful and cheerful.   Afterwards I shall go to London for a few days.   A number of agreeable Russian ladies who were here have mostly disappeared.   Who has got my mare, if I want it here ?

At the end of June Bismarck took a short trip to the

Exhibition in London, and returned to Paris on the 5th of July. On the 14th he wrote to his wife:—

From your letter of the 9th of this month I have learnt with joy that you are well, and I hope to read the same again to-morrow morning. To-day the courier at last arrived, on whose account I left London more than a week ago. I should like to have remained there some days longer—I saw so many pretty faces and fine horses. But the Embassy is a horror; well furnished, but on the ground-floor, besides the staircase, there are only three apartments, one a chancery, another a dining-room, and between both, serving as a common rendezvous for dinner, without a corner in which to take off a dressing-gown, the study of His Excellency. If wash-hand basins, &c., are wanted there, it is necessary to mount the high, tall stairway, and pass through the principal bed-room into a little dog-hole of a living-room. On the first-floor is one great saloon, a small ball-room; next to it the afore-mentioned sleeping-room and dog-hole; that is the whole of the living-room. Two stairs higher there are two rooms for the secretary, and five small places for children, tutor, governess, &c. On the third-floor, under the roof, room for the servants, the kitchen in the basement. I get quite miserable at the idea of being cooped up in such a place. On my application for leave of absence, I have to-day received a reply from Berlin, that the King could not yet determine whether he could give me leave, because the question whether I should accept the Presidency would be held in suspense for six weeks, and I might write whether I thought it necessary to enter the present session of the Chambers, and when, and whether before the commence-ment of my leave I would come to Berlin. The latter I shall endeavour to avoid—shall propose that I be left here in peace till the winter, and during the interval, say the day after to-morrow or Thursday, go to Trouville, west from

Havre-on-the-Sea, and there await the winter. I can
always get here from that place in five hours. Since
yesterday we have had fine weather; until then it was
miserably cold, with endless rain. Yesterday I employed
in dining at St. Germain, a fine wood, two versts long, a
terrace above the Seine with a charming view over forests,
hills, towns, and villages, all green up to Paris. I have
just driven through the Bois de Boulogne in the mildest
moonlight—thousands of carriages in a Corso file, water-
surfaces with gay lights, an open-air concert; and now to
bed. Our carriages have reached Stettin; I shall have
them housed there or in Külz. All my colleagues are
gone, and the only acquaintance with whom I have any
intercourse is old ————, which neither of us dreamt
of twenty years ago. My servants are Lemburg, a
Russian, an Italian Fazzi, who was footman to Stolberg in
Morocco, three Frenchmen (chancery-servant, coachman,
and cook), and an Electoral Hessian, with a Belgian wife,
as porters.

Bismarck went first to Trouville, as he announces;
but he was so uncomfortable there, that he left in a very
few days. On the 25th of July he entered upon that
beautiful journey to the south-west of France into Spain,
where he found strength for the important problem which
fell, two months later, to his lot—that great task he did
not seek, but did not refuse. He enjoyed the pleasure of
this refreshment with keen appreciation, for he well
knew what was before him. He enjoyed the sea-baths of
San Sebatisan and Biarritz particularly; he was all " sea-
salt and sun ;" he lived " as in Stolpmünde, only without sack." He climbed the Pyrenees, and delighted in
the mulberries, olives, and red grapes of Avignon, and
was so industrious a correspondent towards his wife, that
the blue envelopes, in which his letters flew from the
Spanish frontier to Farther Pomerania, did not last. How

many of these letters were written in the open air, upon a rock, upon the grass, with a newspaper underneath them ! Some of these may find their place here.

Bordeaux, 27th July, 1862.

You cannot refuse me the testimonial of being an industrious correspondent ; this morning I wrote to your birthday child from Chenonceaux, and this evening I write from the city of red wine. These lines, however, will arrive a day later than those, the mail only going at noon to-morrow. I have only left Paris the day before yesterday, but it seems to me a week. I have seen some very beautiful castles. Chambord, of which the plans torn from a book give a very imperfect idea, in its desolation corresponds to the fate of its possessor. In the spacious halls and magnificent saloons, where kings and their mistresses held their court amidst hunting scenes, the childish playthings of the Duke of Bordeaux are the only furniture. The guide thought I was a French legitimist, and repressed a tear when she showed me the little cannon of her master. I paid for the tears, according to tariff, with an extra franc, although I have no calling to subvent Carlism. The castle courts were as quiet in the sun as deserted churchyards. From the towers there is an expansive prospect ; but on all sides there are silent woods and broom to the utmost horizon— no town, no village, no farm either near the castle or around it. From the enclosed examples of broom you will hardly recognize how purple these plants, so beloved by me, grow there—the only flower in the royal gardens, and swallows almost the only living tenants of the castle. It is too lonely for sparrows. The old castle of Amboise is magnificently situated ; one can see from the top six miles either way down the Loire. Thence one gradually passes into the south. Wheat disappears, and gives place to maize ; in between rank woods of vines and chestnuts, castles and forts, with many towers, chimneys, and gables, quite white, with high pointed slate roofs. The heat was glowing, and I was glad to have half a coupé to myself. In the evening, splendid sheet lightning in the east, and now a pleasant coolness, which, in our own land, we should think somewhat sultry. The sun set at 7.35. In Petersburg one would be able to see now, about eleven, without lights. Till now, no letter has arrived for me; perhaps I shall find one at Bayonne. I shall stop here some two days, to see where our wines grow.

Bordeaux, Wednesday, 29th July, 1862.

Your letter of the 23rd yesterday reached me safely, and I thank God you are well. Yesterday, with our Consul and a General, I made a charming tour through Médoc. I drank Lafitte, Mouton, Pichon, Laroze, Latour, Margaux St. Julien, Branne, Armeillac, and other wines in their original names, in the cellar. Thermometer 30° in the shade, 55° in the sun; but with good wine inside this is not felt at all. I am just starting for Bayonne, and will write thence more quietly than now, in the custody of the railway.

Bayonne, 29th July, 1862.

I employ the time in which my things are coming from the railway station to perfect my short epistle of this morning from Bordeaux. The country I have just passed through transports me at first sight most vividly into the Government Pskow, or Petersburg. From Bordeaux to this place there are uninterrupted pine forests, broom and moorland, sometimes like Pomerania—as in the Strandwald behind the downs—sometimes Russia. But when I used my glass the illusion vanished; instead of the Scotch fir, it is the long-haired sea-pine, and the apparent mixture of juniper, raspberries, and such plants covering the ground is dissolved into all sorts of foreign-looking shrubs, with leaves resembling myrtle and cypress. The magnificence with which the broom develops its violet-purple blossoms here is astonishing; in between there grows a very yellow furze with broad leaves, the whole forming a gay carpet. The river Adour, on which Bayonne lies, is the frontier of this B. flat of heath, which, in its softer idealization of a Northern landscape, sharpened my home sickness. From St. Vincent the view stretches over the moor and pine-trees to the blue outlines of the Pyrenees, a sort of giant Taunus, but more bold and jagged in profile. The post-office is closed during the hot time of day, until four o'clock, so that I can only receive your letter in an hour, and should be doubly impatient had I not yesterday received your letter of the 23rd; and the one lying here is older. I think of driving to Biarritz towards evening, and bathing there to-morrow, and then continuing my journey to the frontier. In Fuent Arabia I await intelligence as to whether G. is in St. Sebastian, then I shall visit him; but if he has returned to Madrid I shall content myself with having crossed the Bidassoa, shall return hither, and then proceed along the mountains to Pau; thence I shall turn to the right among the mountains, first to Eaux Bonnes and Eaux Chaudes, and next to Cauterets, St. Sauveur, Luz, Barrèges, and Bagnères de Luchon. I cannot say that I am bored; a number of new impressions rise up within me, but I feel like a banished man, and in thought am rather on the Kamenz than the Adour. German newspapers I have not seen for six days, nor do I miss them.

San Sebastian, 1st Aug., 1862.

The road from Bayonne to this place is magnificent. To the left are the Pyrenees, something like Dent du Midi and Moleson; here, however, called Pic and Port, a changing Alp panorama. To the right the sea, a shore like Genoa. The transition to Spain is surprising. In Behobie, the last French place, one could believe that one was still on the Loire. In Fuent Arabia is a steep lane, twelve feet wide; every window has its balcony and curtain, every balcony its black eyes and mantillas, beauty and dirt. On the market-place drums and fifes, and some hundreds of women, old and young, dancing among themselves, while the men stand by smoking and draped. The neighbourhood up to this place is extraordinarily beautiful; green valleys and woody slopes, above them fantastic lines of forts, row after row. Bights of the sea with very small inlets, which, like the Salzburg Lakes in Bergkesseln, cut deep into the land. From my window I am looking at one of these, cut away from the sea by a rocky islet, steeply, fringed by mountains, with forest and houses to the left, below the town and harbour. At about ten I bathed, and after breakfast we walked or slouched through the heat to the mount of the citadel, and sat for a long time on a bank. Some hundred feet beneath us was the sea; next to us a heavy fort battery, with a singing sentinel. This mountain or rock would be an island, did not a low isthmus connect it with the mainland. The isthmus divides two arms of the sea from each other, and thus from the citadel towards the north there is a fine view of the sea. To the east and west are the two arms, like two Swiss lakes; to the south is the isthmus, with the town on it, and behind, towards the land, mountains stretching skyward. I should like to have a picture painted of it for you, and were we fifteen years younger, we would both come hither. To-morrow or next day I return to Bayonne, but shall remain a few days at Biarritz, where the shore is not so beautiful as here, but still prettier than I had thought, and the life is somewhat more civilized. To my great content, I hear nothing from Berlin and Paris. I am very much sunburnt, and should have liked to lie in the sea for an hour. The water buoys me up like a piece of wood, and it is just cool enough to be pleasant. One is almost dry by the time one reaches the dressing-hut; then I put my hat on and take a walk *en peignoir.* Fifty paces off the ladies bathe, after the custom of the country. The customs and passport business are infinite, and the tolls incredible, or I should remain here longer, instead of bathing at Biarritz, where it is necessary to assume a costume.

Biarritz, 4th Aug., 1862.

I fear that I have made some confusion in our correspondence, as I have led you to write too early to places where I am not. It will be better to write to Paris, just as if I were there; the Embassy will then forward them, and I can give quicker information then as to any change in my travelling plans. Last evening I reached Bayonne from St. Sebastian, where I slept for the night, and am now sitting in a corner room of the Hotel de l'Europe, with a charming view of the blue sea, which drives its foam between wonderful cliffs against the lighthouse. My conscience reproves me for seeing so much that is lovely without you. Could I bring you here through the air, we would immediately return to St. Sebastian. Think of the Siebengebirge with the Drachenfels placed on the sea-shore; next to it Ehrenbreitstein, and between both an arm of the sea, somewhat broader than the Rhine, stretching into the land, forming a round cove behind the mountains. Here one bathes in transparent clear water, so heavy and salt that one floats, and can look through the broad rock entrance into the ocean, or landwards, where the mountain chains rise ever higher and more azure. The women of the middle and lower classes are remarkably pretty, some of them handsome; the men are surly and uncivil; and the conveniences of life to which we are accustomed are wanting. The heat here is not worse than there, and I think nothing of it on the contrary, thank God, I am very well. Yesterday there was a storm, the like of which I have never seen. On a stair of four steps on the harbour dam I had to try to mount thrice before I could get up; pieces of stone and halves of trees were flying through the air. Unfortunately, this led me to retract my place on a sailing vessel to Bayonne, little thinking that

in four hours all would be quiet and serene. I thus lost a charming sea passage along the coast, remained another day in St. Sebastian, and yesterday left in the diligence,

somewhat uncomfortably packed between dainty little
Spanish women, with whom I could not interchange a
word. They understood enough Italian, however, for me
to make it clear to them that I was pleased with their
outward appearance. I looked over a travelling plan this
morning, how I could get from here, *i.e.*, Toulouse by railway, through Marseilles to Nizza, then by ship to Genoa,
thence by Venice, Trieste, Vienna, Breslau, Posen, Stargard to Cöslin!—if Berlin were only passable. Just now
I cannot well get by.

Luchon, 9th Sept., 1862.

The day before yesterday we ascended the Col de
Venasque from this place; first two hours through magnificent beech woods, full of ivy, rocks, and waterfalls; then
to a hospice, then two hours of steep riding on horseback
in the snow, with great views, quiet deep lakes between
snow and cliffs, and at a height of 7,500 feet a narrow
portal opened in the sharp comb of the Pyrenees by which
Spain is entered. The land of chestnuts and palms here
shows itself as a rocky basin, surrounded by the Maladetta,
which lay before us, Pic de Sauvegarde, and Pic de Picade;
to the right rushed the waters to the Ebro, to the left to
the Garonne, and towards the horizon one glacier and
snow cap after another stared at us, far into Catalonia and
Aragon. There we breakfasted, pressed closely to the rocks
—red partridges without salt and water; and then rode down
again upon giddy declivities, but with splendid weather.
Yesterday we had a similar expedition to Superbagnères
and to the gates of hell (*le gouffre d'enfer*), into the abysses of
which a magnificent waterfall precipitated itself between
beeches, oaks, chestnuts, and ashes. The waterfalls of the
Pyrenees are certainly superior to those of the Alps, although the latter are decidedly more imposing. To-day we
saw the Lake of Oo, a rock basin like the Obersee, near
Berchtesgaden, but animated by a tremendous waterfall

which tumbles into it. We rowed upon it, singing French *chansonnettes*, alternately with Mendelssohn—*i.e.*, I listened. We then rode home in a pouring rain, and are now dry again and hungry. No day passes without being six or eight hours on horseback. To-morrow the jest is over, and " How so soon it vanishes," &c., was the order of the day. To-morrow evening we shall be in Toulouse, where I hope to find letters from you, *via* Paris. The last I received was yours of the 29th, sent to me by R. It is my fault, as I had appointed that they were only to send on from Paris from the 4th, and then to Toulouse. I thought I should have left Luchon on the 6th, and arrived at T. I know nothing from Berlin ; have not read a newspaper for a fortnight, and my leave is up. I expect a letter from —— in Toulouse, and that I shall be sent for to Berlin, without definitive conclusion.

Toulouse, 12th Sept., 1862.

By some blunder of my own, and post-office pedantry, I somehow got into a mess with your letters, and I am very rejoiced and thankful to receive here your dear letter of the 4th, with good news. I also anticipated a letter from ——, with some clear indications of the future, but only got one from ——. I had no notion of the King's journey to Doberan and Carlsruhe; in happy forgetfulness of the world have I ranged mountains and forests, and am somewhat upset at finding myself, after six weeks, for the first time in a large city. I am going in the first instance with —— to Montpellier, and must reflect whether I shall proceed thence to Paris to make purchases, or whether I shall accompany —— to Geneva, and thence make direct for Berlin. My leave is up; —— writes that the King would be in Carlsruhe on the 9th, but according to your letter it is the 13th. The best thing would be, if I requested extension of leave from here for further — weeks to Pomerania, and await the answer in

Paris, as well as the return of the King to Berlin, before I set out, for certainty is now a necessity, or I shall send in my resignation. At this moment I am not in a state to decide ; I will first take a walk, and perhaps I shall get an idea what to do. I wonder my letters have not reached you regularly. The longest interval I have ever allowed was four days between my last letter from Luchon and the last but one from Bayonne, because we were riding every day from morning till night, eating or sleeping, and paper was not always at hand. Yesterday was a rainy day, fitted for railway travelling, bringing us from Montrejeau to this place—new and bad, a flat country with vines and meadows. I am now writing to —— and ——. If possible, I shall remain in Paris.

With these letters the Apprentice and Journeyman years of Bismarck are at an end ; the next few days conducted him from Avignon to Berlin, to prove his Mastership

Book the Fifth.

———◆———

MINISTER-PRESIDENT AND COUNT.

Staatspräsident

und

Graf.

CHAPTER I.

THE CRISIS.

The Crisis of 1862.—Bismarck Premier.
—The Party of Progress.—The Liberals.
—The Conservatives.—Bismarck's Determination.—"*Voilà mon Médecin!*"—
Anecdotes.—Attitude of the Government.—Refusal of the Budget.—Prudence of the Minister-President.—Official Presentation of Letters of Recall at Saint Cloud.

TWIN-BORN with the active, restless life and labour so typical of our modern days, with the rapid course of political events, we note the natural sisterhood of swift forgetfulness. Most of us would have some difficulty in forming anything like a

clear picture of the decidedly involved situation in which
Prussia stood in the autumn of 1862. It is beside
our purpose to attempt any definition of this situation
here, without taking into consideration the difficulties
surrounding the solution of such a problem at that time;
we must, therefore, content ourselves with cursory hints
and indications.

The Liberal Ministry, which had just resigned, had
left the conflict with the Electoral Chamber of the Diet,
as an inheritance to the Conservative Government now in
power.

King William did not desire a *coup d'état;* he therefore
unweariedly strove to bring about a good understanding,
and found his efforts seconded throughout this stormy
crisis by the loyal zeal and devotion of the Conservatives
as well as the Liberals—especially by his ever-faithful
War Minister General von Roon; but all endeavours,
to the deepest sorrow of the paternal-hearted monarch,
proved unavailing.

It was at last necessary to find some guiding Minister,
sufficiently possessed of devotion, energy, daring, and
circumspection, to carry on the business of the State, despite of the crisis, until, in the course of time, the action of
history should have reconciled these fiery opponents.

The choice of the King fell upon his then representative at Paris—upon Bismarck, who was summoned
by telegraph from the Pyrenees to Berlin.

It was well known to King William that the selection
of this statesman, at any rate for the moment, would tend
to heighten the sharpness of the strife; for, in the eyes of
his opponents, Bismarck then was, and long remained,
the Hotspur of the Junker party—the fiery and energetic
Conservative party leader. Very few knew to what a
statesman Bismarck had ripened in Frankfurt, where he
had thoroughly learnt to know the fox-trap, so dangerous
for Prussia, of German small-statism, with its innumer-

able corners and windings; as also in St. Petersburg, where he had studied under a politician of the first rank, Prince Gortschakoff; and finally in the hot atmosphere of Paris.

"Bismarck! that is the *coup d'état!*" a democratic organ exclaimed; and this was re-echoed in an undertone by many Conservatives, who, perhaps, only saw safety in a *coup d'état*. But Bismarck was by no means a *coup d'état*, but a statesman; and a statesman in whom the King reposed confidence.

After long and well-considered deliberation, the King came to this difficult determination. The appointment of Bismarck, under existing circumstances, was doubly and trebly difficult, for, though Bismarck was intelligible enough to him, the majority of the nation did not understand him, and in every direction, in all circles, and under every political form, opposition arose, with wild cries of resistance.

And when he had actually been summoned, the question presented itself on the other side,—What

conditions would Bismarck impose?   With what programme would he enter upon the situation?

On this, General von Roon, whom Bismarck had
known as a boy, and whom he had accompanied in
surveys through Pomerania, with his little gun, was sent
to meet him. And lo! all this hesitation was perfectly
unnecessary; for the Brandenburg liege faith of Bismarck
responded to the appeal of his feudatory lord with the
simple answer: " Here I am!"

Bismarck imposed no conditions, came forward with no
programme; the faithful vassal of Electoral Brandenburg
placed himself simply at his King's disposal, with that
chivalric devotion which contemplates the most difficult
position as self-intelligible.   The beloved kingdom of
Prussia had to be upheld against the parliamentary spirit;
the new organization of the army, on which the future of
Prussia and Germany depended, had to be saved; such
was the task imposed upon Bismarck.

When Bismarck arrived in Berlin, about the middle of
September, 1862, he found opposite himself the party of
progress, almost certain of victory, clashing onwards like
a charger with heavy spurs and sword, trampling upon
everything that came in its path, setting up new scandals
every day, and acted in such a manner that the wiser
chiefs of that very party shook their heads. Besides the
party of progress, and partially governed and towed along
by it, was the Liberal party, in the greatest confusion after
their recent amazing catastrophe, but possessed, with the
exception of a minority, of an almost still greater dislike
for Bismarck than was entertained by the Progressists:
very easily might this be understood, as it was this party
more than any other that Bismarck had opposed since the
first United Diet.

Bismarck had only the Conservative party in his own
favour, but, during the new era, this had fallen away to
an almost vanishing fraction in the Electoral Chamber;

its political activity was maintained only by the Upper House and by the *Neue Preussische Zeitung*, together with a portion of the provincial press, and was just then once more beginning to express its views in a louder tone by the revival of the conservative associative principle. The new era had shown Conservative politicians that a Conservative party in Prussia, although possessing perfect individuality upon single questions, could only as a great whole be a Government party. "With the Government in courage, without the Government in sorrow, if needs be against the Government with humility; such is the path of the Conservative party!" Such was once the fine and proud axiom of the Conservatives, but only true so far as it concerns special questions. Conservative Prussia can only go hand-in-hand with the Royal Government; but, on the other hand, it is equally certain that a truly Royal Government in Prussia can only be a Conservative Government. The proofs to the contrary imported from France or England are not applicable to the peculiar circumstances of Prussia, and hence act in a manner productive of confusion.

The support which the Conservative party could then give to Bismarck was, as it were, that of a vanquished army, and its ranks required reorganization ere it could be led against the foe. But Conservative support was tendered voluntarily, and with perfect devotion, even by that fraction of the party which was piqued with Bismarck since he had, at Frankfurt, shown a front against Austria, which, indeed, was almost in open hostility towards him, since he had proposed more friendly relations with France, had supported the unpopular doctrine of international interests, and had declared himself for Italy. The acute men of Hochkirchen, the intelligent representatives of conservative idealism, the firm pillars of the policy of the Holy Alliance, the enthusiastic defenders of all legitimacy, from whose ranks Bismarck himself had emerged, had partly become his antagonists; but at the ominous hour when he assumed the head of the Government, they did not deny themselves to

him, and "our azure blues," as the late Baron von Hertefeld used to call them, in his peculiar tone of admiration
and malice, have honestly stood by Bismarck through
difficult years, in the good fight he had fought for the
Prussian monarchy.

What a battle, however, this was may be judged from
the fact that many of the best fellow-soldiers of Bismarck
no longer contended for victory, but, so to speak, sought
only a chivalric death. In all Conservative circles it was
everywhere said that the fight was only continued from a
sense of duty: the victory of progress and parliamentarianism over the old Prussian monarchy was now only a
question of time, but it was necessary to die standing.
The last advocates of the Prussian monarchy at least
desired to win the respect of their antagonists. Such was
the phrase of those days; most of them have probably long
since forgotten it, but it is fitting that they should sometimes be reminded of it. In the year 1863, one of the
most zealous personal partisans of Bismarck determined to
accept an important mission offered by him, with the certain conviction that in so doing he was preparing for an
honourable fall. Certainly there also existed in those days
fresh undejected minds who stood to their imperishable
belief in the Prussian monarchy as in an impregnable fortress, and flung the flag of hope merrily to the breeze; but
of these the number was very small.

Did Bismarck belong to these? Yes. He believed in
his Prussian monarchy, had faith in the future of Prussia
and Germany; but he was also perfectly conscious that he
was engaged in a mortal conflict.

He has not publicly expressed himself on this, but several
isolated remarks which he has, in his characteristic manner,
let drop to various friends, place this beyond a doubt.
Several times he said,—

"Death on the scaffold, under certain circumstances, is
as honourable as death on the battle-field!" and, "I can
imagine worse modes of death than the axe!"

Only six years lie between that time, in which such words were fraught with such terrible significance, and to-day, when that time seems to us like a frightful dream; but that it wears such an aspect to us, is due, under God's mercy and the valour of King William, to the faithful devotion and energetic policy of Count Bismarck.

For the rest, Bismarck entered upon office with strong confidence; he really hoped at first to arrive at some solution of the crisis. All those who saw or spoke to him in those September or October days, remember the unwearied bearing and joyful assurance with which he went to work. " He looks thin, healthy, and sunbrowned, like a man who has traversed the desert on a dromedary!" was the description given of him by a friend at the time. At first he thought it not impossible to win over the hostile party leaders, and he conferred with many of them: whether they were Liberals or Progressists, in the end they were at any rate Prussians. He appealed to their Prussian patriotism; they could not fail, although they sought it by different ways to himself, to have their country's fame and glory as a common goal. But if they desired the well-being of Prussia and Germany, they could not but also desire the means to that end—the newly organized army. No doubt that many of those with whom Bismarck negotiated, or who were negotiated with by others at his instance, felt their hearts beating loudly at this appeal; but he succeeded only in winning a very few. With the majority, the rigid party doctrine prevailed as an insurmountable barrier; with others, every attempt at an understanding was rendered unsuccessful by unvanquishable suspicion; many well understood the hints—and more than hints it was impossible for Bismarck to give—but they did nothing more. He thus finally attained to a summation of undeceptions, which did not discourage him, although this gradually filled his patriotic heart with the deepest sorrow.

But at first, as we have said, he came forward fresh

and full of hope; nor did his first failures and undeceptions disconcert him in any way. His tone towards his opponents was that of reconciliation. For his sovereign's sake he took many a step towards conciliation with sad reluctance, although without desistance.

His wife, who was residing in Pomerania with her parents, he could furnish with meagre reports. The lovely season of the "blue" was past, and the fulness of labour began to increase with rapidity. On the 7th of October he wrote to her at a session of the House of Deputies in the following terms:—"I am sitting at the table of the Chamber, with a speaker, who talks nonsense to me, on the tribune just before me, and between one explanation just given, and another one I shall have to give, I write to you to say I am well. Plenty of work—somewhat tired—not sleep enough—the beginning of all things is difficult. With God's help things will go better, and it is very well so, only it is somewhat uncomfortable, this life on a tray! I dine every day with our good-natured Roons, who will be a real support for you. I see I have commenced on the wrong side; I hope it is not a bad omen." [The letter is written on the inner side of the paper.] "If I had not R. and the mare I should feel very lonely, although I am never alone."

Bismarck was provisionally living at the Ministry of State, in the "Auerswaldhöhle," and only moved to the Foreign Office when the family had returned from Pomerania.

The following letter was also written during those days to his sister. The Bismarckian humour is likewise to be traced in it:—

Berlin, 18th Oct., 1862.

Such good black-pudding I never ate, and seldom such good liver; may your slaughtering be blessed: for three days I have been breakfasting upon the results of it. The cook, Rimpe, has arrived, and I dine at home alone when I am not at His Majesty's table. I got along very well at

Paris. At Letzlingen I shot one stag, one sow, one badger, five brockets, four head of deer, and blundered tolerably, if, perhaps, not as much as my neighbours. But the amount of work here is growing daily. To-day, from eight to eleven, diplomacy; from eleven to half-past two, various Ministerial squabble conferences; then, till four, report to the King; from a quarter past to three-quarters, a gallop in the rain to the Hippodrome; five o'clock, dinner; from seven till now, ten, work of all sorts. But health and sound sleep—tremendous thirst!

It ought not, and could not, remain so long. The strong self-consciousness and feeling of victory with which the Progressist party advanced—and that in a manner the most abrupt, and sometimes even personally insulting—could not fail to convince Bismarck that he would not succeed in solving the crisis. He had now to resolve to leave—in accordance with the King's will—time to solve matters, but, despite of this, to continue, within the constitution, to conduct the Government. With a firm step he pursued this difficult path, and he was able to inspire others with his confidence. Yes; even King William, whose gentle heart suffered severely in this arena of contention, refreshed himself at his Minister's sure bearing—so much so, that on one occasion, when a lovely Russian princess was congratulating him on his healthy appearance, he pointed to Bismarck, and replied, " *Voilà mon médecin !* "

An old acquaintance, who met Bismarck at this time, and asked him how he was, received for reply, "How should I be? You know how I love to be lazy, and how I have to work ! "

The chief of one of the numerous deputations of those days, at which opponents mocked so much as loyalty deputations, although they were of no little significance, was introduced to Bismarck. He summed up the personal impression which the Minister-President made upon him, in his singing Saxon dialect, in the admiring phrase :—

"D'ye hear! one can't talk nonsense when one meets that man!"

"Then I suppose you 've never been in the Chamber?" the Berlin friends of the worthy inhabitant of Wettin, or Löbejühn, observed in reply.

It is certainly evidence in favour of Bismarck's conciliating tendency, that at a session of the Commission he took a twig from his pocket-book and showed it to his antagonists, merrily adding, in a chatty way, that he had plucked this olive-branch at Avignon to present it to the Progressist party in token of peace; but he unfortunately had been forced to learn there that the time for that had not yet arrived.

On the 29th September, 1862, he announced the withdrawal of the budget for 1863, "because the Government considered it their duty not to allow the obstacles towards a settlement to increase in volume." He then announced his intentions, his aims, as clearly as he dared. "The conflict has been too tragically understood," he said, "and too tragically represented by the press; the Government sought no contest. If the crisis could be honourably surmounted, the Government would gladly lend a hand. It was owing to the great obstinacy of individuals that it was difficult to govern with the constitution in Prussia.

A constitutional crisis was no disgrace, it was an honour. We are, perhaps, too cultured to endorse a constitution ; we are too critical. Public opinion changed ; the press was not public opinion ; it was well known how the press was upheld. The Deputies had the task of determining its opinions, and to stand above it. Germany does not contemplate the Liberalism of Prussia, but her power. Bavaria, Würtemberg, and Baden might indulge Liberalism ; but they are not therefore called upon to play the part of Prussia. Prussia must hold her power together for the favourable opportunity which has already been sometimes neglected ; the frontiers of Prussia were not favourable to a good State constitution. The great questions of the day were not to be decided by speeches and majorities—this had been the error of 1848 and 1849 —but by iron and blood ! "

But the Opposition understood this frank language so little, that there was nothing more than plenty of jesting about the iron-and-blood policy, without end.

When the Chamber answered these conciliating steps with the resolutions of the 7th October, by which all expenditure was declared unconstitutional if declined by the national representatives, Bismarck replied with this cutting declaration :—

" According to this resolution, the Royal Government cannot for the present anticipate any result from the continuance of its attempts to arrive at some settlement, but rather expect from any renewal of the negotiation a heightening of party differences, which would render any understanding in the future more difficult."

On the next day, the 8th of October, 1862, Bismarck, who had been named Minister of State and President of the Ministry, *ad interim*, on the 23rd September, was appointed President of the Ministry of State and Minister of Foreign Affairs.

On the 13th of October the session of the Diet was

closed, and on this occasion Bismarck again took an opportunity of expressing his views on his position with great moderation and gentleness. He said :—" The Government is perfectly aware of the responsibility which has arisen from this lamentable crisis ; but, at the same time, it is also observant of the duties it owes to the country, and in this finds itself strengthened to press for the supplies—until the State is settled—necessary for existing State institutions and the furtherance of the common weal, being assured that, at the proper time, they will receive the subsequent sanction of the Diet."

This was the beginning of the loudly-assailed " budgetless" Government ; at the present day, no one will deny that this was precisely the mildest form of opposition. A budget had certainly not come into existence, but the Government was conscientiously carried on according to the principles of the constitution, as the King desired. It was a severe and endless battle which now ensued—a strife wearying both body and soul ; but the Government never appealed to physical force ; it was a war of opinions and convictions, a war of intellectual weapons, such as had never been seen in the political region of the world's history, and such as was really only possible in Prussia.

Perhaps this is the most fitting place to draw attention to one point of Bismarck's policy, that to us does not seem to have been sufficiently valued in general, but which at the same time is highly characteristic of Bismarck's method ; we allude to the great prudence with which he ever upheld the Sovereignty itself above the conflict. Certainly he fought for the Prussian monarchy, on which depended the future of Prussia and Germany ; but the conflict was between him, between the State Government and the Chamber of Deputies, not between the Crown and the Diet, still less between the King and the people. If the King could have dispensed with the reorganization, it was only necessary to dismiss

Bismarck, and the crisis existed no longer. Bismarck was personally identified with the crisis; in this he might fall, but the Crown remained perfectly secure. But in such devotion the constitutional fiction of the irresponsibility of the King had no part whatever; it was the Brandenburg vassal's lealty which covered the feudatory lord with its knightly shield. At the end of October, Bismarck again went to Paris, to take an official leave at the Tuileries; on the 1st of November he had his farewell audience of the Emperor Napoleon at Saint Cloud. It could scarcely have failed that the conversation turned upon the great task, the accomplishment of which Bismarck had so courageously undertaken. Napoleon had then but little belief in success, and probably pointed to the fate of Prince Polignac. Bismarck, however, was fully aware of the difference between the situations of 1830 in France, and 1862 in Prussia.

Immediately after the audience he returned to Berlin.

CHAPTER II.

THE MAN AT THE HELM.

Negotiations with Austria.—Circular of the 24th January, 1863.—Conversation with Count Karolyi.—Prusso-Russian Convention.—The Party of Progress.—Congress of Princes.—Conditions of Prussia.—War in the Distance.—The Danish Campaign.—Treaty of Gastein, 14th August, 1865. —Bismarck elevated to the Rank of Count.—Bismarck and Pauline Lucca. —Correspondence with his Family.—Hunting at Schönbrunn.—Biarritz.

THE action of history would not fail to solve the conflict, but this was only possible if Prussia entered energetically on this action; and thus we see Bismarck, the man at the helm, steering the Prussian vessel of State, undismayed by the daily attacks of the Progressists, through shallows and rocks, firmly and safely towards open water, on which, driven by the breath of God into history, it was to fly in full sail towards the sunrise of victory.

Immediately after assuming the Ministry, in December, 1862, Bismarck entered upon negotiations with Austria. If Austria could decide upon the dismissal of that enemy of Prussian policy, Schwarzenberg, and give Prussia her proper position in Germany, and thus ensure the same to Germany as her right, Bismarck was prepared to enter into a coalition with Austria; but if Austria could not rise to such a policy, Prussia was determined alone to give the *coup de grace* to the unhealthy, troubled state of things, which lay like an Alp on German life, thus terminate the unnatural hesitation, and create for Germany a new and healthy body corporate.

With perfect frankness, as was his peculiar wont, Bismarck explained himself to Austria. The latter was at this time engaged with the project of the so-called delegations to the Bund, *i.e.*, with a reform which was no reform, but an entirely meaningless absurdity, not even an apparent something.

In the famous circular despatch of the 24th of January, 1863, Bismarck says :—

" In order to bring about a better understanding of the two Courts, I took the initiative in the form of negotiations with Count Karolyi, in which I brought the following considerations under the notice of the Imperial Ambassador. According to my convictions, our relations to Austria *must unavoidably change for the better or the worse.* It is the sincere wish of the Royal Government that the former alternative should arise; but if we should not be met by the Imperial Cabinet with the necessary advances as we could desire, it will be *necessary for us to contemplate the other alternative, and prepare for it accordingly.*

" I have reminded ·Count Karolyi that, during the decennial period preceding the events of 1848, there had been a tacit understanding between the two high Powers, by virtue of which Austria was ensured the support of Prussia on European questions, and, on the

z 2

other hand, allowed us to exercise an influence in Germany, unfettered by the opposition of Austria, as manifested by the formation of the Customs Union. By these arrangements the German Diet rejoiced in a degree of internal unity and outward dignity, which has not since then been reached. I have not alluded to the question as to whose error it was that analogous relations were not re-established on the reconstitution of the Diet, as I was concerned, not with recriminations for the past, but with a practical development of the present time. In the latter we find, in those very States with which Prussia, by her geographical position, is interested in maintaining special friendly relations, an opposing influence, promoted by the Imperial Cabinet, with signal results. I put it strongly to Count Karolyi, that Austria in this manner might, perhaps, win the sympathies of the governments of those States, but would estrange from herself those of Prussia, to the detriment of the common interests of the Diet. The Imperial Ambassador consoled himself with the certainty that, in the event of any war dangerous to Austria, the two greater powers would, under any circumstances, be found together again as allies.

" *In this assumption,* according to my view, there exists a *dangerous error,* which may, perhaps, not become apparent until the decisive moment, with a fatal clearness for both Cabinets, and I therefore besought Count Karolyi *urgently* to use all his powers to contradict this in Vienna. I pointed out that already, in the last Italian war, the alliance had not been so valuable to Austria as it might have been if the two powers had not, during the preceding eight years, contended with each other in the field of German politics, in a manner only conclusively advantageous to a third party, and so undermined all mutual confidence. Nevertheless, the fact that Prussia did not seek for any advantage in consequence of the difficulties of Austria in 1859, but rather armed to assist Austria in need, clearly shows the results of the *former more intimate* relations. But should these last not be renewed and revivified, *Prussia would, under similar circumstances, be as little debarred from contracting an alliance with an antagonist of Austria*, as, under opposite circumstances, from forming a faithful and firm alliance with Austria, against common enemies. *I, at least*, as I did not conceal from Count Karolyi, *under such circumstances, could never advise my gracious Sovereign to neutrality.* Austria is free to choose whether she prefers to continue her present anti-Prussian policy, with the leverage of the coalition of the Central States, or would seek an honest union with Prussia. That the latter may be the result, is my most sincere desire. This can, however, only be obtained by the abandonment of Austria's inimical policy at the German Courts.

"Count Karolyi replied that the Imperial House could not relinquish her traditional influences on the German Governments. I denied the existence of any such tradition by pointing out that *Hanover* and *Hesse* had, for a hundred years—from the commencement of the Seven Years' War —been principally guided by Prussian influences; and that, at the epoch of Prince Metternich, the same States had also been guided from Vienna, specially in the interest of the understanding between Prussia and Austria; consequently that the assumed tradition of the Austrian Imperial House *dated only from the time of Prince Schwarzenberg*, and the system to which it pertained has not hitherto shown itself conducive to the consolidation of the German Confederation. I laid stress upon the fact that, on my arrival in Frankfurt, in 1851, after circumstantial conversations with Prince Metternich, then residing at Johannisberg, I had anticipated that Austria herself would see the wisdom of a policy which would obtain us a position in the German Confederation, consonant with the interest of Prussia to throw all her strength into the common cause. Instead of that, Austria has striven to embitter and impede our position in the German Confederation, and, in point of fact, to force us to seek for allies in other directions. The whole treatment of Prussia on the part of the Vienna Cabinet seems to rest upon the assumption that we, more than any other State, are fully exposed to *foreign attacks*, against which we need *foreign assistance*, and that hence we are bound to put up with *contemptuous treatment* from those States from whom we expect aid. The task of a Prussian Government, having the interests of the Royal House and of the country at heart, would therefore be, *to prove the erroneousness of this assumption by deeds*, if words and aspirations are neglected.

"Our dissatisfaction with the condition of things in the Confederation has received fresh aliment during the last few months, from the obstinacy with which the German Governments more closely allied with Austria have *offensively stood out against Prussia* on the delegate question. Before 1848 it had been unheard of that questions of any magnitude should have been introduced in the Confederation, without the concurrence of the two great Powers previously being secured. Even in cases where the opposition had come from the less powerful States, as in the matter of the South German fortresses, it had been preferred to allow objects of such importance and urgency to remain unfulfilled for years, rather than seek to overcome opposition by means of a *majority*. At the present day, however, the *opposition of Prussia*, not only to a proposal in itself, but in reference to its *unconstitutionality*, is treated as *an incident undeserving of notice*, by which no one should be prevented from pursuing a given progress in a deliberately chosen course. I urged upon Count Karolyi to communicate the contents of the preceding conference to Count Rechberg with the utmost accuracy, although in a confidential sense, expressing at the same time my conviction that the wounds sustained by our mutual relations *can only be healed by unreserved sincerity.*

"The second conversation took place on the 13th of December of last year, a few days after the former, in consequence of a despatch of the Royal Ambassador at the Federal Diet. I visited Count Karolyi in order *to draw his attention to the serious state of things at the Diet,* and did not conceal from him that the further advance of the majority in a course regarded by us as *unconstitutional,* would bring us into a position *we could not accept,* and that in the consequences of it we *foresaw the violation of the Confederation;* that Herr von Usedom had left the Freiherr von Kübeck and Baron von der Pfordten in scarcely any doubt as to the construction which we placed upon the matter, but had received replies to his intimations whence we could draw no inferences as to any wish for a compromise, as Freiherr von der Pfordten pressed strenuously for a speedy delivery of our minority vote.

"Upon this I objected that, under such circumstances, a feeling of our own dignity would not admit of our *evading* any longer the conflict induced by the other side, and that I had therefore telegraphed the Royal Ambassador to deposit his minority vote. I indicated that the *passing over the border of legitimate competency by resolutions of the majority, would be regarded by us as a breach of the federal treaties,* and that *we should mark our sense of the fact* by the *withdrawal* of the Royal Ambassador to the Diet, without nominating any successor; and I drew attention to the *practical* consequences likely to ensue upon such a situation in a *comparatively short time,* as it would naturally occur that the *activity of an assembly,* in which, from just causes, we no longer took part, would be regarded by us as inauthoritative on the whole business sphere of the Diet.

* * * * * *

"A few days after this I was confidentially informed that the Imperial Austrian Ambassador at St. Petersburg (Count Thun) was about to return to his post by way of Berlin, and would confer with me upon the pending question. When he arrived, I did not hesitate, despite the recently named lamentable experiences of an endeavour to meet his communications—made for the purpose of some understanding — in the most straightforward manner. I therefore declared myself ready to enter upon different projects, agreed between us, for the settlement of the Frankfurt difficulties. . . . On this Count Thun proposed to me that an interview between Count Rechberg and myself should be arranged, with a view of a further discussion of the matter. I declared myself ready to meet him, but in the next few days received from Count Karolyi confidential communications, according to which, Count Rechberg anticipated, before our interview, the declaration of my adhesion to the reform project in the Diet, regarding which, in my opinion, it was necessary to have longer and more minute negotiations. As the time extending up to the 22nd of December was too short for these, I presumed that it was only possible to employ the proposed conference for the consideration of previous and binding treaties. . . . As Count Rechberg hereupon declared that Austria could not give up the further negotiation of the project in reference to the assembly of delegates without some assured equivalent, the interview until this time has not taken place."

Clearly as it is here stated, so it happened with all negotiations. Prussia ever sought to go hand-in-hand with Austria, but Austria ever evaded the opportunity. She alleged that it was her intention to pursue her German policy alone, in her solitary path—the way of Schwarzenberg—which was to lead, over the entire insignificance of Germany, to the humiliation and oppression of Prussia. Of course Prussia then had no other alternative than to follow its own mission its own way. To this period belongs the conclusion of the Prusso-Russian treaty on the common measures to be pursued for the suppression of the Polish insurrection. This convention, by which the friendly relations of Prussia and Russia were confirmed, has been frequently and unintentionally misinterpreted. The internal meaning of this, and its reaction, require some further explanation, which it is not desirable at present to give.*

The diplomatic campaign, which the other Powers commenced at the instance of the Convention, it is well known, had no result, and was lost in the sands.

But the saddest figure in this business was played by the party of progress, who, in their blind zeal, had seized upon the Convention, on the plea that Prussia by this would become nothing higher than an outpost of Russia. The idea of such a baseless absurdity—had it been so—would have been laughable, if it had not been too sad to see that the opposition to Prussia abroad had again been instigated by an allied party in the actual Prussian camp. This, however, unfortunately was doomed to be frequently repeated on later occasions.

In the summer of 1863 Bismarck had accompanied his King to Carlsbad, and thence to Gastein, when Austria emerged with her new and useless projects of reorganization, in which there was a tinge and tendency of the inoperative Federal principle, as opposed to Prussian Unionistic efforts. King William received the invitation to the Congress of Princes at Gastein, and the Emperor Francis Joseph himself personally handed him a minute memorial on these projects of reform. This contained, although of course it was not acknowledged by Austria,

---

* Why not? I really must here join issue with a writer who assumes too much, and hides his own very small personality, possessing no personal courtesy, behind weighty cloudiness and the permission to copy Bismarck's correspondence.—K. R. H. M.

very little more than the project of delegates long since opposed by Prussia, and which in no way could content the pretensions of Prussia or the wants of the German people.

King William, who had gone with his Premier from Gastein, by way of Munich and Stuttgart, to Baden-Baden, declined to attend the Princes' Congress at Frankfurt, which was then put up upon the scene with skill worthy of recognition, even with taste, but had not the slightest result, although the princes present at it had accepted the fundamental principles of the Austrian project.

And how came it that this illustrious princely congress should have departed to Orcus without any lamentation, so that in only a few weeks, no one ever mentioned it again? Simply because Prussia had taken no part in it.

In Vienna it had been thought that Prussia would have been carried away by it. When that proved unsuccessful, withdrawal was thought undesirable, and every one had to learn, by bitter experience, that nothing was possible in Germany without Prussia. Prussia, as usual, had been undervalued, and thus it was revenged; but, nevertheless, Prussia continued to be slightly esteemed, and the vengeance was to be still greater.

At the present time, the simplest eyes can see that the rivalry of Prussia and Austria was now first coming into public sight, ere it was possible to think of any reconstruction of Germany. Austria had declined all the propositions of Prussia, which aimed essentially at a peaceable separation of Austria from the German Federation, and led to a federal union of the newly constructed union, under the leadership of Prussia, with Austria, but had replied with the Reform Act, containing within itself a nullification of Prussia. Austria, and the Central States allied with her, had given Prussia the alternatives of unconditional submission, immediate nullification, or the exclusion of herself from the new Federation.

Prussia, with quiet dignity, perfected this act of self-exclusion; and, lo! matters did not go on, and the Viennese Reform Act was a blank.

In his report to the King's Majesty of the 15th of September, 1863, and in the Royal reply to the members of the Princes' Congress on the 22nd of the same month, Bismarck promulgated a series of " preliminary conditions" as to the part Prussia might take in further negotiations.

He demanded: 1. The " veto of Prussia and Austria at least upon every federal war *not undertaken in resistance of an attack* upon *federal territory;*" 2. The " entire *equality* of Prussia with Austria in the presidency and government of federal concerns ; " and 3. " A national representation, not to consist of delegates, but of *directly chosen representatives*, in the ratio of the populations of single States, *the powers of which, in resolution,* should, *in any case, be more extensive* than those in the project for the Frankfurt Reform Act." As a plea for this condition he especially insisted, in his report to the King, that " the interests and requirements of the Prussian people were essentially and indissolubly identical with those of the *German people, wherever this element attained its true construction and value; Prussia never need fear* to be drawn into any policy adverse to her own interests." Besides these three points, he also maintained that the " German sovereigns" were bound either " to learn the opinion of the *nation itself* by the *means of chosen representatives*, or to adduce the *constitutional sanction of the Diets of each individual State.*"

But that Bismarck had fully understood the final and actual ends of the Austro-Central policy, may be seen from the following sentence of his report to the King's Majesty :—

" In the entirely remarkable attitude observed by Austria in this transaction, it is impossible to avoid the impression that apparently the Imperial Austrian Cabinet *from the commencement contemplated, not the co-operation of Prussia* in the common enterprise, but the *realization of a separate federation as an end*, already visible in the first propositions of the 3rd of August, *in case* that Prussia would not *join in* the Austrian plans."

There can be no doubt that Bismarck, by his firm attitude towards the Congress of Princes and the Austro-Central policy, has not only saved the future of Prussia, but also that of Germany. At that time people were so confused and dazzled that it was not at all seen. The small fights in the Chamber had robbed people of any understanding of the great things there accomplished. Bismarck was plainly of opinion that war was imminent, as may be clearly read from the report on which he founded the dissolution of the Electoral Chamber of the Diet. It is here said :—" On the basis of the German Federal Constitution *attempts* have come to light, the *unmistakable object* of which is to set down such a power of the Prussian State in Germany and in Europe, which forms a well-earned heritage of the glorious history of our fathers, and which the *Prussian people has not at any time resolved to allow to be alienated from it*. Under these circumstances, it will be a necessity for His Majesty's subjects at the same time to give *expression to the fact*, at the forthcoming elections, that no *political difference of opinion* is so deeply rooted in our country that, *in the face of an attempt to bring down the independence and dignity of Prussia*, the unity of the nation and its unalterable fidelity to the governing house can be shaken."

Perhaps they in the camp of Austria and its allies reckoned on—decidedly they believed in—war ; and war certainly came at the time, but in a remarkable way, not between Prussia and Austria, but, to the inexpressible surprise of the world, Prussia and Austria, hand-in-hand as allies, took the field against Denmark.

It is utterly impossible clearly to state how Bismarck

succeeded in inducing Austria to enter upon this war, how
he managed to get their old rival to draw the sword for
Prussia's interest, in exact contradiction to her entire previous policy. It is quite true to say that the energetic
initiative of Bismarck carried away Austria with him, but
the matter does not grow at all clearer for that. It is
also not inexact, most certainly, to affirm that Austrian
diplomacy might assert that she was obliged to join, in
order to watch over Prussia and bridle her; but it was by
no means false when the Viennese exclaimed, "That
Bismarck drags us by the halter!" when Austria went into
Holstein, to Schleswig, to Jütland, in the interest of
Prussia and Germany. No doubt the magic of Austria's
burning desire to retrieve the Imperial army's lost prestige,
after the misfortune of 1859, contributed to this political
wonder—the desire of hanging fresh laurels on the black
and yellow standard. Such a crown the warriors of Austria
honestly won there in the North. Perhaps the circumstance that the Emperor of Austria always felt a friendly
feeling towards Bismarck personally, had additional influence; and there might be a not altogether groundless feeling
in existence that the conservative policy of Bismarck was
not unlikely in some way to exert a favourable influence in
Austria. It is said that on one occasion the Emperor
Francis Joseph involuntarily exclaimed, when Bismarck
was severely blamed in his presence, "Ah! if *I* but had
him!"

If, however, Bismarck thus led Austria to the North as
the ally of Prussia, and thus prevented interferences from
other quarters, he also created new difficulties for himself
in the sequence of events, which were to assume far higher
proportions than they usually assumed. He knew very
well that, after the victory over Denmark, the old quarrel
with Austria would break out again—must break out again;
nor could he have omitted to see that a victorious war,
carried on in conjunction with Austria, could not fail

mightily to increase all kinds of sympathies possessed by
Austria in the army, and in conservative Prussia. The
deep abhorrence against any rupture with Austria which
Bismarck had to combat in his own camp, emerged still
more into light after the war in a more animated way, and
rendered his position more difficult from day to day. All
the traditions of glorious alliance of the great period of the
War of Freedom had become revivified in the hut as in the
palace, and they possessed real power; for it is an unquestionable fact that Austria would be the best ally for Prussia
from that moment when it determines to allow Prussia to
take her proper position in Germany without malice or
envy. It was the destiny of Germany that Austria could
not resolve to give Prussia what was Prussia's right;
Bismarck's great political task, however, was to compel the
surrender from Austria of that which is the meed of
Prussia and Germany.

That, however, to which we have alluded, could only
become of value after victory. In the beginning of the
Danish campaign it passed only as a fresh breeze through
the sultry political atmosphere of Prussia. The Progressist
party certainly continued in their inimical position, but the
people themselves began to see daylight; those minds, not
entirely blinded by political passion, gradually obtained
some glimpse of the meaning of Bismarck. The cannon
storm of Missunde had awakened Prussian patriotism;
Prussia had never been deaf when the royal trumpet
sounded to battle, and the Prussian heart has ever stirred
when the eagle standards have been unfolded. This
should, however, be attributed to the advantage of the
Minister whose policy led to the battle-field and the
victory.*

* The notice of the Austro-Prussian Campaign in Denmark receives so
little notice on the part of Bismarck's biographer, that I shrewdly suspect he
does not approve of it as a just act on the part of the hero of this book.
Opinions are much divided on the merits of this annexation; in any case, the
limit of aggression seems to be too great, as the German party has not dared

When Prince Frederick Charles had planted Prussia's standard victoriously on the walls of Düppel in April, 1864, King William himself went to the North to honour his brave warriors. On this triumphant progress Bismarck accompanied him, and there he might have learnt that he was no longer the universally hated Minister-President, but that this victory had greatly increased the number of those who honoured him.

In the summer of the same year he accompanied his royal master to Carlsbad, and at this time he put the new companionship of Austria to a severe trial. Saxon and Hanoverian troops then held the Duchy of Holstein in the name of the German Confederation. It is fortunate for us that we need not enter any further upon the terrible Schleswig-Holstein question. Bismarck considered it necessary to remove the Saxons and Hanoverians from the Duchies, which Prussia and Austria had won with the sword, and that at the peace of Vienna had been ceded to Prussia and Austria by Denmark. By the removal of the troops of the Central States the matter was much simplified, and the question brought a step nearer to solution. It was to be expected that Austria, considering her secret treaties with the Central States, would receive this step with very evil grace; but Bismarck put it into

to appeal for justification to any *plébiscite*. In the end, when animosities are healed, it must be confessed that substantial benefit may accrue to the new subjects of Prussia. It is worth while in this place to preserve a political squib, extensively posted in the towns of the Duchies during the war; probably rather an instigation of the Austrians, whom it indirectly compliments, than a spontaneous outburst of Danish satire. All the walls were covered with it one fine morning, thus :—

> " Es giebt nur eine Kaiserstadt,
>   Und es heisst Wien ;
>   Es giebt nur ein Raüber-nest,
>   Und das ist Berlin ! "

> " There is but one Emperor's town, that is called Wien ;
>   There is but one robbers' nest, and that is Berlin ! "

But perhaps annexation was better than such a kinglet as the Prince of Augustenburg.—K. R. H. M.

cution, and on the Austrian side it was allow
ried out, although the press was enraged at it
marck, who went from Carlsbad throug
nna, and then to Gastein, was well
rney.
From Gastein Bismarck returned in
invitation of the Emperor of
ere he took a share in the gre
d park, and had reason to c
ll. On this visit he was re
the Emperor Francis Jo
Exalted Order of St. Stephen.
From Vienna he accompanied the
n went to his peaceful Reinfeld in
urned again to Baden before going to Bu
took sea-baths up till November. After a short
is he returned to Berlin. Here he resumed his one
tle with the party of progress, whose hatred against
Minister-President, as may be very readily understood,
w more intense as he showed himself the more distin-
ished and greater.
After this "elegantly" conducted war—which was at
e an experiment on the newly reorganized army and
needle-gun, and had roused the patriotically warlike
the real, spirit of Prussia—the King invested his
nister-President with the highest mark of honour
ussia can bestow—the Exalted Order of the Black
gle. Among those who felt obliged epistolarily to
igratulate Bismarck on this well-earned distinction, was
former preceptor, the Director, Dr. Bonnell. One
ning Bismarck called on him personally to thank him.
sat pleasantly chatting with Bonnell's family at the
-table. In his decisive manner he related a great deal
ut Biarritz, where he had enjoyed himself thoroughly;
htly alluded to the numerous threatening letters and
rnings of assassination with which he had been incom-

Varzin

Dem Grafen von Bismarck soll es verbleiben.
So lang sie vom Horste die Reiher nicht treiben.

BISMARCK'S ESTATE IN FARTHER POMERANIA.

moded, but which he despised, as no political party had
ever yet received any benefit from murder. He then
related a dream which he had had in Biarritz. In this
dream he thought he ascended a mountain path which
continually grew narrower, until he found himself before
a wall of rock, and beside him a deep abyss. For an
instant he paused, thinking whether he should retrace his
steps; but he then made up his mind and struck the wall
with his cane, on which it immediately disappeared, and .
his road was free again. After talking of many things
in old and new times, he rose and said,—" I must go now,
or my wife will be uneasy again !"

" Dreams are seems," says the proverb, but perhaps not
always, and at the present time every one knows what the
wall was which vanished before Bismarck's blow.

The following year, 1865, arrived. By the Vienna
peace of the 30th October, 1864, the Duchies of Holstein
and Schleswig were ceded to Prussia and Austria—that
is to say, they had returned whither they belonged, to
Germany. This was, however, especially the result of the
daring and skilful policy of Bismarck, for such a conquest
was quite against the intention and desire of Austria. It
was necessary now to deal with this acquisition, and it
soon appeared that Austria was about to substitute, in
place of the great national policy of Bismarck, the ultimate end of which was very openly expressed—to have a
German Confederation under the leadership of Prussia—
the wretched detail of a new Schleswig-Holstein minor
state. No doubt that in such a policy Austria only
thought of contravening Bismarck's German policy—of
rendering the realization of the Bismarck thought of union
an impossibility. Nor was it remarkable that the Central
States did not support the policy of Bismarck, as they
would certainly have to sacrifice a part of that sovereignty
they had so recently acquired to the nation, if Bismarck's
policy should prove victorious. These sovereigns could

A A

not determine to recede to the position they had so long held as German Princes of the Empire; they desired to assert their apparent sovereignty, and they were unable to perceive, that in case Austria should prevail, they would become Austria's vassals at the expense of the German nation—at the price of Germany's future. It was in vain that Bismarck exerted himself at the Federation, as well as at the German Courts, to introduce more healthy opinions—he could not get forward; and the continually abrupter forms in which Austria acted in the conquered Duchies, admitted of no doubt on his part, that the Viennese politicians, with the whole of their partisans in Germany, were determined to force Prussia to submission; to the abandonment of her saving union policy, to the acceptance of the Austrian Federation—in fact, to her humiliation and dependence.

It was sad enough that Austria, in her inimical action, also reckoned upon the internal conflict in Prussia, which was the more zealously stimulated, in proportion as it became clear to the party of progress that the heart of the nation was more and more turning to the statesman who fought his victories, to the greater fame of Prussia and happiness of Germany, upon a field whither they were unable to follow him—upon the field of honour and of deeds. Of what use in the end was it, that they succeeded in victoriously maintaining, by their high-spiced speeches, a majority in the Chamber against the Ministry—that they embittered the daily life of Bismarck and the other Ministers—and rendered their labours more disagreeable, if this Ministry, despite of all, went victoriously on in the world's history?—and that Bismarck, though he might not get the votes of the majority, won the hearts of the people?

We have no doubt that Bismarck, in the summer of 1865, already believed the hour of the great battle between Prussia and Austria to have arrived, and that he was determined to stand up manfully for his sound policy, and with this conviction we arrive at a great riddle—the episode of Gastein.

Bismarck had accompanied the King, in the summer of 1865, to Carlsbad, thence to Gastein and Salzburg, and so to the Emperor of Austria at Ischl.

The deepest veil of secrecy still covers the events which there took place; it is true the historian, A. Schmidt,[*] assures us that already, on the 15th of July, Bismarck, at Carlsbad, had said to the French Ambassador at the Court of Vienna, the Duc de Grammont, that he considered war between Prussia and Austria to be unavoidable—even that it had become a necessity. But this is unquestionably untrue—as untrue as the further statement of the same historian, that Bismarck, on the 23rd July, said openly to the Prime Minister of the King of Bavaria, the Freiherr von der Pfordten, that " in his firm opinion war between Prussia and Austria was *very likely, and close at hand*. It was a question, as the matter appeared to him, of a *duel* between Austria and Prussia only. The rest of Germany might stand by and contemplate this duel as *passive spectators*. Prussia had never contemplated, *and even now did not think of extending its power beyond the line of the Maine*. The *settlement of the controversy* would not long have to be awaited. *One blow—one pitched battle—and Prussia would be in the position to dictate conditions*. The most urgent need of the Central States was to range themselves on her side. *Neutrality*, even that of Saxon soil, would be observed by Prussia. A localization of the war, and that localization confined to Silesia, was not only determined, but, according to the already ascertained opinions of the most competent military authorities, it was possible. The Central States, in addition to this, by the proclamation of neutrality, were an additional means towards securing this centralization of the war. Bavaria ought, however, to weigh well the fact

---

[*] " Preussen's Deutsche Politik "—" Prussia's German Policy," p. 273.

that she was the natural heir of the position of Austria in South Germany."

What Bismarck really might have said to Freiherr von der Pfordten is not recognizable in this acceptation at all.

On the 14th of August the treaty of Gastein was concluded, which divided the co-domination of Prussia and Austria in Holstein and Schleswig. This treaty compelled Austria to leave the Central States a second time in an ambiguous position; the Central States might have learned from the fact how little really was cared for them at Vienna. This knowledge they had dearly to pay for a year later!

What could have induced Bismarck to conclude this truce—for the treaty of Gastein was nothing else? Who can positively say? To the present time it is an enigma not yet solved. Did military exigencies influence the matter? was the season too far advanced? did European politics stand in the way? or the unconcluded negotiations with Italy? was there a threat of intervention on the other side? had the old sympathies for Austria in Prussia, so greatly stimulated by the recent common campaign, to be respected? did King William follow up the old traditional partiality for Austria? did the King and his Minister wish to give Austria a last term of grace, hoping that Viennese politics might change at the twelfth hour? or did the purchase of the Duchy of Lauenburg afford any loophole of escape?

Perhaps all these questions should be answered in the affirmative. As a matter of fact, the treaty became a last experiment, as to whether it was possible for Prussia to go hand-in-hand with Austria. It must not, however, be forgotten, that this much-deprecated treaty was very favourable to Prussia. Despite the co-domination, Prussia already, by geographical position, remained master in the Duchies, and was always stronger.

From Austria, Bismarck went with the King, by way

unich and Frankfurt, to the Rhine, visited Baden-
ι and Homburg, attended the great review in the
ιce of Saxony, near Merseburg, and then set out for
uchy of Lauenburg, the special Minister of which he
l finally sought for recreation at Biarritz.

the 15th September, 1865, he was raised to the
ɔf a Prussian Count.

ɪhort time after he had returned to Berlin by way of
he was taken ill, and remained an invalid through-
he winter, although he carried on business during
hole time with his accustomed energy.

this period belongs a little episode, which we should
ention at all, did it not show very thoroughly how
is to trust rumour, and had, on the other hand, given
ɪrck an opportunity to write a letter to his old friend
ɪ von Roman, which soon appeared in the Berlin
apers. A photographer at Gastein had issued a
e of Count Bismarck, and beside him the royal
ʼ, Pauline Lucca. At this conjunction many friends
ɪmarck were very angry; all sorts of nonsense was
l on the matter, and at last M. André felt himself
ɪlled to write to Bismarck about it. Bismarck thus
ɪ :—

Berlin, 26th December, 1865.

Dear André,—Although my time is very much taken
up, I cannot refrain from replying to an interpellation
made by an honest heart, in the name of Christ. I am
very sorry if I offend believing Christians, but I am
certain that this is unavoidable for me in my vocation.
I will not say that in the camps politically opposed
to me there are doubtless numerous Christians far in
advance of me in the way of grace, and with whom,
by reason of what is terrestrial to us in common, I
am obliged to live at war; I will only refer to what you
yourself say.

"In wider circles nought of deeds or idleness remains concealed."

What man breathes who in such a position must not give offence, justly or unjustly? I will even admit more, for your expression as to concealment is not accurate. I would to God that, besides what is known to the world, I had not other sins upon my soul, for which I can only hope for forgiveness in a confidence upon the blood of Christ! As a statesman, I am not sufficiently disinterested; in my own mind I am rather cowardly, and that because it is not easy always to get that clearness on the questions coming before me, which grows upon the soil of divine confidence. Whoever calls me an unconscientious politician, does me injustice; he should try his own conscience first himself upon this arena. As to the Virchow business, I am beyond the years in which any one takes counsel in such matters from flesh and blood; if I set my life on any matter, I do it in the same faith in which I have, by long and severe strife, but in honest and humble prayer to God, strengthened myself, and in which no human words, even if spoken by a friend in the Lord and a servant of His Church, can alter me. As to attendance at church, it is untrue that I never visit the house of God. For seven months I have been either absent or ill; who therefore can have observed me? I admit freely that it might take place more frequently, but it is not owing so much to want of time, as from a care for my health, especially in winter; and to those who feel themselves justified to be my judges in this, I will render an account—they will believe, even without medical details. As to the Lucca photograph, you would probably be less severe in your censure, if you knew to what accident it owes its existence. The present Frau von Radden (Mddle. Lucca), although a singer, is a lady of whom, as much as myself, there has never been any reason to say at any time such unpermitted things. Notwithstanding this, I should, had I in a quiet moment thought of the offence which this joke has given to many and faithful friends, have withdrawn myself from the field of the glass pointed at us. You perceive, from the detailed manner in which I reply to you, that I regard your letter as well-intentioned, and by no means place myself above the judgment of those with whom I share a common faith. But, from your friendship and your own Christian feeling, I anticipate that you will recommend to my judges prudence and clemency in similar matters for the future— of this we all stand in need. If among the multitude of sinners who are in need of the glory of God, I hope that His grace will not deprive me of the staff of humble faith in the midst of the dangers and doubts of my calling, by which I endeavour to find out my path. This confidence shall neither find me deaf to censorious words of friendly reproof, nor angry with loveless and proud criticism.

In haste, yours,

BISMARCK.

Although this letter may have become public by an indiscretion which, under other circumstances, we should have deplored, we openly declare here that we do not regret the publication; and our readers will be of our opinion, without its being necessary to say more on the subject, or to qualify the contents of the letter.

We will close this chapter with some letters of Bismarck, written by him in his summer journeys of 1863, 4, and 5, when chiefly in attendance on the King, to his family, and generally to his wife.

Carlsbad, 7th July, 1863.

———— has my warmest sympathy; to lose children is worse than dying, it is so against the order of things. But however long it may last, one follows them. I have to-day had a very sunny walk, from 12 to 2, along the Schweitzerthal, behind the Military Hospital, upwards, and by Donitz on the Eger, above Carlsbad and the hills; then to the King, who, thank God, is getting on well, with three glasses of the waters. I am now living at the "Schild," right opposite the Hirschen Sprung, and from my back windows I can see Otto's Höhe, Drei Kreuzberg, &c. It is very fine, and I am very well, but sometimes have a longing for home; to be with you in Reinfeld, and leave the whole Minister world behind me.

Carlsbad, 13th July, 1863.

I think I shall to-morrow go to Schwarzenberg, and thence to the dusty Wilhelmstrasse, and remain there two days, and then meet the King either at Ratisbon or Salzburg, and go with him to Gastein. How long I shall remain there we shall see. I shall often long to be here again, amidst Aberg, Esterhazyweg, Hammer, Kehrwiederweg, and Aich, and I always knew how to get comfortably rid of acquaintances, or, when I met any, to hide myself in the bushes. To-day I have been at work nearly all day.

Berlin, 17th July, 1863.

Since the evening of the day before yesterday I have been vegetating in our empty halls, smothered under the avalanche of papers and visits which tumbled in upon me as soon as my arrival was known. I am now going into the garden for half an hour, and just give you this sign of life. Yesterday I had a Russian dinner, to-day a French one. To-morrow I leave by way of Dresden, Prague, and Pilsen, for Ratisbon, back to the King, and stay with him at Gastein.

Nürnberg, 19th July, 1863.

I do not know whether I shall send this thick paper off from here, but I happen to have an unemployed moment, which I use to tell you that I am well. I yesterday went from Berlin to Dresden, have visited B. and R., who desire their best remembrances (Countess R. also); I then slept at Leipzig for three hours only, but very well, and after five o'clock came on here, where I must await a train which is to bring me, about eleven at night, to the King at Ratisbon. N. N. has desired the presence of all sorts of people here, with whom I wish to have nothing to do, and for this purpose he has engaged the best hotel. I, therefore, selected another, which, as yet, has made no very favourable impression on me; better paper than this it does not possess. Add to this, that Engel has not a clean shirt in the bag, and my things are at the station, so that I sit here in railway dust and discomfort, waiting for a dinner, most probably bad of its kind.

Travelling agrees with me admirably; but it is very annoying to be stared at like a Japanese at every station. Incognito and its comforts have passed away, until some day, like others, I shall have had my day, and somebody else has the advantage of being the object of general ill-will. I should have been very glad to go viâ Vienna to Salzburg, where the King will be to-morrow. I could have lived our wedding-tour over again, but political reasons dissuaded me; people would have attributed God knows what plans to me, if I had reached there at the same time as ————. I shall, no doubt, see R. by chance at Gastein or Salzburg. I must finish this, although my soup has not yet come; but I cannot get on upon this paper, with a steel pen besides, or I shall get cramp in the fingers.

Salzburg, 22nd July, 6 A.M.

From this charming little town I must write you the date at least, in the moment of my departure. The Roons are all below, waiting to say good-bye. Yesterday we were at Königsee, Edelweiss, and Bartholomäus.

Gastein, 24th July, 1863.

I wanted to send you Edelweiss herewith, but it is mislaid. Salzachofen I thought more imposing ten years ago. The weather was too fine. The road hither, which you did not see, is pretty, but not imposing. I here live opposite the King at the Waterfall—a child to that at Golling. I only saw two finer in the Pyrenees, but none greater. I have taken two baths, very pleasant, but tiring afterwards, unfitting one for work. From to-morrow I shall bathe only at midday, and write before. The air is charming, but the neighbourhood rather imposing than friendly. The King is well.

Gastein, 28th July, 1863.

As this day sixteen years ago brought sunshine into my wild bachelor life, so to-day it has rejoiced this valley, and I have seen it on a morning walk for the first time in all its beauty. Moritz would call it a giant dish full of cabbage, narrow and deep, the edges set round with white eggs. Steep sides, some thousand feet high, covered with furze and meadow-green, and huts of thatch, strewed here and there up to the snow-line, the whole surrounded by a wreath of white peaks and bands, richly powdered with snow during five rainy days, and the lower frontier of which the sun is causing gradually to grow higher. Dozens of silver threads run through the green from above—little water streams, tumbling down hastily, as if they were too late for the great fall which they make with the Ache close before my dwelling. The Ache is a river with somewhat more water than the Stolpe has near Strellin, and waltzes swiftly through all Gastein, falling down at different levels some hundreds of feet between rocks.

It is possible to live here in such weather, but I should prefer to have nothing to do, only to walk about on the heights, and sit down upon sunny banks, smoke, and look at the rocky snow-peaks through the telescope. There is little society here. I only mix with the retinue of the King, with whom dinner and tea bring me in daily contact. The rest of the time scarcely suffices for work, sleeping, bathing, and walking. I yesterday evening visited old ———— with the Emperor, who is expected on the second. N. N. will come, and will complain to me that lying is the curse of this world. I have just heard that the King (who is very well, only he has hurt his ankle, and must sit still) keeps the courier till to-morrow, and this letter will not reach by post any sooner, as it would lose a day by being opened. I shall therefore leave it. Good Prince Frederick was yesterday released from his sufferings: the King was much overcome.

Gastein, 2nd Aug., 1863.

Bill's day was kept by me in fine weather, and the King was informed; he asked how old he was, and how industrious his godson might be. To-day the Emperor is coming, flags and garlands are the order of the day, the sun is shining, and I have not yet been out of my room; have been writing for three hours, therefore no more than hearty greetings. If I do not write by way of Berlin, I fall into the hands of the post-office here—certainly I write no secrets, but it is very unpleasant. The mare is in Berlin again. I bathe every day; it is agreeable, but tiring.

Gastein, 12th Aug., 1863.

I am very well, but the couriers are in terror in all directions. Yesterday I shot two chamois at an elevation of seven thousand feet—quite cooked, despite the height. On the 15th we leave here for Salzburg—the 16th, Stuttgart—17th, Baden. On account of the Frankfurt nonsense I cannot leave the King.

Gastein, 14th Aug., 1863.

In order that you may see whether it is really quicker, I send this letter by the post, the courier starting at the same time. I have been writing for four hours, and have got so tired that I can hardly hold my pen. There has been a hot sun for a week, in the evenings storm. The King is well, but the baths have shaken him; he bathes daily, and works as if he were in Berlin; there is no saying anything to him. God grant it may go well with him! To-day I take my last bath—twenty or twenty-one in all, in twenty-six days. I am very well, but worked to death. I am so engaged that I can see very few people. To-morrow evening we sleep at Salzburg—on the 16th, probably at Munich—the 17th, at Stuttgart, Constance, or Baden; it is uncertain. Write to Baden, where I shall probably stay a few days. A letter came from ——— at Spa; perhaps I shall visit her there, but who knows *ce qu'on devient* in a week? Perhaps everything will be different.

———

Baden, 28th Aug., 1863.

I really long to spend a lazy day among you; here, on the most charming days, I never get away from ink. Yesterday I went for a walk till midnight, in the loveliest moonlight, through the fields, but cannot get business out of my head; society also gives no rest. N. N. is charming to see, but talks too much politics to me; ——— naturally is always full of rumours; ———, who is usually so delightful to me, has people about her who disturb my satisfaction; and new acquaintances are very troublesome. A. is especially pleasant. With him and E., who is here for two days, I yesterday dined in my apartment. The King is well, but besieged by intrigue. To-day I dine with Her Majesty the Queen. Schleinitz is here, Hohenzollern expected, Goltz gone to Paris. I think the King will not leave here till Sunday; a few days later I must be in Berlin; perhaps I shall have time in between for a trip to Spa, where I shall find O. Perhaps I shall have to go to the Queen of England, whom the

King proposes to visit at Rosenau, near Coburg. In any case, I hope to have a few days free in September for Pomerania. I wish that some intrigue would necessitate another Ministry, so that I might honourably turn my back upon this ewer of ink, and live quietly in the country. The restlessness of this existence is unbearable; for ten weeks I have had secretary's work at an inn, and again at Berlin. It is no life for an honest country nobleman, and I regard every one as a benefactor who seeks to bring about my fall. With this the flies are humming and tickling and stinging all over the room, so that I really want a change in my position, which in a few minutes the Berlin train will certainly bring me, by a courier with fifty empty despatches.

Berlin, 4th September, 1863.

At last I find a moment to write to you. I had hoped to have a few days of recreation at Kröchlendorff, but it is all the old treadmill over again; last night work till one o'clock, and I then poured the ink over it instead of sand, so that it ran down over my knees. To-day the Ministers were here at nine, and for the second time at one, and with them the King. The question for discussion was the dissolution of the Chamber, for which I had no heart. But it could not be otherwise; God knows what the use of it is. Now we shall have the Electoral swindle! With God's help I am well through it all; but an humble reliance on God is required, not to despair of the future of our country. May He, above all, grant our King good health! It is not very pleasant in this empty house, but I do not notice it on account of work. The horses have arrived to-day in much better condition. The trouble about the mare was groundless.

Bukow. 21st September, 1863.

I wished to-day, on the last day of summer, to write

you a very comfortable and reasonable letter, and full of this idea lay down on the sofa three hours ago, but only woke a quarter of an hour before dinner, which is about six. At seven I had gone out, to ride until half-past one, in the capacity of " Herr Oberstwachtmeister," to see our brave soldiers burn powder and form attacks. I first joined Fritz, who commanded three regiments of cavalry, then went over to the Garde du Corps, stormed like a man over stock and block, and for a long time have had no pleasanter day. I am living next to the King and two adjutants in a nice old house of Count Hemming's; it is a pretty neighbourhood, with hillocks, lakes, and woods, and, above all, there is nothing to do, after finishing my busi- ness with ———— yesterday. To-morrow, I am sorry to say, I must go on the treadmill again: and now to dinner, having slept myself quite stupid, and wrenched my neck on the steep sofa. We have eighty persons at table, all sorts of foreign officers, Englishmen, Russians, besides the whole Federation in the house. I have no mufti clothes with me, so for forty-eight hours am wholly a major.

Berlin, 29th September, 1863.

I was so far ready on Saturday that I had only an interview with the King before me, and hoped to be with you on Sunday at noon. But the interview led to my having four hours of autograph work, and the necessity of seeing the King before his departure for Baden. There was just time for one day at Kröchlendorff, whither I repaired on Saturday evening, after writing myself crooked and lame, to reach there at midnight. Yesterday morning drove to Passow, reached the King by five, and at a quarter to eight attended him to the railroad. To-day I accompany Moritz and Roon to Freienwalde, must see Bernhard about Kniephof, and hope to come to you the day after to-morrow, if there should remain time enough to make it worth while. I am to follow the King to Baden; the "when" will be first known from our correspondence and the business in hand. If there should be time enough for me to remain two or three days at Reinfeld, I will come; if not, the harness-makers will preponderate over my rest, and I shall see you again here in Berlin. On the 17th I then shall probably return with the King from Cologne. M. is sitting opposite, and is working out at my table a joint matter.

Berlin, 27th October, 1863.

It is bitterly cold, but I am quite well. Are you also making fires up at Reinfeld? I hope so; we have been doing so here for more than a week. Yesterday, after dinner, I sat with K. in the blue saloon, and he was playing when I received your letter of Sunday. Indeed the letter you wrote was written in quite a holiday humour. Believe in God, my heart, and on the proverb that barking dogs do not bite. I did not accompany the King to Stralsund, it being a tiring journey, and would retard my work for two days. This evening His Majesty has returned: the threats against his life are far more menacing than those directed against me; but this, too, is in the hands of God. Do not allow the last few fine days to be dimmed by care; and if you are coming, send some feminine being in advance to arrange everything as you wish it. I must go to work. Farewell! This morning, at nine, only three degrees,* and a hot sun. The enclosed† I have twice received this morning from two different quarters.

Babelsberg, 1st November, 1863.

I employ a moment in which I am awaiting the King, who is dining at Sans Souci, to write a line as if from Zarskoe or Peterhof, only to say that I am well,

---

* 35° Fahr.—K. R. H. M.   † A copy of the ninety-first Psalm.

and am heartily rejoiced that I shall soon see you ruling again in the empty apartments at Berlin. On the 9th comes the Diet, with all its worry; but I think, on the day of the opening, I shall go with His Majesty to Letzlingen, and pass two days in the woods. During that time you will, I hope, have done with the hammering and dragging, the necessary accompaniment of your beloved advent, and on my return I shall then find everything in the right place.

For the last few days I have been living alone and industrious, have generally dined alone, and, except for a ride, have not left the house; have been quiet and bored; occasionally there has been a Council of Ministers. This week we shall probably have them daily in the matter of our dear Chambers; and as the King has been a week in Stralsund and Blankenburg, plenty of work has accumulated. I just hear his carriage-wheels, and close with hearty greetings.

Carlsbad, Tuesday, 1864.

God be thanked that you are all well; so am I, but more than ever engaged. At Zwickau on the Perron I met Rechberg; we came on together in one coupé and carriage to this place; thus we talked politics for six hours, and for the first time here. Yesterday evening at tea with the Grand Duchess, King Otho, Archduke Charles Frederick, many diplomatists, and much work with R.

Carlsbad, 20th July, 1864.

The King has just set out for Marienbad, through espaliers of beautiful ladies, with giant bouquets, which more than filled his carriage. R. with "*Vivats*," "hurrah!" great excitement. For me there is now some leisure, all my acquaintances being gone. To-morrow morning early for Vienna; we shall sleep at Prague. Perhaps in a week we shall have peace with the Danes; perhaps this winter again war. I shall make my stay in Vienna as short as possible, to lose as few baths as possible at Gastein. After that, I shall probably accompany the King again to Vienna, then to Baden; then the Emperor of Russia is coming to Berlin in the beginning of September. Before that time there is no prospect of rest—if then.

Vienna, 22nd July, 1864.

Yesterday morning I came with ―――― and ―――― and two others, who lend me their caligraphic aid, from Carlsbad, in a carriage as far as Prague; thence by railway hither to-day; unfortunately this time not to go by water to Linz, especially to worry myself and others. I am living with ―――― for the present; have seen nobody but R. I was rain-bound for two hours in the Volksgarten, and listened to music. Stared at by the people as if I was a new hippopotamus for the Zoological Gardens, for which I consoled myself with some very good beer. How long I shall remain here I cannot tell; to-morrow I have many visits to pay; dine with R. in the country; then, if possible, conclude peace with Denmark, and fly as swiftly as possible to the mountain in Gastein. I wish it were all over. The two days of journeying have somewhat mentally rested me, but in body I am very tired, and say good-night to you.

Vienna, 27th July, 1864.

I have received one letter from you here, and long for the second. I lead an industrious life—four hours a day with tough Danes, and am not at the end yet. By Sunday it must be settled whether we are to have peace or war. Yesterday I dined with M――; a very agreeable wife, and pretty daughters. We drank a good deal, were very merry, which is not often the case in their sorrow, of which you are aware. He has grown grey.

B B

and has cut his hair short. Yesterday, after the conference, I dined with the Emperor at Schönbrunn, took a
walk with R—— and W——, and thought of our moonlight expedition. I have just been for an hour in the Volksgarten, unfortunately not incognito, as I was seventeen
years ago—stared at by all the world. This existence on
the stage is very unpleasant when one wishes to drink a
glass of beer in peace. On Saturday I hope to leave for
Gastein, whether it is peace or no. It is too hot for me
here, particularly at night.

————

Gastein, 6th August, 1864.

Work gets continually worse; and here, where I can
do nothing in the morning after the bath, I do not know
when to get time for anything. Since my arrival on the
2nd, in a storm with hailstones as hard as bullets, I have
just been able, in magnificent weather, for the first time,
to go out by rule. On my return, I wish to employ the
half-hour at my disposal in writing to you. A—— was,
however, here immediately, with plans and telegrams, and
I must be off to the King. I am, however, by the
blessing of God, quite well. I have had four baths, but
shall hardly get more than eleven, as the King sets out
on the 15th. Since yesterday I have been very comfortably lodged, as a large cool corner room, with a magnificent landscape, was vacant; until then I had been living
in a sun-blinding oven, at least by day. The nights are
pleasantly fresh. The King probably goes hence to
Vienna in short day journeys, by way of Ischl, and
thence to Baden. Whether I shall accompany him to
the latter place is uncertain. I still hope to get away for
a few days to my quiet Pomerania; but what is the use
of plans?—something always comes in between. I have
not a gun with me, and every day there is a chamois
hunt; certainly, I have also had no time. To-day seven-

teen were shot, and I was not there; it is a life like that
of Leporello:—

> " Neither rest by day or night,
> Naught to make my comfort right."

Just now I had the whole room full of ladies, flying
from the rain, which relieves guard with the sun to-day.
Fr— from R——, with two cousins, Frau von P——, a
Norwegian. I have long since heard no feminine voice,
not since Carlsbad. Farewell!

It is too strange that I should be living in the rooms
on the ground-floor, abutting on the private reserved
garden where, very nearly seventeen years ago, we intruded
in the moonlight. If I look over my right shoulder I can
see, through a glass door, the dark beech clump-hedge by
which we wandered, in the secret delight of the forbidden,
up to the glass window behind which I am living. It
was then inhabited by the Empress, and I now repeat our
walk by moonlight at greater ease. The day before the
day before yesterday I left Gastein; slept at Radstedt.
The day before yesterday went, in misty weather, to
Aussee—a charmingly-situated place; a beautiful lake,
half Traunsee and half Königssee; at sunset reached the
Hallstädtersee; 'thence, by boat, in the night, to Hall-
stadt, where we slept. Next morning was pleasant and
sunny; at noon we reached the King at Ischl, and so,
with His Majesty, over the Traunsee to Gmunden, where
we passed the night, and I thought a great deal of L——,
H——, and B——, and all those times. To-day, by
steamer, hither, arriving about six. passing two hours
with R——, after convincing myself that ———— is one
of the most beautiful women, of whom all pictures give a

B B 2

false idea. We stay here three days; what follows, whether Baden or Pomerania, I cannot yet foresee. I am now heartily tired, so wish you and all of ours good-night.

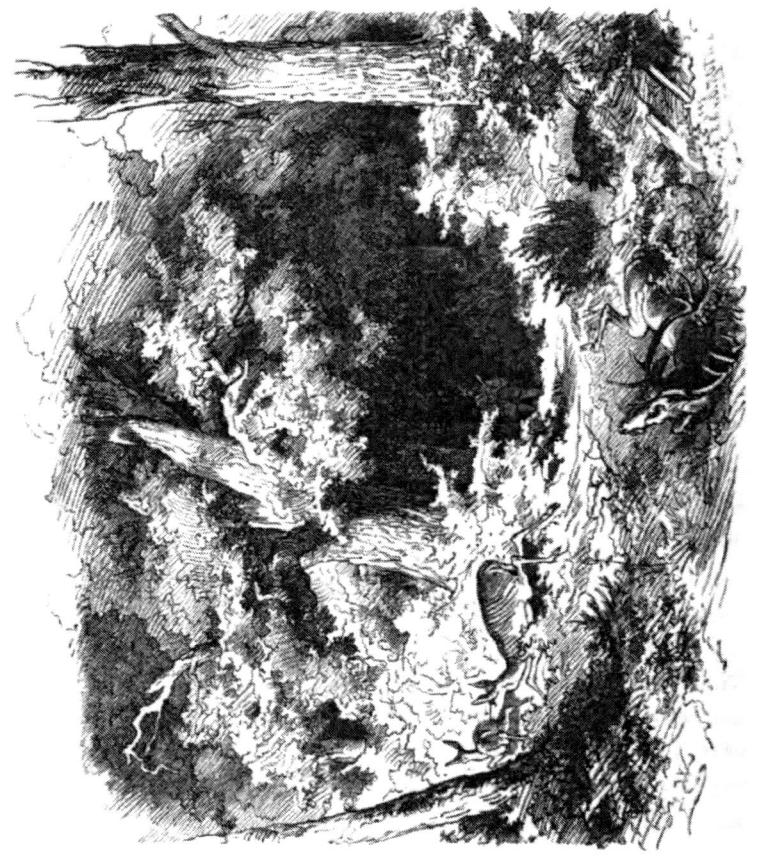

Schönbrunn, Thursday.

The King went early this morning to Salzburg; I follow him to-morrow. This morning I killed fifty-three pheasants, fifteen hares, and one karinckel; and yesterday eight stags and two moufflons. I am quite lame in hand and cheek from shooting. To-morrow evening it will be

decided whether I am to go to Baden, but now I go to **bed.** Good-night all, for I am very tired.

———

Baden, 1st September, 1864.

The King arrived this morning from Mainau, well and cheerful, having been through the rain with the Queen to the races. A.'s busy hand continually shakes over me new blessings of projects, as soon as I have worked through the old ones. I do not know whence I wrote to you last; I have hardly come to my senses since Vienna; slept one night in Salzburg, the second at Munich; conferred much and lengthily with N. N., who has grown thin. I then slept at Augsburg, and thence came, by way of Stuttgart, to this place, in the hope of passing two days in lazy rest, but only had two hours intermission in the forest yesterday morning. Couriers, ink, audiences, and visits, constantly buzz round me without interruption. ——— is also here. I dare not show myself on the promenade; no one leaves me at peace.

———

Frankfurt, 11th September, 1864.

It is long since I have written to you hence, and never from the Zeil. We alighted at the Russian Embassy; the King has driven to the Emperor Alexander at Jugenheim; thence he visits the Empress Eugénie at Schwalbach, and I have got myself free for a day, which I spend with K. at Heidelberg. I accompany her to Heidelberg, shall be back here about two or three—time enough to devote myself to the Diet; to-morrow morning early to Berlin, whence, after the necessary cavilling, I shall start for Pomerania.

———

Bordeaux, 6th October, 1864.

Excuse this scrawl, but I have no paper at hand, and only wish to apprise you that I have reached this place safely. It seems almost like a dream to be here again. Yesterday morning I started from Baden, slept very well at Paris, set out this morning about eleven, and now at eleven P.M. am here. I think of leaving for Bayonne to-morrow morning at eight, to reach Biarritz by two. In Paris it was still cold; in Baden yesterday there was an early frost; on this side of the Loire things grew better; here it is decidedly warm—warmer than any night this year. I am, in fact, already quite well, and would be *quite* cheerful if I only knew that all was well with you. At Paris I felt very much inclined to live there again; he had arranged the house there very well, and the life I lead at Berlin is a kind of penal servitude when I think of my independent life abroad. If it agree with me, I think I shall take about fifteen baths, so that on the 21st or 22nd I shall set out on my return journey; if God wills, you will then be— or perhaps somewhat earlier—at Berlin. In his care, Engel has locked me in; there is no bell, and this letter will lose a day, as it cannot be sent to the post to-night. It is so warm that I have the window open.

Biarritz, 9th Oct., 1864.

When I remember how assiduously we lighted fires in Baden, and even in Paris, and that here the sun graciously requests me to take off my paletot and drawers, that we sat till ten by the sea in the moonlight, and this morning breakfast in the open air, and that I am writing to you at the open window, looking at the blue and sunny sea, and on bathing folks who are wandering about in very slight costumes, paddling with naked feet in the water, I cannot help saying that southern nations possess a peculiar grace of God in their climate. I shall not yet bathe more than once, but shall soon venture upon two, if not, *à la* ———, upon more. The only comfort I require is to hear from you. If we were free people, I should propose to you to come with child and baggage to this place, and remain here the whole winter, as many of the English do, from reasons of economy, which prevails here in the winter season.

Biarritz, 12th Oct., 1864.

My dear Sister!—I am so delightfully disengaged that I can send a few lines in the direction of my thoughts! I am well, particularly since I have yesterday and to-day at last received news of Johanna's gradual recovery. I reached here on the forenoon of the 7th—in Paris we still had fires, from Bordeaux an agreeable temperature, and here heat so that summer clothing was necessary. Since yesterday there has been a north wind, and it is cooler, but still warmer than I have felt it all the summer. A very light summer coat was too hot for me on my evening's walk by the shore. Until now I have taken seven baths, and now proceed with two *per diem*. I am writing to you by the open window, with flickering lights, and the moonlit sea before me, the plash of which is accompanied by the carriage bells on the road to Bayonne. The lighthouse in front of me changes its light from red to white, and I am looking with some appetite at the clock to see whether the dinner hour of seven has not arrived. I have not for a long time found myself in such comfortable climatic and business conditions, and yet the evil habit of work has rooted itself so deeply in my nature, that I feel some disquiet of conscience at my laziness— almost long for the Wilhelmstrasse, at least if my dear ones were there. "*Monsieur, le diner est servi,*" is the announcement.

The 13th.—I could not yesterday write any farther. After dinner we took a moonlight walk on the southern shore, from which we returned, very tired, at about eleven o'clock. I slept till nine; about ten bathed in water of 14° warmer* than ever I had found the North Sea in August; and now we are going together to Fuent Arabia, beyond the frontier; shall dine on our way back at St. Jean de Luz. The weather is heavenly to-day, the sea quiet and blue; it is almost too hot to walk in the sun.

Izazu, 17th October, 1864.

Although I have this morning sent you a letter by the courier, *pour la rareté du fait*, I must write to you from this remarkable place. We breakfasted here, three miles to the east of Biarritz, in the mountains, and

* 55° Fahr.

are seated in charming summer weather at the edge of a rushing stream, the name of which we cannot learn, as nobody speaks French—nothing but Basque. There are high narrow rocks before and behind us, with heather, ferns, and chestnuts all around. The valley is called Le Pas de Roland, and is the west end of the Pyrenees. Before we went off we took our baths—the water cold, the air like July. The courier despatched, we had a charming drive through mountains, forests, and meadows. After eating and drinking, and climbing ourselves tired, our party of five are sitting down reading to each other, and I am writing myself on the lid of the box in which were the grapes and figs we brought with us. At five we shall return with the sunset and moonlight to Biarritz, and dine about eight. It is too pleasant a life to last. The 20th, the evening before last, we went to Pau. It was heavy and sultry there, and at night storm and rain; we were in the railway, but came from Bayonne hither by carriage; the sea magnificent. After it had been as smooth as a duck-pond for some days with the land winds, it now looks like a boiling cauldron, and the wind is warm and moist with it; the sun alternates with rain—very Atlantic weather.

To-day I take my fourteenth bath; I shall hardly get more than fifteen, for it seems I must to-morrow leave this warm shore. I am still striving between duty and taste; but I fear the first will conquer. I will first take my bath, and then decide whether it shall be the penultimate one. Anyhow, the fourteen days I have spent here have done me good, and I only wish I could transport you, without travelling discomfort, hither or to Pau.

Paris, 25th October, 1864.

Before going to bed, after a tiring day, I will announce to you my fortunate arrival here. Yesterday noon I left dear Biarritz; they were making hay in the meadows when I started in the hot sun. Friends accompanied me as far as Bayonne; at about six A.M. I arrived here. Plenty of politics, audience at St. Cloud, a dinner at Drouyn de Lhuys's, and now I am going to bed tired out.

Carlsbad, 12th July, 1865.

I am ashamed that I did not write to you on your birthday; but there is so much of "must" in my life that I scarcely ever get to "will." The treadwheel goes on from day to day, and I seem as if I were the tired horse in it, pushing it along without getting any forwarder. One day after the other a courier arrives, one day after the other another departs—between while come others from Vienna, Munich, or Rome; the burthen of papers increases, ministers are all at odds, and from this centre I am obliged to write to each of them singly.

The review I hope to stop; as far as I know, the actual return has not yet reached the King; but I have brought the matter forward, and His Majesty has promised to examine into the provision question for man and horse. To-morrow I will inquire in the military cabinet as to how far the writing has got.

Late in the evening, the 13th.

The whole day I have been writing, dictating, reading, going down and up the mountain as to the report to the King. The courier's bag and my letter are both closing. Across the table I see the Erzgebirge, along the Tepl by the evening twilight, very beautiful; but I feel leathery and old. The King starts from here on the 19th, five days off, for Gastein, whither the Emperor designs to come. On the road I will see ——— somewhere in Bavaria. "Neither rest by day nor night." It looks ugly for peace—it must be settled at Gastein.

I begin to count the days I shall have to sit through in this fog chamber. As to what the sun looks like, we have only dark reminiscences from a better past. Since this morning it has at least been cold; until then sultry moist heat, with a change only in the form of rain, and continued uncertainty as to whether one gets wet with rain or perspiration, when one stumps up and down the esplanade steps in the mud. How people with nothing to do can endure it I do not understand. What with bathing, work, dinner, reports, and tea at His Majesty's, I have scarcely time to realize the horrors of the situation. These last three days there has been a theatre of comedians here; but one is almost ashamed to go, and most people avoid the passage through the rain. I am very well through it all, particularly since we have had Kaltenhaüser beer. ——— and ——— are dreadfully cast down from not knowing what to drink. The landlord gives them bad beer in order to force them to drink worse wine. Other news than this there is none from this steam-kitchen, unless I talk politics.

———

For some days I have had no time to send you any news. Count Blome is here again, and we are zealously labouring at the maintenance of peace and the repair of the fissures in the buildings. The day before yesterday I devoted a day to the chase. I think I wrote you word how fruitless the first was. This time I have at least shot a young chamois, but saw no others in the three hours during which I abandoned my motionless self to the experiments of the most various insects; and the prattling activity of the waterfall beneath me convinced me of the deep-rooted feeling which caused some one before my time to express the wish, "Streamlet, let thy rushing be!" In my room, also, this wish is justified both by day and by night

—one breathes on reaching any place where the brutal noise
of the waterfall cannot be heard.   In the end, however, it
was a very pretty shot, right across the chasm; killed
first fire, and the brute fell headlong into the brook, some
church-steeple's height beneath me.   My health is good, and

I feel myself much stronger.   We start on the 19th—that
is Saturday—for Salzburg.   The Emperor will probably
make his visit there, and one or two days will be spent
besides at Ischl.   The King then goes to Hohenschwangau.
I go to Munich, and join His Majesty again at Baden.
What next may follow depends upon politics.   If you are

in Homburg long enough, I hope to take a trip over to you from Baden—to enjoy the comforts of domesticity.

Baden, 1st September, 1865.

I reached this place the day before yesterday morning, slept till half-past twelve, then had much hard work; dinner with the King—long audience. In the evening a quartette at Count Flemming's with Joachim, who really performs on his violin in a most wonderful way. There were many acquaintances of mine on the racecourse yesterday whom I did not very well remember.

September begins rainy. Two-thirds of the year are gone just when one has grown accustomed to write 1865. Many princes are here. At four ——— wants to see me; she is said to have grown very beautiful. The King leaves at five—it is undecided whether to Coblenz or Coburg, on account of Queen Victoria, whom he desires to meet. I hope in any case to pass by way of Frankfurt on the 5th or 6th. Whether, or how long, I can be in Homburg, will soon be seen—longer than one day in no case, as I must be with the King in Berlin.

Baden, Sunday.

That you may see what a husband you have, I send you the route. We go to-morrow morning, at six o'clock, to Coburg, to the Queen of England. I must go too, and I am sorry to say Spa is all over for me; but it cannot be otherwise.

CHAPTER III.

THE GREAT YEAR 1866.

Disputes with Austria.—The Central States.—Mobilization of the Army.—
Bismarck shot at by Kohn-Blind, 7th May, 1866.—Excitement in Berlin.—
War Imminent.—Declaration.—The King sets out on the Campaign.—
Sichrow.—Litschen.—Battle of Sadowa, 3rd July, 1866.—Bismarck with
His Majesty on the Battle-field.—Negotiations of Nicolsburg.—Treaty of
Prague.—Illness of Bismarck.—Consolidation of Prussia.—Triumphant
Entry of the Army into Berlin.—Peace.

ERE the year 1865 was at an end, Bismarck had become
firmly convinced that Austria had lapsed from the Treaty
of Gastein and had returned to the Central State policy,
the advocate of which was the Freiherr von Beust. This
policy, which could only ultimate in eternizing the old
vacillating system at the Federation between Prussia and
Austria, as this was the only way in which the existence of
the Central State sovereignties could be prolonged, was
skilfully guarded by the Freiherr von Beust, and always

presented the seductive appearance of moderation, as it neither conceded anything to Prussia nor Austria, but kept the one constantly in check against the other. That Germany was certainly being imperilled by it, politicians entirely overlooked. At the moment Prussia had the preponderance, not only actually, as Bismarck in fact and truth pursued a national policy, but also formally, as it had separated Austria by the Treaty of Gastein from the Central States. According to the principles of the Central States, Prussia had now to be depressed, and Austria elevated. Here was the point at which Bismarck awaited his diplomatic opponents. Had they been the German patriots for which they were so anxious to pass—and perhaps they quite honestly deemed themselves such—they would have come to the material point, and demanded more from Austria for Germany than Prussia had offered. Austria was in the position to accede to the German princes—perhaps to the German people—more than Prussia could do, whose whole position was much more awkward. Austria did not imperil her entire autonomy as Prussia did. Bismarck, however, knew his Pappenheimers —the Central State policy did not go upon the material, but the formal point—and only used their federation with Austria to force Prussia to the acceptance of a new Augustenburg minor State north of the Elbe.

So little a policy necessarily would come to destruction in face of the energy with which Bismarck clung to his national programme. This also became very ominous for Austria, for she saw herself obliged to give battle upon a basis which tottered under her. Faithful to the traditions of her old policy, Austria sought to win the Courts by promises, and she succeeded ; but she knew very well that little or nothing was gained thereby. The result has shown how little worth Austria set upon the German Confederation. Prussia, while she asked, promised nothing. Bismarck adhered to his policy, which only

demanded sacrifices on the part of the princes—sacrifices
for Germany, not for Prussia, who was ready to bring far
greater ones than any minor State.

Thus approached the hour of decision—a decision
whether in future the German people, under the leadership
of Prussia, should assume her proper place in Europe, or
whether it should coalesce into a weak federation of im-
puissant territories, under Austrian satraps, and be blindly
obedient to every signal from Vienna.

Preparations were made in every direction; but it was
certain that in Vienna, in a scarcely credible misapprehen-
sion of Prussia, the authorities had armed for a long time
only because it was believed that Prussia was to be terrified by such armaments. At Vienna, the peaceable disposition of the venerable King William, who, to the last
moment, hoped for a peaceful termination, which was
indeed possible until the firing of the first cannon shot,
was looked upon as fear. Was it impossible for Austria,
without any stain upon her honour, to concede to Prussia
and Germany in May all that which she had solemnly
acknowledged at Prague in August?

It would be far beyond the limits of this book to enter
upon the fomented quarrels in the Elbe Duchies and at the
Diet on the diplomatic recriminations concerning the earlier
or later armaments. We conceive that we have already
sufficiently set forth Bismarck's policy; for our purpose it
is quite unimportant whether Austria really desired war, or
whether her object was to terrorize. King William did *not*
wish for war; but he wished to be free from Austria, for the
present and future, in the interests of Prussia and Germany.
Prussia had seriously armed; for whoever desires to attain
an end must have the means to attain it, and Bismarck
had not forgotten what had caused the fall of the Radowitz
policy. But Radowitz had not been wrecked upon the
insufficiency of the Prussian military system of his day,
but on the actual course of foreign policy.

VICTORY !

How had this changed since the days of Erfurt and Olmütz?

In judging of the rupture with the Diet, it must be here again borne in mind, what had become of it since 1851, what position it had assumed towards Prussia. Count Bismarck, on the re-establishment of the Diet in 1851, had been sent to Frankfurt as a friend of Austria. Prussia desires to co-operate openly and freely with Austria, and that this was also the endeavour of Count Bismarck, his whole political behaviour had testified at the very time in the most unequivocal manner, when Austria, weakened by internal revolution, was obliged to resort to foreign assistance. He soon perceived, however, that such co-operation was impossible. The necessary condition of it was the equalization of Prussia with Austria, and this had also been promised at Olmütz. Count Bismarck could not allow Prussia to be the *second* German power. He used to say that as Austria was " one " so also Prussia was " one ;" nor could he interpret the treaties in any other way than as they were understood until 1848 ; that Prussia, no more than Austria, could subordinate themselves to resolutions of the majority.

But this principal condition Austria allowed only to herself : a hegemony over Germany was the policy of Prince Schwarzenberg, and his successors adhered to this word. Count Bismarck soon convinced himself that all federal complaisance only called forth further demands, that gratitude and sympathy in the policy of the empire were as little thought of as national feelings and German interests.

Austria did not desire any nearer approach to Prussia ; she would come to any understanding. She began by securing to herself an obedient majority at the Diet, and believed that she could dispense with extending the competency and sphere of action of the Federation, after making the Diet, by the institution of the influence of the

c c

majorities, and the suppression of the right of protest in the minority, a serviceable instrument of Viennese policy, and thus gradually do away with the right of protest and the independence of the individual States, and thus also that of Prussia. The Austrian Ministers went so far as to assert that Austria alone in the Federation had any right to a foreign policy; and this Austrian policy should be endowed with the semblance of legality by the resolution of the servile majority in the Diet. In such an aspiration Austria found from the Central States an only too willing sympathy. To the ambition and thirst for action of the Ministers of the latter, the territorial dimensions of their own country and the circle of activity assigned to them seemed not important or distinguished enough. It flattered them to be engaged in questions of European policy. This, indeed, they could enter upon without danger or a necessity for reciprocity; and they speedily found a natural consequence of the principle of federal law in the fact, that the members of the Federation need follow no foreign policy of their own, but would only have to follow such as might be dictated by the majority.

But the mediatization of the foreign policy of Prussia was not the only object held in view. If the course of European politics admitted of it, it was proposed as a further consequence to declare as an undoubted issue of federal jurisprudence, that the constitution and laws of Prussia should be subject to the determination of the majority.

The Central States saw themselves placed on an equality with Prussia with the highest satisfaction. They were ready to make any sacrifice otherwise so obstinately refused, except independence, if Prussia were only subjected to the same. They could not forgive Prussia her greatness and high position, and therefore they experienced an especial delight in making Prussia feel the importance of the Federation. The securer they felt of the majority, the less concealed and bold were their pretensions, and every demand of Austria on Prussia, however unjust, found ready support from the Central States, especially if the question were to combat the estimation and influence of Prussia in Germany. The majority was always to decide, even as to the question of their own right of decision, and there was no hesitation in doing violence to words and sound common sense to prove a united vote as to such a proceeding. They endeavoured to deceive the world and themselves by the fallacy that "Federal Diet" and "Germany" were identical ideas, and the opinions of Prussia were stigmatized as being non-German, while Prussia was accused of stirring up strife in the Federation, when she declined unconditionally to submit to the arbitrary decisions of the majority in the Diet, while Austria allowed herself to be praised to the skies in her paid press as the exclusive representative of Germany and German interests. But even at that time did many believe this? Had not Austria betrayed her real views and intentions in the secret despatch of the 14th of January, 1855, in a most unequivocal manner? Openly and without any reticence she had declared in that document that she would have no hesitation in destroying the Federation to carry through her policy. She had invited the Federal Governments, in contravention of the articles of federation, to enter into a warlike alliance with her and place her troops at the disposition of the Emperor of Austria, and promised them advantages at the expense of those who refused such an alliance—that is, by way of territorial aggrandisement.

The political life of Count Bismarck in Frankfurt was an uninterrupted fight against such a system as above described. He was never weary in pointing out and warning them that the elements ruling at the Diet were tending towards conditions which Prussia could not accept as permanent. He had also predicted at Frankfurt that the plan took a direction towards placing Prussia, as soon

c c 2

as the fruit was believed to be ripe, in the position that it would have to reject a resolution of the majority, then to commit a breach of the Federation, which should be ascribed to Prussia.

So also was the event. Prussia remained faithful to the Federation till it was violated by others, and when they had done, they blamed Prussia with the breach of the Federation:

The spring of the great year 1866 was the most difficult in Bismarck's life. The terrible load of responsibility pressed heavier and heavier upon him. Serious and well-intentioned, as well as perfidious, attempts at peace, lamed and impeded his activity. Intrigues of all kinds hovered about his person. His position was now openly assailed, now secretly undermined. More than once he felt the ground trembling beneath him—he could not get forward; and in addition to this he was corporeally ill; rheumatic pains increasing in an alarming way. Doubt very often, it is probable, assailed the strong mind of Bismarck, the ghastly ray of suspicion fell upon his courageous heart. The man who had to fight for his King and country, with all the powers, the traditions of ancient brotherhood in arms, the ties of princely relationship, the intrigues of diplomatists, the falling away of old friends, with the wrong-headedness, cowardice, low-mindedness of others, down to the pacific overtures of his opponents, in so superhuman a manner, now gradually grew into a more and more intensified battle with himself. On this the Almighty, the Lord of him and of Prussia, had mercy on him. He gave him a great sign.

On the 7th of May, 1866, at five in the afternoon, Count Bismarck was walking abroad for the first time after his severe illness, returning from an interview with the King, and proceeding up the centre allée of the Unter den Linden. Almost opposite the hotel of the Imperial Russian Embassy, he heard two rapidly following reports behind him. As it was afterwards found, one bullet had just grazed his side. Count Bismarck turned swiftly round, and saw a young man before him, who was raising his revolver to fire a third time. Bismarck met the man quickly, and seized him by the arm and by the throat; but

before he reached him the man fired the third shot. It was a glance shot on the right shoulder, which Bismarck felt for a long time afterwards. Then the wretch passed the revolver, as quick as lightning, from the right to the left hand, and close to him fired two other shots at the Minister-President. One shot missed him in consequence of a quick turn, only burning his coat; but the other struck him, and at this moment Count Bismarck believed himself mortally wounded, for he felt that one of the bullets had struck him right on the rib. The rib probably feathered, as they say in deer-shooting — *i.e.*, it bent elastically. Count Bismarck at once mastered the sensation of weakness which had come over him by the concussion of the vertebræ through the rib for an instant. He handed over the criminal—whom he had held with an iron grasp—to the officers and men of the First Battalion of the Second Foot Guard Regiment, who were just marching down the street, and walked on in the direction of his house in the Wilhelmstrasse, where he safely arrived before the news of the attempt was known.

During the whole period preceding the war, there was nothing extraordinary in the Minister-President's being with the King longer than usual, so that the dinner usually fixed for five was often half an hour late, or even longer. Nobody, therefore, was surprised at the Count's late appearance on this occasion. No one in the house had even an idea at the terrible attempt at murder on the Unter den Linden—of the wonderful preservation of the master of the house. There was some company assembled in the salon of the Countess, awaiting the Minister-President; at last he entered. Nobody noticed any disquietude or excitement in his manner; it only seemed to some as if his greeting were heartier than usual. Saying, "Ah! what a pleasant party!" he went to his study, where it was his habit to remain for a few moments before sitting down to table. He this day made a short report of the event to His Majesty the King. Then he returned to the dinner-party, and said, as he very often did when he came late, in a merry scolding tone to his wife, "Why *don't* we eat our dinners to-day?" He approached a lady to lead her to the dining-table, and then, as they went out of the salon, he went up to his wife, kissed her on the forehead, and said, "My child! they have shot at me, but there is no harm done!"

Tenderly and prudently as this was said, terror naturally displayed itself on all countenances. Every one crowded round the honoured gentleman in trembling joy at his wonderful escape. He, however, would not delay, entered the dining-room, and, after a short grace, sat down to his soup, which no doubt tasted all the better to him the less that he, in all human probability, seemed likely to have any right to it again half an hour before.

The surgeon who was called in said afterwards, when all sorts of theories were attempted to account for the non-success of the attempt, with great justice :—" Gentlemen! there is but one explanation. God's hand was between them!"

In fact, the dinner on that day was frequently interrupted ; nobody ate any dinner at all, except Bismarck himself. Before six o'clock, only half an hour after the crime, the King himself arrived, having risen from his own dinner to congratulate his Minister. Bismarck received his royal master on the stairs, and remained alone with him for a short time. No doubt it was a touching meeting for both of them ; for the dear Lord who still could press his tried servant by the still warm hand, as for the Minister, ready at any moment to die for his King, be it on the battle-field or in the street! There was very little ceremony at the Ministry of Foreign Affairs that day. Scarcely had the King departed ere, one after the other, the Princes of the Royal House who happened to be in Berlin appeared, and sat down at the family table, drinking a glass of wine to Bismarck's safety. The company increased as the news of the criminal deed grew known farther of ; the venerable Field-Marshal Count Wrangel was one of the first who hastened to express sympathy. Generals, ministers, ambassadors, friends, and all who respected him, even political opponents, thronged round the precious personage so wonderfully preserved to his native land. At the threshold of the door crowds of persons of all conditions were assembled, who inscribed their names in lists prepared for the purpose, in token of their sympathy. Supplements of the *Gazettes* then appeared, telling in brief periods what had taken place ; and rejoicing multitudes thronged the Wilhelmsplatz and Wilhelmstrasse till far into the evening. Conservative clubs serenaded him, and, for the first time in his life, Bismarck addressed from the window the people of Berlin.

From that day all vacillation in Bismarck was at an end. The Lord God, in his wonderful salvation, had vouchsafed him a sign, and he again felt the full and strong conscience of his historical mission; he knew that he was the sentinel whom God had placed at a post, from which alone He could relieve him. Nor was this a Divine signal to Bismarck alone.

It is known that the political enthusiast who attempted the murder, the stepson of a democratic fugitive named Blind, whose name he had assumed, ended his career by suicide before any examination could take place. There were traces of a conspiracy certainly discovered, but they were not pursued; the attempt at assassination therefore cannot be regarded as the crime of an individual. It was sad enough to see that the fanatical hatred of Bismarck went so far in Austria and South Germany; that voices were raised, trying to elevate the murderer into a martyr. The Austrian press dishonoured itself by the publication of an advertisement in which an obscure advocate set a price on Bismarck's head. It was very silly that the *Ritter von Geist* in Vienna endeavoured to account for Bismarck's wonderful escape by changing his shirt into a suit of chain mail, and then with wonderful wit declared that the Prussian Minister-President bought his linen from the ironmonger!

The times were growing more serious; minds began to feel that stillness which precedes the storm.

Mit Gott für König und Vaterland—"With God for King and Fatherland"—the ancient royal battle-cry of olden time, first crept softly and then louder and louder from heart to heart, from mouth to mouth, until at last it thundered in the roaring of a thousand cannon throughout the trembling world. It seems sad that in those very days a valiant archduke in Italy, most infelicitously altering our old dear Prussian cry, closed an order of the day with the words: "For God with Emperor and Fatherland!"

It was just during these days of omen that Bismarck, although very serious, was more gentle and kind than ever to his relatives and friends. There was expectation, often expectation to the greatest tension, but no vacillation, no doubt in him; he was a brave man from head to foot. In the later hours of evening he was often in the beautiful garden of the Minister of Foreign Affairs, of which garden he was very fond; under its old trees he used to take counsel with Moltke, with Roon, and others; there he often walked up and down restlessly for hours, in deep thought, waiting for a royal message. There, too, the eventful thought flashed upon him, in the night of Thursday to Friday, from the 14th to the 15th of

June, to set the Prussian columns in motion twenty-four hours sooner than had been intended. Immediately General von Moltke was sent for, and the telegraph was at work.

In the enthusiasm at the first results, and in the restless activity of those days, Bismarck seemed to have lost every trace of illness. An old partisan of his, who was invited to dinner by him in those days, found him fresher and more vigorous than ever. During the most animated conversation, the news came in that telegraphic communication with Italy was broken off. Bismarck turned to Legations Councillor von Keudell and said, "Dear Keudell, please give directions that telegrams be sent viâ London," and continued his conversation. Immediately after dinner General von Moltke was announced. Bismarck went out, but returned in ten minutes, quite at ease, and invited his guest to accompany him into the garden, although no doubt those ten minutes had been spent in a conference of the most important eventful character. General von Werder was announced. Another conference, and then Bismarck related, in strolling about the garden, how on that forenoon, worn out by continued exertion to the greatest extent, and waiting in the ante-chamber of the King, he had fallen asleep on a sofa. He delighted in his garden, and got on the ice-house, from which he could overlook the whole of the green thickets of the fine large garden behind the palace in the Wilhelm-strasse.

A few days later, on Friday, the 29th of June, the first news of victory arrived. No one, no one will ever forget that day! As if by enchantment, the whole of Berlin was dressed in black-and-white flags; in every street resounded, in joy, "*Ich bin ein Preusse, keunt ihr meine Farben?*"—"I am a Prussian; do you know my colours?"* In thousands the multitude pressed to the palace of the King, who greeted his faithful people from the window, while the General-Intendant von Hülsen read the victorious news from the balcony. There was no end to the

---

* See the Appendix for this stirring national song, and a version I have attempted.—K. R. H. M.

rejoicings bursting joyfully from full hearts. It was indeed a Prussian day!

When Count Bismarck, at about 2 P.M., left the royal palace, he was besieged on all sides. Every one wanted to shake hands; on that day, in that hour, every one felt and knew what Count Bismarck was to Prussia; some have already forgotten it, and there are others who would fain have it forgotten.

Bismarck was visibly in deep emotion, but he maintained his serious carriage. The first victories did not intoxicate him; his prudence, indeed, had apparently increased in power. In this hour he thought of the sacrifice, and was humble in his heart.

In the evening, the multitude returned to the palace of the King, and sang Luther's hymn,—"*Ein feste Burg ist unser Gott*,"—"A fortress firm is our God." The King returned thanks. Only the few persons close to him could hear the words—the roaring ocean of human voices drowned them—and yet every man knew what the King had said. Prussia's King could only express what every Prussian felt and thought at this moment. Thence the multitude rushed to the Crown Prince's palace, and greeted with hoch and hurrah the victorious leader of the second army, which had stood so well against the enemy; thence to the palace of Prince Charles, the eldest Prince of the royal house, whose son, Prince Frederick Charles, had penetrated so gloriously into Bohemia with the first army, and had won "first blood" for Prussia in this war. Next the mass stood head to head in the Wilhelmstrasse, before Bismarck's hotel; the never-ending cry of triumph forced the Minister-President to the window. He raised his hand in token that he would speak; all were silent beneath; from the distance on both sides the muffled roaring of the shores of this popular mass toned along. For the second time, Count Bismarck addressed the people of Berlin, in powerful but proudly moderate words; he ended with a

salute to the King and his army. At the moment a tremendous peal of thunder reverberated over the royal city,
a flash of forked lightning illuminated the scene, and,
with a strongly ringing voice, Bismarck shouted above
the multitude, "The heavens fire a salute!"

No one will ever forget it who heard that peal of
thunder. The reply was returned as with one voice;
then the rejoicing mass got again into motion to greet
"old Roon," the faithful warrior, at the Ministry of
War.

On the 30th of June Bismarck left Berlin in the suite
of the King, with Generals von Roon and von Moltke.
The King was also accompanied by the General Feld
Zeugmeister, Prince Charles of Prussia, Herrenmeister of
Balley Brandenburg, for the seat of war. The carriages
rolled by the statues of the Great Frederick, the heroes
of the War of Freedom, and the great Elector on the Long
Bridge. Bismarck was serious and firm, looking like an
iron statue, and more taciturn than ever. The first

night's quarters the King passed at the Castle of Reichenberg—a few days before the head-quarters of his victorious nephew, Prince Frederick Charles, who had already penetrated far into Bohemia, and was encamped in the fields, where Prussian hearts were throbbing to the Almighty, and their arms smiting the foe, according to the brave phrase of the Maccabees, which the Prince had used in General Orders, but which contradictory ignorance could not find, and still prates enough about it to this day, as a Prussian "Bible forgery." * Count Bismarck, at the first night's lodging at Reichenberg—and, it is said, not without reason—evinced great anxiety as to the safety of his royal master. Of himself he thought much less; perhaps he does not know, to this moment, that it was only towards the morning it was found possible to disembark his horses and bring them up. We have heard that a surprise of the royal head-quarters by a strong body of cavalry advance was not beyond the bounds of possibility. Sufficient reason for Bismarck's anxiety! From Sichrow and Jitschen, Bismarck wrote the following letters to his wife :—

Sichrow, 1st July, 1866.

To-day we have started from Reichenberg, and have just reached this place. It is uncertain whether we shall remain here, or proceed to Turnau. The whole journey was dangerous. The Austrians, yesterday, had they sent cavalry from Leitmeritz, might have caught the King and all the rest of us. Charles, the coachman, has had a severe fall with the mare, which ran away with him. At first he was thought dead; he is lying in the hospital here, near Sichrow, in the next village. Kurt had better come for him.

Everywhere we meet prisoners; according to the returns there are already above fifteen thousand. Jitschin was

* 1 Maccabees iii., 58, 59.—K. R. H. M.

yesterday taken by us at the point of the bayonet by the Frankfurt Division; General Tümpling was severely wounded in the hip, but not mortally. The heat is terrible. The carriage of provisions is difficult. Our troops suffer from weariness and hunger. There are not many traces

of war here, except the downtrodden cornfields. The people are not afraid of the soldiers; they stand in their Sunday clothes at their doors, with wife and children, in astonishment. At Trautenau the inhabitants murdered twenty defenceless oboists of ours, who had remained behind the front after the passage of their regiments. The criminals are at Glogau, before court-martial. At Münchengrätz a brewer enticed twenty-six of our soldiers into the spirit vault, made them drunk, and set it on fire. The distillery belongs to a convent. Except such things we learn little more here than you do in Berlin. This castle, which is very splendid, belongs to Prince Rohan, whom I saw every year at Gastein.

Jitschen, *not* Gitschin, 2nd July, 1866.

We have just arrived from Sichrow; the battle-field here was still full of corpses, horses, and arms. Our victories are much greater than we thought; it seems we have already more than fifteen thousand prisoners, and with dead and wounded the Austrian loss is stated at a higher figure—about twenty thousand men. Two of their corps are completely dispersed, some regiments destroyed to the last man. Till now I have seen more Austrian prisoners than Prussian soldiers. Send me cigars by the courier every time—a thousand at a time, if they can be had, price twenty dollars, for the hospitals. All the wounded beg them of me. Then by clubs, or our own resources, subscribe for some dozens of Kreuzzeitungs for the hospitals—for instance, the one at Reichenberg; the other places can be learnt at the Ministry of War. What is Clermont-Tonnere about? is he not coming? I have no news by the post. Send me a revolver of wide calibre, a saddle pistol. Charles, the coachman, is better; he will not suffer permanently, but for some time will not be fit for service .Charles B. is much to be praised; he is the active principle of our travelling household. I greet you heartily. Send me a French novel to read, but only one at a time. God keep you.

Your letter with the Homburg enclosure has just arrived; a thousand thanks. I can understand how you feel the quiet of our departure. In our hurry here one feels nothing of the position—perhaps a little in bed at night.

On the road to Jitschen, on the battle-field, Prince Frederick Charles came to meet his royal uncle. What a meeting! The Prince drove into Jitschen with the King about 2 P.M., where the King alighted at the Golden Lion. The guard of honour here consisted of Pomeranian Grenadiers of the regiment of the late King.

We are not here writing a history of the famous campaign ; we will only observe that on the 2nd July no battle was expected at the royal head-quarters for the next day ; the King visited the wounded, and Bismarck accompanied him.

About 11 o'clock P.M. the chief of the staff of Prince Frederick Charles, General von Voigts-Rheetz, arrived in

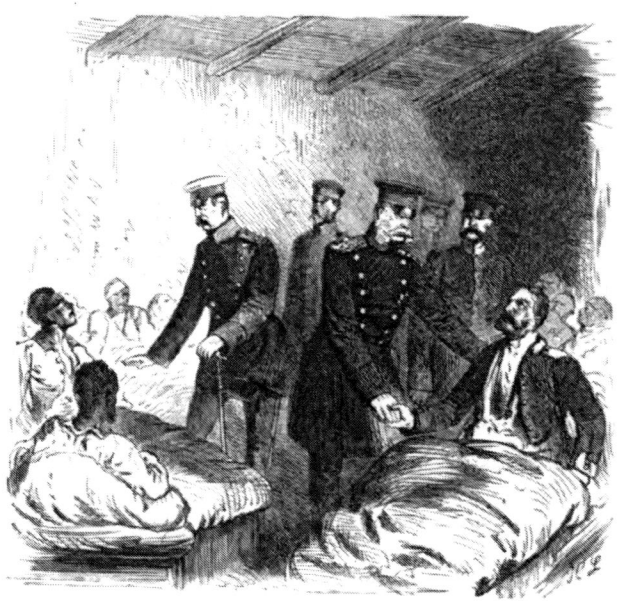

Jitschin from Kamenitz, the head-quarters of the Prince, bringing with him the plans and positions of battle, settled by the Prince in consequence of the daring reconnoissance of an officer on his staff, Major von Unger, which plans were submitted to the King. Immediately upon the arrival of General von Voigts-Rheetz the Council of War was summoned to the King, the battle dispositions of the Prince were entirely accepted, all arrangements made, and Count Finck von Finckenstein rode off on his historical ride to the army of the Crown Prince, to summon it up. The plan was exceedingly simple. Prince Frederick

Charles was to throw himself on the front of the enemy, seize it, and if possible, overcome it until the Crown Prince arrived with the second army, to give the *coup de grace*.

Very simple—alas! how much looks simple upon paper!

On the 3rd of July, amidst fog and rain, Prince Frederick Charles set out to battle against the overwhelming force of the enemy; in the first dawn of the day his troops were in their assigned position. At eight the Prince began the battle. "Too early!" critical voices have said; but military authorities have said, "at the right moment!" for any longer delay would have allowed General Benedek to take up a much stronger position. The Prince bravely took the enormous responsibility on himself, and commenced the battle. At nine a ringing shout of joy announced the arrival of the King on the battle-field, and with him came Count Bismarck, the great Major of Landwehr.

Certainly it created a fine impression, to see the faithful First Councillor on the mare Veranda—since that time known as "Sadowa"—on the field of honour, "where the bullet whistles, and the lance is couched, and death is rush-

D D

ing round in every shape "—behind the venerable King. Whoever had seen Bismarck only under the cross-fire of the disdainful speech of a political opposition in the debates of the Chamber, firm, half-contemptuous, and mighty, had never seen him as a whole; he was seen to best advantage amidst the bullets of Sadowa. There he sat, his high form upright in the saddle, upon a very tall roan, with a plain paletot over his uniform, while his piercing eyes scanned each movement from beneath his helmet. And thus he sat and rode for hours, for momentous hours, behind his royal master, in thunder and in smoke. Behind him again the musical and gallant Legations Rath von Keudell, also an officer in the Landwehr cavalry. Noon arrived, but no decisive news from the Crown Prince. The battle went burning on, and many a brave heart feared at that time for beloved Prussia. Dark were the looks in the neighbourhood of the King; old Roon, and Moltke of the bright face, sat there like two statues of bronze. It was whispered that the Prince would have to loose his Brandenburgers—his own beloved third corps, whom he had till now held in reserve; his stormers of Düppel— against the foe, which meant that he would have to set his last hazard on the die to gain the victory. Suddenly Bismarck lowered the glass through which he had been observing the country in the direction from which the Crown Prince was approaching, and drew the attention of his neighbours to certain lines in the far distance. All telescopes were pointed thitherward, but the lines were pronounced to be ploughed fields. There was a deep silence, and then the Minister-President lowered his glass again and said, decidedly, " Those are not plough furrows; the spaces are not equal; they are marching lines!" Bismarck had been the first to discover the advance of the second army. In a little while the adjutants and intelligence flew about in every direction—the Crown Prince and victory were at hand!

Prince Frederick Charles sent forward his major, Von Unger-Manstein, and the Brandenburg brigade of Düppel marched forward, playing, " *Heil dir im Siegerkranz !*"*

The rest need not be told here. Bismarck followed his King in the battle. The warlike monarch dashed into the

grenade fire of the enemy, on which Bismarck made him

* At the important battle of Königsgrätz, according to a recent number of the *Preussische Jahrbücher*, the Prussians lost in dead, wounded, and missing, 359 officers and 8,794 men; the Austrians 1,147 officers and 30,224 men. The proportions seem thus to have been: for the Prussians, $\frac{1}{11}$; for the Austrians, $\frac{1}{7}$; average loss on both sides, $\frac{1}{10}$. In the battle of Malplaquet

that he was riding towards the silent battle-field where *he* was commander-in-chief, and where *he* had to be the victor. On his road he wrote the following letters to his wife :—

Hohenmauth, Monday, 9th July, 1866.

Do you remember, my heart, how, nineteen years ago, we passed through here on the road from Prague to Vienna? No mirror showed the future—not even when I passed over this railway, in 1852, with the kind Lynar. We are all well. If we do not become extravagant in our demands, and do not imagine that we have conquered *the world*, we shall obtain a peace worth the having. But we are as easily intoxicated as cast down, and I have the unthankful office of pouring water into this foaming wine, and to cause it to be understood that we do not inhabit Europe alone, but with three neighbours. The Austrians are encamped in Moravia, and we are already so daring as to affirm that our head-quarters will to-morrow be where theirs are to-day. Prisoners are still arriving, and cannon since the 3rd to the number of one hundred and eighty. If they bring up their southern army, with God's gracious assistance, we will beat that also. Confidence is general. Our people are worthy to be kissed; every man is brave to the death, quiet, obedient, moralized, with empty stomachs, wet clothes, little sleep, boot-soles falling off—friendly towards every one, no plundering and burning, paying what they are able, and eating mouldy bread. There must exist a depth of piety in our common soldier, or all this could not be. It is difficult to obtain any news of friends. We lie miles away from each other; no one knows where the other may be, and there is no one to send—that is to say, plenty of men, but no horses. For four days I have been seeking for Philip,* who has been slightly wounded in the head by a lance-thrust, as G. wrote me word, but I cannot discover where he lies, and now we have proceeded

* Bismarck's nephew.

eight miles farther. The King exposed himself very greatly on the 3rd, and it was well that I was with him, for all the warnings of others were in vain, and no one else would have dared to have spoken as I did on the last occasion, when I succeeded, after a knot of ten cuirassiers and fifteen horses of the 6th Cuirassier Regiment were rolling around in their blood, and bombs were flying about in very unpleasant proximity to our Sovereign. The worst of them, fortunately, did not explode. Yet I would rather have it so than that he should be over-prudent. He was full of enthusiasm at his troops, and justly; so that he never remarked the noise and fighting around him, and sat quiet and comfortably, as if at Kreuzberg, continually coming across battalions whom he had to thank and say " Good night" to, until we had got under fire again. He had to listen to so much on the subject, however, that he will let it alone for the future, and you may rest quite tranquil. I hardly believe in another *real* battle.

If you receive no news from any one, you may be assured that he is alive and well, for any wounds to friends we hear of in less than twenty-four hours. We have not as yet come into contact with Herwarth and Steinmetz; therefore I have also not seen Sch., but I know that both are well. G. leads his squadron quietly forward with his arm in a sling. Farewell. I must go to duty.

Your most faithful,
V. B.

Zwittau in Moravia, 11th July, 1866.

I am in want of an inkstand, all being in use; otherwise I am well, after sleeping well on a field-bed and air-mattress, and awakening at eight to find a letter from you. I had gone to bed at eleven. At Königsgrätz I rode the tall roan; was thirteen hours in the saddle without fodder. He behaved very well, was frightened neither at the firing nor the corpses, ate corn-tops and plum-leaves with satisfaction at the most difficult moments, and went thoroughly well to the end, when I seemed more tired than the horse. My first bed for the night was on the roadway of Horic, without straw, with the aid of a carriage cushion. Every place was full of the wounded; the Grand Duke of Mecklenburg found me, and then shared his chamber with me, R., and two adjutants—which, on account of the rain, was very welcome to me. As to the King and the bombs, I have already informed you. The generals all were full of the superstition that, as soldiers, they dared not speak to the King of danger, and always sent me to him, although I am a major. The rising trigger of the revolver covers the sight point, and the notch in the top of the cock does not show in the line of sight. Tell T. of this. Good bye, my dearest; I must go to S.

Your faithful,
V. B.

Nicolsburg! It was there that Bismarck fought his quiet battle, there he accomplished his Sadowa, and chivalrously strove for victory and peace, not alone against the diplomacy of his antagonists, but against the proud daring of triumph in his own camp, which encircled him in so heart-warming and so seductive a manner. Perhaps Bismarck never showed himself a greater statesman than in those days; the billows of victory could not overthrow him, mightily as they dashed over him; he stood like a tower in the torrent of rancour, anger, even of most malicious suspicion, which rose up against him. But he perceived the hollow-eyed ghost of pest silently creeping through the armies, and pitilessly strangling out the life of the victors; he knew what the climate of Hungary was in August, and he looked boldly at the cloud which was rising, pregnant with calamity, in the far west. Hail to the faithful and brave hearts who in so terrible an hour clung firmly to Bismarck!

It was a strange coincidence that the magnificent castle of Nicolsburg had passed through the female line from the inheritance of the great house of the Princes of Dietrichstein to General Count von Mensdorff-Ponilly, of Lothringian descent, like the Austrian Imperial House itself, so that peace was actually negotiated in the very mansion of the Imperial Minister for Foreign Affairs himself. Has not the Count Mensdorff-Ponilly, as the heir of the Dietrichsteins through his wife, been recently raised to princely rank under the title of Nicolsburg?

As Napoleon the First resided here after the battle of Austerlitz, so did William I. reside here after the battle of Sadowa; the castle has historical recollections enough. Count Bismarck contemplated the magnificent pile on his arrival intently, and then said with grave mirth to his companions:—"My old mansion of Schönhausen is certainly very insignificant in comparison with this splendid

ilding, therefore I am better pleased that we should be
re at Count Mensdorff's, than that he should now be at
y house!"

In these final days of July the preliminaries of Nicols-
arg were completed, which resulted in the peace of
'rague.

* * * * * *

The battle was over, victory had been attained; then
weakness and illness assailed Bismarck worse than ever.
The old pains of nervous rheumatism came more terribly
than before; but he kept himself up by the power of the
will, for his King was still in want of him.

On the 3rd of August Bismarck wrote to his wife, on
his return from Prague—" that fated city, where heroes
sicken"—as follows:—

Prague, 3rd August, 1866.

I have stolen away from the railway station, and am
waiting here alone, and without luggage, until the King
arrives, and after him my packages. This moment of
compulsory inactivity I employ in greeting you from
hence, and telling you that I am well, and hope to be in
Berlin to-morrow night. The King is in excellent health.
The multitudes between here and the station are so
packed that I fear there will be accidents.

Evening.—The King came quicker than I expected, and
since then we have had business of all kinds, and then
dinner. I have just returned from a drive with His Majesty
through Hradschin, the Belvedere, &c., and have seen all
the beauties of the Prague neighbourhood. In a few days it
will be just nineteen years since we saw all these things
together. How many wonders had to take place ere I
should find myself to-day in the same place, without B.
Hei cerstwa! I had remembered to my coachman's great
satisfaction. To-morrow we hope to be in Berlin. There
is great controversy as to the speech from the throne.
The little people have all of them not enough to do; they

see no farther than their own noses, and exercise their powers of natation on the stormy waves of eloquence. One can manage to settle with one's enemies—but alas for one's friends ! They have all got blinkers on, and only see a spot of the earth.

This reference to the speech from the throne in the letter probably touches especially on the question of indemnity.

There was something peculiar about this indemnity which Bismarck demanded and obtained from the Diet which was immediately summoned after the war. The word sounded very harsh to the ears of the victors ; and there are many honourable men at the present day who still painfully feel that Bismarck considered it necessary then to obtain this indemnity. Certainly the wearied statesman did not fight this new fight for the indemnity from any affection for the doctrine of Constitutionalism.

On the 4th of August Bismarck returned, in the suite of the King, to Berlin, amidst the nameless rejoicings of the nation. On the next day came the solemn opening of the Diet, and a torrent of work overwhelmed the Minister-President. Then ensued the peace-treaties with individual States, the consolidation of the conquered provinces, the formation of the North German Confederation, cares as to envious malice ; and through all this the suffering man held himself up, pale, but firm, sustained by his high sense of duty, by the consciousness of his supreme mission. For days and hours the powers of Bismarck, stretched to their utmost tension, gave way, but he always recovered himself, presenting an undaunted front in every direction.

This, indeed, was necessary ; for the victorious war had brought him no rest. The relations towards the West were growing more and more menacing ; the cloud he had perceived from Nicolsburg was assuming form. It could no longer be compared at will to a weasel or a camel. Had the cloud obtained a name, a new war on the Rhine was almost unavoidable, a war in which Prussia would unquestionably have to shed her blood only for the laurels, without winning the fruits, of victory. Such a war, however, Bismarck desired—was indeed forced—to avoid from a sense of duty. Let us allow a Frenchman to relate in what manner he accomplished this task.

A long essay was published in the *Revue Moderne* of Paris, by J. Vilbort, under the title of "Germany since Sadowa." Contained in this is the speech on territorial compensations, demanded by France in August, 1866, at the very time when the rejoicings in Prussia were at their height.

"On the 7th of August," says M. Vilbort, "we took our leave of M. de Bismarck, from whom we had received, before, during, and after the war, a consistently kind reception, for which we are bound to express our liveliest acknowledgments. About 10 P.M. we were in the study of the Premier, when M. Benedette, the French ambassador, was announced. 'Will you take a cup of tea in the salon?' M. de Bismarck said to me. 'I will be yours in a moment.' Two hours passed away; midnight struck; one o'clock. Some twenty persons, his family and intimate friends, awaited their host. At last he appeared, with a cheerful face and a smile upon his lips. Tea was taken; there was smoking and beer, in German fashion. Conversation turned, pleasantly or seriously, on Germany, Italy, and France. Rumours of a war with France were then current for the tenth time in Berlin. At the moment of my departure, I said:—'M. le Ministre, will you pardon me a very indiscreet question? Do I take war or peace with me back to Paris?' M. de Bismarck replied, with animation, 'Friendship, a lasting friendship with France! I entertain the firmest hope that France and Prussia, in the future, will represent the dualism of intelligence and progress.' Nevertheless, it seemed to us that at these words we surprised a singular smile on the lips of a man who is destined to play a distinguished part

the necessity of great armaments against France, while, at the same time, his refusal to give up the smallest portion of German territory elevated the dignity of Prussia in the eyes of all patriots; nor did it benefit the Minister less, who thus upheld the national standard high and firmly in the sight of the foreigner. Thus it happened that, after half a century, the Napoleonistic policy for the second time divided two great nations, who, by their intellectual, moral, and material development, by all their interests and aspirations, are destined to form a fraternal alliance, and thus ensure the freedom and peace of Europe on an irrefrangible basis."

On the 20th of September, 1866, Bismarck, after a short rest, was able to assume the place of honour which was his due in the memorable triumphant entry of the troops to Berlin, as Major-General and Chief of the Seventh Heavy Landwehr Regiment of Horse, to which his grateful Sovereign had appointed him. Immediately before the King there rode, in one rank, Count Bismarck, the War Minister General von Roon, General von Moltke, the Chief of the General Staff, General von Voigts-Rheetz as Chief of the General Staff of the First Army, and General von Blumenthal as Chief of the General Staff of the Second; while the King was immediately followed by the Royal Princes and other commanders. There was a great and intelligent recognition in this Royal order of arrangement.

As may be understood, the loud rejoicings on the occasion of this magnificent festival of victory were in honour of the Army and its Royal Commander-in-Chief; but many an eye followed, with grateful admiration and emotion, the powerful form of the Minister-President, in the white uniform, with the yellow collar and accoutrements of his regiment, wearing the orange sash of the Exalted Order of the Black Eagle on his broad chest, his flashing helmet being deeply pressed over his forehead, astride of his tall horse, riding along in so stately a manner, and occasionally saluting a friend, here and there, in a courteous way. Scarcely one of the multitude whose acclamations met his ear even suspected that the mighty man, in intolerable pain, could scarcely keep himself upright in the saddle.

Nor could Bismarck altogether withdraw himself from the patriotic festivals which accompanied and followed the triumphant entry of the army. Too much was wanting where he was absent. We then saw him at the monster dinner which was given in honour of him, and to Generals Von Roon and Von Moltke, by an enthusiastic assembly, formed of men of all parties. Zealous democrats then applauded the great statesman, and whoever was present on that occasion would have believed that Bismarck was also popular, in the ordinary sense of the word. When the Minister-President, in the pithy speech in which he acknowledged the toast pledged in his honour, said that the Berlin people, as this war had shown, had their hearts, words, and hands in the right place, the enthusiasm knew no bounds, and the guests rushed from all quarters to pledge him again. When the storm had become somewhat allayed, the Director, Dr. Bonnell, of the Friedrich's Werder Gymnasium, was seen to step forward.

Bismarck seized his early teacher by both hands, and thanked him heartily for a poetic greeting with which he had presented him on his return, merrily regretting that he had not been able to reply in Alcaic verse. The Chief Burgomaster, sitting opposite him, asked whether the Minister-President sent his sons to the same institution. "Certainly," answered Bismarck; "and I myself was also a scholar of Bonnell!" And so introduced his old teacher in the heartiest manner.

After this festival, Bismarck's last strength failed him. He went into the country to Patbus, when he fell very ill, and only gradually recovered after a long time, and then not wholly, but just enough to admit of his return to business at Berlin in December.

..... people, as this was
..... hands in the I......
....., and the pre.....
..... again V......
..... the I......

General Major.

Bundeskanzler.

Unter Preußens Königsfahnen,
Unter Friedrichs stolzem Aar,
Auf des Sieges blut'gen Bahnen
Wurde sein Geheimniß klar:

MAJOR-GENERAL AND CHANCELLOR OF THE CONFEDERATION.

His air is that of the aristocrat and courtier, improved by all the charm of the most polished courtesy. He advanced to receive me, took me by the hand, led me to a seat, and offered me a cigar.

" ' Monsieur le Ministre,' I said to him, after a little preliminary conversation, ' I, like many of my countrymen, am most anxious to be thoroughly enlightened on the true interests of the German nation. Permit me, therefore, to express myself with entire frankness. I am glad to confess that, in her foreign policy, Prussia seems, at the present time, to be pursuing objects with which the French nation sympathizes in no ordinary manner, such as the complete emancipation of Italy from Austrian influence, and the establishment of an united Germany, based on universal suffrage. But is there not a flat contradiction between your Prussian and German policies? You declare a national parliament to be the only fountain in which Germany can find rejuvenescence, the only form of supreme authority by which she can realize her future destiny. Yet, at the same time, you treat the Second Chamber at Berlin in the manner of Louis XIV., when he entered the Houses of Parliament whip in hand. In France we do not admit the possibility of any association between absolutism and democracy ; and, to speak the whole truth, allow me to state to you that in Paris your plan of a national parliament has not been considered as a serious one. It has been looked upon as an acutely constructed engine of war, and it is generally believed that you are quite the man to break it up when it has served your purpose, the moment it seems to have become inconvenient or useless.'

" '*A la bonne heure*, you go at once to the root of things,' replied M. de Bismarck. ' In France, I know, I am as unpopular as in Germany. Everywhere I am held responsible for a state of things I did not create, but

E E

which has been forced upon me as upon every one else. I am the scapegoat of public opinion; but that does not much trouble me. I follow out a plan, with a perfectly calm conscience, which I consider useful to my country, and to Germany.

"'As to the means to this end, I have used those within my reach, for want of others. Much might be said as to the internal condition of Prussia. To judge of it impartially, it is necessary to study the peculiar character of the people of this country in the most thorough way. France and Italy are now compact social polities, each animated by one spirit and one sentiment; while, on the contrary, Germany is given up to individualism. Here, every one lives apart in his own narrow corner, with his own opinions; his wife and children round him; ever suspicious of the Government, as of his neighbour; judging eerything from his personal point of view, and never from general grounds. The sentiment of individualism and the necessity for contradiction are developed to an inconceivable degree in the German. Show him an open door, and, rather than pass through it, he will insist on breaking a hole in the wall at its side. No government, however it may act, will be popular in Prussia; the majority in the country will always be opposed to it; simply from its being the government, and holding authority over the individual, it is condemned to be constantly opposed by the moderates, and decried and despised by the ultras. This has been the common fate of all successive governments since the beginning of the dynasty. Neither liberal ministers, nor reactionary ministers, have found favour with our politicians.'

"And while thus passing in review the various governments and forms of rule which have existed since the foundation of the monarchy, M. de Bismarck strove to prove to me, in brilliant, graphic language, sparkling with wit, that the Auerswalds and the Manteuffels had shared the same fate as himself, and that Frederick William III., surnamed the Just, had succeeded as little as Frederick William IV. in satisfying the Prussian nation.

" ' They shouted,' he added, ' at the victories of Frederick the Great, but at his death they rubbed their hands at the thought of being delivered from the tyrant. Despite this antagonism, there exists a deep attachment to the royal house. No sovereign or minister, no government, can win the favour of Prussian individualism. Yet all cry from the depths of their hearts, " God save the King !" And they obey when the King commands.'

" ' Yet some say, M. le Ministre, that this discontent might grow into rebellion.'

" ' The Government does not believe this need be feared, and does not fear it. Our revolutionists are not formidable. Their hostility exhausts itself in invectives against the Prime Minister, but they respect the King. It is I who have done all the evil, and it is with me alone that they are angry. Were they a little more impartial, perhaps they might see that I have not acted otherwise, simply because I could not. In Prussia's present position in Germany, and with Austria opposed to her, an army was an imperative necessity. In Prussia it is the only force capable of discipline. I do not know if that is a French word ? '

" 'Certainly, M. le Ministre, and in France can also be applied.'

" ' A Prussian who got his arm broken in a barricade,' continued M. de Bismarck, ' would go home crestfallen, and his wife would look upon him as a madman ; but in the army he is an admirable soldier, and fights like a lion for the honour of his country. A party opposed to the Government has not chosen to recognize the necessity imposed on us by circumstances of maintaining a large military force, evident as that necessity has been. But

I could not hesitate, for my own part; by family, by
education, I am the King's man; and the King adhered to the idea of this military organization as firmly
as to his crown, being convinced, heart and soul, of its
indispensibility. No one could make him yield or compromise the point. At his age—he is seventy—and with
his traditions, people persist in an idea; above all, if they
feel it to be good. On the subject of the army, I should
add, I entirely agree with his view.

"'Sixteen years ago I was living as a country gentleman, when the King appointed me the Envoy of Prussia
at the Frankfurt Diet. I had been brought up in the
admiration, I might almost say the worship, of Austrian
policy. Much time, however, was not needed to dispel my
youthful illusions with regard to Austria, and I became
her declared opponent.

"' The humiliation of my country; Germany sacrificed
to the interests of a foreign nation; a crafty and perfidious
line of policy—these were not things calculated to give
me satisfaction. I was not aware that the future would call
upon me to take any part in public events, but from that
period I conceived the idea, which at the present day I
am still pursuing, the idea of snatching Germany from
Austrian oppression, or at least that part of Germany
whose tone of thought, religion, manners, and interests,
identify her destinies with Prussia—Northern Germany.
In the plan which I brought forward, there has been no
question of overthrowing thrones, of taking a duchy from
one ruler, or some petty domain from another; nor would
the King have consented to such schemes. And then there
are all the interests of family relationship and concessions,
a host of antagonistic influences, against which I have
had to sustain an hourly warfare.

"' But neither all this, nor the opposition with which I
have had to contend in Prussia, could prevent my devoting

myself, heart and soul, to the idea of a Northern Germany, constituted in her logical and natural form, under the ægis of Prussia. To attain this end I would brave all dangers, exile, the scaffold itself! I said to the Crown Prince, whose education and natural tendencies incline him rather to the side of parliamentary government, what matter if they hang me, provided the rope by which I am hung bind this new Germany firmly to your throne?'

"'May I also ask, M. le Ministre, how you reconcile the principle of freedom, embodied in the existence of a national parliament, with the despotic treatment to which the Berlin Chamber has had to submit? How, above all, have you been able to induce the King, the representative of the principle of divine right, to accept universal suffrage, which is *par excellence* the principle of democracy?'

"M. de Bismarck answered with animation: 'That is a victory achieved after four years of struggle. When the King sent for me, four years ago, the situation of affairs was most critical. His Majesty laid before me a long list of liberal concessions, but not one of these concerned the military question. I said to the King, "I accept; and the more liberal the Government can prove itself the stronger it will be." The Chamber has been obdurate on one side, and the Crown on the other. In the conflict I have remained by the King. My respect for him, all my antecedents, all the traditions of my family, made it my duty to do so. But that I am, either by nature or from principle, an adversary of national representation, a born enemy of parliamentary government, is a perfectly gratuitous supposition.

"'During those discussions when the Chamber of Berlin set itself in opposition to a line of policy imposed on Prussia by circumstances of most pressing necessity, I would not separate myself from the King. But no one has a right to insult me by the supposition that I am only mystifying Germany in bringing forward my project of a parliament. Should the day come when, my task being accomplished, I find it impossible to reconcile my duties to my Sovereign with my duties as a statesman, I shall know how to retire without denying the work I have done.'

"Such are substantially," says M. Vilbort in conclusion, "the political opinions expressed to me by M. de Bismarck. His thoughts conveyed by my pen, in another form, may have lost to some extent their emphasis; but I have anxiously endeavoured faithfully to reproduce them."

We have placed this report of the intellectual Frenchman here on purpose, because Count Bismarck, independently of other interesting remarks, has given indications as to the course of his future policy not easily to be misunderstood; for it may readily be conceived that we do not feel called upon to enlarge upon Bismarck's policy in the last three years. What he has done in this period, and how he has done it, is vivid before the eyes of every one, and fresh in every one's memory, and there is scarcely time yet to incorporate it with history. Our readers will have convinced themselves, that in contradistinction to others, we do not find the last deeds and speeches of Bismarck inconsistent with his earlier acts and speeches; and we think we have demonstrated that the Bismarck of to-day has developed consequently from the Bismarck of 1847—that the great aristocratic statesman is still the "King's man," as he then was the "Junker Hotspur," or conservative party leader. The demand for the so-called indemnity, the amnesty, the direct elections, and all those things which are sometimes praised and sometimes blamed and designated "Bismarck's contradictions," are only apparent contradictions, at once to be explained if thoroughly examined. It is very easy to hold very different opinions on many points from those of Bismarck, and warmly as we admire him, we do not regard him as infallible; but we think that it is necessary to be very careful in censuring his individual political acts, even where such unpleasant surprises occur, for actually a quite incomparable political instinct has fitted him for leadership, and has caused him to discover ways and means not existing in any programme, sometimes coming into severe collision with theory, but in practice either have or will have great blessings in them for the Prussian kingdom and the German people.

We have depicted Bismarck in person at various ages; of latter years he has altered but little at first sight. Those who have only seen him in the distance at the Chamber or the Diet, looking round with his eye-glass, looking through papers, or playing with his pencil, will only have seen the tall form in the King's plain blue uniform, with a single Order—a cross hanging from the neck. It is necessary to draw nearer to observe that time has done more than pass with a friendly greeting by the Chancellor of the Diet. Such years of service as those of Bismarck, in this period of his life, count double, like soldiers' years. Bismarck, according to this calculation, is more than fifty-four years of age.

As an orator, too, the Chancellor of the Diet is almost the same as of old, only he has grown quieter. A member of the Diet, Herr L. Bamberger, describes him in his book as follows[*] :—"Count Bismarck is certainly no orator in the usual sense of the word, yet, in spite of many defects in his delivery, he commands the attention of his audience by the evident force with which his thoughts work within him. It seems, besides, as if the habit of speaking in public, and especially the certainty which is so requisite, and which he now possesses, of obtaining the ear of his audience, has materially contributed of late years to the development of his parliamentary faculty. Yet in the year 1866, one of his admirers, who had attended a sitting of the Reichstag, drew his portrait in the following terms :—' No oratorical ornamentation, no choice of words, nothing which carries the audience away. His voice,

[*] L. Bamberger. Monsieur de Bismarck, Paris, 1868. Graf von Bismarck, Breslau. Count Bismarck, London, 1869, p. 39, sq.

although clear and audible, is dry and unsympathetic, the
tone monotonous; he interrupts himself, and stops frequently; sometimes even he stutters, as if his recalcitrant
tongue refused obedience, and as if he had difficulty in
finding words in which to express his thoughts. His
uneasy movements, somewhat lolling and negligent, in no
wise aid the effect of his delivery. Still, the longer he
speaks, the more he overcomes these defects; he attains

more precision of expression, and often ends with a well-
delivered, vigorous—sometimes, as every one is aware, too
vigorous—peroration.'" "It should be added," observes
Herr Bamberger,* "that his style, although unstudied, is
often not wanting in imagery. His bright and clear intel-

* Count Bismarck, p. 41.

lect does not despise colouring, any more than his strong constitution is free from nervous irritability."

The same author says at another part of his book*, "To an opponent he can be provoking, malicious, even malignant; but he is not treacherous; he offends against morality and justice, but against good taste, by pathetic appeals, never. He is not of the tribe of paragraph writers who imagine that the world is governed by fine phrases, and that public evils are to be mastered by wrapping them up in pompous commonplaces. On the contrary, he is one of those who delight in heightening a contrast by exaggeration, and who thus overshoot their mark. What induced him to confess his principle of blood and iron at that committee meeting?" The instance is very unhappily chosen, without considering that by a blunder the so-called blood and iron theory is written, *Principe du fer et du feu*,† for Bismarck never proclaimed this theory, with which Philisters are made to shudder, at all. In an actually peaceable sense there was a reference at that committee meeting of the 1st September, 1862, as to sparing the effusion of blood and the use of iron. But it is useless to say this, and to reiterate it; Bismarck has been credited with the blood and iron theory, and his it will remain, for it has been proverbial as a " winged word."‡

Another description of Bismarck as an orator (by Glagau) we extract from the *Daheim*.

"The chivalrous personality of Count Bismarck, his easy carriage, and, above all, his universal fame as a diplomatist and statesman, lead us to expect him also to be a brilliant speaker; either one who could bring forth a deeply meditated, well arranged speech without hesitation or trouble, in an elegant flow, or, still more, a speaker of

* Count Bismarck, p. 117. It should be named here that though I have quoted the authorized English translation, I do not agree with its exactitude. —K. R. H. M.

† But not so in the English edition as quoted.—K. R. H. M.

‡ *See* Büchmann, Geflügelte Wörter (Winged Words), 4th edition, p. 224.

natural eloquence, whose thoughts and figures arise in the
soul during his speech, the play of whose words and
rhetorical figures, born of the moment, leap in winged
dance from the lips, who poetizes in his speech like an
improvisatore, whose lightning thoughts and catchwords
hit the mark, moving and burning the hearts of his
auditors. Neither of these. Certainly, a few moments
before, with a swift pen, he has written a few notes on a
narrow slip of paper, which looks like a recipe, over which

he, while turning his thumbs one over the other, balancing
the upper part of his body backwards and forwards, and
speaking to the House, occasionally casts a glance; but,
nevertheless, he stops, and hesitates, even sometimes

stammers and repeats himself; he appears to struggle with his thoughts, and the words clamber over his lips in a half-reluctant way. After two or three words he continually pauses, and one seems to hear an inarticulate sob. He speaks without gestures, pathos, and intonation, without laying a stress on any particular word; sometimes he accentuates the final syllable or the halting verb in a manner totally wrong. Can this be the man who has now a parliamentary career of twenty years behind him?—who already belonged in the Diet of 1847, as Deputy of the Saxon chivalry, to the leaders and promptest speakers of the then exceeding extreme right; who set the liberal majority into excitement and rage in 1849 and 1850, as a member of the Second Chamber and of the Erfurt Union Parliament; who, finally, has, almost singly, opposed a closed phalanx of progressists, as Minister-President, since 1862, repaying their emotional speeches, full of self-confidence and security, in almost the same coin, replying to their mocking and malicious attacks upon him on the spot, and with flashing presence of mind even exciting them to the combat by witty impromptus and cutting sarcasms, often wounding them to the soul?

" Yes, it is the same man; and, when requisite, he is as acute and biting as of yore, although, since his great victories, he has adopted more of statesman-like earnestness, quiet objectivity, and a conciliating carriage, corresponding to his present universally admitted greatness. Gradually his speech begins to flow and to warm, and soon unfolds its especial charm—that original and fresh, free and straightforward mode of expression to which we, in our commonplace days, were quite unaccustomed. Hence it has been called by his opponents ' paradoxical,' ' frivolous,' and ' scholastic.' We are indebted to them for a whole vocabulary of sentences, such as ' Catiline existences,' ' People who have missed their vocation,' ' Blood and iron,' ' Austria should transfer her centre of gravity to Ofen,' 'This conflict must not be taken too tragically,' and which soon became proverbially current, and, in the meantime, have revealed their deep truth and apposite precision. How true and exact, and, at the same time, how coloured and tangible, is his definition of the national character of the Germans, on the occasion of the introduction of the Bill for the Constitution of the Confederation, which has hitherto prevented the attainment of a great united fatherland. 'It is, as it seems to me,' says Count Bismarck, 'a certain superfluity in the feelings of manly self-consciousness which in Germany causes the individual, the community, the race, to depend more upon their own powers than upon those of the totality. It is the deficiency of that readiness of the individual and the race to merge itself in favour of the commonwealth, that readiness which has enabled our neighbour nations to secure, at an earlier period, those benefits after which we are striving.' And when the orator, at the end of his speech, exhorts the House to fulfil their task as soon and as perfectly as possible, he continues :—' For the German nation, gentlemen, has a right to expect from us that we should preclude the possibility of a recurrence of such a catastrophe (*i. e.* a German war); and I am convinced that you, together with the allied government, have nothing so nearly at heart as to fulfil this just anticipation of the German nation.' With this beautiful exhortation, simply, but worthily and warmly, uttered, like the greatest of orators, he electrified the whole assembly, for tumultuous applause resounded from all the benches."

Next to the Reichstag of the North German Confederation, the Luxemburg question, in the year 1867, principally drew attention to Bismarck. Probably many of those who in the pride of recent victory then demanded war for the former Federal fortress, have become convinced that Bismarck's measured attitude was full of high political wisdom. At Bismarck's dinner-table, a short time after Luxemburg had been declared neutral, a learned man gave it as his opinion that Prussia ought to have made it a *casus belli* with France. Bismarck answered very seriously: —" My dear Professor, such a war would have cost us at least thirty thousand brave soldiers, and in the best event would have brought us no gain. Whoever has once looked into the breaking eye of a dying warrior on the battle-field, will pause ere he begins a war." And, after dinner, when he was walking in the garden with some guests, he stopped on a lawn, and related how he had paced to and fro upon this place in disquiet and deep emotion in those momentous days of June. He awaited the royal decision in an anguish of fear. When he came indoors again, his wife asked what had happened that he looked so overcome. " I am excited for the very reason that nothing has happened," he replied, and went into his study. A few minutes later, shortly before midnight, he received the royal decision—the declaration of war.

From the 5th to the 14th of June, 1867, Count Bismarck remained at Paris in the suite of the King, where he became an object of general attention. The Parisians could not picture our Minister-President in any other way than in his white uniform of Cuirassiers. A regular flood of generally horribly bad pictures of him were sold at a sou per copy—the white uniform alone showing that Bismarck was the subject.

From the end of June to the beginning of August he visited his family at Varzin, an estate in Farther Pomerania, which he had bought in the spring.

On the 14th of July, 1867, he was appointed Chancellor of the North German Confederation, went in the beginning of August to the King at Ems, and on the 15th of August opened the session of the Council of the Federation at Berlin. On the 15th of November the Diet was opened, and on the 29th of February, 1868, it was closed. On the

23rd of March the Reichstag of the North German Confederation was opened, and to this the Customs Parliament
was added; it was no wonder, therefore, that under the
gigantic load of work the strength of the Minister-President at last gave way altogether. In the June of 1868 he
was taken seriously ill, and it was only at the end of the
month that he was able to go to Varzin, where, in complete
retirement and entire abstinence from all regular business,
he very slowly mended; but was not able to regain his
strength, in consequence of nervous sleeplessness. He
seemed to feel the obstacles to his activity even more than
all his illness. "Send me no secretary hither, or I shall
go to work again!" he was heard querulously to exclaim.
Despite of all public notifications, a flood of letters pursued
him to Varzin; the whole correspondence, as might be
naturally supposed, had to be returned unopened to Berlin,
where it was estimated that during this stay at Varzin the
Minister-President had been solicited for aid to the extent
of not less than a million and a half of thalers.*

When at last he had grown somewhat better, Bismarck
had the misfortune, on the 21st of August, to have a
dangerous fall from his horse. He had gone out riding
with his friends, Moritz von Blankenburg and the Legation's Rath von Keudell, on a meadow near Puddiger, one
of his farms, a German mile and a quarter from Varzin;
his horse put his foot into a hole, fell, and fell with all its
weight upon his body. So severe a fall might have had
still sadder results, but such as they were they were sad
enough, and weeks of severe pain again had to be endured,
often not unmixed with many fears. At the very time
when the foreign newspapers were picturing the most
secret and wonderful activity in the Chancellor, he was
lying prostrate in the most dangerous state. It need
hardly be said that most anxious looks were directed
towards Varzin—that general excitement eagerly antici-

* Say £225,000.—K. R. H. M.

pated news from thence, and that many hearts breathed lightly again when better intelligence arrived. The news was better than, properly speaking, it had any right to have been, but, fortunately, it has been justified by time.

The delight at the good news from Varzin was shown in the most various ways, especially in presents of remedies against sleeplessness. Bismarck was particularly amused with an old soldier, who advised him to smoke a pound of Porto Rico tobacco every day: he sent the old warrior a pipe and a quantity of tobacco, with the request that he would be so good as to smoke for him.

On the 1st of October, the Burgomaster of Bülow arrived, with a deputation of the magistracy and town council, and brought the Minister-President the honorary diploma of the citizenship of the town. Bismarck received the gentlemen from Bülow with special friendliness, and said, among other things, that he accepted the diploma with the greater satisfaction, as Bülow had ever shown itself a patriotic and loyal city. After dinner, he offered the deputation the hospitality of his house for the night. But the respectable citizens declared that they had promised their careful and inquisitive wives to return before midnight, and that they must, therefore, keep their words. On this the Countess turned merrily to her husband and said: " As you are now also a citizen of Bülow, I should be very glad if you would, from this time, follow the good example of your colleagues of Bülow ! " Bismarck laughed, and shrugged his shoulders, but returned no answer.

The fresh and vigorous manner with which Bismarck has since returned to his duties, allows us to hope that his long and severe illness is quite at an end. He has certainly never thought of sparing himself when duty called ; but he takes part freely in hunting parties, for the free air of the forest is his best medicine, and in the month of December he was present at several parties in the province of Saxony, in the Mark, and even in Holstein. In Holstein, at Ahrensburg, where he hunted for two days with Count Schimmelmann, a brilliant torchlight procession was formed in his honour.

On the 13th of December, shortly before the Count's departure, a long train of several hundred people, young and old, with two hundred flaming pitch torches, appeared in the castle-yard, preceded by a band, and followed by sixty mounted yeomanry. After the leader of the procession had announced that they had come to pay their respects to the Minister - President, Count Bismarck approached the window, before the crowd, and spoke to the following effect :—

" I am rejoiced that you thus salute me as a fellow countryman, and I thank you for the honour you do me. I see in it a proof that the feeling of solidarity has also grown stronger and stronger with you ; and of this I shall joyfully inform the King. We have always belonged to each other as Germans—we have ever been brothers—but we were unconscious of it. In this country, too, there were different races : Schleswigers, Holsteiners, and Lauenburgers ; as, also, Mecklenburgers, Hanoverians, Lübeckers, and Hamburgers exist, *and they are all free to remain what they are*, in the knowledge that *they are Germans*—that they are brothers. And here in the north we should be doubly aware of it, with our Platt Deutsch language, which stretches from Holland to the Polish frontier : we *were* also conscious of it, but have not proclaimed it until now. But that we have again so joyfully and vividly been able to recognize our German descent and solidarity—for that we must thank the man whose wisdom and energy have rendered this consciousness a truth and a fact, in bringing our King and Lord a hearty cheer. Long live His Majesty, our most gracious King and Sovereign, William the First ! "

A threefold cheer was heard throughout the castle-yard.

The torch-bearers and pedestrians then accompanied the honoured man to the railway station hard by, where the farmers, who had led the procession on horseback, were introduced to the Count, and were greeted by him in friendly accents. A hurrah of many hundreds of voices followed the train as it glided away.

CHAPTER V.

A BALL AT BISMARCK'S.

Beauty and might,
With honour bedight,
Assembled by night,
Shining so bright:
And what was not flower a plant would be—
Come not for dancing, but just to see.

Interior of Bismarck's House at Berlin.—Arrival of Guests.—The King.—
The Queen.—The Royal Princes.—The Generals.—Committee of Story-
tellers in the Refreshment Room.—Supper.—The Ball.—Home.

WE have entitled this chapter, "A Ball at Bismarck's,"
for reasons of brevity and alliteration, for in truth, at these
great evening assemblies, with supper after midnight, the
ball is a secondary object for the majority of the guests.
This arrangement, entirely imported from England, pleases
us as little as the English expression "rout," for the principal peculiarity of it is that double the number of guests
are invited than can find room in the apartments, and such
a system is very much at variance with our old-fashioned
notions of German hospitality. The institution of a "rout"
is only tolerable when the greater number of the guests
only come for a quarter of an hour, and then disappear to
attend another "rout." The continual arrival of fresh
individuals, the continual variation in the faces, may
then possess a charm of its own. But this does not take
place at Bismarck's, for when the "Minister-President and
the Countess of Bismarck-Schönhausen" send out their
invitations, no house in Berlin has the courage to vie with

them and open its door on the same evening. The consequence of this is, that all the guests arrive early and stop as long as ever they can. Now, as we have already said, the apartments at the Ministry of Foreign Affairs are exceedingly small, and thus there is a crush of which it is impossible to form any idea unless one has seen it. Add to this the temperature of the dog-days in the brilliantly lighted saloons, and the impossibility of sitting down; an enjoyment only appreciated to its full extent by the members of the Reichstag and Deputies of the Diet, who here find ample opportunity, after their long plenary and committee sittings, to stand.

The guest reaches the first saloon by the stairs, through a forest of tropical plants and orange groves, with livery servants sprinkled in, to the place where the Minister-President, in his white uniform, with the star and collar of his Order, aided by his wife, receives the guests, interchanging a few friendly expressions with them, and then they enter. But after this the guest literally founders in the ocean of dazzling light and crowds of people; it is only after a considerable interval that a person, unless accustomed for years to these parties, recovers his self-possession. At first he hears single words in the noise around him; gradually he learns to understand them; and then come long sentences which he is able to comprehend. Next comes the second stage; he observes that he is swimming between rosy red and pale blue, clouds of garments of various textures; he recognizes with absolute ecstasy the golden threads which pass through these clouds; the soft sounds of the yielding substances are varied by the sharp rustling of silk, and the brilliant gleam of crackling satin; then he perceives rounded shoulders, shining necks, wavy locks, smiling faces—the happy man sees them all, for he is walking towards a group of ladies. He walks? No, he rather creeps, or pushes himself forward without lifting his feet. Beautiful Mother Nature in her wisdom has

F F 2

instinctively taught him that he must necessarily tread
upon some lady's train if he raise his foot a quarter of a
line from the floor.　Thus he shoves himself along on the
left flank of the battalion, whence beautiful eyes are flashing in competition with gold and jewels.　This danger he
can encounter, for all this fire is not directed at him, the
worn-out man of fifty.　He is looking round in astonishment, and then comes a sudden block, for it is impossible
to break through the new group standing right in front.
Court gala uniforms, black coats with broad bands of
various orders, civil uniforms with golden embroidery, and
officers with silver—every place is taken up, and the
wearers are standing shoulder to shoulder in humming
conversation.　Nothing but strange faces!　Suddenly a
very large hand, but of course in a delicate glove, certainly
specially made for this great, good hand, is laid upon the
arm of the anxious undecided one, a well-known face greets
him in a friendly way, and a well-known voice says,—
"Good evening, dear old fellow!"　But he scarcely
recognizes his tried patron and friend, for he had never
seen him in full uniform with the orange and white sash.
When, however, he sees who it is, a great feeling of satisfaction comes over him—he is no longer alone, and he
is safe.　Other acquaintances appear, remarks are inter-
changed, there is even recreation, but under difficulties.
People push here and there, and are pushed in return;
it is impossible to penetrate to the ball room, but the
music of the Cuirassier Guard Regiment can be heard
very well, and sometimes a servant with a tray full of
ices is captured by the more daring—a real grace in this
heat.　It is very comical to hear every one complaining of
want of room and heat, and yet none of the complainants
seem to have any idea of getting rid of these disagreeables
in the simplest manner in the world, by going away!

　Suddenly all the heads, decked with feathers, flowers,
and jewels, bow slowly and then rise again; it is as if the

evening breeze passed gently over the meadow, the flowers all bending up and down, hither and thither.

King William is entering, conducted by the Minister-President. The stately royal man bows with chivalrous politeness, now to this lady, now to that; he pronounces kind words, which are really more kind and fewer in number than is usually the case. Here he shakes hands with one general, there he nods to another gentleman—the path by which the King has passed is marked by proud and happy faces. Those who feel disposed to jeer, cannot in the least know how a Prussian feels when the King's hand touches his own, and the King's eye looks so grandly and mildly into his.

But to enjoy a really heart-warming sight, King William and Bismarck must be seen together. The great hero, Prince Eugene, or Eugenio von Savoye, as he wrote it in Italian, German, and French, once said of the three

Emperors whom he had served—"Leopold was my father, Joseph my friend, Carl is my sovereign!" In Bismarck's

conduct towards the King may be seen the reverence for a father, the attachment of a friend, and the fullest respect for a sovereign. An unique spectacle, this!

Now the Queen passes through the brilliant throng, dressed with royal simplicity; she speaks with several of the members of the Reichstag. When the sailing boat passes through the waves of the sea, when the swan glides over the shining mirror, a silver line marks the passage they have taken. Such a line denotes the path which the Queen had followed through the throng.

The whole Royal House is present.

The tall stately man yonder, with the brave handsome countenance, who looks still taller in his light blue dragoon

uniform with the yellow collar, in which he is not often seen, is the Crown Prince. He is engaged in animated conversation with a foreign diplomatist, in a golden full dress, and is evidently in the best of tempers. Prince Albrecht, the King's younger brother, passes swiftly in a frank military manner, shaking one or the other person cordially by the hand. His elder brother, Prince Carl, the Commander-in-Chief, is a singular contrast to him.

He stands erect and proudly in the middle of a circle, but without stiffness. A mocking smile plays over his features; there is a remarkable intermixture in his eyes of sharp observation and indifference. How he brings first this person and then that to his side, without raising his hand! This is the reproachless manner of a *grand seigneur* of days gone by; one cannot but feel that Prince Carl still retains whole and undivided the princely consciousness of former times. In his eyes every one—not of princely rank— stands on the same level. Rank, titles, honours, have no distinction in his eyes. He is as gracious to the ministers and high dignitaries, as to the author whom he has just summoned to him. He alone really exercises the *métier de prince.*

Yonder stalwart form, with the good brave countenance, in the admiral's uniform, is Prince Adalbert, a cousin of the King, he is talking with Herr von Selchow, the Minister of Agriculture, who at a distance looks like an officer in the cavalry. All the princes of the Royal House wear the Cross of the Order *pour le mérite*, and therefore have all been under fire.

Prince Frederick Carl yonder is talking with Count Eulenburg, who has made his way through typhoons and Japan to the Ministry of the Interior. The Prince, with his high forehead, firm bearded countenance, large eyes with their lonely quiet expression, and spare form, in the red jacket of the Ziethen Hussars, is the hero of Düppel and Sadowa, also a member of the North German Reichstag.

All the faces in yonder group are well known, for their portraits hang in every window; they have written their names in the book of history with the sword. At every step here one may greet a hero. Certainly, designed and undesigned mistakes sometimes happen, as, for instance, that pretty young lady cannot sufficiently wonder that the valiant old Steinmetz, the famous hero of Nachod and Skalitz, is still so young, and dresses in private clothes.

They had pointed her out a Reichstag Deputy from Pomerania as the famous General, and left her in the error.

Through the brilliant throng and excitement, in the

dazzling illuminations and heat, children wise in their generation, and lucky dogs who know everything, have discovered the way to obtain a thorough course of refreshments, which is hidden in a dark thicket yonder, and slily wins in semi-concealment. In noble silver vases there is cool—deliciously cool—beer. All the thirsty souls who drink at this fount sing the praises of Bismarck, for he has introduced this innovation. Bismarck first made beer fashionable in Berlin *salons*. And so readily has it been received within a short time, that even tender ladies and high princes no longer hesitate to pay their court openly to King Gambrinus.

There is lively conversation over the beer. A wit has spread a rumour that the delicious drink has come from

Schwechat, and is a present from the Austrian Imperial Chancellor to the Chancellor of the North German Confederation. Some give a friendly assent to this, others kindly add, that Bismarck has already, in return, sent some Neunaugen and Flunder from Pomerania, to his colleague in Vienna; and why should it not be believed? Formerly, at any rate, the most friendly and social relations existed between Bismarck and Beust.

An old Colonel D—— mutters something like "*timeo Danaos*," but swallows the rest of the words, as he cannot immediately find the Latin terminations in the lumber-room of his memory, but instead, enjoys another goblet of the supposed gift. He is almost frightened when his neighbour remarks, that Beust as well as Bismarck is a descendant of an Alt Mark family; Büste, the family seat of the Beust family, is only distant a few miles from Bismarck; certainly, the family had not lived there for a long time. Colonel D—— begins to have a better opinion of the Austrian Chancellor, and drinks up his beer in comfort.

Another is telling how Bismarck laughingly said, that "his colleague, the Minister of Finance, would to-day convince himself that this dwelling was much too small for the Minister-President, and would think of how he could get him out of the difficulty." Thus the little circle got happily into the downward way of telling anecdotes, whence there is no return.

To a somewhat complaining deputation from the new provinces, Bismarck good-humouredly explained, that Prussia was like a woollen jacket, very unpleasant at first, but when people got accustomed to it they found it very comfortable, and at last came to think it a great benefit.

Bismarck allowed another deputation to whine for a long time about universal military service and the weight of taxation; he then said, very seriously and in a tone of

the greatest astonishment, "Dear me, these gentlemen probably thought they could become Prussians for nothing!"

A well-known politician promulgated a very paradoxical statement at Bismarck's dinner-table; some one present started forward to refute it. "Pray don't trouble yourself," exclaimed Bismarck, "if you will only have patience for two minutes, the learned Herr Professor will at once contradict himself in the most brilliant manner!"

In the year 1848 there was a great deal rumoured about a falling away of the Rhine Provinces. "Where are they going to fall to?" asked Bismarck.

"And in France they no longer say, '*travailler pour le roi de Prusse*,' to indicate a lost labour of love, but '*travailler pour le maître de M. de Bismarck!*'" whispered a fat diplomatist cautiously to his neighbour.

"How is it," King William merrily once asked the Minister-President and his cousin Herr von Bismarck-Briest, "that the Bismarcks of Schönhausen are all such tall, strapping fellows, and those of Briest the contrary?" Count Bismarck replied, "Because my ancestors all served the King as soldiers in battle, while my cousins were engaged in civil affairs!" Herr von Bismarck-Briest added, with presence of mind, "That is why I have put my seven sons into the army."

It was true that six Bismarck-Briests fought in the last war under the King's standard; a pity that the seventh was not there, but as a Landrath he was "exempt."

"But," whispered a pale assessor, who has been guilty of innumerable verses, "Bismarck is deficient in æsthetic culture; I have heard from the best authority, that once at Frankfurt, when Goethe's pearl, 'Happy he who closes up his door without hatred of the world!' was performed on the piano, Bismarck burst out with, "What a tailor's soul this Goethe had!'"

The pale assessor looked as if such barbarism froze him; some laughed, others shrugged their shoulders.

"The ideas of the moment were confused with opinions or meaning!" said a Provincial Government Councillor, who knew how to combine his reverence for Bismarck with his æsthetic aspirations; for in fact he only knew Bismarck and Goethe.

"I remember you in my boyish days very well," said Bismarck, in 1864, to the Body-Physician of Prince Albrecht, the Privy-Councillor Dr. von Arnim; "you then enormously struck me with your energy."

"This is completely altered now," replied Arnim, quietly, "you now strike me enormously with yours."

The negroes in America are very fond of assuming fine names of famous men, such as Cæsar, Scipio, Hannibal, Aurelius, Washington, King James, Abraham Lincoln, and so forth. One of these black gentlemen got very drunk, and shouted like a madman; he was seized and put into prison, but brought sober before the magistrate the next morning. "What is your name?" The negro answered, with great dignity, "Count Bismarck." There was Homeric laughter. The magistrate said, "You are discharged; one must overlook a little from any one bearing so great a name; but for the future take care to do your illustrious god-cousin in Berlin more credit!"

There was no end to this. Anecdote succeeded anecdote, one joke the other; each departing story-teller leaving another in his place, until the circle round the altar of Gambrinus was broken up by the news that their Majesties and the Court, after having partaken of supper in the Countess's salon, had taken their departure. This was the signal for supper for the rest of the guests.

A buffet supper is the saddest conclusion of a "rout"— it is almost somewhat humiliating to stand with one's hat under one's arm and the plate in one's hand, after having had great difficulty to procure knife, fork, and all the other utensils employed in civilized nations for the business of eating! But humanity can even support this, and with a little care and patience it is possible gradually to

get a complete supper, from a cup of soup to a fruit ice.
Modest minds content themselves certainly by absorbing
a gigantic portion of ham pie with a spoon—or whatever
the fortune of war has favoured their plates with—ask

for nothing more—but "go in " for the wine which is
foaming in any quantity.

In the meantime the dance music is beginning again,
and with it the actual period of enjoyment for dancers,
and the terrible hour for chaperonizing mothers and aunts,
who sit out the last cotillon with a heroism brave unto
death.

The non-dancing guests now really begin to enjoy
themselves—the crowd being no longer so thick, there is
more room, as the saloons reserved for the Court are now
open, and there are plenty of seats.   Presently a smoking-
room suddenly opens—a smoking-room with noble cigars,
iced champagne, and hot coffee.   Everywhere one sees the
Minister-President busy among his guests, conversing in
the most agreeable tone, seeing that there is nothing
wanting, inviting every one to drink, and himself rejoicing in the gaiety he disperses.   And whoever departs at
about five in the morning, with a hearty shake of the
hand from Bismarck, will certainly carry away with him
the impression that the First Minister of Prussia is also
the most delightful host in Prussia.

CHAPTER VI.

BISMARCK'S HOUSE AT BERLIN.

'Tis but a hut or little more,
The threshold narrow, slim the door—
And yet within this space so wee,
Proudly uprears the laurel tree.

Bismarck's House in Ordinary Costume.—Its History.—"Sultan Uilem and Grand Vizier Bi-Smark."—"Bismarck, *grand homme*, Bakschisch!"—The Cuckoo Clock.—Daily Habits.—Sunday at Bismarck's.

In that portion of the Wilhelmstrasse at Berlin, which has remained comparatively quiet, although it is bounded on one side by the animated and famous street Unter den Linden, and on the other by the noisy and busy Leipziger Strasse, one of the arteries of Berlin circulation, not far from the Wilhelmsplatz, stands a plain one storied house, with twelve windows in the front—the Ministry of Foreign Affairs—since 1862 the official residence of Count Bismarck.

It is the most modest ministerial residence in Berlin; in no large State of Europe does the Foreign Minister live so quietly as Count Bismarck does here. To the right of the Minister-President is the Hotel of Prince Radziwill—*entre cour et jardin*—with its railings and stately front court; to the left is the building of the Royal Privy Court Printing-office of Messrs. Von Decker; opposite the former Palace of the Order of St. John of Balley Brandenburg, so magnificently restored by Schinckel, and now the property of Prince Carl of Prussia. One advantage Bismarck's dwelling enjoys with all the aristo-cratic houses of the Wilhelmstrasse—it has a large garden with fine old trees in it, which extends as far as the Königsgrätzer Strasse.

The whole extent of the Wilhelmstrasse, from the Linden to the Leipziger Strasse, formerly belonged to the Thurgarten—the freehold being the King's. On the enlargement of the city by Frederick William I., this site was given to the generals and higher officials as free building ground, and was supported by the King with his well-known energy by building materials and other subven-tions. The present site of Wilhelmstrasse and Königs-grätzer Strasse, by the privilege of the 21st of September, 1736, was covered by a free house, respecting the builder of which there is still some question. It was unquestion-ably the work of one General von Pannewitz; probably Wolf Adolf von Pannewitz, born the 13th March, 1679, at Great-Gaglov, in Lower Lausitz, who had been Page and Equerry to King Frederick I., and had joined the regiment of Gensdarmes in 1714, from the disbanded Garde du Corps. He became lieutenant-colonel of this regiment in 1719, in 1725 commander, and in 1728, after the death of Field-Marshal General von Natzmer, its Chief. Pannewitz had gained renown on the Rhine, in Italy, and Brabant, and had so distinguished himself in the first Silesian war, that the great King allowed him to retire from the service on account of bodily illness, very honorably, with a pension of three thousand thalers. How the ownership of this old hero, who had honestly served three Kings of Prussia, passed to the well-known Countess Barbara Campanini, the married Presidentess von Cocceji, we cannot tell; but according to the register she sold the house on the 10th April, 1756, to the Actual Privy State and Directing War Minister and Grand Master of the Robes, Herr Count von Eickstedt. After the death of this nobleman it became the property of his widow, the

Countess von Eickstedt-Peterswaldt, Caroline-Friedrike, born von Grumbkow; then that of her daughter, the widowed Obermarshallin von Wangenheim, Philippine Juliane, born Countess von Eickstedt-Peterswaldt. This lady was, however, Bismarck's grand-aunt, having been married first to the Royal Captain Ernst Friedrich von Bismarck, at Schönhausen (born 1729, died 1775), a grand uncle of the Minister-President—so that in the last century a Bismarck lived both at Schönhausen and in the Wilhelmstrasse. In the year 1804 the Hanoverian Councillor of Finance, Johann Crelinger, bought the house, but soon sold it to the wife of the Russian Imperial Minister and Ambassador at the Royal Prussian Court, Herr Maximilian von Alopeus, Luise Charlotte Auguste Friedrike, born a Von Veltheim. From her it passed into the possession in 1815 of her husband, Baron Alopeus, who sold it in 1819 to the Government.

The family of Alopeus, originally derived from a learned family of Finland, have long played a great part in Berlin society. Baron Maximilian was thrice Russian Ambassador for several years in 1790, 1802, and 1813 at Berlin, and was succeeded in the post by his younger brother, who has been raised to the rank of Count—Daniel Alopeus, who died here in 1831. Public attention has been very recently drawn to this younger Alopeus by a book which has passed through dozens of editions in France, and has been translated into almost all languages. The principal personage of this specifically Roman Catholic book is Alexandrina, Countess Albert de Laferronays, the only daughter of Daniel Alopeus and the lovely Johanna von Wenckstern, who married for the second time the Prince Paul Lapuchin of Korsie in the Ukraine.

The Fiscal Board bought the house originally for the then Minister of State, Count von Bernstorff, together with all its furniture and fittings. Since that time all the Foreign Ministers of Prussia have resided there, with the exception of Ancillon, who remained in a private house, Unter den Linden.

It has been long known that the apartments are not sufficient for the requirements of the service. The Ministerial bureaux, grown too unwieldy for the ground floor, had to be transferred to another building, scarcely saving much trouble in the transaction of business. The apartments form a very · fitting dwelling-place for a nobleman in private life, but are by no means suitable for the Prussian Prime Minister and Chancellor of the North German Federation. Bismarck has naturally felt this inconvenience more than any one else ; but, as far as we know, he has taken no steps towards any alteration, but usually contents himself with a good-humoured joke about it.

To the left, on the first floor, are two spacious saloons, having a view of the court and garden. These are very convenient, and are decorated with old family portraits, some of which we have mentioned in our previous chapter on Schönhausen. It is not usual to decorate official residences with ancestral portraits ; but, as everything of the kind was wanting, Bismarck had his portraits brought from Schönhausen. In the second saloon stands the Countess's piano, and here there is an excellent likeness of Bismarck's sister, Frau von Arnim, as a child. Next to this is the sitting-room of the Countess, with a good picture of Bismarck in the Frankfurt period. From the first saloon one passes to the right into a large reception-room, where the Ministerial Council is also held. This is very simply decorated by a portrait of the King, and a gigantic porcelain vase, presented by the King to Bismarck. To the right of this saloon is Bismarck's dining-room, with its old carpet, of which so much has been said in Berlin, although we really cannot say why. Next to this is a ball-room, over the hall, where the very large dinners also are served. To the left, next to the Ministerial saloon, is

the comfortable but simple study of Bismarck.   A double
writing-table with a low-backed chair on either side, is the
principal object.   In the corner, by the stove, is a *chaise-
longue*, with a lion's skin over it.   This lion's skin was
brought to the Minister-President by the celebrated
traveller Rohlfs, from Africa.   We are indebted to him also
for the following anecdote :—Rohlfs was on board an Egyp-
tian ship, and was obliged to tell the officers a great deal
about "Sultan Uilem" and his Grand Vizier "Bi-Smarck,"
which seemed like a new edition of Haroun-ar-Reschid
and the Vizier Djaffar to the Orientals.   The name
Bismarck pleased them wonderfully, as Bi-Smarck in Arabic
signifies "Swift Fire," "Rapid Action."

In the "Wochenblatt der Johanniter Ordens-Balley-
Brandenburg," another traveller thus relates his ride from
Cairo to the Pyramids—we there read: "Every one who
has been in the East or has read a book of travels knows
the events of the next hour.   The visitor to the Pyramids
is seized like an irresponsible being by four brown shapes,
each clad in a single garment; two of them drag him up
the irregular steps of the Pyramid of Cheops, while the two
others assist by shoving and pushing.   It is of no use to
beg and pray—always forward, forward !   The eye roves
giddily on the depths, and anxiously glances up the
uneven steps, the worn and slippery blocks of stone—
upward, upward, until one falls exhausted on the little
platform, and without any power of assembling moral
courage.   The guides then dance round with the customary
cry of 'Bakschisch ! bakschisch !' (Money ! money !).   Dark
traditions concerning an Englishman who declined to pay,
and was precipitated into the depths, do not make the
situation any the pleasanter ; and had I not understood the
Arab people, having left my companions far behind, I
should have felt very uncomfortable.   But I alleged weariness, and would bind myself to nothing.   But when all
appeals in German, Arabic, English, and Italian had

failed (for these fellows smatter all languages), the tallest
fellow, who had guessed my nationality, placed himself
before me, and, holding up his forefinger, pathetically
exclaimed, '*Signor! Bismarck grand homme! Bakschisch!*'
At this appeal to my patriotic feelings, laughter got the
upper hand, and I divided my copper money among these
gentlemen, just as the heads of my companions became
visible at the edge of the topmost stone ridge."

In this study hang pictures of the Great Elector and
the Great King, with some other portraits of King
William. Otherwise the room is quite without decoration.
A side door leads into the boudoir of the Countess,
another into Bismarck's bedroom, and the dressing-room
beyond.

Beside the door leading from the study to the bedroom,
is a cuckoo clock, which every quarter of an hour reminds those whom Bismarck receives here, in an appealing
and unmistakable manner, that they are not to forget they
are in the presence of a man whose precious time belongs
to his King and country. With some this warning is
unnecessary, but in other cases it is very useful, and
should any one neglect its appeals, the possessor of the
cuckoo clock is quite the man to support them in the
politest manner in the world. Softly and cautiously various
stories are whispered of the important influence this
cuckoo clock has exercised on the fates of many.

Such are the apartments inhabited by Prussia's Premier;
his children live in a wing of the house.

When at Berlin, Bismarck is accustomed to breakfast,
entirely dressed in a blue uniform overcoat, about ten
o'clock. At this time he opens all the letters which have
come in, runs through the telegraphic despatches and
the latest news of the morning papers, and then receives
his councillors in the study, rides for an hour, and then
proceeds to the Royal presence. At his return from the
Palace, about five, the family dines; but it is a rare

circumstance not to find friends present. Bismarck has always an excellent appetite, and prefers the red wine of Bordeaux, which he once on the tribune of the Second Chamber called "the natural drink of the North German," to Rhenish wine. The greatest punctuality prevails at his table. He especially delighted in exhorting his sons while they were young, to sit upright; and a person who for a long time had the honour of being Bismarck's table companion, asserts in full seriousness, that owing to the continual directions Bismarck gave his sons on this point, which he also profited by himself, he had, according to his own calculation, himself grown two inches taller in the time. Conversation is sparkling, open, and almost always

illustrated by the humorous manner of the host and the witty animation of the Countess. The language employed

G G 2

is always German, very seldom a little French or English. Bismarck's family table has an especial charm at Christmas time, when a great tree stretches its branches over the guests. After dinner the Minister-President stays for a short time in his wife's salon, where he drinks a cup of coffee and smokes, during which time he runs through the *Kreuzzeitung* and the *Norddeutsche Allgemeine*. He then retires to his study, and receives the Ambassadors, or a Council of Ministers is held, and after that he works by himself. About midnight he returns into the salon to his wife, and is pleased if he finds any company there. This rarely fails, especially when the Diet or Reichstag is assembled. It may be very well understood that this arrangement is often altered, according to circumstances : the Council of Ministers often sits in the morning, and

then the Count can scarcely find time, after his audience of the King, to get his accustomed ride in the Thiergarten.

In the warmer seasons of the year he often goes into the garden after dinner, where the trees are; he was very commonly, here every day with Roon and Moltke before the war of 1866. The trees could tell some strange mysteries, but of course they are "sworn," as is proper with ministerial trees. Sometimes Bismarck mounts the ice-house; there he gets a "view"—it certainly is not very extensive, but still green and pleasant—over the large neighbouring gardens. The Minister-President attends divine service with his family in the Holy Trinity Church, in which he was once confirmed. The Communion he receives at the hands of the Consistorial Councillor Souchon, who has also confirmed his children. If Bismarck, from personal illness, is unable to attend public worship, he likes to have a private service read for him and his by some young divine. But it is a rule to receive no one in the morning—for it is Sunday in Bismarck's house.

CHAPTER VII.

VARZIN.

Purchase of Varzin.—The Veranda.—The Park.—The Name of Bismarck
famous.—House Inscriptions.—Popularity of Bismarck.—In an Ambush
of School-girls.—Conclusion.

IN the April of 1867 Count Bismarck went to see the
Estates of Varzin (consisting of Varzin, Wussow, Puddiger,
Misdow, and Chomitz), near Schlawe, in Farther Pomerania, and soon afterwards purchased them. In the
autumn of that year, as we have said, he spent some weeks
at Varzin, but in the following year he remained there,
unfortunately in great illness, from June to December.

He soon made himself at home there, and is fond of
Varzin, as may be readily understood from its being close
to the birthplace of his wife—beloved Reinfeld. Nothing
is wanting there to his enjoyment—there are trees, and
plenty of good riding and hunting. He converses with
every one who meets him, in forest and field, in a
friendly manner, and is fond of talking "platt" with the
country people. Recently he said to an old labourer
known to him, who had been ill: "*Nu seid Ihr wohl wieder
ganz auf dem Tüge?*" (You're all right on the main again?)
"*I ja,*" replied the old man, "*Sie sollten man ok hie
blieven, den würden Sie noch mal so frisch!*" (Ay! O,
you'd a vast deal better ztop 'ere; yow'd be eer zo mooch
vresher!) Bismarck laughed. "Yes—if one could be as
you are, and always stop in Varzin, I believe you!"

If one turn south on the Cöslin-Danzig road, by the
large village of Carwitz—recently marked as a station on
the railway from Cöslin to Danzig—after a short drive on
a good road, some three German miles, one reaches the
Bismarck estates with great ease. It is a very pleasant
neighbourhood, alternating with wooded hillocks, meadows
and waters, wood and plough-land. There is nothing very
magnificent about it, nothing very pretentious; but it is
a pleasant spot, and the Countess Bismarck once merrily
called it, very appropriately, "a pretty little humpy
countrykin."

Varzin cannot be seen from the distance; it is hidden
by woods. The descending road divides the mansion, to
the right, from the farm-buildings on the left, forming a
long parallelogram.

Varzin does not look nearly so aristocratic as Schönhausen, which Bismarck calls his "old stone-heap." A
building of one story, with two wings, all painted pale
yellow, surrounds a somewhat roomy courtyard, open to
the road. On the principal building, on the gable, are the
arms of Blumenthal. The steps of the stairway are

occupied by orange-trees, myrtles, and laurels.   We saw a
young donkey running about, who was eating the fallen
laurel leaves with a very good appetite.   The possessor of
Varzin must feel very much flattered that laurels abound
so much in his house that there are enough to feed
donkeys!

On this open staircase, or rather veranda, Bismarck
receives his guests, like a simple country nobleman, in a
green coat, white waistcoat, and yellow neckcloth, and

with a hearty shake of the hand makes them free of the
hospitality of his house.   On this veranda the Countess
stands with her daughter, and looks with beaming eyes
and happy face after the three sportsmen who are proceeding towards the forest, and wave their hands in

THE PARK AT VARZIN.

greeting back to her. And for others—for every one—it is a pleasant sight to see Count Bismarck walking between his sons, his rifle over his shoulder, or riding on horseback. On this veranda also the last farewell takes place between mother and sons. After the longest possible holiday, they return to school at Berlin, while Bismarck himself orders the postilion to make haste, that he may not lose the midday train at Cöslin. The honest Pomeranian, with the well-fed face above his orange collar, has no idea that there exists an intimate bond between himself and the great Minister—that in his capacity, as Chancellor of the North German Confederation, he is his highest representative.

The interior of the mansion of Varzin is habitable and comfortable, but there is nothing otherwise remarkable about it. To the right of the hall on which you enter, is the dining-room, which is connected with the kitchen and servants' rooms in the left wing; to the left is the Count's room, the large centre table of which is covered with maps. Maps, especially those of a minute kind, are an old hobby of Bismarck's; if a trip is projected, or guests are departing, the road is accurately measured off beforehand on the map. This zealous study of maps has always seemed to us very characteristic of Bismarck's whole nature; he always desires to know the road he is travelling in the most accurate manner; he considers the advantages, and weighs them against the annoyance. The windows of this apartment look out on the courtyard. To the right again is the Countess's room, the windows opening on the park, and thence there is a really magnificent view: in the bright summer moonlight nights, one would think that one had, by enchantment, some fragment of early French court life, from Meudon or Rambouillet. On the other side of a prattling little brook, crossed by a pretty little bridge, the park, with its fine old trees—oaks and beeches—rises in terraces up the hill-side, and the white statues contrast well with the green foliage. At such a sight, one thinks of the "Enchanted Night" of Tieck; and indeed there is somewhat of the "wondrous world of faërie" in the whole aspect of the scene—in its antique but eternally youthful splendour.

Our readers know, from the letters we have given, how passionately Bismarck loves such scenery. There is a great deal more of the romantic poet and sentimental German in the great statesman, than would appear at first sight. He sometimes recognizes this himself with a smile.

The park of Varzin by moonlight has indeed a peculiar old-fashioned appearance; very little imagination is necessary to people it with gentlemen in court uniforms and swords, hats under their arms, and ladies with towering head-dresses, hoops, and high shoes. On these terraces, over the pretty flower banks, and round the white statues, there breathes the whole inspiration of a life which, for a long time, was unjustly contemned, and afterwards was properly derided, when fashion became its distinguishing trait, after the *petit maître* style—a life we cannot wish back again, but which we cannot but love, it having been that of our grandfathers and great-grandfathers, and containing in it, with many traits of insignificance, some great and admirable features. We may laugh at it, but it contains some pretty ideas!

To return to our description. Next to the Countess's drawing-room are the bedrooms, and to the right of these again is a hall, where an enormous black oak staircase, reminding one of the other staircase at Schönhausen, leads to the upper story. In this hall, and in the ante-chamber, one sees the horns of two immense moufflons, two tremendous stag antlers, and some others of different ages. These all belong to Bismarck's hunting expedition in the park at Schönbrunn, when he hunted there after the Danish war, with his royal master, as the guest of the

Emperor of Austria. The Emperor Francis Joseph at that time very graciously sent these trophies to Bismarck at Berlin.

On the other side of this hall, by way of a small room, one passes behind the dining-room into a large garden saloon and conservatory, with a pretty pavilion. In one of the guest-chambers of the right wing, on the ground floor, there is a picture, ghastly to look upon, of the master of the house, in life-size, which as Friedrich Gerstäcker, the unwearied traveller, informs us, is sold in great numbers in Venezuela. A worthy transatlantic Correggio, the name not yet known to fame, has depicted the Count in a sky-blue miller's coat and bright green trousers, red neckerchief, and rosy red gloves, such as the dandies of Caraccas probably wear, after a photograph. There is not a trace of likeness in the face, and yet there is something so characteristic in the attitude, that one immediately knows who one has before one—something so like that the very dogs bark at it. Bismarck, it is well known, is an especial favourite among the Germans in America. Several new cities have been named after him; there is a Bismarck on the Conchos in Texas, and a Bismarck in Missouri; the locality of a third we do not recollect. A considerable trans-oceanic trade is carried on in terribly bad photographs of the Minister-President, and a German cutler has made himself a little fortune by his Bismarck knives; these knives are distinguished by a very sharp and strong blade. Nor has the old world remained behind the new in its admiration. German vessels bear Bismarck's name and likeness, under the black and white and red flag, to the farthest shores. Acute champagne-makers compete with Veuve Clicquot and the Duc de Montebello under the designation of Bismarck-Schönhausen, and from Cannes, in Southern France, to Rügenwaldermünde, in Farther Pomerania, speculative hotel-keepers announce that " Rooms have just been engaged here for Count Bismarck." After the English style, the name of Bismarck has been bestowed as a baptismal name; we ourselves know a little Fräulein von X., named Wilhelmine Bismarck Sadowa, born the 3rd of July, 1866. In Spain the lucifer-match boxes significantly bear the portraits of Bismarck and his Royal master.

We have been especially pleased at finding Bismarck's name in the true German household phrases. Thus, a dear and lately deceased friend, the Privy Councillor Dr. von Arnim, wrote over his door:—

> Lang lebe und blühe König Wilhelm, mein Held;
> Mit ihm soll behalten Graf Bismarck das Feld!

Long live and flourish King William, my hero; with him shall Count Bismarck keep the field.

Several house proprietors in Berlin have adopted this sentence; but still more apposite is the following inscription on the house of a master weaver:—

> Als Wilhelm wirkt und Bismarck spann,
> Gott hatte seine Frende dran. 1866.
> As William worked and Bismarck spon,
> God had his joy thereon. 1866.

Gardeners have started a Bismarck rose, and a giant Bismarck strawberry, and the fashionable world attires itself in Bismarck brown. At our request, the management of the Bazaar, the most competent house for such things, has kindly shown us fourteen shades of this colour in silk, and informed us at the same time that there are many more of such Bismarck shades; that Bismarck *foncé* is not nearly so dark as Bismarck *courroucé*. This colour originally was called *hanneton* (May beetle), and soon drove the *Vert Metternich* from the field; while in Austria a small cake (*semmel*), strewn with a little poppy seed, shaped like a pigtail, holds its sway with the Radetzky Köpfel. On the Paraná and Paraguay the steamer Count Bismarck runs up and down the river. At Alexandria the Passage Bismarck is full of brown and black forms. At Blumberg, in the South Australian colony of Adelaide, the Germans assemble in the Bismarck Hall, and to keep up their national enthusiasm over a drink, they smoke cigars "Conde de Bismarck." These are considered highly elegant, but cost one hundred and thirty dollars a pound, although there is a cheaper medium Bismarck cigar.

In the Grand Duchy of Posen, by a Cabinet Order of the King, the four places Karsy, Bobry, Budy, and Zwierzchoslaw, in the circle of Pleschen, have been, at the desire of the inhabitants, incorporated as Bismarcksdorf.

In Berlin the Bismarckstrasse unites the Roonstrasse with the Moltkestrasse; while in 1865 the malice of the Berlin wits wanted to change the name of the Wasserthorstrasse, when the terrible fall of the houses took place there, into Bismarckstrasse.

In South Germany the belief that Bismarck does everything and can do everything, down to the Spanish Revolution, and perhaps even directs the weather, is continually spreading. Oddly enough, the Ultramontane enemies of Bismarck especially take care to spread the name of the Minister-President. They certainly paint black over black, but they make the nation familiar with his fame, and though they may ever depict him as a sort of devil, truth will break through at last.

Is Bismarck really popular? This may be a curious question to ask, but it may still be legitimately put, for in the ordinary sense of the word Bismarck is not popular, despite his world-wide fame. For instance, he is not popular as in our days Cavour and Garibaldi have been. He has not the popularity of the ruling party opinion and that of the day, but, in place of it, his is the historical popularity which will preserve his memory to a grateful posterity. A correspondent of the liberal Paris paper *Le Temps* very excellently expresses our meaning in the

following remarks:—"The Chancellor of the North
German Confederation is not what we can call a popular
man; the Prussians, or at least the Berlinese, entertain
for him a similar feeling to that entertained by the other
Germans for Prussia. They do not love him; they love to
exercise their wit upon him, and you know how biting
and salted the Berlin wit is; but they acknowledge him
and wonder at him, showing him tolerance. They look
upon him as the greatest statesman of the present day;
are proud of him, although he often presses hard upon
them. M. de Bismarck has for the Prussians an incomparable magic, particularly since he opposed the
policy of Napoleon. Since 1866, a change has taken
place which has surprised me, although there is nothing
very surprising in it. Before 1866, the Premier in everything he did had the world pretty much against him—to-
day every impulse is expected from him, and if he gives it,
almost every one is at his back."

The question of popularity, as far as the great world is
concerned, may well be left here; but in Varzin and the
neighbouring districts it has long since been determined.
Only ask his farmers and labourers! And with the daring
blacksmith—(or was it a miller?)—who secretly poaches on
Bismarck's preserves, the Minister-President is, perhaps,
the most popular of any.

It is a real pleasure to see Bismarck at Varzin among
his trees; not during those restless nocturnal wanderings
in the park, to which his sleepless illness only too
frequently impels him, but when he is pleasantly pointing
out his favourites to his guests. It was an event when
the North German Chancellor, the summer before last,
discovered three magnificent beeches in the midst of a
thicket.

On a declivity with a beautiful view, there is a rich deer
preserve. Bismarck might even erect a falconry, and hunt
with hawks—there are plenty in the Netherlands still.

But this Imperial and Royal amusement is for him too—reactionary.

One day Bismarck thought, as he was riding to the Crangener frontier, whither he had sent his gamekeeper, that he caught a glimpse of a peculiar blue animal which fled before him. But when he came up with it, it proved to be a blue parasol, and he himself had fallen into an ambuscade, for he found himself suddenly surrounded by a crowd of young ladies, who received him with songs. The pastor in Crangen kept a young ladies' school, who, having heard that Bismarck was coming, thus paid their respects to him in so unexpected a way, and left him, delighted with his amiability. Crangen, an ancient hunting castle of the Dukes of Pomerania, standing picturesquely, with its four stately towers and high gables, between three lakes and high mountains, is, without doubt, the most beautiful spot in this neighbourhood. It belongs to the Royal Major Retired Rank Freiherr Hugo von Loën, who is Bismarck's nearest neighbour in that direction.

The long residence of Bismarck at Varzin during the summer before last, has directed the eyes of all Europe on this modest seat in Farther Pomerania. Varzin was an old fief of the family of Von Zitzewitz, who possessed many estates in this neighbourhood. It is said that it came *per fas et nefas* into the possession of the very powerful Privy Minister of State and War and Principal President of Pomerania, Caspar Otto von Massow, who then sold it to Major General Adam Joachim, Count of Podewils. Count Podewils and his brothers received a renewal of the fief, and it was a heritage in their family, until in this century it passed through an heiress to a Von Blumenthal, Werner Constantine von Blumenthal, who was raised to a Countship in 1840. Bismarck purchased the Varzin estates from the younger sons of this Blumenthal. They form, with Varzin, Wussow—where the church is situated, Puddiger, Misdow, Chomitz, and Charlottenthal, a considerable property.   The soil is not equal throughout ; the forests are very fine and stately ; the wood in good condition.   The game is very plentiful—few stags, but plenty of roes, hares, and smaller game.   The Wipper, which falls into the Baltic at Rügenwaldermünde, five German miles from Varzin, serpentines through the forests of the Bismarck property, and in part forms the boundary of the estate, and is very useful for the transportation of the timber.

Formerly there were considerable glass factories in Misdow and Chomitz, but they are no longer worked, nor is any spirit distilled there ; but a wood factory it is said is in use—certainly a profitable business in this neighbourhood, so full of wood.

APPENDIX A.

It has been thought desirable to give the originals of the two poems translated respectively at pages 46, 47, and pages 99, 100, by the present Editor, for the benefit of those who may like to see them.

Das Blatt, das grün und kräftig
Des Wandrers Blick entzückt,
In purem Golde prächtig
Den Schild der Bismarck schmückt;
Das Kleeblatt gülden leuchtend,
Das ist im blauen Feld
Von Nesselblättern dräuend
Gar scharf und blank umstellt.
  Es was vor alten Zeiten
Ein Fräulein wonnesam,
Durch die der Nessel Zeichen
Ins Schild der Bismarck kam.
Um Fräulein Gertrud warben
Viel Edle, kampferprobt,
Die auf Geheiss des Vaters
Dem Vetter schon verlobt.
Dar kam ein Fürst der Wenden
Herab vom nord'schen Meer,
Er kam mit hundert Pferden—
Jung Gertrud sein Begehr;
Jung Gertrud lehnte höflich
Die hohe Ehre ab,
Der Fürst, erzürnet höchlich,
Erhub den güld'nen Stab;
Er winkte seinen Knechten
Und rief, von Zorn entbrannt;
" Ich will das Kleeblatt brechen
Mit meiner eignen Hand!
Ja, wär's noch eine Nessel,
Gäb's doch ein kleines Weh,
Doch lustig ist's zu brechen,
Grün oder gold den Klee!"—
Und noch am selb'gen Tage,
Dar stürmt mit reis'gem Tross

Der Fürst vom Wendenstamme
Jung Gertruds festes Schloss.
Der Burgvogt, überfallen,
Fiel fechtend in dem Tross,
Und über Wall und Graben
Der Wende drang ins Schloss.
Des leichten Siegs frohlockend
Der Fürst schaut freudig drein,
Und trat mit stolzem Worte
In Gertruds Kämmerlein:
" Ich komme, Dich zu brechen,
Du güldner Herzensklee,
Du brennst ja nicht wie Nesseln,
Das Kleeblatt, thut nicht weh!"
Drauf that er sie umarmen,
Wie brünst'ge Liebe thut,
Doch plötzlich schrie er: "Gnade!"
Und sank ins heisse Blut.
Jung Gertrude, wunderprächtig,
Schwang über ihm den Stahl.
Den Dolch stiess sie ihm kräftig
Ins Herz zum andern Mal,
Und rief: " Das sind die Nesseln,
Die Nesseln brennen, weh!
Wer hat noch Lust zu brechen
Der Bismarck güldnen Klee!"
Und seit jung Gertruds Zeiten,
Dräut in der Bismarck Schild
Der Nesseln blankes Zeichen,
Rings um des Kleeblatt Bild;
Mit scharfem Stahl sie haben
Ihr Kleinod stets bewahrt
Ja, seit jung Gertruds Tagen
Blieb das der Bismarck Art!

H H

From Dr. G. Schwetschke's " Bismarckias." *See* pages 99, 100.

Abgeschüttelt von den Sohlen
Ist der Schulstaub; hohe Wogen
Tragen jetzt das Schiff des Jünglings.
Alle Anker sind gelichtet,
All Segel aufgezogen
Und der Burschenfreiheit Flagge
Lustig flatternd zeigt die Inschrift:
" Nitimur in vetitum ! "

Schöne Tage wilder Freiheit !
Fröhlich sammelt ihr die Jünger
Der kastalischen neun Schwestern
Auch in andrer Götter Hallen.
An den duftenden Altären
Eines Bacchus und Gambrinus,
Edler Säfte milder Spende,
Opfert froh der Neophyt.

Auch des Kampfesfrohen Mavors
Heiligthum erschliest sich prangend.
Hört ihr dort den Schall der Waffen ?
Hört ihr dort des Kampfes Tosen ?
Hei ! wie blitzen scharfe Klingen,
Hei ! wie pfeifen Terz und Quarten,
Wie so mancher haut so manchem
Ueber's Maul, und wird gehau'n.

Und so schlang ein rother Faden
(Nämlich der von Blut und Eisen)
Damals schon durch unsres "Burschen
Erdenwallen" sich ; es melden
Göttingen, Berlin und Greifswald
Kühnen Muthes hohe " Thaten
Von vergangner Jahre Tagen"—
Wie einst Ossian es sang.

APPENDIX B.

THE PRUSSIAN CONSTITUTION OF 1847.

(p. 144.)

THE great interest and importance of the following documents, from their forming the absolute point of departure of Bismarck's political activity, has induced their republication in this volume, together with some few other papers bearing upon various matters in relation to German and Prussian politics. At the present day they cannot fail to be read with interest, inasmuch as they illustrate in a remarkable degree the impolicy of hasty concessions. The Prussia and Germany of 1847 was hardly prepared by political education and enlightenment for such concessions, and the immediate effects, which the "English editor of these pages personally witnessed, was a stimulant to the ultra party to demand more and more at the hands of the King. The text amply illustrates the excited state of public opinion at the time, which culminated in the days of March, 1848, and has required the steady and fearless hand of Count Bismarck to rein in. Political students can make their own comments.

The following is a translation of a decree dated Berlin, February 3, 1847 :—

We, Frederick William, by the grace of God, King of Prussia, &c., give notice, and herewith ordain to be known :—

Since the commencement of our government we have constantly applied particular care to the development of the relations of the States of our country.

We recognize in this matter one of the weightiest problems of the kingly calling bestowed on us by God, in the solution of which a twofold aim is marked out for us—namely, to transmit the rights, the dignity, and the power of the Crown, inherited from our ancestors of glorious memory, intact to our successors on the throne; but at the same time to grant to the faithful States of our monarchy that co-operation which, in unison with those rights, and the peculiar relations of our monarchy, is fitted to secure a prosperous future to our country.

In respect whereof, continuing to build on the laws given by His late Majesty our Royal Father, now resting with God, particularly on the Ordinance respecting the national debt of the 17th of January, 1820, and on the law respecting the regulation of the Provincial Diets of the 5th of June, 1823, we decree as follows:—

1.—As often as the wants of the State may require either fresh loans, or the introduction of new taxes, or the increase of those already existing, we will call together around us the Provincial Diets of the monarchy in an United Diet, in order, firstly, to call into play that co-operation of the Diets provided by the Ordinance respecting the national debt; and secondly, to assure us of their consent.

2.—We will for the future call together at periodical times the Committee of the United Diet.

3.—To the United Diet, and, as its representative, to the Committee of the United Diet, we entrust—

(a). In reference to counsel of the Diet in legislation, the same co-operation which was assigned to the Provincial Diets by the law of June 5, 1823, Sect. 3, No. 2, so long as no general assemblies of the Diet take place.

(b). The co-operation of the Diets in paying the interest on, and liquidation of, the State debts, provided by the law of January 17, 1820, in so far as such business is not confided to the deputation of the Diet for the national debt.

(c). The right of petition upon internal, though not merely provincial, matters.

All the above, as is more closely defined in our Ordinances of this day respecting the formation of an United Diet, the periodical assembling of the Committee of the United Diet and its functions, and the formation of a deputation of the Diet for the national debt.

While we thus far refer to the promises of that Gracious Sovereign our Royal Father, on the raising of new loans, as well as the increase of existing taxes, which are founded on that system of the German Constitution, bound up with the assent of the States, and in thereby giving to our subjects a special proof of our royal confidence; so we expect in return the like confidence from their often-proved fidelity and honour, as was shown when we ascended the throne of our Father, and also we expect that they will support us and our efforts directed solely to the welfare of the country, on which efforts success under God's gracious assistance cannot fail to await.

Officially authenticated by our own subscription, and sealed with our royal seal,

FREDERICK WILLIAM.

Given at Berlin, Feb. 3rd, 1847.
(L.S.)

ORDINANCE OF THE 3RD OF FEBRUARY, 1847, FOR THE FORMATION OF THE UNITED DIET.

We, Frederick William, by the grace of God, King of Prussia, &c., having taken the opinion of our Ministers of State, make the following Ordinance, in pursuance of our letters patent of this day, in the matter of the affairs of the Diets, respecting the formation of an United Diet :—

Section 1.—We shall unite the eight Provincial Diets of our monarchy in one Diet, as often as is necessary, according to the tenour of our letters patent of this day, or on any other occasion when we think it needful on account of urgent matters of State.

With regard to the place of assembly, and the continuance of the Session of this United Diet, as well as with regard to its opening and close, we will make a special determination in each particular case.

Section 2.—We grant to the Princes of our Royal House, as soon as, according to the prescriptions of law, they have attained majority, the right of sitting and voting in the Estate of Princes, Counts, and Lords, at the United Diet. The Estate of Nobles in this Diet is composed, besides, of the Princes and Counts of the old Imperial Constitution, who have seats in the Provincial Diets, as well as of the Silesian Princes and noblemen, and all other founders, Princes, Counts, and Lords of the eight Provincial Diets, who are entitled either to a single or collective vote in those Assemblies.

The Princes of our House may, under our sanction, in case of hindrance, intrust some other Prince of our House with the disposal of their votes.

Single members of the Estate of Nobles, who are invested with full powers in the Provincial Diet, retain this privilege in like manner for the United Diet.

In respect to the organization and enlargement of the Estate of Nobles, we reserve to ourselves the right of further regulations.

Section 3.—The Deputies of the Estate of Knighthood, and the Commoners of the eight Provinces of our monarchy, are to appear in the United Diet in the same numbers as in the Provincial Diets.

Section 4.—To the United Diet we entrust the co-operation reserved to the Provincial Diets in case of State loans by Article 2 of the Ordinance relative to the national debt, dated January 17, 1820; and, accordingly, no new loans, for which the collective property of the State may be assigned. as security (Article 3 of the Ordinance of January 17, 1820), shall be contracted without the concurrence and guarantee of the United Diet.

Section 5.—If new loans, of the nature mentioned in Section 4, are required for covering the expenses of the State in time of peace, we will not contract them without the consent of the United Diet.

Section 6.—If, however, in the event of expected war, or war already broken out, the funds in our Treasury, and other reserve funds, are insufficient for the requisite purpose, extraordinary supplies and loans must therefore be raised; and if urgent political circumstances should not admit of our appeal to the United Diet, the said loan shall be raised with the concurrence of the deputation for the national debt, which concurrence shall stand in lieu of the co-operation of the States. Loans for the above-mentioned objects, contracted with the concurrence of the deputation, will be raised on the same security as that which, in Article 3 of the Ordinance of January 17, 1820, is assigned for the national debt.

Section 7.—Should a loan be raised in the manner mentioned in Section 6, we will, on the removal of the obstacles which prevented an appeal to the United Diet, call it together, and explain the object and application of the loan.

Section 8.—Moreover, the United Diet, conformably with Article 9 of the Ordinance of January 17, 1820, must propose to us the candidates for vacant posts in the chief department for the administration of the national debt; and, conformably with Article 13 of the said Ordinance, the accounts for the administration of the national debt, drawn up by the deputation, must be carefully examined by the United Diet, and submitted to us for discharge in separate resolutions.

When the United Diet is not sitting, this business must be transacted by the Committee of the United Diet.

Section 9.—Without the consent of the United Diet we will not introduce any new imposts, nor increase the amount of the existing taxes, either generally or in any particular province.

This condition does not, however, extend to import, export, and transit duties, nor to those indirect taxes, the specification, levying, or administration of which may be the subjects of an understanding with other Powers; neither does that condition refer to domains or royal property (whether the arrangements relate to income or to substance), or to taxes for objects relating to provinces, circles, or communes.

Section 10.—In the event of a war, we reserve to ourselves the right of levying extraordinary taxes without the assent of the United Diet, when urgent political circumstances do not permit us to call it together. In such cases, however, we will, as soon as circumstances permit, or at latest on the termination of the war, make known to the United Diet the object and application of the extraordinary taxes which may have been levied.

Section 11.—Should the Diet be called together on any of the occasions specified in Sections 4—10, copies of the finance estimates and the accounts of the State for the intervals between the sittings of the Assembly shall be submitted to the members for their information.

The fixing of the finance estimates, as well as determining the employment of the State revenue, and the application of the surplus to the wants and welfare of the State, remains an exclusive privilege of the Crown.

Section 12.—Conformably with the law of the 5th of January, 1823, we reserve to ourselves the right of demanding extraordinary counsel from the United Diet in framing laws relating to alterations in the rights of persons and property, or on other matters than those alluded to in Section 9, which have for their object alterations in the taxes, whether those laws concern the whole monarchy or several provinces. The Diet is authorized to give the required counsel, with full lawful effect.

Should we deem it necessary to seek counsel of the Diet concerning changes in the constitution of the Diet—changes which, not being limited to any particular province, are not to be arranged by the Diet of that province —we shall demand an opinion from the United Diet, for whose consideration changes in such matters of State are exclusively reserved.

Section 13.—To the United Diet belongs the right of laying before us petitions and complaints relating to the internal affairs of the whole kingdom, or of several provinces; on the other hand, petitions and complaints which concern merely the interests of particular provinces must be referred to the Provincial Diets.

Section 14.—When the United Diet has determined on raising new State loans (Section 5), or the introduction of new taxes, or increasing the existing rate of taxes (Section 9), the Estate of the Nobles must take part with the other estates in the discussion and decision. In all other cases the deliberations and votes of the Estate of the Nobles in the United Diet are to take place in a separate assembly.

Section 15.—Every member of the Estate of the Nobles is entitled to a full vote in the United Diet, but when (as mentioned in Section 14) the Estate of the Nobles is united with the other estates in one Assembly, the members of that Estate, taking part in the discussions of the United Diet, have only that number of votes which belongs to them in the Provincial Diets.

Section 16.—Resolutions are to be carried by the majority of votes.

Petitions and complaints are only to be brought under our cognizance when they have been deliberated on in both Assemblies (that is, in the Assembly of the Estate of Nobles, and in the Assembly of Deputies of the Knighthood and Commoners), and when in each of these Assemblies at least two-thirds of the votes have been in favour of such petitions or complaints.

When the two above-named Assemblies, or one of them, after the discussion of a law, or of certain articles of a law, shall decide against that law by a majority less than that above-named, the views of the minority shall be submitted to our consideration.

Section 17.—If on a subject in respect to which the interests of two different estates or provinces may be at variance with each other, a particular estate or province should have reason to complain of a resolution according to the terms of Section 16, a separation of the Assembly into its component parts takes place, if a majority of two-thirds of the said estate or province be obtained.

In such case the estate or province must discuss the matter separately, or pass a separate vote, and the various views entertained on the subject will afterwards be submitted to our decision.

Also, in other cases, we reserve to ourselves the privilege of requiring, when we think fit so to do, a separate opinion from each of the estates and provinces.

Section 18.—For the Estate of Nobles of the assembled Diet, as well as for the Assembly of the Knighthood and Commoners, we will appoint a Marshal to conduct the business and to act as president. The places of both these Marshals may, in the event of their being disabled from attending, be supplied by Vice-Marshals.

When, as mentioned in Section 14, the Estate of Nobles and the other estates unite together, the Presidency of the Assembly devolves on the Marshal or Vice-Marshal of the Estate of Nobles.

Section 19.—The United Diet is not connected in its functions with those of circles, communes, or corporations; its functions are likewise independent of the classes or persons which it represents; and these are not allowed to give to the Deputies either instructions or commissions.

Section 20.—Petitions or complaints must not be presented or delivered by any except the members of the United Diet.

Section 21.—Petitions and complaints which we have once rejected must not again be presented to us by the said Assembly, and must only be renewed when new causes give occasion for them.

Section 22.—In all deliberations of the United Diet, or of single estates or provinces of the same (Sections 14 to 17), our Ministers of State, and also such of our high officers as we appoint to attend during the whole sitting, or for particular occasions, shall be present, and shall take part in the discussions when they think necessary. They are not, however, to vote, except when they are authorized to do so as members of the Diet.

Section 23.—The business of the United Diet is to be regulated according to rules approved by us.

Given under our autograph signature and royal seal,

FREDERICK WILLIAM.

Berlin, Feb. 3, 1847.

ORDINANCE OF THE 3RD OF FEBRUARY, 1847, RESPECTING THE PERIODICAL ASSEMBLING OF THE COMMITTEE OF THE UNITED DIET AND ITS PRIVILEGES.

We, Frederick William, by the grace of God, King of Prussia, &c., after having taken the opinion of our Ministers of State, make the following Ordinance, in pursuance of our letters patent of this day, in the matters of the affairs of the Diet, respecting the periodical assembling of the Committee of the United Diet and its functions :—

Section 1.—The Committees of the Provincial Diets are to be convened to form the Committee of the United Diet, according to the regulation laid down by the Ordinances of June 21, 1842. The former Princes of the Empire in the province of Westphalia, as well as those in the Rhine Province, are to be entitled to depute from amongst themselves two members each to the Committee of the United Diet, who may participate in its proceedings either in person or through plenipotentiaries from the members of the Estate of Nobles of the United Diet. Besides this, a Deputy is to proceed to the Committee of the United Diet from each of the provinces of Prussia, Brandenburgh, Pomerania, and Posen, to be elected by and from the members of the First Estate entitled to single or collective votes. As regards the province of Pomerania, the Prince of Putbus is to assume this post without election, so long as he remains the only nobleman in the province possessed of the qualification specified.

The election of the other members of the Committee is to take place at the United Diet, in accordance with the Ordinances of the 21st of June, 1842, through the representatives of the several provinces; but in the interval between one United Diet and another as hitherto, viz., at each Provincial Diet.

Section 2.—The Committee of the United Diet will be convened by us as often as a necessity arises therefor, but, at the farthest, four years after the close of the last assembly of the same; or, if a United Diet has been held in the meantime, within the same lapse of time after the close of the latter.

We shall require, as a general rule, from the Committee of the United Diet, requisite advice, according to the general law of the 5th of June, 1823, respecting the laws which have for their object alterations in the rights of persons and property, or others than the alterations in taxation designated in Section 9 of the Ordinance of this day, upon the formation of the United Diet, if these laws concern the whole monarchy or several provinces; and we hereby confer upon it the privilege of giving such advice, with full legal effect. The regulation in Article 3, No. 2, of the above-mentioned law is annulled by the present regulation.

As, however, we have already reserved to ourselves, in the Ordinance concerning the formation of the United Diet, the right to acquire from it opinions of the same kind, in appropriate cases, we will equally reserve to ourselves the right to submit laws of the above-mentioned description which concern the whole monarchy or several provinces, in exceptional cases, for the opinion of the Provincial Diets, if this should appear advisable for particular reasons—for example, for the sake of despatch.

Section 4.—The Committee of the United Diet, as the representative of the United Diet, is to attend to business relating to the State debts, pointed out in our Ordinance of this day, on the formation of the United Diet.

Section 5.—The right of petition appertains to the Committee of the United Diet to the same extent as to the United Diet itself. Herefrom are excepted, however, all proposals having alterations of the constitution of the Diet in view.

Section 6.—Should we find ourselves induced to make communications to the said Committee of the United Diet upon the State finances, the regulations of the 11th Section of the Ordinance on the formation of the United Diet are to come into full operation.

Section 7.—The conduct of business and the presidency of the Committee of the United Diet is to be assumed by a Marshal, to be appointed by us, who will be represented, in case of need, by a Vice-Marshal, to be similarly appointed.

Section 8.—The Committee of the United Diet is to deliberate as an undivided assembly. Its resolutions are, as a general rule, to be adopted by a simple majority of votes.

Petitions and complaints are only to be laid before us if they have been voted by at least two-thirds of the members.

If the Committee of the United Diet declares itself, on the deliberation of a law, against the law, or some of the provisions of the same, by a less majority than that above mentioned, the views of the minority are also to be laid before us.

Section 9.—The Provincial Diets are to communicate to their several Committees no instructions or proposals for the Committee of the United Diet.

Section 10.—The regulations of the 17th, 19th, 20th, 21st, 22nd, and 23rd Sections of the Ordinance of this day, on the formation of the United Diet, are also to come into full operation in the Committee of the United Diet.

Given under our royal hand and seal, at Berlin, February 3, 1847,

FREDERICK WILLIAM.

ORDINANCE FOR THE FORMATION OF A DEPUTATION OF THE DIET FOR THE AFFAIRS OF THE STATE DEBTS.

We, Frederick William, &c., ordain as follows :—

1. In the execution of the co-operation proposed in the 6th Section of the Ordinance of this day, relative to the formation of the United Diet, in the contraction of State loans in times of war, and for the current co-operation of the Diet in the reduction and extinction of the State debt.

A deputation of the Diet shall be formed for the affairs of the State debt.

2. This deputation to consist of eight members, of whom one is to be chosen in each of the eight provinces, by the States of the province, for a period of six years.

The election to take place at the United Diet, but in the interval between one Diet and another, at the Provincial Diets, according to the regulation relative to the proceedings in election of Diets of the 22nd June, 1842. The election must only fall on persons who are members of the Diet in question. If one of the elected members loses the qualification before the lapse of the sexennial period, he is also to secede from the deputation. If, however, his secession is caused by his not having been re-elected as a Deputy of the Diet, he is to remain a member of the deputation till the next Diet.

To each member of the deputation two *locum tenentes* are to be chosen, of whom one is to replace him in case of emergency, as well as in the event of a vacancy occurring in the interval between one Diet and another. The choice of these *locum tenentes* is to be made conformably with the regulations respecting the actual members.

3. The members of the deputation are to be sworn to the fulfilment of their duties in their summons.

Section 4.—To the province of the deputation appertain the following duties, exclusively of the co-operation in the contraction of war loans conferred by the six sections already mentioned.

1. The deputation is to take charge of the redeemed State debt documents, according to the regulation of Article 14 of the Ordinance of 17th January, 1820, and to effect their deposit in the Judicial Chamber.

2. It is to audit the annual accounts of the interest and extinction of the State debts, after they have been previously revised by the upper chamber of accounts, and to cause them to be presented to us for our approval by the

United Diet, or the Committee thereof, on its next assembly, according to the 14th Article of the Ordinance of January 17th, 1820.

3. It is authorized to undertake extraordinary revisions of the fund for the extinction of the State debts and the control of the State papers, on the occasion of its meeting.

The deputation for the affairs of the State debt will regularly meet once a year, and besides this, as often as occasion demands; the summons to be made by the Minister of the Interior.

6. The deputation is to elect a President at each meeting, who must be presented to the Minister of the Interior.

The presence of at least five members will be requisite to constitute a valid act of the deputation.

Given under our hand, &c.,

FREDERICK WILLIAM.

Berlin, Feb. 3, 1847.

OPENING OF THE PRUSSIAN DIET.

THE KING'S SPEECH.

April, 1847.

[King Frederick William IV., on opening the Diet, made the following speech, of sufficient importance to be added here, when the circumstances of the grant of the Constitution are considered.]

ILLUSTRIOUS noble Princes, Counts, and Lords, my dear and trusty Orders of Nobles, Burghers, and Commons, I bid you from the depth of my heart welcome on the day of the fulfilment of a great work of my father, resting in God, never to be forgotten, King William III., of glorious memory.

The noble edifice of representative freedom, the eight mighty pillars of which the King of blessed memory founded deep and unshakably in the peculiar organization of his provinces, is to-day perfected in your Assembly. It has received its protecting roof. The King wished to have finished his work himself, but his views were shipwrecked in the utter impracticability of the plans laid before him. Therefrom arose evils which his clear eye detected with grief, and, before all, the uncertainty which made many a noble soil susceptible of weeds. Let us bless, however, to-day the conscientiousness of the true beloved King, who despised his own earlier triumph in order to guard his folk from later ruin, and let us honour his memory by not perilling the existence of his completed work by the impatient haste of beginners.

I give up beforehand all co-operation thereto. Let us suffer time, and, above all, experience, to have their way; and let us commit the work, as is fitting, to the furthering and forming hands of Divine Providence. Since the commencement of the operation of the Provincial Diets, I have perceived the defects of individual portions of our representative life, and proposed to myself conscientiously the grave question, how they were to be remedied? My resolutions on this point have long since arrived at maturity. Immediately on my accession I made the first step towards realizing them by forming the Committees of the Provincial Diets, and by calling them together soon after.

You are aware, Lords and Gentlemen, that I have now made the days for the meeting of those Committees periodical, and that I have confided to them the free working of the Provincial Diets. For the ordinary run of affairs their deliberations will satisfactorily represent the desired point of union. But the law of January 17, 1820, respecting the State debts, gives, in that portion of it not as yet carried out, rights and privileges to the Orders which can be exercised neither by the Provincial Assemblies nor by the Committees.

As the heir of an unweakened crown, which I must and

I I

will hand down unweakened to my descendants, I know that I am perfectly free from all and every pledge with respect to what has not been carried out, and, above all, with respect to that from the execution of which his own true paternal conscience preserved my illustrious predecessor. The law is, however, carried out in all its essential parts; an edifice of justice has been built upon it, oaths have been sworn on it, and it has, all unfinished as it is, maintained itself as a wise law for seven-and-twenty years. Therefore have I proceeded, with a cheerful heart indeed, but with all the freedom of my kingly prerogative, to its final completion. I am, however, the irreconcilable enemy of all arbitrary proceedings, and must have been a foe, above all, to the idea of bringing together an artificial arbitrary assembly of the Orders, which should deprive the noble creation of the King, my dear father—I mean the Provincial Diets—of their value. It has been, therefore, for many years my firm determination only to form this Assembly, ordained by law, or by the fusion together of the Provincial Diets. It is formed; I have recognized your claim to all the rights flowing from that law; and, far beyond—yes, far beyond—all the promises of the King of blessed memory, I have granted you, within certain necessary limits, the right of granting taxes—a right, gentlemen, the responsibility of which weighs far more heavily than the honour which accompanies it. This august Assembly will now denote important periods in the existence of our State, which are treated of in my patent of February the 3rd. As soon as those periods occur, I will assemble the Diets on each separate occasion round my throne, in order to deliberate with them for the welfare of my country, and to afford them an opportunity for the exercise of their rights. I have, however, reserved the express right of calling together these great Assemblies on extraordinary occasions, when I deem it good and profitable; and I will do this willingly and at more frequent intervals, if this Diet gives me the proof that I may act thus without prejudice to higher sovereign duties.

My trusty and free subjects have received all the laws which I and my father have granted them for the protection of their highest interests, and especially the laws of the 3rd of February, with warm gratitude, and woe to him who shall dare to dash their thankfulness with care, or to turn it into ingratitude.

Every Prussian knows that for twenty-four years past all laws which concern his freedom and property have been first discussed by the Orders, but from this time forward let every one in my kingdom know that I, with the sole necessary exception of the occurrence of the calamity of war, will contract no State loan, levy no new taxes, nor increase existing ones, without the free consent of all Orders.

Noble Lords and trusty Orders, I know that with these rights I intrust a costly jewel of freedom to your hands, and that you will employ it faithfully. But I know, as certainly, that many will mistake and despise this jewel—that to many it is not enough. A portion of the press, for instance, demands outright from me and my Government a revolution in Church and State, and from you, gentlemen, acts of importunate ingratitude, of illegality—nay, of disobedience. Many also, and among them very worthy men, look for our safety in the conversion of the natural relation between Prince and people into a conventional existence, granted by charters and ratified by oaths.

May, however, the example of the one happy country, whose constitution centuries and an hereditary wisdom without a parallel, but no sheets of paper, have made, not be lost upon us, but find the respect which it deserves. If other countries find their happiness in another way than that people and ourselves, namely, in the way of "manufactured and granted" constitutions, we must and will praise their happiness in an upright and brotherly manner. We will, with the justest admiration, consider the sublime example, when a strong will of iron consequence and high intelligence succeeds in delaying, in mastering, and allaying every crisis of serious importance; and above all, when this tends to the welfare of Germany, and the maintenance of the peace of Europe. But Prussia, gentlemen, Prussia cannot bear such a state of things. Do you ask why? I answer, cast your eyes at the map of Europe, at the position of our country, at its component parts; follow the line of our borders, weigh the power of our neighbours, throw before all an enlightened glance on our history. It has pleased God to make Prussia strong by the sword of war from without, and by the sword of intellect from within; not, surely, by the negative intellect of the age, but by the spirit of moderation and order. I speak out boldly, gentlemen. As in the camp, unless in cases of the most urgent danger or grossest folly, the command can only be rested in the will of one, so can the destinies of this country, unless it is to fall instantly from its height, only be guided by one will; and if the King of Prussia would commit an abomination, were he to demand from his subjects the subserviency of a slave, so would he commit a far greater abomination were he not to demand from them the crowning virtue of freemen—I mean obedience for the sake of God and conscience. Whoever is alarmed at the tenor of these words, him I refer to the development of our laws for a century back, to the edicts of the Orders, and finally, to this Assembly and its rights; there he may find consolation if he will.

Noble Lords and trusty Orders, I am forced to the solemn declaration, that no power on earth will ever succeed in moving me to change the natural—and, in our own case, so imperatively necessary—relation between Prince and people, into something merely conventional or constitutional; and that, once for all, I will never suffer a written sheet of paper to force itself in, as it were a second providence, between our Lord God in Heaven and this people, in order to rule us with its paragraphs, and to replace by them our ancient and time-hallowed trusty reliance on each other. Between us be truth. From *one* weakness I feel myself entirely free—I strive not for idle popular favour; who could do so if he has read history aright? I strive alone to fulfil my duty, so as to satisfy my understanding and my conscience, and to deserve the thanks of my people, even though it be never my lot to obtain it.

Noble Lords and trusty Orders, it has often caused me care and impatience during the first years of my reign, that I could not remove hindrances which opposed an earlier convocation of your Assembly. I was wrong. On both sides we should have been poorer by many experiences, poorer by experiences in part of a costly nature; but all of them, if not always good, yet for us of priceless worth. We have now lying open before us the experiences of seven years, and, by God's good pleasure, not in vain. The working of parties on one side, and the temper of my people on the other, are now clear and indubitable. It is a splendid privilege of the kingly office, that it can on all occasions call things by their right names without fear. I will do this to-day before you, as a duty which I have to fulfil. I beg you now to follow me a moment, while with a sharp eye we consider the state of things at home.

The dearth which has visited Europe of latter years has also penetrated to us, if with less severity than in other countries. It has, however, found us well prepared, and I can give my Government the honourable testimonial that it has honestly done its part towards alleviating the calamity. There are, also, means further to resist it, if God spares us from new failures in the crops. Here I must mention private benevolence, which, in these times, has manifested itself anew so nobly, so cheeringly; and I pay it here, before you, the tribute of my admiration and my gratitude.

The extinction of the national debt is progressing. The taxes are diminished, the finances are put in order. I have to-day the happiness to offer the provinces, for the use of their treasuries, a donation of 2,000,000 rix-dollars.

The management of affairs, and the administration of justice, are with us in a purer condition than almost in any other country; publicity is established in our Courts; roads, canals, all kinds of improvements of the land are proceeding to an extent before unknown; science and art are in the most flourishing condition; the national prosperity is increasing; trade and industry, if, alas! not protected against their European vicissitudes, are comparatively satisfactory; paternal care and goodwill are certainly nowhere to be mistaken; the press is as free as the laws of the Confederation permit; the freedom of confession is associated with animating power to our old liberty of faith and conscience; and our just pride and strong shield, my army of the line and militia, may be called incomparable.

With our neighbours and with the Powers on this and the other side of the ocean we stand on the best terms, and our relation to our allies, in combination with whom we once freed Germany, and from the happy concord of whom depends the maintenance of a thirty-two years' peace in a great part of Europe, is firmer and closer than ever.

I could add much which would be calculated to bend our knees in thanks towards God, but this will suffice. For it is quite sufficient to found this gratitude, and a state of contentment, which in an honest comparison, in spite of many just wishes, appears quite natural. Before all, one would think that the press must diffuse gratitude and contentment on all sides, for I venture to say that it is the press which, to a particular extent, owes me thanks. Noble lords and faithful States, I require your German hearts to grant me those thanks. While recognizing the honourable endeavour to elevate the press by a noble and conscientious spirit, it is yet unquestionable that in a portion of it a dark spirit of destruction prevails, a spirit that entices to revolution, and that deals in the most audacious falsehood, disgraceful to German fidelity and Prussian honour. I know that the genuine sense of the people remains firm, but we do not deceive ourselves as to the evil fruits of the evil tree, which meet us in the shape of dissatisfaction and want of confidence, attended by still worse facts, such as open disobedience, secret conspiracy, a declared revolt from all which is sacred to good men, and attempted regicide. Even in our churches are seen those fruits, together with the twofold death in indifference and fanaticism. But ecclesiastical matters do not belong to the States. They have their legitimate organs in the two confessions. One confession of faith I am, on this day, unable to suppress, bearing in mind the frightful attempt to defraud my people of its holiest jewel—its faith in the Redeemer, Lord and King of itself and of us all. This avowal is as follows. [Here His Majesty arose, and spoke the words standing, and with right hand uplifted] " I and my house, we will serve the Lord."

I turn my troubled glance from the aberrations of a few to the whole of my people. Then does it grow bright with tears of joy ; there, my lords, amid all the heavy troubles of government, is my consolation. My people is still the old Christian people—the honest, true, valiant people— which has fought the battles of my fathers, and the honourable qualities of which have only grown with the greatness and fame of their country, which once, like no other, in the days of trouble, bound itself to its paternal King, and bore him, as it were, upon its shoulders from victory to victory,—a people, my lords, often tempted by

the arts of seduction, but always found proof against them
Even out of the strongest of these trials it will come forth
pure.   Already is the impious sport with Christianity, the
abuse of religion as a means of distinction, recognized in
its true form as sacrilege, and is dying away.   My firm
reliance upon the fidelity of my people, as the surest means
of extinguishing the conflagration, has been ever nobly
rewarded both by the older and the younger sons of our
Prussian country, even where another language than ours
is spoken.

Therefore, hear this well, Lords and faithful States, and
may all the country hear it through you.   From all the
indignities to which I and my Government have been
exposed for some years, I appeal to my people!   From all
evils which perhaps are still in reserve for me, I appeal
beforehand to my people!   My people knows my heart,
my faith and love to it, and adheres in love and faith to
me.   My people does not wish the association of representatives in the Government, the weakening of rank, the
division of sovereignty, the breaking up of the authority
of its kings, who have founded its history, its freedom, its
prosperity, and who alone can protect its dearest acquisi-
tions, and will protect them, God willing, as heretofore.

Know, my lords, I do not read the feelings of my
people in the green arches and huzzahs of festivity;
still less in the praise and blame of the press, or in the
doubtful, sometimes criminal, demands of certain addresses
which are sent to the Throne, and States, or elsewhere.   I
have read them with my own eyes in the touching thanks
of men for benefits scarcely promised, scarcely begun;
here, where broad districts of land stood under water;
there, where men scarcely recovered from hunger.   In
their grateful joy, in their wet eyes, did I read their
feelings three years ago, when the lives of myself and the
Queen were so wonderfully preserved.   This is truth—
and in my words is truth, when I say, that it is a noble

people; and I feel entirely the happiness of presiding over such a people. And your hearts will understand me and accord with me, when in this great hour I urgently call upon you—"Be worthy of this people!"

Illustrious Princes, Counts, and Lords, you will have recognized in the position assigned to you by law in this United Diet, my intention that that position should be a dignified one, at once answering to the conception of a German order of nobles, and also beneficial to the whole community. I rely upon your deeply feeling at this hour, and in these times, what is meant by being the first of a nation, and also what is required at your hands. You will repay my confidence.

You, my Lords of the nobility, and my faithful Burghers and Commons, are, I am firmly persuaded, impressed with this truth, that on this day, and in this hour, you are the first of your respective Orders; but, therefore, also the protectors of your ancient renown. Look at this throne! Your fathers and mine—many princes of your race, and of mine, and myself—have fought for the preservation, the deliverance, and the honour of that throne, and for the existence of our native land. God was with us! There is now a new battle to be fought on behalf of the same glorious possessions—a peaceful one, indeed, but its combats are not a whit less important than those of the field of war. And God will be with us yet again, for the battle is against the evil tendencies of the age. Your unanimity with me, the prompt expression of your wish to aid me in improving the domain of rights (that true field for the labour of kings), will make this Diet a pitched battle gained against every evil and lawless influence that troubles and dishonours Germany; and the work will be to your renown and that of the country, and the contentment and satisfaction of the people.

Representatives of the Nobles, be now and for the future, as of old, the first to follow the banner of the Hohen-

zollerns, that for three centuries has led you on to honour.
And you, Burghers, give to the whole world a living
testimony that the intelligence—the great mass of which
you are proud to represent—is, among us, that right and
true one which ennobles by the development of religion
and morality, and by the love of your King and country.
And you, representatives of the Commons, you and your
Order are never the last when your country and your
King call on you, whether it be in peace or in war. Hear
the voice of your King, that tells you they require you
again!

In my kingdom, neither of the three Orders ranks
above or beneath the other. They stand beside each
other on an equality of rights and honour, but each
within its limits, each with its own province. This is a
practicable and reasonable equality. This is freedom.

Noble Lords and trusty Orders, a word more on the
question—yes, the question of existence between the
Throne and the different Orders. The late King, after
mature consideration, called them into existence, according
to the German and historical idea of them; and in this
idea alone have I continued his work. Impress yourselves,
I entreat you, with the spirit of this definition. You are
German Orders, in the anciently received sense of the
word—that is, you are truly, and before all, "representatives and defenders of your own rights," the rights of those
Orders whose confidence has sent here the far greater
portion of this Assembly. But after that you are to
exercise those rights which the Crown has recognized as
yours; you have, further, conscientiously to give the
Crown that advice it requires of you. Finally, you are
free to bring petitions and complaints, after mature deliberation, to the foot of the throne.

Those are the rights, those the duties, of German
Orders; this is your glorious vocation. But it is not
your province to represent opinions, or bring opinions

of the day, or of this or that school, into practical operation. That is wholly un-German, and, besides, completely useless for the good of the community, for it would lead necessarily to inextricable embarrassments with the Crown, which must govern according to the law of God and the land, and its own free, unbiassed resolution, but which cannot and dares not govern according to the will of the majority, if "Prussia" would not soon become an empty sound in Europe. Clearly recognizing my office and your vocation, and firmly resolved to treat that recognition faithfully under all circumstances, I have appeared among you, and addressed you with royal freedom. With the same openness, and as the highest proof of my confidence in you, I here give you my royal word that I should not have called you together had I had the smallest suspicion that you would otherwise understand your duties, or that you had any desire to play the part of what are called representatives of the people. I should not have called you together for that purpose, because, according to my deepest and most heartfelt conviction, the Throne and State would be endangered by it, and because I recognize it as my first duty, under all circumstances and events, to preserve the Throne, the State, and my Government, as they at present exist. I remember the axiom of a royal friend, " Confidence awakens confidence." That is this day my brightest hope. That my confidence in you is great, I have proved by my words, and sealed by my act. And from you, gentlemen, I expect a proof of confidence in return, and an answer in the same manner —by your acts. God is my witness, I have summoned you as your truest, best, and most faithful friend ; and I firmly believe that, among the hundreds before me, there is not one who is not resolved, at this moment, to preserve that friendship. Many of you were at Königsberg on the 10th of September, 1840 ; and I can even now hear the thunder of your voices as you pronounced the oath of fidelity, that then penetrated my soul. Many of you, on the day on which I received the homage of my hereditary estates, joined with thousands in the still echoing " Yes !" with which you replied to my demand whether you would, " in word and deed, in heart and spirit, in truth and love, help and assist me to preserve Prussia as it is, and as it must remain, if it would not perish ; that you would not let or hinder me in the path of considerate but vigorous progress, but endure with me through good days and through evil." Now redeem your word—now fulfil that vow !

You can do it by the exercise of one of your most important duties—namely, by choosing from among you faithful and upright friends of the Throne and of our good purpose for your Committees—men who have comprehended that at this time it is the first duty of the Orders to encourage and support the good disposition and fidelity of the country by their own example, and, on the contrary, to strike down and discountenance every kind of many-headed faithlessness—men who, enemies of every kind of slavery, are, above all, enemies of that shameful yoke which a misguiding opinion (branding the name of freedom of thought) would lay upon your necks. This selection is a very critical act—one pregnant with consequences. Weigh it in your hearts, and choose conscientiously.

Remember, also, that the day of uncertainty as to the form which the activity of the Orders is to take is passed. Many things, which, under this uncertainty, forbearance could excuse, have henceforth no excuse remaining. The 3rd of February of this year, like the 3rd of February, 1813, has opened to the real children of our fatherland that path they have now to pursue; and the same unspeakable happiness which then fell to the lot of my glorious father is now also mine—mine in this moment. I speak, as he did, to the hearts of German—of Prussian men !

Go, then, illustrious Princes, Counts, and Lords—dear and faithful Orders of Nobles, Burghers, and Commons—proceed, with God's help, to your task. You will, I am certain, in this moment, when all Europe is gazing on you, and through all the future labours of the Diet, prove yourselves true Prussians; and that one thing, believe me, will not be absent—namely, God's blessing, on which all things depend. Out of our unanimity it will descend on the present and future generations, and, I hope, on all our glorious German fatherland, in one broad stream, beside which we may dwell in peace and safety, as by the shores of the blessing-bringing rivers that water the earth. And now, once more, and out of the fulness of my heart,—welcome!

APPENDIX C.

(p 394.)

ICH BIN EIN PREUSSE!

Ich bin ein Preusse, kennt ihr meine Farben?
Die Fahne schwebt mir weiss und schwarz voran;
Dass für die Freiheit meine Väter starben,
Das deuten, merkt es, meine Farben an;
Nie werd' ich bang verzagen; wie jene will ich's wagen:
    Sei's trüber Tag, seis heitrer Sonnenschein:
    Ich bin ein Preusse, will ein Preusse sein!

Mit Lieb' und Treue nah' ich mich dem Throne,
Von welchem mild zu mir ein Vater spricht;
Und wie der Vater treu mit seinem Sohne,
So steh' ich treu mit ihm und wanke nicht.
Fest sind die Liebe Bande: Heil meinem Vaterlande!
    Des König's Ruf dringt in das Herz mir ein;
    Ich bin ein Preusse, will ein Preusse sein!

Nicht jeder Tag kann glühn im Sonnenlichte
Ein Wölkchen und ein Schauer kommt zur Zeit;
Drum lese keiner mir es im Gesichte
Dass nicht der Wünsche jeder mir gedeiht.
Wohl tauschten nah' und ferne, mit mir gar Viele gerne.
    Ihr Glück ist Trug, und ihre Freiheit Schein;
    Ich bin ein Preusse, will ein Preusse sein!

Und wenn der böse Sturm mich einst umsauset,
Die Nacht entbrennet in der Blitzes Gluth:
Hat's doch schon ärger in der Welt gebrauset,
Und was nicht bebet, war der Preussen Muth.
Mag Fels und Eiche splittern, ich werde nicht erzittern
    Es sturm und krach; es blitze wild darein!
    Ich bin ein Preusse, will ein Preusse sein!

Wo Lieb' und Treu' sich so dem Konig weihen,
Wo Fürst und Volk sich reichen so die Hand:
Da muss des Volkes wahres Glück gedeihen,
Da blüht und wächst das schöne Vaterland.
So schwören wir auf's Neue, dem König Lieb'und Treue!
    Fest sei der Bund! Ja, schlaget muthig ein!
    Wir sind zu Preussen, lasst uns Preussen sein!
                    THIERSCH.

This noble song, perhaps, emphatically—but rather in
the sense of England's "Rule Britannia" than its "God

save the Queen"—may be regarded as the national anthem of the Prussians. The air to which it is sung is wild and martial; derived undoubtedly from an ancient Polish hymn, to which it bears a striking affinity, and of which it may be regarded as a musical synonym. The present editor offers a version which is tolerably close, although he cannot hope to preserve the actual tone of the original author.

I AM A PRUSSIAN.

I am a Prussian ! see my colours gleaming—
The black-white standard floats before me free ;
For Freedom's rights, my fathers' heart-blood streaming,
Such, mark ye, mean, the black and white to me !
Shall I then prove a coward ? I 'll e'er be to the toward !
    Though day be dull, though sun shine bright on me,
    I am a Prussian, will a Prussian be !

Before the throne with love and faith I 'm bending,
Whence, mildly good, I hear a parent's tone ;
With filial heart, obedient ear I 'm lending—
The father trusts—the son defends the throne !
Affection's ties are stronger—live, O my country, longer !
    The King's high call o'erflows my breast so free,
    I am a Prussian, will a Prussian be !

Not every day hath sunny light of glory ;
A cloud, a shower, sometimes dulls the lea ;
Let none believe my face can tell the story,
That ev'ry wish unfruitful is to me.
How many far and nearer, would think exchange much dearer ?
    Their Freedom's naught—how then compare with me ?
    I am a Prussian, will a Prussian be !

And if the angry elements exploding,
The lightnings flash, the thunders louder roar,
Hath not the world oft witnessed such foreboding ?
No Prussian's courage can be tested more.
Should rock and oak be riven, to terror I 'm not driven ;
    Be storm and din, let flashes gleam so free—
    I am a Prussian, will a Prussian be !

Where love and faith so round the monarch cluster,
Where Prince and People so clasp firm their hands,
'Tis there alone true happiness can muster,
Thus showing clear how firm the nation's bands.
Again confirm the fealty ! the honest noble lealty !
    Be strong the bond, strike hands, dear hearts, with me,
    Is not this Prussia ?   Let us Prussians be !

KENNETH R. H. MACKENZIE.

INDEX.

Woodfall and Kinder, Printers, Milford Lane, Strand, London, W.C.

York Street, Covent Garden.
London, *December*, 1869.

JAMES HOGG AND SON'S

NEW BOOKS AND ANNOUNCEMENTS.

In the press, demy 8vo., about 500 pages, with numerous Illustrations, price 15s.

A DICTIONARY

OF

RITUAL AND OTHER ECCLESIASTICAL TERMS.

BY THE REV. FREDERICK GEORGE LEE, D.C.L.;

F.S.A. London and Scotland ; S.C.L. Oxon ; Vicar of 'All Saints', Lambeth ; F.A.S.L. ;
Editor of the " Directorium Anglicanum ;" Author of the " Beauty of Holiness,"
" Ecclesiastical Vestments," &c.

In this publication it has been the aim of the compiler to bring together, in a comparatively small compass, as much information as possible concerning the meanings and applications of the many Ritual Terms and other Ecclesiastical Words bearing on the study of Ritual—a detail of Lituriology to which much attention is now being directed. With this aim, the Editor, who for many years has been collecting materials for this volume, has consulted nearly two hundred MS. Church and Churchwardens' Accounts of the period of the Reformation, which tend to throw so much light both on the statute-law and custom of our National Church of that period. Neither ordinary nor extraordinary sources of information have been overlooked ; both Latin and Eastern terms are included, and authorities produced for almost every fact or statement that is given. The illustrations are mainly taken from " Ornamenta " and " Instrumenta Ecclesiastica " existing and used in the Church of England ; while the representations of pre-Reformation ceremonies, rites, and observances have been selected from Anglican rather than from foreign examples and authorities.

"The Services of the Church cannot be done and celebrated with too great care and anxiety. When we remember to Whom they are offered, we cannot be too decent and over-much orderly in rendering them with seemliness and reverence."—DR. SOUTH.

BY THE REV. FREDERICK GEORGE LEE, D.C.L.

In the press, small crown 8vo., cloth, with a Frontispiece, price 7s. 6d.

THE MANUALE CLERICORUM;

A GUIDE FOR THE REVERENT AND DECENT CELEBRATION OF DIVINE SERVICE, THE HOLY SACRAMENTS, AND OTHER OFFICES,

According to the Rites, Ceremonies, and Ancient Use of the United Church of England and Ireland.

Abridged from the "Directorium Anglicanum," with Additions of special value in the practical rendering of the Services of the Church.

PREFATORY NOTE.

This Guide is published with the intention of supplying the Clergy, Choristers, Lay Readers, Choir-masters, and Acolytes with a series of plain directions and suggestive hints for the decent and orderly celebration of the public Services of the Church. Only in a few instances are the authorities given at length for the recommendations and directions provided, and this for the obvious reason of being enabled to issue the book in a convenient and portable form, and at such a reasonable price as to bring it within the reach of a large and increasing class—decency and order in conducting divine service being no longer peculiar to one theological school.

The Editor acknowledges with gratitude the value of many important suggestions in its preparation, and is deeply obliged to those several friends who have taken the trouble to give him the benefit both of their theoretical knowledge and practical experience.

[Nearly Ready.

In the press, Fourth Edition, with Illustrations, demy 8vo., cloth, price 12s. 6d.

CAREFULLY REVISED, WITH NUMEROUS EMENDATIONS, AND IN HARMONY WITH THE PRESENT STATE OF THE LAW.

THE DIRECTORIUM ANGLICANUM;

BEING A MANUAL OF DIRECTIONS FOR THE RIGHT CELEBRATION OF THE HOLY COMMUNION,

For the saying of Matins and Evensong, and for the decent and Orderly Performance of all other Rites, Functions, Offices, and Ceremonies of the Church, according to the use of the Church of England.

With Plan of Chancel, and Illustrations of "such Ornaments of the Church and of the Ministers thereof at all times of their ministrations (as) shall be retained, and be in use as were in this Church of England by the authority of Parliament, in the second year of the reign of King Edward the Sixth."

The general approbation with which this book has been received has induced the publishers to prepare for publication a Fourth Edition, which has been very carefully revised by the Editor, and brought into harmony with the Privy-Council Judgment in the St. Alban's Case. The Psalms in some of the Services not given at length in the Third Edition are now printed in full, so as to render the work in all respects complete.

"The existence of one such work of credit and reputation must do something to diminish the varieties of Ritualism into which the taste or studies of independent explorers might lead them. . . The book must be admitted to stand without a rival in its own line; and if there are few who are prepared to adopt its system as a whole, there are fewer still who might not gather from its pages some hints for the more decent and orderly performance of their own public ministrations in Church."—*Guardian.*

[Nearly Ready.

In fcap. 8vo., cloth, price 2s. 6d.

A HANDY BOOK OF REFERENCE AND QUOTATION.

MOTTOES AND APHORISMS FROM SHAKESPEARE.

A selection of Two Thousand Seven Hundred Mottoes and Aphorisms from Shakespeare, with a copious Index of upwards of Nine Thousand References to Words and Ideas. The whole is numbered and arranged alphabetically, so that any word or idea can be traced at once, and the correct quotation (with the name of the play, act, and scene) given without going further. This is not simply a key to Shakespeare, but a book which it is believed will be found generally useful for quotation and reference.

In fcap. 8vo., cloth, price 2s. 6d.

THE RULES OF RHYME;

A GUIDE TO VERSIFICATION.

With a Compendious Dictionary of Rhymes.

BY TOM HOOD.

This guide to English Versification gives the strict rules and correct rhymes for that style of composition, touching upon the peculiar requisites of song-writing, and the necessities of comic and burlesque verse. The Dictionary of Rhymes distinguishes between such words as are admissible in serious verse; such as, being archaic and Shakespearean, are only available for exceptional use; and those which simply answer the purpose of comic verse. Classical measures are examined, with a view to their adaptability to English verse, taking into consideration the relations of quantity and accent.

ADVENTURES IN THE ICE:

A comprehensive summary of Arctic Exploration, Discovery, and Adventure, including Experiences of Captain Penny, the Veteran Whaler, now first published. With portraits of Sir John Franklin, Captain Penny, Dr. Elisha Kent Kane, Dr. Isaac I. Hayes, and fourteen other Illustrations.

By JOHN TILLOTSON.

Black and gold binding, gilt edges, price 3s. 6d.

" A fairly written and concise summary. . . Containing a stirring account of the several voyages of Captain Penny, and of his adventures with shoals of whales."—*Athenæum*.

" A book that cannot but be popular with boys. Mr. Tillotson has epitomised very ably all the accounts of Arctic adventure."—*Fun*.

" We could scarcely imagine a better or more enjoyable book for boys than this. It consists of stories, adventures, and illustrations, with this advantage, that the stories are all instructive, and the adventures actually took place, and the illustrations are all from real life. . . . It will almost infallibly chain the attention."—*Edinburgh Courant*.

PIONEERS OF CIVILIZATION.

By the Author of " Lives of Eminent Men," &c.

Black and gold binding, gilt edges, price 3s. 6d.

Chap. I. The Soldier-Pioneer.
,, II. Pioneers of Enterprise and daring.
,, III. Exploring Pioneers.
,, IV. Peaceful Pioneers.

Chap. V. Trading Pioneers.
,, VI. Settling Pioneers.
,, VII. The Pioneers of Faith.

With Portraits of Dr. Livingstone, Captain Clapperton, William Penn, Captain Cook, Lord Robert Clive, Captain Flinders, Rev. Henry Martyn,
and ten other page Illustrations.

" This is a most agreeable book, well and sensibly written."—*Art Journal*.

" It is a good little book."—*Daily Telegraph*.

" In ' Pioneers of Civilisation.' Messrs. Hogg follow up their book of Arctic exploration, and continue a series which will delight our boys, and even the ' boys of a larger growth.' "—*Fun*.

. A Catalogue of Choice Illustrated Books, for young readers, suitable for School Prizes, &c., will be forwarded on application.

OUR COLONIES AND EMIGRATION.

DEDICATED BY PERMISSION TO THE RIGHT HONOURABLE EARL GRANVILLE, K.G.,
SECRETARY OF STATE FOR THE COLONIES.

In One Vol. crown 8vo., price 6s.

THE STORY OF OUR COLONIES.

WITH SKETCHES OF THEIR PRESENT CONDITION.

BY H. R. FOX BOURNE.

Author of "Famous London Merchants," "English Seamen under the Tudors," &c.

In this work, the chief incidents in the History of the Colonial Possessions of Great Britain are detailed, and some account given of their Present Circumstances, with a view of illustrating both their Value to the Mother Country, and their "Importance as Fields of Emigration." Our North-American and West-Indian Settlements, the Australian Colonies, and our other possessions, are described in turn.

In one handsome volume, crown 8vo., cloth, price 7s. 6d.

THE CHURCH SEASONS, HISTORICALLY AND POETICALLY ILLUSTRATED.

BY ALEXANDER H. GRANT, M.A.

Author of "Half-hours with our Sacred Poets."

The aim of this volume is to trace the origin and history of the Fasts and Festivals of the Ecclesiastical Year, and to illustrate in poetry the circumstances under which they began and continue to be celebrated, and the principal ideas and doctrines which they severally incorporate. Whatever authorities promised to throw light upon any question of historical interest, have been consulted indifferently and at first hand; whilst the selection of illustrative poetry has been so wide and impartial as to embrace contributions from the Christian muse of all ages and nations.

The work seeks to combine the advantages of a manual of historical authority, with those of an anthology of verse applicable to the seasons which have been already systematically celebrated (to exclude the mention of any but departed names) by Wither, Ken, and Keble.

CPSIA information can be obtained at www.ICGtesting.com
224568LV00003B/13/P